Peacebuilding Legacy

Peacebuilding Legacy

Programming for Change and Young People's Attitudes to Peace

SUKANYA PODDER

OXFORD
UNIVERSITY PRESS

OXFORD
UNIVERSITY PRESS

Great Clarendon Street, Oxford, OX2 6DP,
United Kingdom

Oxford University Press is a department of the University of Oxford.
It furthers the University's objective of excellence in research, scholarship,
and education by publishing worldwide. Oxford is a registered trade mark of
Oxford University Press in the UK and in certain other countries

© Sukanya Podder 2022

The moral rights of the author have been asserted

Impression: 1

Published in the United States of America by Oxford University Press
198 Madison Avenue, New York, NY 10016, United States of America

British Library Cataloguing in Publication Data
Data available

Library of Congress Control Number: 2021952416

ISBN 978–0–19–286398–0
DOI: 10.1093/oso/9780192863980.001.0001

Printed and bound by
CPI Group (UK) Ltd, Croydon, CR0 4YY

*This book is dedicated to Neil Skylar,
and to all the children and young people who make us curious.*

Preface

This book tackles three important questions encountered by the peacebuilding community in countries recovering from war and violent conflict. How can the long-term effects of post-war peacebuilding be studied? Are there any lasting effects on the normative beliefs and institutional structures that result from the application of liberal peace solutions? How do these norms and institutions shape (if at all) children and young people's attitudes towards peace? These questions have piqued my interest for more than a decade, both during and in the years following my extensive fieldwork on child soldier reintegration after the Liberian civil wars. My training at the Post-war Reconstruction and Development Unit (PRDU) (2007–2010), University of York, subsequent commissioned work for the British government, a range of international and intergovernmental organizations like the Organization for Economic Cooperation and Development (OECD), the North Atlantic Treaty (NATO), the International Organization for Migration (IOM), the United Nations Mission in Liberia (UNMIL), the United Nations Development Programme (UNDP), and periodic interactions with international non-governmental organizations (INGOs) and charities like Save the Children, Search for Common Ground, War Child, Saferworld, the International Rescue Committee among others, have provided me ample practical experience to embark on this study.

Based on this experience, in this book I develop the concept of peacebuilding legacy to address normative, institutional, and organizational questions around the long-term effects of donor-funded peacebuilding projects for children and young people. I demonstrate why the peacebuilding community must shift away from doing peace as an impatient peace. Why they must change their approaches from short-term wins to more strategic, long-term, and sustainable objectives. I demonstrate how this is possible while operating within the straitjacket of technocratic peacebuilding, using both archival and contemporary data from the field.

I had several goals for this book. First, I hope that the analytical framework applied for the study of peacebuilding legacy will enable peacebuilding practitioners to engage critically with the question of legacy early in their programming cycle. From considering the long-term livelihoods potential of the various activities that are implemented, to thinking about how best to link these efforts with national government departments through an explicit commitment to institutionalization of the short-term peacebuilding gains, the legacy framework will become their go to guide for designing sustainable and impactful programmes.

Second, I wish to underline the urgent need across the sector for a shift away from the donor-defined, short-term understanding of how peacebuilding should be done as a technical activity, to considering the long-term and transformative potential within technocratic peacebuilding. For the most part, projects are implemented in tandem, by multiple agencies, in their own atomized islands, and, without the strategic thinking necessary to determine how they can feed into the bigger objective of conflict transformation. Disconnected or one-off projects without sufficient follow-up, means, often the gains or short-term positive effects become lost, or simply do not multiply in ways that could create broader ripples or long-lasting multiplier effects.

Third, I have tried to highlight the missing balance between the tendency to chase donor-funding for survival purposes and the importance of defining the overall purpose (of country presence and programming) and the long-term contribution that large peacebuilding INGOs intend to leave behind. This is where strategic thinking and learning from evaluation steps in. By designing focused interventions in the same communities over longer periods, peacebuilders can commit to depth rather than breadth in their programming choices. Such an approach can help navigate the problem of 'fleeting presence', that inevitably produces limited transformative effects in norms, behaviours, and attitudes of individuals and groups. This also allows for the long-term monitoring of peacebuilding outcomes. Continuity in staffing, local partnerships, and through focused and consistent programming in key areas, peacebuilding INGOs can support a more strategic commitment to transformative peace.

Fourth, I wish to emphasize that the road to transformative peace lies through the formalization of peacebuilding efforts. Creating affordable, sustainable, locally owned, and locally funded structures and institutions as part of project legacies is important. Planning exits early with succession plans in place through the handover of peace projects to local organizations or to the national government can help build a stronger organizational legacy as well. This also applies to the programming focus with young people. While youth are often engaged in the informal sphere, through creative projects, the lack of donor funding support and the limited engagement of young people with formal politics becomes a limiting factor for long-term inclusion and active citizenship. Linking their efforts in the informal sector with the formal sphere requires support and co-operation on the part of both the adults and the youth.

Finally, learning and reflection is an important piece of the puzzle for sustainable peace. Learning for peacebuilding INGOs must be internally guided rather than externally imposed, through donor stipulated accountability requirements. Internal reflection on data generated through monitoring and evaluation

(M&E) processes, must become part of the moral compass of peacebuilding practice. This can be achieved by regularly revisiting the theory of change for each
project; making the necessary adjustments along the way, actively archiving the
institutional memory, documenting internal communications, and analysing the
evaluative evidence. Through post-closure evaluations and follow-up research, the
commitment to learning from evaluation can be built into the programming life-
cycle. Such an explicit commitment to learning from evaluation holds the key to
developing a conscious and concerted push towards 'programming for change'.

Acknowledgements

Turning now to thanking those who made this research possible. I am grateful to the British Academy for funding this research during 2016–2018. Many people have helped me think through the project in order to operationalize it. First and foremost, I am indebted to the partner INGO and their staff, in particular Saji Prelis, Joseph Jimmy Sankaituah, and Vilma Venkovska Milchev, and members of the institutional learning team for sharing their time, necessary documents, and for offering inputs that informed the project design. In the field, I remain indebted to my research participants for their time and willingness to take part in the research. In Macedonia, I remain grateful to the country office staff, the *Mozaik* alumni, parents, teachers, evaluators, and the Ministry officials for sharing their time and views that allowed me to triangulate the findings. In Sierra Leone, the country office staff (past and present) were incredibly helpful and accommodating during my field trip and during follow-up meetings via Skype. Community members in Sinjo, Bamba (Pujehun district) and in Kemen and Maconteh (Port Loko district) entrusted me with their stories. Several of the former project beneficiaries including the former radio reporters offered candid accounts about the long-term effects of their exposure to liberal peace norms. In the civil society sector and in the government, Alithur Freeman, Frances Fortune, Ambrose James, Ngolo Katta, Jo Rahall, Sonkita Conteh, Ensah Bockarie, Ibrahim Bangura, Andrew Lavali, Charles Lahai, and Anthony Koroma provided valuable insights that helped me triangulate my findings. I am thankful to Alison Brettle and Miranda Melcher, both previously graduate students at King's, for research assistance.

Among my academic friends and colleagues, I have had the opportunity to learn and absorb ideas from many brilliant and generous scholars over the years. I will name a few of them here. Roger MacGinty with whom I started fleshing out the skeleton of the project back in 2014 has been a firm influence on my thinking since our York years. Andy Knight, a distinguished scholar of high standing has offered kind mentorship over the years. Gearoid Millar, a source of tremendous intellectual energy, has proven to be a reliable collaborator and sounding board for my ideas. Myriam Denov, an inspirational scholar, offered encouragement and insightful comments on the proposal that made it much stronger. Walt Kilroy has offered sound advice and much needed humour on difficult days. Elke Krahmann, Anna Jarstad, Giuditta Fontana, Krijn Peters, and Caitlin Ryan read parts of the book and offered valuable feedback. At King's, Mats Berdal, Funmi Olonisakin, Matt Uttley, Nick Lloyd, Chris Kinsey, Jonathan Hill, Ellen Hallams, Lynda Hobbs,

Danni Macdivitt, and John Fogarty, have offered friendship, support, and enthusiasm for my ideas. Finally, every book needs a publisher. I am grateful to Dominic Byatt at Oxford University Press, for recognizing the potential and value of the research.

Most importantly, I would like to thank my family, for their moral support, and confidence in my abilities and for their trust in my adventures. They have cheered me on at every hurdle, to try again, do better, and reach further. In particular, I am indebted to my late mother for bestowing us with many gifts and simple joys during summer vacations in India. In Caversham, Sanjay, deserves special mention, for his stoic support, that has made my work-life more manageable. This project would not however be what it is today without my son Neil. His smile, his curiosity, intelligence, and unconditional love, inspires me every day to be a better person, to lead a kinder, more joyful life. His timekeeping on my chapters kept me on track to finish the manuscript, so that I could make more time for the games and toys that he wanted to share. I dedicate this book to him.

Contents

List of Figures	xvi
List of Tables	xvii
Abbreviations	xviii
Introduction	1
The Puzzle of Peacebuilding Legacy	3
Argument in Brief	8
A Few Words on Research Design and Methodology	11
Significance and Relationship to the Existing Literature	13
Theme 1: Measurement of Peacebuilding Effectiveness	13
Theme 2: Learning and Reflection from Peacebuilding Evaluation	14
Theme 3: Sustainable Peace and Local Ownership	15
Theme 4: The Role of Children and Youth in Peacebuilding	17
Theme 5: Media and Peace Education for Building Peace Norms	18
Case Specific Literature and Significance	19
Organization of the Book	21
1. Peacebuilding Legacy	24
Introduction	24
Conceptualizing Peacebuilding Legacy	26
Time	27
Transformation	29
Intergenerational Peace	31
Capturing Peacebuilding Legacy	33
Cues for Capturing Legacy	35
Transmission of Peace Norms: Resonance and Retention	36
Institutionalization, Sustainability, and Timely Exits	40
Organizational Learning and Reflection	43
The Transformative Potential of Technocratic Peacebuilding	47
2. Data and Methods	52
Introduction	52
Research Design	54
Case Study Research	55
Meta-ethnographic Synthesis	56
Reading and Translating the Studies	57
Reflections on the Process	60
Challenges of Fieldwork in Post-war Countries	61

Ethical Considerations   63
Field Research in Sierra Leone   64
Research with Child Reporters and Young People in Freetown   65
Land Conflicts and the Rural Hinterland   67
Fieldwork in Macedonia   70
Observations from the *Mozaik* Groups in Struga, Debar,
    and Skopje   71
Mozaik Alumni in Debar and Skopje   73
Potential Limitations and Biases   74

3. Peacebuilding through Pre-school Education and Media
   Programmes in Macedonia   76
Introduction   76
War, Peace, and Interethnic Relations in Macedonia   78
Language Rights and the Demand for Education in the Mother
    Tongue   81
Educational Segregation and Early Years' Provision: Integrated
    Education for Conflict Prevention   82
The School System and Monolingual Instruction   83
Policy and Practical Developments on Integrated Education   85
Early Years' Education   87
Evolution of the *Mozaik* Bilingual Immersion Groups: A Story
    of Shocks, Adaptation, and Institutionalization   88
The Conflict of 2001 and After   89
Dwindling Resources and Quality   92
Standardization Measures   93
Training and Monitoring   93
Adjustments   94
Lessons   95
Norm Transmission and Retention: Social Capital,
    Inter-regional Difference, and the Limits of Diffusion   95
Mozaik Values and Behaviour Change over Time   97
Social Capital and Norm Retention   98
Blockages to Transformative Peace   99
Intergenerational Values   101
Complementing *Mozaik* through Media and Theatre   103
   Nashe Maalo   104
   Bridges for the New Balkans   105
   The Balkan Theatre Network   106
Shortcomings of the Media Projects   107
Social Capital Dynamics and the Media Projects   108
Conclusion   110

4. Children and Youth-Focused Radio in Sierra Leone   112
   Introduction   112
   Background and Context Leading to the Civil War   113
   Intergenerational Tensions and the Sierra Leone Civil War   114
   Post-war Liberal Peacebuilding and Youth Empowerment   115
   Radio and Media in Promoting Peace and Reconciliation   116
   Studying Children and Youth Focused Radio and Its Legacy   118
   Making Local Voices Count: Radio Led Reconciliation after
       the War   119
   From an Authentic to a Manufactured Peace: Shifting to a
       Formulaic Narrative   123
   Programming for Change? The Evolution of the Studio's Radio
       Programmes   124
   Theme 1: Rights and Participation of Children, Women, and
       Youth   125
   Theme 2: Governance and Anti-corruption   129
   Theme 3: Democracy Promotion and Electoral Participation   137
   Radio Based Norm Transmission: Variable Resonance, and
       Inauthentic Norm Adoption   141
   Institutionalization of the Gains: Caught Between a Diffused
       and an Accidental Legacy   143
   A Few Accidental Legacies: Community Radio, IRN, and the
       BRU   144
   Conclusion   146

5. Learning and Reflection from Sierra Leone and Macedonia   148
   Introduction   148
   The Push for Adaptive and Agile Peacebuilding   149
   Barriers to and the Limits of Learning from M&E   152
       Disciplinary Disconnect   154
       Technocratic Dominance   155
       Fear of Failure and Limited Consequences of Not Learning   156
       Managing the Institutional Memory   157
   Organizational Learning Practices of the Partner INGO   158
   Macedonia Country Office Learning Trajectory   159
   Learning from Evaluation in Macedonia   167
   Sierra Leone Country Office Learning Trajectory   169
   Learning from Evaluation in Sierra Leone   175
   Variation in Country Office Learning Behaviour   176
       Staff Continuity   177
       National Government Buy-in   178
       Local Partnerships   179
       Donor Rules   180
   Conclusion   181

6. Programming for Change: Media and Peace Education in
   Shaping Young People's Attitudes to Peace   182
   Introduction   182
   Children and Young People's Attitudes to War and Peace   183
   Media and Peace Education: Norms, Persuasion, and Attitude
      Change   185
   Norms and Attitude Change   186
      Media Persuasion and Peace Education for Norm Messaging   188
   Second Order Interpretations on Norm Persuasion and
      Attitude Change   188
   Macedonia   190
      Intercultural Communication: Minority Language, Intergroup
         Contact, and Socialization   190
      Quality Pre-school Education: Enrolment,
         Institutionalization, and Pedagogy   191
      Citizenship and Ethnic Identity: Segregation, Integrated
         Education and Social Cohesion   193
   Sierra Leone   194
      Access and Acceptance: Information, Sensitization, and
         Dependence   194
      Agency and Behaviour: Voice, Capacity, and Participation   196
      Citizenship and Democracy: Governance, Accountability, and
         Elections   198
      The Limits of Persuasion and Young People's Attitudes to Peace   199

Conclusion: Transforming Peacebuilding for Transformative
Peace   203
   The Study of Peacebuilding Legacy: Conceptual and Analytical
      Dimensions   205
   Operationalizing the Logics of Legacy for Peacebuilding
      Practice   208
      The Institutional Aspects of Peacebuilding Legacy   208
      Linking Informal Advocacy with Formal Systems   208
      Material and Non-material Resonance   209
   The Normative Aspects of Peacebuilding Legacy   209
      Norms Transmission, Resonance, and Retention is
         Intergenerational   211
      Policy Articulation is Not the Same as Norm Internalization   212
   The Organizational Aspects of Peacebuilding Legacy   212
      Documenting Field Level Changes   213
      Continuity in Local Partnerships   214
   Peacebuilding with Children and Young People: From
      Instrumental to Transformative Participation   215
      1. Youth as Partners Rather than Targets   215
      2. Youth as Agents of Change   217

3. Integrating Youth Activism into the Formal Sphere   219
4. Adopting an Ecological Model of Peace   220

Bibliography   222
Appendix 1: Evaluation Based Recommendations and Follow-up
  Actions in Macedonia   269
Appendix 2: Evaluation Based Recommendations and Follow-up
  Actions in Sierra Leone   271
Appendix 3: Macedonia Meta-ethnographic Synthesis and
  Concepts   273
Appendix 4: Sierra Leone Meta-ethnographic Synthesis and
  Concepts   283
Index   302

List of Figures

1.1. Conceptualizing peacebuilding legacy 36

1.2. Relationship between norm resonance, compliance behavior, and retention 39

1.3. Results of norm transmission by peacebuilding organizations: explaining resonance and retention 40

1.4. Binaries in transformational and technical peacebuilding 48

2.1. Community meetings, Sinjo, Pujehun (Photo courtesy of the author, March 2017) 68

3.1. *Mozaik* kindergarten in Struga (Photo courtesy of the author, 5 September 2017) 90

3.2. *Mozaik* timeline: financial shocks and adaptation 92

4.1. Radio programme timeline 121

4.2. Support for democracy in Sierra Leone (2015) 138

5.1. Typical peacebuilding M&E activity flowchart 153

List of Tables

2.1. Country office learning behaviour   59

2.2. Norm concepts and second order interpretations for norm transmission   59

2.3. Details of FGDs   65

3.1. Macedonia timeline: evolution of ethno-national violence, 1989–2001   80

3.2. Timeline of *Mozaik's* development   91

5.1. Timeline and types of learning behaviour   160

6.1. Second order interpretation of norm concepts   189

Abbreviations

ALNAP	Active Learning Network for Accountability and Performance in Humanitarian Action
ASC	Advancing Social Cohesion
APC	All People's Congress
AFRC	Armed Forces Revolutionary Council
BTN	Balkan Theatre Network
BRU	Bike Riders' Union
BiH	Bosnia and Herzegovina
BNB	Bridges for the New Balkans
BBC	British Broadcasting Corporation
BDE	Bureau for Development of Education
CCNY	Carnegie Corporation of New York
CHRCR	Center for Human Rights and Conflict Resolution
CCG	Centre for Common Ground
CPD	Centre for Peacebuilding and Development
CCYA	Centre for the Coordination of Youth Activities
CTC	Children's Theatre Centre
CDF	Civil Defence Forces
CSO	Civil Society Organization
CDA	Collaborative for Development Action
CPU	Community Peace Building Unit
CR	Community Radio
CTAs	Community Teachers' Associations
CSR	Corporate Social Responsibility
CCSL	Council of Churches of Sierra Leone
CVE	Countering Violent Extremism
DPMNE	Democratic Party of Macedonian National Unity
DRC	Democratic Republic of Congo
DNA	Deoxyribonucleic Acid
DfID	Department for International Development
DME	Design, Monitoring, and Evaluation
DDR	Disarmament, Demobilization, Reintegration
DDRR	Disarmament, Demobilization, Reintegration, and Rehabilitation
DJ	Disc Jockey
DBOCs	District and Budget Oversight Committees
EU	European Union
ERP	Evaluation Research and Practice
FSU	Family Support Unit

FGDs	Focus Group Discussions
FDI	Foreign Direct Investment
MSW/GCA	Gender and Children's Affairs Unit within the Ministry of Social Welfare
GKN	Golden Kids News
GoSL	Government of Sierra Leone
IMC	Independent Media Commission
IRN	Independent Radio Network
IM&E	Indigenous Monitoring and Evaluation
IPA	Innovation for Poverty Actions
ILT	Institutional Learning Team
IIEP	Interethnic Integration in Education Programme
IMRO	Internal Macedonian Revolutionary Organization
IDPs	Internally Displaced Populations
IDRC	International Development Research Centre
IFC	International Finance Corporation
INTRAC	International NGO Training and Research Centre
INGO	International Non-Governmental Organization
IOM	International Organization for Migration
IR	International Relations
IRC	International Rescue Committee
LSLAs	Large-Scale Land Acquisitions
Lean MERL	Lean Monitoring, Evaluation, Research, and Learning
LPC	Liberian Peace Council
LURD	Liberians United for Reconciliation and Democracy
LNGOs	Local Non-governmental Organizations
Log-frames	Logical Frameworks
MTV	Macedonian Television
MALOA	Malen Affected Land Owners and Users Association
MIT	Massachusetts Institute of Technology
MP	Member of Parliament
MAFFS	Ministry of Agriculture, Forestry, and Food Security
MoES	Ministry of Education and Science
MEST	Ministry of Education, Science, and Technology
MoLSP	Ministry of Labour and Social Policy
MSW	Ministry of Social Welfare
M&E	Monitoring and Evaluation
MSC	Most Significant Change
MODEL	Movement for Democracy in Liberia
NDC	Nansen Dialogue Centre
NCDDRR	National Commission for Disarmament, Demobilization, Reintegration, and Rehabilitation
NDA	National Democratic Alliance
NDI	National Democratic Institute
NEC	National Election Commission

USAID	National Liberation Army
NPFL	National Patriotic Front of Liberia
NATCOM	National Telecommunications Commission
NLA	National Liberation Army
NGO	Non-Governmental Organization
NATO	North Atlantic Treaty Organization
OFA	Ohrid Framework Agreement
OFF	Open Fun Football
OSIWA	Open Society Initiative for West Africa
OECD	Organization for Economic Cooperation and Development
OECD-DAC	Organization for Economic Cooperation and Development-Development Assistance Committee
OPARD	Organization for Peace, Reconciliation, and Development
OSCE	Organization for Security and Cooperation in Europe
PRA	Participatory Rural Appraisal
PCS	Peace and Conflict Studies
PEC	Peacebuilding and Evaluation Consortium
PMDC	People's Movement for Democratic Change
PtPT	Pikin to Pikin Tok
POLCOMMFEST	Police Community Music Festival
PCE	Post-Closure Evaluation
PRSP	Poverty Reduction Strategy Paper
PIVOT	Promoting Information and Voice for Transparency on Elections'
RACAP	Rural Agency for Community Action Programme
RCTs	Randomized Control Trials
RUF	Revolutionary United Front
RSPO	Roundtable on Sustainable Palm Oil
SMCs	School Management Committees
SfCG	Search for Common Ground
SSR	Security Sector Reform
SRH	Sexual and Reproductive Health
SMS	Short Message Service
SLA	Sierra Leone Agriculture
SLA	Sierra Leone Army
SLBC	Sierra Leone Broadcasting Corporation
SLIEPA	Sierra Leone Investment and Export Promotion Agency
SLPP	Sierra Leone People's Party
SAC	Socfin Agricultural Company Ltd.
SEI	State Education Inspectorate
SDGs	Sustainable Development Goals
SIDA	Swedish International Development Agency
SADC	Swiss Agency for Development Cooperation
ECOMOG	The Economic Community of West African States Monitoring Group
ToC	Theory of Change
UNDP	UN Development Programme

UNHCR	UN High Commissioner for Refugees
UNPHR	United for the Protection of Human Rights
UK	United Kingdom
ULIMO-K	United Liberation Movement of Liberia for Democracy-Krahn
UN	United Nations
UNICEF	United Nations Children's Emergency Fund
UNCRC	United Nations Convention on the Rights of the Child
UNDESA	United Nations Department of Economic and Social Affairs
UNESCO	United Nations Educational, Scientific and Cultural Organization
UNGA	United Nations General Assembly
UNMIL	United Nations Mission in Liberia
UNAMSIL	United Nations Mission in Sierra Leone
UNPBC	United Nations Peacebuilding Commission
UNSC	United Nations Security Council
UNSG	United Nations Secretary General
USIP	United States Institute for Peace
USA	United States of America
USAID	United States Agency for International Development
USD	United States Dollars
OIC-VET	Vocational and Educational Training for the Organization of Islamic Cooperation
VSO	Voluntary Services Overseas
WHO	World Health Organization
WFOV	Worst Forms of Violence
YES	Youth Education and Life Skills
YPS	Youth, Peace, and Security

Introduction

It was the winter of 2008; I was in Monrovia, Liberia as an intern with the International Organization for Migration (IOM) Liberia office, supporting an evaluation of their waste management programme with ex-combatants. Liberia had witnessed two episodes of civil conflict, first during 1989–1997, and then during 1999–2003, following a period of conflict relapse. Ethnic persecution against ethnic Mandingos and Krahns, after Charles Taylor's electoral victory in 1997, forced ex-fighters from groups like the United Liberation Movement of Liberia for Democracy-Krahn faction (ULIMO-K), and the Mandingo dominated Liberian Peace Council (LPC) into exile. External support for two new insurgencies between 2000 and 2002, namely the Liberians United for Reconciliation and Democracy (LURD), and the Movement for Democracy in Liberia (MODEL), saw these ex-fighters re-recruited into the new armed formations along ethnic lines (Pugel, 2007). The second civil war formally ended with the signing of the Accra Accords in August 2003. It provided for the creation of the United Nations Mission in Liberia (UNMIL), which was entrusted with the responsibility for comprehensive security sector reform (SSR), and a large-scale disarmament, demobilization, reintegration (DDR) programme (Podder, 2019). The outcome of the DDR effort soon became the framing narrative for peacebuilding success in Liberia.

The reintegration phase was caught between the choice of expedience in the form of short-term training projects lasting six to nine months versus the pursuit of reconciliation through the transformation of wartime social relations. Targeting of ex-combatants through DDR support created new 'haves' and 'have nots' in the post-war period. It strengthened stigma over the 'combatant' label; creating community hostility towards ex-combatants, and weakening social reintegration in the initial stages. During 2008–2009, the focus was on training a further 23,000 ex-combatants as part of a 'residual caseload' list prepared by the National Commission for Disarmament, Demobilization, Reintegration, and Rehabilitation (NCDDRR). Funding to the tune of United States dollars (USD) 20 million was provided by the Norwegian government for this final phase.[1] The IOM office was located on UN drive near the upmarket location of Mamba point. Along a long, winding road close to the beach, lead DDR implementing

---

[1] NCDDR Programme Coordinator for the Residual Caseload (Monrovia, 7 December 2008).

Peacebuilding Legacy. Sukanya Podder, Oxford University Press.
© Sukanya Podder (2022). DOI: 10.1093/oso/9780192863980.003.0001

agencies like the United Nations Children's Fund (UNICEF), the UN Development Programme (UNDP), the UN High Commissioner for Refugees (UNHCR), and other key partners like Save the Children and IOM were located next to each other.

As part of my attachment, I met and interacted with these agencies and their staff, I grew familiar with their top-down understanding of liberal peacebuilding during formal interviews and informal discussions. To understand the situation outside the capital, I travelled by road to Lofa county in the northwest, where the LURD insurgency began. It was a short visit, but enough for me to realize that several of the beneficiaries in the different DDR training projects were proxies (Munive and Jakobsen, 2012). When I returned to Liberia in August 2009, I visited rural communities across six counties with a range of peacebuilding organizations working with youth and civilian communities, and not only with ex-combatants. A wider coverage of the country with a more extensive mix of respondents, complemented by the use of multiple gatekeepers, offered a richer narrative of peacebuilding experiences (Podder, 2012). In Nimba, Taylor's home county, I visited Ganta, Flumpa, and Kawee with Equip, a Canadian international nongovernmental organization (INGO). In Flumpa, a Mano village, 75 minutes-drive from Ganta, in Saclapea district, although the civilians maintained superficial civility, a certain amount of covert hostility towards ex-combatants and child soldiers bubbled under the surface. Through participatory rural appraisal (PRA) techniques, such as timeline exercises, landscape mapping, and institutional diagramming analysis, I found that the selective targeting of ex-combatants through the DDR programme created deep animosity.

In other places like Sackiebomo and Gbolokie's Town in Margibi county, which could be easily accessed from the capital, ex-combatants who had fought for the Taylor militia and the National Patriotic Front of Liberia (NPFL) factions, had opted to self-demobilize. The fear of stigma, and anticipated problems with cross-border travel linked to the profiling of DDR participants had made them hesitant to take part. In Koon Town, and Toe's Town, in Toddee district, Montserrado county, communities benefited from youth focused community development initiatives like the United States Agency for International Development (USAID) funded Youth Education and Life Skills (YES) project, but similar to Margibi, the ex-NPFL soldiers had opted to self-demobilize. They deeply regretted the decision. Through my ethnographic fieldwork during 2008–2012, I acquired a nuanced understanding of the different motivations underlying ex-combatant demobilization. I also became privy to the worldview of international, governmental, and non-governmental agencies implementing peacebuilding and development initiatives for ex-combatants and non-combatant children and youth, and the ways in which these initiatives were received by the local populations. It also made me aware of the research puzzle around peacebuilding legacy.

The Puzzle of Peacebuilding Legacy

While in Liberia, it was my job to determine whether these internationally funded programmes had been successful in supporting the reintegration of ex-combatants, and the reconciliation processes between them, and the civilian communities. What was not clear to me at that time was how far the different peacebuilding initiatives had been transformational, how far they had a lasting effect on the beliefs, and structures that shaped children and young people's attitudes towards peace. How could the long-term effects of these projects be captured? To what extent had these projects made ex-combatants and the broader youthful population truly peaceful over time? Did the liberal norms introduced through the different peacebuilding projects resonate with the locals? How far were they retained by the direct beneficiaries of these efforts and the wider communities where they resided? What sort of direct institutional legacies of these projects were retained by the national actors? And finally, what was the organizational legacy for the different peacebuilding organizations implementing these projects, and what did they learn from their experiences? Little if any thinking around legacy concerned the donors, national government departments, and the international and local civil society organizations (CSOs) that implemented the many projects that I included in my research on child soldier reintegration. The long-term effects of peacebuilding programmes from a normative; institutional, and organizational perspective became a central puzzle that emerged from my numerous field visits to West Africa (2008–2017), and one that motivates this book. It was clear to me that the monitoring and evaluation tools available for measuring short-term project impact were not fit for purpose in studying long-term effects. This motivated me to engage in conceptual scoping around peacebuilding legacy, and to develop observable cues for approximating long-term effects.

In this book, I focus on how liberal norms around peace, non-violence, and reconciliation transmitted through multi-year children and youth focused media and peace education projects, transformed intergenerational and intergroup relations in the cases of Sierra Leone and Macedonia[2] respectively. To operationalize the study, I entered into a knowledge production partnership with a leading international peacebuilding organization based in Washington, D.C. In collaboration with their Director of Children and Youth Programmes, Sierra Leone and Macedonia were selected for the research, because the partner INGO has run projects relating to children and youth for over 15 years in these cases,

---

[2] The official name has changed to the Republic of North Macedonia following the Prespa agreement of June 2018. I will use the shorter version, Macedonia, throughout this book.

and their programmes were either sunsetting (Macedonia), or near sunsetting (Sierra Leone), offering the necessary historical aspects that enabled a study of peacebuilding legacy. Given the ambiguous, elastic, and politicized nature of peacebuilding as a concept, and as a practice, delineating peacebuilding effects, whether over the short or long term, is not simple (Bush and Duggan, 2014: 3). The administration of parallel peacebuilding processes creates additional complexity about how norms around non-violence and peaceful co-existence are understood, interpreted, and applied (Millar, 2013: 189–91). This is because, the long-term effects of peacebuilding can denote a wide variety of things, ranging from attitudinal change, perceptual change, structural change, policy change, to behavioural change at the individual, and, or, the collective levels (Bush and Duggan, 2014: 6).

The peacebuilding field is made up of multiple organizations that implement overlapping as well as complementary types of programming (Millar, 2014a). Most peacebuilding programmes are organized and executed into time-bound projects serving specific communities and target groups. Projects can be thematic, focusing on issues such as human rights, child protection, education, gender, and the like. They may vary in their duration, last anywhere between nine and twelve months, or extend over several years on a rolling basis. The accumulated knowledge from the implementation of peacebuilding activities is rarely centralized. Projects are delivered through a combination of international and local non-governmental organizations (INGOs and LNGOs) with little planning, or at times interest on the part of donors to coordinate the accumulated learning across implementing organizations (Chigas, Church, and Corlazzoli, 2014). Project-based models of learning rather than thematic or longitudinal studies dominate the field (de Coning, 2018). In addition to learning gaps, each of the main actors (donors, recipients, local elites, and non-elites) can have different expectations from peacebuilding (Campbell, 2018). There can also be a mismatch between project-level results (programme effectiveness), and outcomes at the country level (peacebuilding effectiveness); or between the country level, and the 'peace writ large' (societal transformation) (Autesserre, 2017). As a consequence, the question of legacy will be different depending on who one asks, and the level of analysis, at which we seek to capture the long-term effects.

Methodologically, capturing legacy poses several complex, and as of yet, insurmountable challenges. Each intervention has more immediate effects as well as longer-term ones. These can be direct or indirect, intended or unintended, and positive but also negative (Brabant, 2010: 1–3; Lemon and Pinet, 2017: 254). Common monitoring and evaluation (M&E) tools are only capable of assessing the short-term outputs of individual peacebuilding projects. They cannot, and generally do not even attempt, to provide any assessment of the long-term legacy of broader peacebuilding interventions made up—as they are—of many projects implemented over time by a diversity of organizations. The delayed nature of causality requires synthetic qualitative approaches, that can juxtapose analytical versus subjectivist approaches (Neufeldt and Fast, 2005; Blum, 2011; Campbell, 2011; Kawano-Chiu, 2012; de Coning, 2018). Within the peacebuilding field, there is still a quest to find appropriate methods and ways of dealing with planning, monitoring, and evaluation over the longer-term (Scheers, 2008: 5). Given these limitations, studying legacy at a scale larger than the project level becomes difficult to map over time, especially beyond that of a single organization.

The choice of a single peacebuilding organization for operationalizing this research was also determined by practical considerations around data access and the depth of analysis. Researchers need to establish trust to access the institutional memory across digital, human, and print formats. In addition to access, the longitudinal data must be of a manageable scope to allow in-depth and comparative analysis. It demands a narrower scope. This was achieved by shifting the frame of reference from understanding the 'peace writ large', or the cumulative effects of peacebuilding on societal transformation in each case, to that of the partner organization's experiences and contributions to long-term peacebuilding through its multi-year projects in each context. Such a design allowed controls to be put in place with regard to timelines and target groups.

While such an approach could be attempted with more than one organization, there remains the danger of losing analytical depth for breadth. Besides, very few peacebuilding organizations are open about their institutional memory; or are willing to share relevant evaluative data linked to past projects. Working closely with the country teams and with the institutional learning teams based in the regional offices (Brussels and Dakar), and at the headquarters in Washington, D.C., I could tap into staff perspectives, strategic planning processes, and the organizational planning and implementation choices. This, in addition to my access to the document archives relating to various M&E exercises in the two cases, made it possible to control for variation over time. By focusing on the evolution, shifts, and the processes of adaptation between projects, the external and internal influences shaping peacebuilding legacy became clear.

A note of terminology is warranted here. Although there is overlap, there are important distinctions between the terms' 'children', 'youth', and 'young people' that will be used in this book. The UN General Assembly (UNGA) has defined 'youth' as the age between 15 and 24 years. However, there is no single agreed definition. For example, the lowest age range for youth is 12 years in Jordan, and the upper range is 35 years in a number of African countries including Sierra Leone. The World Health Organization (WHO) and UNICEF use the term 'adolescent' for those aged 10–19 years, and young people for those 10–24 years (Podder and Özerdem, 2015: 2). There is also a degree of overlap between the international definition of youth and that of children. The UN Convention on the Rights of the Child (UNCRC) (1991), defines a child as everyone under the age of 18 years unless the law of a particular country is applicable to the child, in which case adulthood is attained earlier (Hilker and Fraser, 2009: 9).

A range of national and international NGOs promote children's rights both in conflict and non-conflict settings (Watson, 2006: 229). During conflict this entails a responsibility to protect children from harm, and to stop their use as soldiers (D'Costa and Glanville, 2019). The dominant framework for children emphasizes protection. It privileges the victim frame. Such a protectionist framework also informs the peacebuilding projects with children in the post-war period (Shepler, 2005). UNICEF, UNDP, and various INGOs like Save the Children, the International Rescue Committee (IRC), and War Child among others focus on the rehabilitation of child soldiers and children affected by armed conflict, through projects relating to their education, mental health, and early childhood development.

Norms and stereotypes as well as programmatic approaches vary between these categories. Policy discourses on youth for example presents a polarized discourse. On the one hand, young people are viewed as powerless, and in need of protection much like children. On the other hand, they are feared as threats to security: dangerous, violent, apathetic, and a 'lost generation' (O'Brien, 1996). The dangers posed by 'the youth bulge' or a large youthful population (Urdal, 2006; Pruitt, 2020), are seen as increasing a country' susceptibility to political violence and crime. These assumptions align closely with the broader thinking on new wars and the new Barbarism thesis (Kaplan, 1994; Kaldor, 1999). By advancing such a negative and violent image, youth, and young people as a conceptual category are 'othered' in the discourse on conflict. They are characterized as vandals or perpetrators of criminal and political violence, rather than as victims in need of protection (Abbink and van Kessel, 2005).

Such a negative or securitized framing has encouraged interventions aimed at keeping youth busy, or off the street, through a range of short-term vocational and educational projects to disarm, demobilize, and reintegrate ex-combatants and child soldiers. During the post-war reconstruction phase, relief programmes and international aid efforts have made youth a major beneficiary or development target. Donor funded projects reinforce the narrative of youth insecurity. Their overall effect has generated greater exclusion rather than positive youth integration into society (Podder, 2012; McMullin, 2013). At the other end of the spectrum, youth are gendered, infantilized, and categorized as 'at-risk'. Through labels such as teenage mothers, sex slaves, school drop outs, and children born of wartime rape, varying degrees of vulnerability are espoused, thereby requiring interventions that aim to secure or protect young people from the risks of physical, sexual, and domestic violence (Podder and Özerdem, 2015: 7).

In recent years, the predominantly negative framing around youth has shifted towards acknowledging their important and positive role in peace processes. On 9 December 2015, the United Nations Security Council (UNSC) resolution 2250 was adopted unanimously. It is the first international policy framework to recognize the important and positive role young people play in preventing and resolving conflict, countering violent extremism (CVE), and building peace. This was followed by two further resolutions, 2419 (2018) and 2535 (2020), which recognize the role of young people as partners for peace. This trio of resolutions represents the youth, peace, and security (YPS) policy framework in international politics (Podder, Prelis, and Sankaituah, 2021). In response to this policy shift, at a practical level, peacebuilding efforts have shifted towards advocating for youth's change agentry and towards encouraging their inclusion in peace processes (McEvoy-Levy, 2006; Sommers, 2012).

Finally, a word on the choice of studying the legacy of peacebuilding projects targeting children and youth. While the analytical framework on peacebuilding legacy will apply to diverse categories of post-war peacebuilding projects, this choice to focus on media and peace education projects with children and young people was informed by the following considerations. First, barring ad hoc observations about the potential of youth as a powerful peace constituency, very little analytical work exists for explaining the long-term transformation of young people's attitudes towards peace (Podder and Özerdem, 2015: 3–10). The longitudinal study of media and peace education projects with children and youth is used here to identify and capture the processes whereby peace and conflict-related actions, narratives, attitudes, beliefs, and stances are transmitted from the older generation to the younger generation; and how far they aid or inhibit conflict transformation.

Second, such a focus also furthers the study of temporality in peacebuilding. Issues of peace and conflict are often examined through events and incidents (violent outrages, elections, new constitutions, peace accords, and the like) rather than through processes, especially long-term processes. The focus on peacebuilding legacy allows us to explore how conflict issues become redundant or change over time, and new issues become part of the conflict-scape particularly for the younger generation. It enables us to address the question of intergenerational peace, understood here not simply as peace between generations but at a more practical level, as the designing of peace interventions that can cater to the needs of different generations during the post-war phase.

Finally, such a focus allows us to assess the quality of peace experienced between generations. Often the younger generation in long-duration conflicts are born after a peace accord has been signed. Yet they may continue to experience various forms of structural and everyday forms of violence, when the quality of peace delivered by the accord is ephemeral or unstable. The longitudinal study of children and youth focused peacebuilding interventions allows us to analyse how, if at all, peacebuilding efforts can trigger a durable transformation of the struc-tures of violence over time (Sewell, 1996: 844). We turn now to the book's core argument.

Argument in Brief

This book makes the argument that there is immense transformative potential at the heart of technocratic peacebuilding. To unpack this potential, scholars and practitioners must engage with, and invest in the study of peacebuilding legacy. Conceptualized through the lens of time, transformation and intergenerational peace, peacebuilding legacy is understood as the longer-term effects of peace-building programmes. It is captured through the cues of norm transmission, their resonance and retention; the formal institutionalization of peacebuilding gains, and the organizational learning and reflection from the monitoring and evalu-ation of peacebuilding. Through this conceptual and analytical framework, the study of peacebuilding legacy links with live debates around peacebuilding effec-tiveness; sustainable peace; intergenerational justice, and local ownership in the field of peace and conflict studies.

Legacies can be direct, indirect, and interrupted in nature. Direct legacies repre-sent the physical, institutional, and structural remnants that are the more tangible representations of peacebuilding efforts. Indirect legacies are linked to processes initiated during periods of intervention when international actors and their local partners take major decisions and actions in key policy areas. Interrupted legacies are processes and actions marred by short-term interventions and patchwork pro-gramming. Without consistent investment or follow-up, certain interventions do not portend long-lasting changes; rather they may inspire only temporary shifts in behaviours (Gledhill, 2020: 4). This book is specifically concerned with the direct legacies of peacebuilding work with children and young people, and uses data from projects implemented over 15+ years by the partner INGO's country programmes in Sierra Leone and Macedonia to illustrate its argument.

I find that peacebuilding legacy is strongest if there is dedicated programming in a specific area for multiple years, followed by some form of institutionalization or handover into the national system. Successful institutionalization can contribute to sustainable peace, through the transfer of peacebuilding models to national organizations, whether government agencies or national civil society organiza-tions who act as an invested peace constituency. Succession and handover can enhance local ownership of the peacebuilding gains. Peacebuilding legacy is likely to be weak and diffused even accidental, if programmes are running on multiple tracks and pursue thematic approaches with ad hoc project designs. The legacy of the multiyear youth focused media and education projects in Sierra Leone and Macedonia, present different trajectories and behaviours relating to intergroup and intergenerational conflict resolution because of the variable commitment to institutionalization. In Sierra Leone, institutionalization as a goal was missing with regard to the various radio programmes; but present in Macedonia with regard to the *Mozaik* preschool bilingual immersion groups.

The *Mozaik* model of intercultural communication was adopted by the government into its national preschool curriculum in 2012. Understanding the 'success' of *Mozaik*'s nationalization, required deeper enquiry into the motivations of the relevant stakeholders. I found that the government's coalescence with donor agendas around social cohesion and integrated education encouraged institutionalization of the bilingual groups into the national system. Continuity in staffing, together with their efforts to keep the programme afloat in the face of multiple external and internal shocks offered important lessons around agency, ownership, and adaptation at the country office level. In Sierra Leone, by contrast, both governmental and international actors were responsible for the ad hoc nature of engagement with children and youth issues. A piecemeal approach to the multifaceted intergenerational issues in Sierra Leone, and weak local ownership meant that the agenda around youth and peacebuilding was defined for Sierra Leone rather than emerging organically from it.

From a norm transmission, resonance, and retention perspective, close identification with the cultural and institutional milieu encourages the internalization or retention of norms. Conversely, weak resonance is likely to invite greater resistance to and contestation both at the individual and the group levels. Processes of media persuasion and norm transmission in Sierra Leone and Macedonia had different long-term effects. In pursuing a *learning and belief focused* programming model that targeted individuals' ingrained beliefs and values, the role of group social norms in shaping intergroup relations was underemphasized in Macedonia. In Sierra Leone, radio programming adopted a *social norms model* by targeting the normative climate of relevant social models. When introduced in neo-patrimonial societies in West Africa, liberal ideas interacted with pre-existing concepts and practices in peculiar ways. They were differently socialized and acculturated by individuals and groups in ways that both empowered and disempowered youth. The lesson here is that radio-based sensitization in itself cannot sustain long-term change in group norms. Changes in the legal, political, economic, and other social institutions are critical for long-term and meaningful transformation. Without changes in how youth access resources such as land, and without removing the structural barriers to youth's employment in the formal sector, new norms around rights and participation triggered mixed results.

From a programming perspective, I find that media-led peacebuilding produces more diffused normative and institutional legacies compared with peace education projects. Media programmes are often reactive to emerging political, economic, and social events, and this can result in a discontinuous programming strategy, leaving only limited scope for institutionalization. In Sierra Leone, no transition processes were put in place through which the various children and youth focused radio programmes and the complementary community engagement work could be absorbed or continued in some form by the government. This presented weak institutionalization of the gains from the advocacy around child rights and child protection. In Macedonia, similarly, the media projects implemented by the Macedonia country office did not conclude in ways that could integrate the learning from them into the national networks of NGOs working in the media sector. In both cases, projects resulted in only limited professionalization of the media sector. As a result, strengthening the capacity-building work of local media organizations did not take place.

From a learning and reflection perspective, I argue that capturing the organizational legacy of the work that peacebuilding INGOs implement over multiple years in a given context requires commitment to, and rigorous application of self-reflection and learning. This can be achieved not only through the use of standard M&E tools that are part of routine accountability measures to donors (Mika, 2002; MacGinty, 2012a; Campbell, 2018). Deeper reflection on the processes of adjustment, adaptation, and change requires meticulous archiving of the institutional memory; commitment to sustained programming on specific themes, and being responsive to evaluation results (Heideman, 2016; de Coning, 2018). By adjusting theories of change in response to beneficiary feedback, and by commissioning follow-up research with beneficiaries in the form of post-exit studies (Hayman, 2016), peacebuilding INGOs can build stronger organizational legacies of their work in a specific context.

With regard to the dimensions of time, transformation, and intergenerational peace, I find that in conflict affected societies, the cultural values of the older generations may be resisted by the younger generation as traditional, archaic, and irrelevant. Equally, the latter may present or align with cultural values that are Western, modern and thereby dismissive of tradition. Intergenerational conflict also exhibits important structural tensions. Structural violence excludes younger generations from access to resources like land, and from political power (Galtung, 1969: 170–1; Sooros, 1976: 175). When political and economic systems are geared to the short-term interests of contemporary elites, the interests of the future generations are compromised (Valentine, 2019).

Integrating futures consciousness into peacebuilding involves broadening peacebuilding approaches to include an active intergenerational dimension (Boulding, 1966; Hutchinson, 1999). For example, in Sierra Leone, external, donor-driven peacebuilding norms created new expectations about how youth should be treated, engendering the hope of a shift from their erstwhile liminal status in society. A perceived improvement in their social status in the post-war years reinforced the desire to be less marginalized and more central to decision-making. Such changes were less forthcoming however, given that the structural which was less forthcoming barriers to young people's access to resources such as land and political power remain intact. Community elders and chiefs have viewed civil society activism as disrespectful and disruptive of the traditional ways of life. They saw the advocacy around human rights as pitting children against adults, encouraging them to demand rights and opportunities from adults as a given, while denouncing the importance of traditional values and communal duties.[3] Therefore, the diffusion and adoption of rights-based norms emanating from donor discourses were seen as erosive of established norms around reciprocity, obligations, and hierarchy. This in turn gave rise to new forms of intergenerational tensions.

Finally, new ideas are not introduced into normative voids. They enter into spaces that are monopolized by a defined normative space that can be resistant to change (Björkdahl, 2008: 139). In Macedonia, national level adoption of donor stipulated policies on social cohesion and integrated education did not translate into societal adoption of these norms. The media and peace education projects founded on the values of intercultural communication did not translate into greater intergroup interaction. Friendships forged during the *Mozaik* years were transient, and the depth and longevity of intergroup social relationships were embedded in the family, and in broader social capital dynamics. Even with successful institutionalization of the *Mozaik* groups, in terms of norm resonance and retention there were important gaps. Though better suited to institutionalization, peace education efforts in themselves cannot reorient the values, practices, norms, and beliefs around peace, reconciliation and tolerance for the future generations unless the mindset of the older generation, of the families, and wider communities are also targeted. Fundamental social change—such as of the intergenerational and inter-group kind—takes a long time, even generations, and cannot easily be delivered within the scope, funding, and timeframe of specific donor-led interventions. Society does not change profoundly and rapidly within a short period of time; this makes it imperative to reflect on the issues of time, transformation, and intergenerational peace when studying peacebuilding legacy.

A Few Words on Research Design and Methodology

Peacebuilding projects are implemented in complex, intricate, and transitional environments (Bächtold, 2021). Individual peace initiatives are often decontextualized by external peace interveners through the application of standard tools and measurements that are not designed for addressing the complexity inherent in post-war interventions (Stave, 2011; Danielsson, 2020). Methodologically

---

[3] Interview, female staff, local CSO focusing on child protection issues led by former child reporter trained by the partner INGO.

speaking, the challenge with evaluations of peacebuilding programmes is that they are rooted in the short-termism that plagues the wider field. From impact assessments to mid-term and end of project reviews, rarely is there the time to take a pause and reflect back on the implementation process and the learning derived from them. The longitudinal study of programmatic effects runs contrary to the DNA of the peacebuilding industry. The question of legacy from a normative, institutional, and organizational learning perspective is neglected not only by donors, but also by the implementing organizations such as international and local NGOs and their staff.

In a recent webinar, Patricia Rogers (2018) underlined that 'there is an ongoing need for innovation in evaluation, given the changing nature of programs and policies, the United Nations sustainable development goals (2030), and the context in which they are implemented' (see, Esser and Vanderkamp, 2013). Innovation can be in the form of: new technology (such as using social media data or machine learning for analysis); a bricolage, or a patchwork, of previous ideas and techniques or borrowing ideas and methods from other disciplines and professions (Campbell, et al., 2014). Recent efforts to ground the definitions of peacebuilding success in the perceptions and reality of the communities or beneficiaries (Firchow, 2018), suggest that such an anthropological approach can be potentially extended to the study of learning and reflection across peacebuilding INGOs, and their local partner organizations. Ethnographic methodology is considered the hallmark of anthropology. Several scholars have urged the development of ethnographic approaches in order to actualize the anthropological potential for the study of peacebuilding, and for furthering our understanding of the non-state aspects of peace such as the importance of relationships, personal attitudes, and professional mindsets (Chambers, 2006; Oda, 2007: 8–9; Davies, 2008; Bräuchler, 2018; Millar, 2018b).

Combining existing information sources with anthropological ones also allows for the undertaking of an 'ethnography for meta-data'. This would require scholars and practitioners to combine methods from conventional peace and conflict studies, political science, international relations, and social anthropology in order to examine stories interwoven within each peacebuilding project to examine how these intersect with top-down processes and bottom-up involvement over time and across generations. This is something that I attempt here. While I was well-experienced in primary fieldwork, having conducted ethnographic studies and survey research in Liberia and Mindanao, Philippines during 2008–2012, I had not used project archives for studying peacebuilding effects before. In this book the choice of meta-ethnographic synthesis has allowed me to understand the complex relationships between projects and programmes, and as Dirksmeier and Helbrecht (2008) suggest, this requires a completely different positionality of the researcher, and of her or his views on causality. By combining the archival ethnography of project proposals, periodic reports, internal and external evaluations with primary fieldwork, I could analyse data found in the various project archives, and in the institutional memory of the staff and external evaluators personnel stretching back over time (Lee et al., 2015).

While some limitations of using evaluations as meta-data must be acknowledged, a meta-ethnographic study of this type offers a highly interpretative method, one that demands considerable immersion in the individual evaluation studies to achieve a synthesis. Findings from the meta-data, combined with primary fieldwork with the project beneficiaries, offered rich lessons to be drawn, which would not be possible without the combination of methods, the use of multiple projects, and a multi-year lens. In summary, the meta-ethnographic synthesis approach proved to be a powerful and flexible tool for synthesizing archival data, through which different phenomena and dynamics of project planning, and implementation could be captured over time (Gracy, 2004). Programmatic documents when studied in synthesis offered insights into the interconnections that cannot be tracked in standalone reports. It also helped to trace the evolution of organizational priorities and strategies that influenced the sustainability, local ownership, and responsible exit decisions within a given context.

Significance and Relationship to the Existing Literature

In terms of its scholarly significance and relationship to the existing literature, this book straddles several live debates and themes in the field of peace and conflict studies. Here I outline how the book relates to and advances these different strands of scholarship through its new and important contributions.

Theme 1: Measurement of Peacebuilding Effectiveness

This book contributes to the literature on peacebuilding effectiveness by developing the new conceptual model on peacebuilding legacy and the novel analytical cues for capturing legacy. Unlike disciplines such as economics and health, macro-indicators of peace are not easily quantifiable. Community trust, tolerance, and social reconciliation are intangibles, process-oriented objectives, not products. These are essentially elements of psychological change, rather than physical transformations or developments. They involve public perceptions and everyday adaptations to evolving circumstances and manifest fully over the longer term. Given these characteristics, understanding the results of peacebuilding over time, moves against conventional project management logic. The latter assumes a clear hierarchy of goals, a demonstrable relationship between inputs and outputs, and the delivery of results matched to a defined timetable. Implementing agencies and their partners find themselves pressured to demonstrate impact, to market their activities, and to promote a deliberate narrative of success. However, practitioners in the field are well aware that on the ground things are often not so clear cut. Changes tend to be more qualitative than quantitative; they may affect attitudes and relations in the short-term, but not have long-lasting influence. Structural changes are even more difficult to orchestrate and usually bear fruit only in the long-term (Leonhardt, 1999; Bush and Duggan, 2015; de Coning, 2018).

The success and failure of peacebuilding therefore depends on how these effects are captured and assessed over time. Is it about the reduction of violence, post-war economic recovery, democratic progress, non-recurrence of civil conflict or the re-establishment of public security and the rule of law (Walter, 2004; Doyle and Sambanis, 2006; Call, 2008; Firchow, 2018: 18–19)? One simple approach can be to use the positive results of a single activity in terms of its support for personal change as an indicator of micro-success. If the project can become more influential and begins to shape wider relationships, then it can be considered as achieving a higher degree of success. If personal or relational change then leads to structural change, then it may have an even greater peacebuilding effect (Campbell, 2007: 6). So, there are both lateral and hierarchical models of effectiveness (Anderson, 2004; Hoffman, 2004; Paffenholz and Reychler, 2007). This book contributes to the literature on measurement by developing the conceptual and analytical model on peacebuilding legacy. Through the examination of norm retention and formal institutionalization it draws on the experience of multi-year media and peace education efforts with children and young people in Sierra Leone and Macedonia to demonstrate how these interventions have shaped young people's attitudes towards peace over time.

Theme 2: Learning and Reflection from Peacebuilding Evaluation

By synthesizing meta-data in the form of the partner INGO's institutional memory, together with primary field research, this book combines a top-down and a bottom-up perspective on learning from evaluation. In the field, there is wide acknowledgement of the challenges regarding how different actors think of, apply, and learn from peacebuilding M&E (Bush and Duggan, 2015; Campbell, 2018; de Coning, 2018). This is because different actors have different needs and requirements. For donors, evaluation provides financial accountability for aid investments (Campbell, 2018). For practitioners, evaluative data and findings help demonstrate performance to donors and governments that fund their work (Galama and Van Tongeren, 2002: 23; Grimes, 2003: 35). In short, the relationship between M&E and institutional learning and reflection is not always straightforward or obvious. The current indicators and M&E tools, while usefully capturing immediate changes cannot measure the degree or extent of change over time. These include for example, the International Development Research Centre's (IDRC) 'outcome mapping technique', the 'most significant change approach' (MSC), 'appreciative inquiry', and the 'randomized control trials' (RCTs) developed by the Poverty Action Lab at the Massachusetts Institute of Technology (MIT); and the Carnegie Corporation of New York (CCNY) funded 'Everyday Peace Indicators' project (Davies and Dart, 2005; Campbell, 2007: 16; Bush and Duggan, 2013; Firchow and MacGinty, 2017).

There is a growing recognition in the field that to capture long-term effects, researchers need to shift away from top-down designs and use more grounded and interpretive methodologies. Socio-cultural anthropology that primarily studies non-state social forms can provide useful avenues for interpretive research with international non-governmental organizations (INGOs), and local peacebuilding organizations and the communities, and groups that they serve (Clastres, 1974). Barring a few studies on bureaucratic rationality, organizational learning routines, and the institutional memory of specific organizations such as the UN and specific NGOs (Benner and Rotman, 2008; Campbell, 2008; 2018; Gready, 2013; Williams and Mengistu, 2015; Heideman, 2016; Linde, 2018), the field is relatively nascent in its development. Theoretically informed empirical research with peacebuilding organizations can offer valuable insights into the lesser known aspects of knowledge generation, project implementation, and adaptation from an organizational perspective.

An 'ethnography of peacebuilding' can allow for a more empirical and grounded approach to the study of peacebuilding organizations (Goestchel and Hagmann, 2009: 68; Denskus, 2012). It can allow researchers to capture whether the norms underlying the projects were contextually relevant, how far they resonated with local value systems, the extent to which they were retained, if the project structures were formally absorbed into the national institutions, and whether the exit was timely and responsible in ways that built sustainable local capacities. Project archives offer a useful and underutilized resource for explanatory and exploratory analysis over the long-term. Through the application of meta-ethnographic synthesis, the learning from individual project evaluations can be synthesized in ways that allows the meta-data to be compared and related over time (Church and Shouldice, 2003: 7). This is where the book makes an original methodological contribution.

Theme 3: Sustainable Peace and Local Ownership

The book advances scholarly understanding around sustainable peace and local ownership through an examination of decisions around institutionalization;

nationalization, and succession. This contribution also speaks to the concern around sustaining peace that animates current policy discourses. Encompassing the entire gamut of its activities, the UN's sustaining peace agenda urges UN bodies including the UN Peacebuilding Commission (UNPBC) to advance, explore, and consider sustainable peace as part of its post-war reconstruction efforts.[4] To achieve sustainable peace requires thinking about timely and responsible exits in ways that empower local agency and ownership of the peace. The UN Secretary General's report *No Exit Without Strategy* (2001) argues that peacebuilding should be understood as fostering the capacity to resolve future conflicts by (1) consolidating security, (2) strengthening political institutions, and (3) promoting economic and social reconstruction (Doyle, 2007: 9). Ideally speaking, an exit strategy should be built into every project design by incorporating capacity-building and preparing successor organizations within the life-cycle of a given project.

This is rarely the case, however. Exit strategies are usually not addressed early enough in the design of projects because it is not realistic for implementing INGOs to have these in place at the start of the programming cycle. Things change, contexts differ, and if strategies are developed at the start, they can soon become outdated. Donors are equally disinterested in thinking about exit beyond the needs of accountability linked to specific funding cycles. Without strategic planning, an INGO's country operations can meander on for many years in an auto-pilot mode. The latter largely stems from a survivalist streak, making INGOs more focused on prolonging operations rather than adopting a strategic approach about exit and handover (Gardner et al., 2005; Hayman et al., 2016). The tendency to prolong operations by pursuing evolving donor interests weakens the organizational footprint. It can result in a lack of focus regarding projects that are pursued over time and can create a weak resonance of the projects with the local needs. To address this tension, strategic accountability regarding the duration and direction of country operations is necessary (Brehm, 2001: 57). National partners and local NGOs need to be trained to take on tasks that they must manage independently, relatively early on in the capacity-building cycle, rather than late in the programming life-cycle (James, 2015). Encouraging community-based fund-raising, local ownership, and self-sustaining capacities for training and development in a given country can help create a sustainable training loop critical for designing a sustainable and locally owned legacy (Popplewell et al., 2016: 3, 9).

---

[4] The UN's sustaining peace agenda was defined by identical resolutions adopted by the Security Council (UNSC) and the General Assembly (UNGA) through resolutions A/RES/70/262 and S/RES/2282 (2016). This was followed by the adoption of resolution 2413 (2018); the General Assembly's high-level meeting on peacebuilding and sustaining peace, and a high-level briefing to the UNSC was followed by the UN Secretary General Antonio Guterres' report A/72/707-S/2018/43 in 2018.

Theme 4: The Role of Children and Youth in Peacebuilding

The book advances the scholarship on the role of children and youth in peace-building by operationalizing the concept of intergenerational peace. It identifies the factors that enable young people to become change agents through the creation of links between the informal sphere of youth activism, and the formal sphere of policy making. Most youth focused projects are stop-gap in nature, they are neither focused on sustainable livelihood generation nor do they invest in building young people's relationship with the state (Munive, 2010). There is a tendency to pay lip service to instrumentalize or even 'programmatize' youth's participation in post-war contexts without enabling their meaningful involvement in the formal institutions of policy-making (Altiok and Grizelj, 2019). While democratic rights and participation can in theory be empowering for young people, their inclusion and involvement is much more complex. Practising democracy takes time, as does the willingness, opportunity, and confidence to engage with formal institutions like national youth councils, youth parliaments, and national youth commissions for example. Young people's ability to realize democratic participation, access to resources, and civic rights is circumscribed by the structural barriers to their meaningful inclusion. Instead of taking an indirect approach to youth participation through informal, short-term projects that are politically non-controversial; youth focused projects need to be used in incremental ways for building young people's civic engagement with formal institutions and local government actors (Oosterom and Shahrokh, 2016).

Without engaging in formal processes, young people will continue to remain marginalized or feel left out. Meaningful youth engagement in post-war societies demands a long-term commitment to youth-led and adult supported processes that encourage youth inclusion and participation (Prelis, Shelper, and Sankaituah, 2012: 4). We see this powerfully at play in Sierra Leone. Young people's peacebuilding experiences are situated within a social landscape of power, rights, expectations, and perceptions. It is intergenerational, and linked to how generational consciousness is constituted. This is a point that comes forth in the Macedonia case study. Adult attitudes to intergroup relations and to intergenerational interactions present considerable structural barriers to youth inclusion in the socio-economic and political realms (Collison et al., 2017). From both cases, we find that, while the adults need to be willing to facilitate and enable youth inclusion, the youth also need to cooperate with these adult supported processes to create the necessary changes in the organizational, institutional, and societal politics, structures, values, and norms. Without establishing a two-way communication between youth needs and the important formal institutions, without repairing state–citizen relations, the gains of short-term technocratic peacebuilding will not be transformative or long-lasting (von Kaltenborn-Stachau, 2008).

This is where the book makes an original contribution. It outlines the ways in which the formal and informal spheres can be linked to enhance young people's meaningful inclusion, and therefrom, their attitudes towards peace.

Theme 5: Media and Peace Education for Building Peace Norms

Both media and education projects are commonly used tools in relation to children and youth focused peacebuilding. Media's adoption as a tool for peacebuilding has been part of a top-down push from donors such as the United States, that has spent nearly USD 600 million on media development during 1994–2004 (Hume, 2004:19). Bratić, (2008) reviewed 40 media projects in 18 countries to argue that radio, newspapers, television, magazines, and the internet or digital media are critical in shaping our understanding of political, economic, and social events. They constitute the 'symbolic sphere of our existence' (Gerbner et al., 1986). Media effects theory suggests that while media does not have the power to directly alter or mould individual behaviours (Katz and Lazarsfeld, 1955; Klapper, 1960), there is wide recognition that the effects of the media are not negligible either. Children and young people are known to acquire knowledge from media programmes, and often mimic behaviour through the creation of role models or through the imitation of superhero characters on radio and television (Bandura, 1986; Lemish, 2005; Lemish and Gotz, 2007; Davies, 2010).

Educational responses to conflict, based on the principles of integration and co-existence represent the hope that through educating young people to respect others, to make friends, to see beyond negative stereotypes, and to learn tools for resolving disputes, we can hope to prevent future violence and atrocities (Minow, 2002: 2). Scholars have examined the barriers to education in conflict affected societies, the role of education in reconstructing civil society, and its importance in encouraging co-existence and peacebuilding, especially in countries recovering from intergroup, and identity-based conflicts (Weinstein, Freedman, and Hughson, 2007; Smith, 2010; Justino, 2014; Bush and Saltarelli, 2000; Gallagher, 2010; McGlynn, Zembylas and Bekerman, 2013). Betty Readon (1988), a well-known American peace educationist, categorizes the field of peace education into specific topical areas. These include conflict resolution, cooperation, non-violence, multicultural understanding, human rights, social justice, world resources, and the global environment. Across the spectrum of topics, peace education can promote either a cognitive or fact-oriented education about peace, or it can fulfil a broader approach premised on promoting an 'education for peace' (Rosandic, 2000: 10).

The role of peace education and integrated education has been researched extensively in the context of deeply divided societies such as Northern Ireland,

Cyprus, and Israel (Bekerman and Horenczyk, 2004; Bekerman and McGlynn, 2007; Donnelly, 2008; Hayes and McAllister, 2009; McGlynn and Zembylas, 2009). By reorienting the learning and socialization processes that support the psychological leanings towards violence, peace education seeks to promote a culture of peace, across diverse levels of the family, community, ethnic, and religious groups (Galtung, 1969; Danesh, 2006; Salomon, 2002: 4). Donor funded project reports on education and conflict reduction, and ethnic education and instruction in the mother tongue, deal with the implication for education and language policy in divided societies (Smith and Vaux, 2003; South and Lall, 2016).

Very little research, however, has been undertaken to examine the long-term effects of media and peace education projects in shaping young people's attitudes towards peace. I find that radio and media related norm persuasion can generate limited attitude change in societies characterized by exclusive forms of social capital such as Macedonia. They are more persuasive, however, in societies with lower resistance to external norms such as Sierra Leone. I also find that media projects are issue driven, and transient in nature. These rarely contribute to the creation of formal structures, offering only a weak commitment towards the professionalization of the media sector. In short, they offer a limited scope for institutionalization. Peace education projects by contrast create formal structures and processes, that can be more readily absorbed into national systems in ways that can shape the future of educational provision. In explaining why media programmes tend to produce diffused peacebuilding legacies compared with peace education projects, this book makes an original contribution.

Case Specific Literature and Significance

The analytical framework on peacebuilding legacy developed here offers original insights for peacebuilding with children and youth groups in the Sierra Leone and Macedonia cases. In the Sierra Leone case, the literature on post-war peacebuilding is quite substantial. In particular Catherine Bolten's research on sensitization messages, social capital, and INGO resources (2012, 2014), Gearoid Millar's research on compound friction (2013), and Boersch-Supan (2012) and Patrick Tom's (2013) work on youth and intergenerational tensions help frame some of the issues around intergenerational peace. More specifically, scholars have examined different aspects of the Lome peace process (1999), peacekeeping, and the state-building processes after the civil war ended in 2000 (Davies, 1996; Francis, 2000; Hanlon, 2005; Curran and Woodhouse, 2007; Olonisakin, 2008). In the years following the UN led post-war reconstruction effort, themes such as the elite capture of donor resources in a neo-patrimonial society, and the hiccups with implementing a liberal peace framework, including developmental shortfalls, have been the focus of several studies (Castañeda, 2009; Labonte, 2011; Cubitt, 2012; Enria, 2012; Pemunta, 2012; Bah, 2013; Millar, 2013; Lawrence, 2014).

In Sierra Leone, support for the reconstruction effort was organized into specific sectors such as mass media, democratization, health, education, transitional justice, gender, livelihoods, and ex-combatant reintegration to name a few. Studies reflect this sectoral focus. Some have examined the effects across health (Rushton, 2005), education and vocational training (Smith Ellison, 2014; Matsumoto, 2018; van der Veen and Datzberger, 2020), media (Cole, 1995; Kargobai, 2017), ex-combatant reintegration (Humphreys and Weinstein, 2007; Peters, 2007a; Denov, 2010; Bolten, 2012), democratic politics and institution-building (Fanthorpe, 2005; Bellows and Miguel, 2006; Christensen and Utas, 2008; Shepler, 2010; Fortune and Blah, 2012; Reed and Robinson, 2012; Bangura and Kovacs, 2017), rural governance (Jackson, 2005; Jackson, 2007; Millar, 2016) and land conflicts (Rahall and Schäfter, 2011; Millar, 2016, 2017, 2018a; Ryan, 2018).

Studies on youth agency (Bøås, 2013; Cubitt, 2012; Stasik, 2016); youth employment (Bürge, 2011; Menzel, 2011; Machonachie, 2011; Drew and Ramsbotham, 2012; Enria, 2015; Fortune et al., 2015) and intergenerational conflicts are quite extensive as well (Manning, 2009; Boersch-Supan, 2012; Tom, 2013, 2014; Finn and Oldfield, 2015). On the role of civil society in Sierra Leone, scholars have focused on the complexities of NGO led peacebuilding, and the sustainability of these efforts, emphasizing the problems linked with a progressive depoliticization of the civil society sector, problems with corruption, patronage, and a lingering dependency on external support (Neethling, 2007; Lambourne, 2008; Solà-Martín, 2009. 2009; Bolten, 2014; Datzberger, 2015; Bøås and Tom, 2016). These studies do not, however, examine the long-term effects of radio-based sensitization and community engagement on young people's attitude to peace. A gap that is addressed here.

Published literature on early years education and media in Macedonia includes a range of books, journal articles, and policy reports (see Tankerseley, 2001; Shochat, 2003; Brunnbauer, 2004; Karajkov, 2008; Ramet, 2013; Milchev, 2013; Spasovska and Rusi, 2015; Fontana, 2016a; Fontana, 2016b). To review the existing literature briefly, barring a handful of studies on the institutionalized ethnicity in the Western Balkans (Bieber, 2005; Spaskovska, 2012), the politics of ethnicity (Brown, 2000; Pearson, 2002; Piacentini, 2019) the crisis of inter-ethnic relations leading to the 2001 conflict in Macedonia (Hislope, 2004; van Hal, 2005; Petroska-Beska and Najcevska, 2004; Van Hal, 2005), and post-war power sharing in Macedonia (Westrick, 2011; Koinova, 2013; McEvoy, 2014; Fontana, 2016b), the literature is limited compared to that on peacebuilding in Sierra Leone. A few studies, specifically focus on the Ohrid Framework agreement (OFA) (Reka, 2008; Aleksovska, 2015); and the role of external actors like the European Union (EU) in conflict resolution (Archer, 1994; Ilievski and Taleski, 2009). Other studies examine the issue of segregated education, language, literacy, and history (Jachova, 2004; Barbieri,

Bliznakovski, and Vrgova, 2013; Arraiza, 2014; Todorov, 2016; Loader et al., 2018). There is a limited literature on integrated education (Krstevska-Papic and Zekolli, 2013; Bashkim, Dimitrova, and Brava, 2016), education policy, student identity, and interethnic attitudes (Dimova, 2006; Koneska, 2012; Lyon, 2013; Kavaja, 2017; Cvetanova, 2016; Tomovska et al., 2019). A few studies also examine children's understanding of interethnic symbols and early years education (Tomovska, 2009; Tomovska et al., 2019), and only three studies look specifically at the *Mozaik* bilingual immersion groups (Tankersely, 2001; Milchev, 2013; Fontana, 2016b). None of these studies look at the long-term effects of the integrated education efforts from a peacebuilding legacy perspective, nor do they examine the role of social capital in influencing attitude change, an area where this book makes an original contribution.

Organization of the Book

The ensuing chapters are organized as follows. Chapter 1 develops the concept of peacebuilding legacy through the lens of time, transformation, and intergenerational peace by engaging with the relevant critical scholarship in international relations (IR) and peace and conflict studies. Peacebuilding legacy is captured through three qualitative cues in an ideal typical model, given the considerable methodological challenges encountered with measuring long-term change. The model anticipates that high norm resonance, will elicit high compliance and high retention of external norms. Neutral resonance will prompt non-participation and mixed retention, while low resonance will encourage non-compliance, resistance, and rejection, leading to weak retention. Institutionalization or formal adoption of peacebuilding models by national agencies and successor organizations allows for the transfer of knowledge and supports local ownership and capacity-building. Organizational frameworks for long-term monitoring of outcomes beyond project life-cycles would require investing in meticulous archiving of institutional memory, and in post-closure evaluations. It also demands a shift from accountability driven approaches to M&E to more long-term and sustainable models. In place of technocratic approaches that privilege international expertise and scientific knowledge, we must shift to the use of indigenous monitoring and evaluation (IM&E) and local knowledge for sustainable and long-term monitoring of results.

Chapter 2 discusses the methods and approaches taken. It outlines the key challenge faced by academic researchers in transferring knowledge from research to policy by considering the pros and cons of knowledge production partnerships. The chapter then presents the research design. The approach taken for reading and translation the evaluative studies as part of the meta-ethnographic synthesis is explained, before turning to the tools used for field data collection in the two cases. A discussion on research in post-war environments is followed by an examination of ethical concerns in conducting primary research with children and young people. This is followed by some critical reflections on how my positionality as an academic of South Asian origin working at a British university was negotiated in the field. In particular, I reflect on the issues of research access, the reliance on gatekeepers, translators, and the use of purposive and snowball sampling. Possible biases and limitations of the research are acknowledged together with the steps taken to mitigate them before making some concluding reflections.

Chapter 3 presents the data from Macedonia. The chapter begins with a contextual background around interethnic relations and educational segregation. It proceeds to discuss the role of early years educational interventions in managing interethnic conflict before presenting the case of the *Mozaik* kindergartens and complementary regional and national media projects. The Macedonia case study provides critical insights for understanding the benefits and drawbacks of institutionalization and the national absorption of INGO projects in the area of peace education. It also underlines the important role of staff continuity in preserving the institutional memory, although this may not result in more effective learning and reflection. The chapter concludes with some noteworthy findings around norm resonance and retention, and their interaction with social capital dynamics in shaping long-term attitude change among children and young people.

Chapter 4 highlights the perils of seeking breadth over depth in addressing long-standing intergenerational tensions using the case of Sierra Leone. Chasing donor funding to ensure longevity of presence, without consideration of whether donor strategic priorities resonate with local issues, gave rise to a 'manufactured' rather than an 'authentic' peace. The role of community radio and radio soap operas like *Atunda Ayenda* and Golden Kids News (GKN) in articulating local issues was powerful. Children's participation as journalists enabled them to voice their concerns on radio. This experience did not translate into sustainable livelihoods however. Ad hoc involvement of the national government agencies in youth focused activities meant that projects did not conclude in ways that resulted in the sustainable transfer of project related learning. There was no commitment to institutionalization, or the creation of successor organizations. Patronage dynamics have overtaken organically formed youth focused associations like the Bike Riders Associations (BRAs). These are now highly politicized. Similar tensions permeate land conflicts in the rural hinterland in a period of liberal marketization, triggering new tensions both intergenerationally, and amongst different categories of youth.

Chapter 5 examines the data from an organizational learning and reflection perspective. It provides a state-of-the-art review of developments in the field of learning from peacebuilding M&E, before examining the learning practices of the partner INGO. Learning behaviours in the two country cases are classified into four types and are examined across the different phases of programming over 15+ years. The meta-ethnographic synthesis results from Macedonia highlights the importance of continuity both in terms of programming staff, and the project

focus for preserving the institutional memory and for successful institutionalization. I find that this was possible even when the Macedonia country office was not
particularly learning oriented.

For example, periodic evaluations had advised a revision of the theory of change
underlying the *Mozaik* bilingual groups, urging that families rather than children
should be made the target of the intervention. This did not happen with *Mozaik*
or the related media efforts that remain focused mainly on the children and youth
groups. In Sierra Leone, the breadth of work undertaken by the country office
presented a far from organic evolution. The country office was more dynamic and
committed to learning from evaluation across its media and community outreach
work. Despite a steady staff turnover, adjustments were made where possible and
the digital memory of projects were well-preserved. This learning orientation did
not translate however into an explicit commitment to institutionalization due to
weak formal links with government agencies that could help institutionalize their
efforts.

Chapter 6 presents the second order interpretations from the meta-
ethnographic synthesis regarding norm persuasion. It examines the role of
media and peace education norms in shaping young people attitudes to peace
over time. Nine specific second order learning concepts are analysed in each case,
across the broad themes of 'access and acceptance', 'agency and behaviour', and
'citizenship and democracy' in Sierra Leone and 'intercultural communication',
'quality pre-school education', and 'citizenship and ethnic identity' in Macedonia.
I reflect on the limits of norm persuasion in precipitating long-term attitude
change among young people without incorporating an ecological model of child
development. Different actors across the multiple levels of programming need
to be targeted at the same time inorder to foster meaningful and lasting attitude
change across society.

In the conclusion, I revisit the main arguments of the book. I examine the logics
of institutional, normative, and organizational legacy operative across the suite of
children and youth focused media and peace education projects in Sierra Leone
and Macedonia. This helps examine the broader conceptual, methodological, and
analytical value of these logics for peacebuilding practice. Thereafter, relying on the
book's empirical, and analytical insights, broader debates around youth and peacebuilding programming are debated. The findings urge a shift from instrumental
to transformative participation of young people. In terms of practical implications, the chapter encourages vertical and horizontal integration of young people's
participation in peacebuilding; a stronger engagement with the formal sphere;
enhanced intergenerational responsibility; repairing state-citizen relations, and
adopting an ecological model of peace.

1

Peacebuilding Legacy

Introduction

Over the past three decades we have seen the development of ever more sophisticated peace-support interventions by international organizations, bilateral donors, and INGOs. From Cambodia and the former Yugoslavia in the early post-Cold War years, to the latest interventions in South Sudan, we have seen enormous energies and significant material, political, and symbolic resources (one estimate would suggest USD ten billion) expended in the name of peacebuilding (Global Peace Index Report, 2017: 3). Much of this has been targeted at children and young people, who are significant actors in relation to conflict and violence globally (Pruitt, 2020). We have little idea, however, if these resources are 'well spent' beyond a programme specific M&E of short-term outputs. Even after 20 years of peacebuilding work, commonly used M&E tools are still designed primarily to assess the outputs of single peacebuilding interventions, and over short time-periods. Whether we consider methods common among international organizations (Rogers, Chassey and Bamat, 2010; OECD, 2012) or those advanced by scholars (Anderson 1996; Bush 1998; Paffenholz and Reychler 2007; Firchow and Mac Ginty, 2017), there appears to be no existing process able to assess the cumulative outcomes of multiple peacebuilding interventions within societies recovering from conflict. In fundamental ways, the core puzzle that plagues the discipline of peace and conflict studies is to ascertain how technocratic approaches to peacebuilding that are rooted in short-term, project-based execution of activities and outputs can further longer-term transformative outcomes that aim to alter young people's attitudes and beliefs about peace and violence.

To unpack this dichotomy at the heart of the real work of peacebuilding, it is worthwhile considering what scholars and policymakers envisage successful peacebuilding to entail. Lederach (1997: 20) defines peacebuilding as 'a comprehensive concept that encompasses, generates, and sustains the full array of processes, approaches, and stages that are needed to transform conflict toward more sustainable, peaceful relationships.' In this, peacebuilding is both relational and political (Vayrynen, 2019: 3). Goodhand and Hulme (1999: 15), suggest that 'peace requires social transformation and must be done slowly'. Recognition among scholars that peacebuilding is a long-term process; and that a longer and

Peacebuilding Legacy. Sukanya Podder, Oxford University Press.
© Sukanya Podder (2022). DOI: 10.1093/oso/9780192863980.003.0002

more sustained international commitment is necessary has been consistent since the end of the Cold War (Tschirgi, 2004: 9; Doyle and Sambanis, 2006: 27; Donais, 2009: 9; de Coning, 2010: 10). From a policy perspective, in the report *An Agenda for Peace* produced by the UN Secretary General (UNSG) Boutros Boutros-Ghali (1992, para 21), consistent investment, policy continuity, and programme continuity were identified as critical to peacebuilding success (de Coning, 2010: 21). More recently, *The Challenge of Sustaining Peace* report (2015) produced by a group of experts appointed by the UNSG, Ban Ki Moon, helped to define the 'sustaining peace' concept as the forward-looking and transformative alternative to peacebuilding (see also, Langer, Langer and Brown, 2016). Sustainable peace refers to an absence of not only physical violence, but also structural, psychological, cultural, environmental, and temporal violence (Reychler, 2015a: 20). For peace to be sustainable, it must evolve gradually and be locally owned (Ricigliano, 2015).

In pursuit of their transformative agenda, peacebuilding INGOs design and deliver thematic 'projects and programmes', around good governance, democratization, transitional justice, reconciliation, SSR, and economic restructuring that form part of the transition between post-war reconstruction and long-term development (Tschirgi, 2003). Trainings, and the development of manuals for child soldiers and ex-combatant youth may fit within the 'project' approach, but may not generate adaptive processes (Duckworth, 2016: 5). Designed as short-term projects lasting anywhere between nine and twelve months, thematic programmes are constructed on loosely conceived theories of change that anticipate, how and why a desired change is expected to occur in a particular context (Vogel, 2012: 26). For some time, critiques of the liberal peace have expressed suspicion towards peacebuilding strategies as effective technical solutions to the problems of violent conflict, underdevelopment and state weakness (Götze and Guzina, 2008, Chandler, 2013; Autesserre, 2014: 78). This is because technocratic approaches to peacebuilding draw on the purported a-temporal universalism of modern social scientific knowledge (Wallerstein, 1997: 100). The continuous demand for better, more accurate knowledge to improve interventions is part of the managerial rationality of donors (Bakonyi, 2018: 586).

The bureaucratic pressure to deliver value for donor aid sourced through the taxpayers' money has normalized the deployment of a battery of neoliberal technologies of management and control (Duffield, 2001; Duffield, 2007; Denskus, 2007a; 2007b; Bächtold, 2021). The knowledge produced in, and around peacebuilding interventions perpetuates Eurocentrism's epistemic avatar and establishes a hierarchy of knowledge. Within this frame, experts from the Global North speak authoritatively about solutions for the Third World's problems, even when they lack the necessary contextual and historical knowledge (Escobar, 2004: 207–30; Mignolo, 2007: 155–67; Ndlovu-Gatsheni, 2013; Sabaratnam, 2013: 262–3). These hierarchies appear to replicate colonial and exclusive regimes of knowledge production (Cohn, 1996). Technocratic approaches to peacebuilding and the dominance of M&E as managerial tools for measuring peacebuilding effectiveness are part of this regime that offers temporary fixes and incomplete solutions (Denskus, 2007a; Goetschel and Hagmann, 2009; Mac Ginty, 2012a, 2013; Sabaratnam, 2013; Autesserre, 2014).

For example, while speaking the language of empowerment and rights, peacebuilding projects generate a plethora of informal and temporary structures (child welfare committees, micro-credit groups, community patrols, and women's groups) rather than institutions that link into national and formal agencies and departments. This project-based culture of most donor organizations creates considerable pressure for the achievement of tangible and measurable results, and limited concern for their long-term effects (Donais, 2009: 9). Activity focused peacebuilding linked to external financing is attuned to meeting the short-term needs of beneficiaries, whether they are specific target groups (victims of sexual violence, disabled children, ex-combatants, the internally displaced) or specific rural communities. Even if successful in mobilizing participation, project linked structures often dissipate or become defunct once the project-related funding runs out. Urgency to produce results, can and does undermine strategic thinking, it encourages an 'impatient' peace (Barnett, Zürcher, and Fang, 2014: 608; Hom, 2018: 306). Beneficiaries return to their old patterns of life and the learning derived from their involvement in the different project activities may, or may not, encourage shifts in their behaviour over the longer-term. As a result, an overarching focus on time-bound achievements and project focused outputs runs contrary to the long-term process of transformation necessary for sustaining peace.

Conceptualizing Peacebuilding Legacy

Measuring progress towards the achievement of longer-term goals that go beyond the identification of programme outputs requires long-term investment in building the resilience of local mechanisms that emphasize sustainability and affordability of local initiatives (Juncos and Joseph, 2020: 292–5). It necessitates thinking about legacy. By 'peacebuilding legacy', I mean the long-term effects of various peacebuilding interventions attempted in the context of post-war reconstruction that are non-linear and difficult to predict. Legacies can be direct, indirect and interrupted in nature. Direct legacies represent the physical, institutional, and structural remnants that are the more tangible representation of peacebuilding efforts. Indirect legacies are linked to processes initiated during periods of intervention when international actors and their local partners take major decisions and actions in key policy areas. Interrupted legacies are processes and actions marred by short-term interventions, and patchwork programming. Without consistent investment or follow-up, certain interventions do not portend long-lasting changes, rather only temporary shifts in behaviours (Gledhill, 2020: 4). This book is specifically concerned with the direct legacies of peacebuilding work with children and young people implemented over 15+ years by the partner INGO in Sierra Leone and Macedonia.

Peacebuilding legacy is conceptualized here through the lens of 'time'; 'transformation', and 'intergenerational peace'. Conflicts change over time and across generations. Intractable conflicts, as in South Sudan, Palestine, and Afghanistan, pose different experiences of conflict and peace for different generations. The current format of M&E activities is time-bound and organized into six-month cycles over two-three-year blocks. They do not accurately present the results of peacebuilding efforts that manifest many years after projects have closed and after the donors and implementing organizations have folded their operations and left (Bamat, 2012). Therefore, understanding the true, long-term effects of peacebuilding activities presents a misalignment of principles and priorities between 'donor time' and the time necessary for conflict transformation through societal norm change from violence to peace (Bush 1996; Kwano-Chiu, 2012). The transmission of values from one generation to the next is a central plank in social sustainability, but it can also involve the perpetuation of partisan views, militarism, and social systems of exclusion and violence (Fargas-Malet and Dillenburger, 2016; Joireman, 2018). There is a need for adopting a more long-term and generational view of peacebuilding effects due to the different needs and experiences of different generations, and their evolving needs and expectations from peace (Sooros, 1976). I examine each sub-concept in turn.

Time

On paper, peacebuilding activities are structured so that they deliver results to an appropriate temporal strategy (Miall, 2004: 7). Peacebuilding success however cannot be predicated on any specific type of action, or sequencing of activities (Christie and Algar-Faria, 2020: 161). Recent critical IR scholarship on the role of time in world politics and sociological and anthropological theories of time offer some valuable insights for scoping the role of time in shaping peacebuilding legacy (Shapiro, 2000: 79–98; Hutchings, 2007: 71–89; 2018: 253–8; Lousley, 2016: 310–28). For conceptual purposes, time can be cyclical, circular, or linear in character. As such, there is no unique ontological manner of registering time nor of perceiving it. Adam (2004: 144–5) suggests that we think of temporal relations as 'clusters of temporal features', such as timeframes, tempo, timing, sequence, and patterns. The measurement of time and the notions of temporality therefore are dynamic, culturally defined, and contextually dependent. In sociological theories of time, a distinction is often made between social time and inner time. Social time is linear, predictable, as well as regular and uniform. Social events reflect dominant temporal expectations (Zerubavel, 1982; 1987), and a non-elite understanding of time (Mac Ginty, 2016: 1–12). Inner time is more discontinuous and multifaceted. It is cyclical time, in which events recur, and repeat themselves. Cyclical time is often imposed on traditional or small-scale societies. In anthropological accounts, the notion of time is used to govern, and to construct social meanings (Schwartz, 1974; Bergmann, 1992; Adam, 1990, 2004; Mueller-Hirth and Oyola, 2018: 2).

Despite the complexity and richness in the social study of time, Western normative and teleological notions of time are predominantly linear. The dominant understanding of time is clock time, a forward moving, globally unified time with discrete units for measurement and coordination (Hall, 1959: 28; Hutchings, 2008: 18; Hutchings, 2018: 253-8). Linear and sequential notions of time are hardwired into the formal, political, diplomatic, and security worldviews and practices. Political time relates to the ripeness for peace negotiations, and the willingness of the political and military elites to engage in a negotiated compromise (Christie and Algar-Faria, 2020: 159). It represents elite understandings of time. These top-down institutionalist, and externally driven notions of time that drive peace processes intersect with social time, or the everyday activities of ordinary people in the villages, streets, and workplaces giving rise to the hybridized nature of time (Mac Ginty, 2016: 1–12). Time is therefore relational, connected to understandings of the past, and the future, as well as the present. For the victims of wartime violence, time is crucial for the understanding of social questions related to the legacies of violence (Teitel, 2003). Changes in the personal, structural, relational, and cultural aspects of conflict over different periods (short, medium, and long-term) in the conflict cycle, are experienced differently by the different age groups. Acknowledging this difference, recent peace studies scholarship has adopted time sensitive perspectives in the study of transitional justice, to examine conflict experiences that are both public and private (Read and Mac Ginty, 2017: 151).

In the context of peacebuilding, Barbara Adam (2004) alludes to the importance of time literate thinking about the issues that affect peacebuilding. Pluralities of time co-exist and operate simultaneously with respect to how peacebuilding is implemented by different CSOs. Temporament, or the way persons or organizations deal with time in conflict management and peacebuilding situations, shapes the duration of peacebuilding engagement on the ground (Reychler, 2015a: 19). Peacebuilders for the most part remain subservient to policy time, which refers to the time considerations of donors, and these can be very different from that of local communities where peacebuilding is implemented. Policy time emphasizes how peacebuilding practices are regulated and constrained due to the demands of bureaucratic clock-time, which determine project budgets, time horizons, and time rules in the design and implementation of peacebuilding policies and practices (Christie and Algar-Faria, 2020:159). Bureaucratic clock time has a linear, unidirectional flow that is independent of human experience. Communities who are the beneficiaries of peacebuilding interventions rarely have control over the timing or duration of peacebuilding activities. Such an approach results in a disconnect between the enforced timeframes of activities that often need to be completed within '9–12–18-month cycles', and the evolving needs, expectations, and experiences of the beneficiaries or the communities of intervention (Hutchings, 2008).

There are also inequalities in how time is used and whose time is valued (Bastian, 2014). Giordano Nanni in his book *The Colonization of Time* (2012) illustrates the link between power and time. To be kept waiting is a social assertion that one's time and social worth are less valuable (Schwartz, 1974: Bourdieu, 2000). Because waiting is bound up with social status and power, it is often experienced by the poor and the powerless (Auyero, 2011: 5-8; Harms, 2013). Donor states, international organizations, and INGOs decide on the timing and duration of support for local communities in conflict-affected areas. They rarely take the bottom-up and local perspectives into account (Read and Mac Ginty, 2017). Policy time therefore equates with control; it is a form of hierarchical power and governance within peacebuilding. It is aligned with Western time that is linear and sequential in character and is imposed on local communities who follow a different sociological and anthropological understanding of time, be it social time, inner time, or cyclical time (Igreja, 2012; McLeod, 2013). The time sequence adopted by donors and INGOs also differs from the timeframe across which changes in behaviour, attitudes, and beliefs take place in societies under transition. Short-term projects with little or no follow up result in a superficial or partial transformation of attitudes. Long-term, in-depth, and sustained engagement holds the key for the lasting transformation of conflicts; and for building sustainable peace. It is also the key to building stronger peacebuilding legacies.

Transformation

The idea of transformation is implicitly built into the notion of progress towards peace (Richmond, 2005). Some of the main scholars of conflict transformation theory such as John Paul Lederach (1997; 2005), Adam Curle (1971), and Johan Galtung (1976) address transformation in terms of 'system-wide' and 'structural' changes. For Väyrynen (1991), these can include actor transformation, issue transformation, rule transformation, and structural transformation. These changes are rooted in an overarching shift from a culture of violence to a culture of peace. The idea of a culture of violence, as developed by Johan Galtung (1969), implies a dynamic system of reciprocally reinforcing physical, psychological, and structural influences that can impede peaceful relations. Transformative peacebuilding is primarily concerned with transforming these influences and establishing new conditions that are enabling for peace. Only focusing on structural changes through top-down or headquarters driven strategic planning has limited transformative potential. Liberal marketization when introduced without transforming unequal social or power relations can reinforce pre-existing sources of structural violence (Galtung, 2000). Equally, problem-solving through advocacy around appropriate behaviours would not transform structural inequalities of social relations and institutions or their social meanings (Cox, 1981: 129–30).

The transformative work of peacebuilding involves reforming both the psychological (inner), and the structural (outer) triggers for conflict. Social problems can be discursively perpetuated; therefore, any transformation would need to address discursive practices as well (Fetherston, 2000: 22). Critics of the top-down approach to building peace propose a more locally owned, bottom-up variant that allows local voices to be heard (Curle, 1994; Lederach, 1997; Paffenholz, 2014). Towards this end, peacebuilding in the 1990s nurtured the idea of the 'peace from below' with a focus on striving for social justice, ending violent conflict, and building healthy, cooperative relations in local communities (Lederach and Appleby, 2010: 27). The 'local turn' recognizes that the best peace-making potential is to be found in the communities themselves (Dietrich, 2013; Mac Ginty and Richmond, 2013; Leonardsson and Rudd, 2015). 'All self-sustainable peace is context specific, indigenous, and bottom-up' (de Coning, 2013: 6). Thereby justifying the efforts to build on indigenous socio-cultural structures and practices, and for empowering, and developing local peacemakers (Curle, 1994: 96–105). The local turn in peacebuilding intersects with a growing emphasis on local capacity-building, and local ownership of the transformative agenda pursued by the UN, and other international peacebuilding actors or partners (Paffenholz, 2016).

Critics of the liberal peace expose the instrumentalization of the local; or its use in a rhetorical sense, thereby undermining the potential of the local for transformative peacebuilding (Mac Ginty and Richmond, 2013: 771). Not all local-level grassroots peace efforts are equally consequential for the purposes of national or society wide transformations. Constructive linkages through vertical integration of local level and national level peace efforts do not emerge organically but must be consciously planned (McCandless, Abitbol, and Donais, 2015: 4). Vertical integration must grapple with hierarchical relationships and power asymmetries. Critical peacebuilding scholars have critiqued how the civil society is used in relation to liberal peacebuilding, and the constrained worldview of donor funded CSOs marked by compliance and pacification (Richmond, 2011: 433–4). INGOs are resourceful and can exercise both bureaucratic and coercive power over communities, generating 'haves' and 'have nots' through the selective delivery of services to certain geographic locations (Riehl, 2001).

Conflict transformation theory has been influenced by the debate on timing and sequencing of interventions (Reychler, 2015b; Langer and Brown, 2016). The transformative peace agenda is rooted in the assumption that transformation can take place gradually through processual logics; rather than through concrete discernible actions or events (Mitchell, 2010: 641–2). Yet in practice, peacebuilding is about activity or actions, and less about looking into the future or thinking about the long-term effects. Peace is processed or 'worked upon' by external norms and practices that shape outcomes into a desired state of affairs. There is a certain compartmentalization of transformation into specific reform tasks. Peacebuilding actors like the UN, the EU, various donor governments, and INGOs operate as change agents, that use technocratic liberal peacebuilding processes as a means for restructuring the economy, electoral procedures, and the civil society landscape. This becomes the focus of transformation, rather than the changes in personal, structural, relational, and cultural aspects of conflict brought about over different time periods and affecting the different system-levels (Diamond and McDonald, 1996).

For example, the EU has made externally guided reform a centre-piece of its intervention in countries like Bosnia and Herzegovia (BiH), Kosovo, and Cyprus among other cases (Chandler, 1999; Ker-Lindsay, 2009; Visoka, 2011; Pogodda et al., 2014; Groß, 2015). Lederach (1997: 94) notes that the role of external peacebuilders is limited to supporting internal actors, coordinating external peace efforts, engaging in a context-sensitive way, and respecting local culture. In Lederach's theory, the greatest resource for sustaining peace in the long term is always rooted in the local people and their culture. Without an explicit commitment to local ownership, no amount of local engagement or community level peacebuilding can generate sustainable peace (Mac Ginty, 2008; Taylor, 2010; Richmond, 2011; Belloni, 2012: 32). Conflict transformation requires a more considered and strategic approach, taking account of both the structural and the local level transformative processes. In place of overlapping, imperfectly coordinated activities across different levels of intervention, we require strategies that maximize the long-term effects of initiatives across these multiple levels to effect the constructive structural changes necessary for transformative peace (Lederach and Appleby, 2010: 22).

Intergenerational Peace

Intergenerational realities manifest in various ways in the context of war and conflict. War-induced flight, migration, and resettlement create important physical (rape, injury, torture, crime, starvation) and psychological effects (stress, depression, isolation, unemployment, discrimination) on families and between generations (Denov et al., 2019: 18–20). Resilience and adaptive capacities are passed on, in an intergenerational sense, as is intergenerational trauma. For example, children born of wartime rape may both consciously and unconsciously absorb the abuse, trauma, and discrimination faced by their mother into their lives (Carpenter, 2010; Denov, 2015: 64). The cumulative effects of trauma passed down along generational lines, are often amplified, in that they can give rise to unpredictable impacts as noted for example amongst the survivors of the Holocaust

(Danieli, 1998; Evans-Campbell, 2008: 316). In Rwanda, the intergenerational fallout of genocidal rape resulted in a loss of identity, and social exclusion for the children due to the father's perpetrator status, and the shame surrounding rape, that undermined their maternal identity (Carpenter, 2000, cited in Denov et al., 2017: 3293).

Intergenerational resilience by contrast involves learning from, and honouring the lived experiences of each generation (Rawluk, 2012: 108; Atallah, 2017). Children and families of refugees often exhibit resourcefulness, and the ability to cope well amidst profound adversity (Denov et al., 2019: 23). Both intergenerational trauma and resilience brought forth by war and armed conflict, require socio-ecological approaches to the study of vulnerability and adaptation as they can shape the nature of conflict between generations (Boothby, Crawford, and Halperin, 2006; Tyrer and Fazel, 2014). By way of definition, intergenerational conflict involves different generations regardless of whether there is a lag between the time at which mutually exclusive interests become operative (Soroos, 1976: 175). Intergenerational relations are longitudinal when interests of different generations are operative at different times, and considerable time may elapse between the actions of one party, and the impact of the actions on a second party (Soroos, 1976: 174).

In conflict-affected societies, clashing value systems with the older generation can create different standards for actions; and thereby regulate day-to-day behaviours as well as important and critical life decisions of the young in ways that can elicit the latter's disapproval (Gaerling, 1999). Intergenerational conflict can also present important structural tensions. The political and economic systems when geared toward the short-term interests of contemporary politically active groups, compromises the interests of the future generations (Galtung, 1969: 170–1). Scholars concerned with the study of African neopatrimonialism draw on 'Big Men' or 'Great Men' research to explain how power, control, and distribution of resources in these societies exacerbate structural inequalities long after the conflict subsides (Godelier and Strathern, 1991 cited in Utas, 2012: 1; Tom, 2014: 332; Podder, 2015).

Concern for future generations is necessary for engendering intergenerational peace defined as the approach through which different generational needs in conflict-affected societies can be accommodated into peacebuilding thinking; and incorporated into peacebuilding programming (Boulding, 1967). Intergenerational peace can be pursued by adopting norms, behaviours, and policies that can shape the direction and experience of peace for the future generations, and by implementing peacebuilding in ways that creates a meaningful normative and institutional legacy (Hutchinson, 1999). When peacebuilding is rooted in long-term thinking, outcomes are extended beyond the interests or needs of the current generation to thinking about the future generation, and in anticipating their needs (Sooros, 1976: 177). Futures thinking can help adjust the assumption that human progress is inevitable, and that each generation leaves behind an enriched legacy for the next (Howker and Malik, 2013; Vladimirova, 2014: 66; Humphreys, 2015: 1–14; Kaplan, Sanchez, and Hoffman, 2017).

Interests of different generations are operative at different times, and considerable time may elapse between the time one party acts, and the impact of that action on a second party manifests (Soroos, 1976: 174). In long-drawn, protracted conflicts, peacebuilding initiatives and how their effects unfold over time can lead to new problems between generations; as each generation is likely to have distinct peacebuilding needs. In practice, peacebuilding activities rarely take into account, or take stock of the generational differences, or, of the specific generational needs (Christie and Algar-Faria, 2020: 160). For example, in Israel, intergroup contact programmes between Arabs and Jews have mostly targeted children and youth, while involving very few elders. Few scholars reflect on the importance of understanding the generational differences in relation to peace. Intergenerational narratives of historical pasts can play a crucial role in slowly building new intergroup relations after the termination of conflicts (Leone, 2018: 458). Without addressing the values and prejudices of the older generations, efforts to transform the attitudes of younger generations can prove to be futile in intergroup conflicts (Leitner, Scher, and Shuval, 1999: 25; Axelrod, 2006).

Peace with intergenerational justice or equity involves developing initiatives that aim to bring the older and younger generations together in purposeful ways, through mutually beneficial activities that promote greater understanding and respect between generations (Hutchinson and Milojević, 2012: 15; Finn and Scharf, 2012: 2; Scharf, Timonen, Carney, and Conlon, 2013: 19). From encouraging cross-cultural dialogue, to sharing knowledge on ethics, rights, civic responsibilities, and well-being (Hicks and Holden, 1995; Groff and Smoker, 1997; Inayatullah, 1997, 1998; Hutchinson, 1997, 1999, 2005a, 2005b), it is urgent to recognize the intergenerational character of peacebuilding work (Boulding, 1966; Russett, 1974; Hutchinson and Ivana Milojević, 2012: 165). Such a reorientation lies at the heart of legacy thinking.

Capturing Peacebuilding Legacy

The study and measurement of long-term effects including the question of appropriate methodologies for capturing conflict transformation is a critical one in thinking about peacebuilding legacy (Millar, 2018b; Podder, 2021). While some aspects of legacy are linked to specific outcomes, such as large-scale job creation (positive), or violent protest (negative), that may be relatively easy to observe and measure, many important impacts (on personal experiences, in remote communities, or over extended periods), are less visible and largely ignored. Although some longitudinal survey research has been in operation for many years in Northern

Ireland and Israel/Palestine, these are the exceptions (Hughes and Donnelly, 2003; Gvirsmann et al., 2016). For the most part, the current suite of conflict analysis, and M&E tools used by both practitioners and scholars, while well-suited to 'snap-shot research', is less well-equipped for examining longer-term change. Given the current methodological constraints, what do we need to capture peacebuilding legacy, and how might we attempt to do that?

Capturing the legacy of peacebuilding in any one case requires; first, that we rec-ognize and assess the interconnections, points of articulation, and relationships between different projects claiming to have peacebuilding effects; and second, that we then assess their collective impacts on dynamics central to sustainable peace, such as the development of sustainable communities, intergroup relation-ships, and the longer-term processes of statebuilding and development closely associated with peacebuilding in post-conflict and conflict-affected societies. The nub of the problem, therefore, is to identify, observe, and 'measure' the cumu-lative and incremental impacts of peacebuilding interventions broadly defined (Millar, 2021). From a macro perspective, this primarily involves assessing the extent to which peacebuilding processes have collectively served to support a 'neg-ative peace', or deter conflict recidivism (Mac Ginty, 2010: 400), and the extent to which they contributed to 'positive peace' or supported intergroup reconciliation, civil society strengthening, smooth political transitions, and the development of conflict-ameliorating forms of governance (Pouligny, 2005).

Long-term change, it can be argued, is fundamentally non-linear and complex, compounding the challenge of attributing a specific change to a specific interven-tion, and by a specific actor. Even after 20 years of peacebuilding work, commonly used M&E tools such as logical frameworks (logframes) are still designed pri-marily to assess the outputs of single peacebuilding interventions over short time periods. Activities and outputs guided by logframes constitute part of project 'per-formance' or the 'showing of doing' in an anthropological sense of how change will manifest over time (Grimes, 2003: 35). A certain commodification or reduction-ism becomes inevitable (Neufeldt, 2007: 10–11; Benner and Rotman, 2008: 43–62; Bush, 2001; Mac Ginty, 2012a: 287). Embedded in technocratic peacebuilding, the overall approach of current M&E tools is embedded in bureaucratic processes that are deterministic or linear in design. The outcome is more or less guaranteed if the design is followed. The focus is on achieving pre-set outcomes and impact.

Theories of change are often perceived as a way to move away from the rigid templates associated with the logframe approach (Eriksen, 2009: 662 cited in de Coning, 2018: 2). Many organizations today talk about contribution analysis, based on the development of a postulated theory of change for a given interven-tion. For example, in my research with child soldiers in Liberia, I found that DDR projects expected short-term vocational training would lead to the regeneration of livelihoods, and contribute to the long-term social transformation by building the capacity of an economically active youthful population (Jennings, 2008: 327-330).

Project evaluations were designed to either confirm or verify the theory of change or suggest revisions by testing it against the given logic, and the evidence available (Mayne, 2012: 271). Considerable donor and government pressure on CSOs to fit within particular narratives, in order to operate in a specific country, means, loosely conceived theories of change are used as an accountability and funding tool (Campbell, 2018). This was very much the case with DDR projects I evaluated in Liberia. Even when it was possible to verify or confirm with empirical evidence, that any given intervention made a difference to youth livelihoods (Blattman and Annan, 2011), what happened to the ex-combatant youth years after they enrolled in a DDR related vocational training programme remained largely outside the scope of donor interest, creating important gaps in the measurement of peacebuilding legacy.

Linear causal logic is ill-suited for examining the dynamic and complex social systems that peacebuilding interventions seek to influence (Brussett, De Coning, and Hughes, 2016: 2). Without situating or relating project contributions into the larger eco systems of social change, only a superficial process of critical thought and limited learning and reflection can take place (Lewis, 2016: 12–18). This is because peace is difficult to quantify beyond the absence of violence. It emerges from messy political processes that are unique to each society, and its cultural belief system (Brussett, De Coning, and Hughes, 2016: 2). Measuring transformational change, such as attitude change requires the development of innovative methodological tools to assess less visible outcomes (Scharbatke-Church, 2011: 471–5; Christie and Algar-Faria, 2020: 156). Given the delayed nature of causality, synthetic qualitative approaches that juxtapose analytical versus subjectivist approaches to understand 'effects' need to be developed.

Cues for Capturing Legacy

In this book, I use three cues for capturing peacebuilding legacy qualitatively. The first cue is norm transmission, resonance, and retention by project participants, and their families and communities; the second cue is the progress with institutionalization and adaptation of project models through their successful handover to national agencies; and the third cue is the depth of learning and reflection from the M&E of projects by the peacebuilding organization itself. These three cues enable us to evaluate the long-term effects of peacebuilding on post-war environments in terms of norms, institutions, and organizational practices. Studying peacebuilding legacy through these three cues offers a simplified ideal type conceptualization of complex causal or path dependent processes of change with some heuristic value. Observed outcomes along these three cues intersect with the live debates on local ownership, local capacity building, and sustainable peace that inform the goal of transformative peace (Figure 1.1). I discuss each analytical cue in turn.

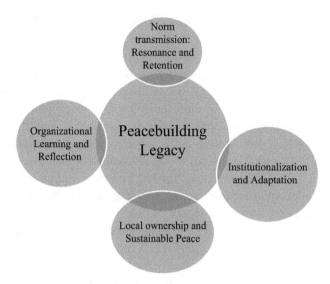

Fig. 1.1 Conceptualizing peacebuilding legacy

Transmission of Peace Norms: Resonance and Retention

Norms are rules of behaviour which are jointly held and sustained by social groups (Elster, 1989; Krupkar and Weber, 2013). More specifically, they represent collective expectations regarding the appropriate behaviour and actions within a given social milieu (Katzenstein, 1996: 6; Laffey and Weldes, 1997: 210). How norms spread in the international system has been studied through a social constructivist lens within the discipline of IR. Several waves of norm research can be identified, moving progressively from the study of the role of transnational advocacy networks and norm entrepreneurs in the process of norm emergence, to that of norm internalization in domestic and transnational settings (Finnermore and Sikkink, 1998; Risse and Sikkink, 1999; Björkdahl, 2002b; Acharya, 2004). The first generation of norm scholarship developed models to explain the ways in which states have adopted international norms, thereby supporting their socialization into international regimes (Keck and Sikkink, 1997; Risse et al., 1999). The second wave of norm scholarship focused on the adoption by, and meeting of the normative criteria set on countries seeking accession to the EU, by the latter.

These studies examine how the EU has influenced the domestic, organizational, political, and cultural scope conditions for successful norm diffusion (Björkdahl, 2002a; Björkdahl, 2005; Schimmelfennig, Engert, and Knobel, 2006; Magen and Morlino, 2009; Tholens and Groß, 2015: 251), while also highlighting the possible domestic constraints to norm diffusion (Checkel, 1999; Cortell and Davis, 2000). The third wave of norm research has seen a diversity of critical scholarship on how norms travel, alongside an examination of the processes of contestation, resistance, and localization that are part of the norm internalization process. This has included research into the domestic side of norm diffusion in post-war states, including the interactive and inter-relational nature of norms (Acharya 2004: 241; Katsumata, 2011: 558–60; Björkdahl and Gusic, 2015: 269–70; Tholens and Groß, 2015: 249–50; Zimmerman, 2016: 98). It is this third wave of norm research that I draw on for capturing the link between norm transmission, resonance, and retention for measuring peacebuilding legacy.

Given the focus here on post-war peacebuilding, and due to the limited application of norm diffusion frameworks from IR literature to post-war contexts, this study assumes norms transmission in the context of peacebuilding to be liberal in character, tied to donor funded reform programmes, and therefore more in the nature of policy transfer (Dolowitz and Marsh, 1996; Jenkins, 2008). New norms can spread more easily in post-war societies as the normative space is often under renegotiation, with new social groups scrambling to gain ascendance in the post-war order (Tholens and Gross, 2015: 255). The modes of norm transmission can include schools and curriculum, family, beliefs, or religion and through media, culture, art, literature, and political economies (Finnermore and Sikkink, 1998: 887–917; Acharya, 2011: 95–123). Transmission in itself does not encourage adoption or the retention of norms. The influx of new ideas must resonate with local populations, and for that, norms must identify with or incorporate local meaning to generate and maintain legitimacy within a broader social context before they can be adopted and implemented in the long run (Wiener, 2007: 6).

The idea around norm resonance gains salience here. Resonance refers to the cultural or institutional match of a specific external rule with the already existing domestic values, norms, practices, and discourses in a specific issue area. The higher the degree of normative fit, the more likely the target groups or civilian communities will conceive the norm as familiar, legitimate, and trustworthy (Cortell and Davis, 2000: 69). A missing cultural match can produce outright resistance to norm adoption (Zimmerman, 2016: 98). Therefore, the processes of norm transmission can be inherently hybrid in nature, resulting in a clash between liberal (international) and at times illiberal (local) norms. This tension is accepted as part of the operational reality of norm transmission and norm diffusion by critical peace studies scholars (Mac Ginty, 2010; Jarstad and Belloni, 2012; Millar, 2015; Zimmerman, 2016). Compliance, contestation, resistance, localization, participation, and non-participation are identified as the possible outcomes of norm transmission efforts (Mac Ginty, 2012b: 167–70; Zimmerman, 2016: 98–115; Wolff and Zimmerman, 2016: 1–22).

The likelihood of compliance to external norms increases with stronger resonance of the norms with local values, i.e. norms do not contradict basic societal beliefs and local legitimacy, or when the local identification with the introduced values is high (Schimmelfenning, 2005: 2). In IR scholarship, contestation is put forward as an analytical concept to grasp the diverse practices by which the recipients of external norms dispute the validity, the meaning, or the application of norms (Wolff and Zimmerman, 2016: 6). Oliver Richmond uses the terms 'resistance' and 'critical agency' to conceptualize how local actors can challenge, work against, reject, co-opt, or usurp international peacebuilding efforts in a way that aims to reclaim it as a locally owned process, or 'a reclaimed peace' (Richmond, 2011; Richmond, 2012a: 117; Richmond, 2012b: 354-355). Local actors can either sidestep the liberal peace project, or divert symbolic and financial resources intended to buttress efforts such as democracy promotion in ways that undermine the liberal peace (Zahar, 2012: 74).

A certain amount of bargaining between international and local actors in order to promote their own values, norms, and practices ensues (Jarstad and Belloni, 2012). Richmond (2010) views resistance to be a positive emancipatory force, with the potential for enhancing sustainable peace. In arguing for a post-liberal peace, Richmond's vision is for a via media that emerges from the encounter between local knowledge, and international prescriptions, and assumptions, about peace. In what he describes as an 'eirenist' approach, contestation, and resistance are absorbed into a hybridized version of peace, that transforms but does not replace the liberal peace (Richmond, 2009a; 2009b). By contrast, Antje Wiener's work on contestation refers to the conflicts over the meaning of norms. Because the meanings of norms are created through interactive processes, and are based on social practices in specific contexts, norms are part of a continuous cycle of reinterpretation (Wiener, 2014: 59; Wiener, 2007: 1-17). In her scholarship, contestation is seen as central to establishing the legitimacy of the compliance process and is constitutive towards social legitimacy (Wiener, 2004: 218). Amitava Acharya focuses on the localization of norms, defined as the processes of framing and grafting by local actors that give a norm legitimacy, 'by infusing it with local characteristics; and by making it congruent with the local context' (Acharya, 2014b: 101). Global norms including the promotion of human rights norms in post-war societies are interpreted, changed, and resisted in new contexts, in particular in the non-Western/Third World regions (Acharya, 2013). For Acharya, localization involves a dialogue based on which locals can adapt norms to their specific local context (Wolff and Zimmerman, 2016: 15).

For local communities and CSOs, 'conformity to rigid technocracy, the acceptance of Western bureaucratic norms, and local compliance in projects that are conceived, designed, funded and evaluated by external actors' is interpreted as participation in peacebuilding (Mac Ginty, 2012b: 171). Non-participation in civil society projects by contrast can be both voluntary (agency and choice driven) and involuntary (restricted by structural or legislative constraints), and has important implications for norm transmission. Resistance to CSO-driven sensitization and the advocacy of external norms manifest as a form of local agency. Although it can have temporal specificity, linked to a certain stage in the liberal peace transition, resonance with individuals and groups who hold strategic positions (elites) in societies and institutions, can at best encourage the legal adoption of external norms. However, such a legal adoption of norms is unlikely to translate into a broader internalization or attitude change at the societal level, unless most individuals and groups (non-elites) identify with these norms (Mac Ginty, 2012b: 172–5).

While each of the perspectives reviewed here focuses on the outcome of norm diffusion, little attention, however, has been given to the issue of norm retention. The extent to which the values and norms underpinning international peacebuilding projects resonate with the local context at any given point in time is important because missing resonance can become a major constraint for norm adoption both at an individual, and at the group level. Building on the existing scholarly arguments about the possible outcomes of norm transmission, it is anticipated that high resonance will elicit high compliance and high retention of external norms over the longer term. Mixed resonance will prompt minimal involvement or non-participation and mixed retention. Low resonance of external norms will encourage resistance, rejection, and non-compliance, leading to weak retention (Figure 1.2).

High resonance it is anticipated will be matched with legal or de jure adoption of the norms at the national level, policy implementation at the societal level, and norm internalization at the individual level. While the legal adoption and implementation of a norm relates to the collective level of the state, the internalization or long-term retention depends on the conviction and identification of individuals and groups with the values being transmitted through various peacebuilding programmes (Risse et al., 1999 cited in Björkdahl, 2008: 136). Norm adoption can vary between the spectrum of high resonance and low resonance through the stages of superficial adoption, non-adoption, rejection, and low retention on the low resonance spectrum. On the high resonance spectrum, norm adoption ranges from instrumental adoption, de jure adoption to internalization and high retention of norms. Instrumental adoption may involve a tactical decision to adopt norms that advances one's position in society. It can be part of a wider strategy of tactical

High Resonance	High compliance	High Retention
Mixed Resonance	Non-participation	Mixed Retention
Low Resonance	Non-compliance	Weak Retention

Fig. 1.2 Relationship between norm resonance, compliance behaviour, and retention

Low Resonance	←————————————————→			High resonance
Superficial Adoption	Norm Internalization	De jure adoption	Policy Implementation	Instrumental adoption
Non-Adoption	Individual	National	Society	De jure adoption
Rejection				Internalization
Low retention				High retention

Fig. 1.3 Results of norm transmission by peacebuilding organizations: explaining resonance and retention

agency and navigation used by subaltern or marginalized subjects like women and youth in a post-war society (Shepler, 2005: 197–211; Utas, 2005: 403–6; Podder, 2015: 43–6). Non-adoption follows resistance or rejection of external norms due to weak resonance and retention. Full adoption aligns with the high resonance and the high retention of internalized norms. Low resonance encourages low retention (Figure 1.3).

Lack of resonance and weak norm retention have implications for peacebuilding legacy in three ways. First, even when there are policy changes at the national level, and the participation of target populations in activities that speak to, or align with donor concerns, without norm resonance a meaningful shift in behaviours that can be transformative for people's everyday realities is unlikely. This can be observed in the Sierra Leone and Macedonia case studies to different degrees. Second, weak norm resonance can result in diverting resources and attention away from locally relevant issues, thereby resulting in a manufactured rather than an authentic peace, an issue that I tackle in the case study of Sierra Leone. Finally, low resonance, can be one of the many reasons for superficial adoption and weak retention of values transmitted through peacebuilding projects. Unless projects speak to the intrinsic issues that separate groups in society, project participants can fall back on their learned or established patterns of behaviour. Wider societal tendencies around segregation and the role of social capital on the weak resonance and retention of values around intercultural communication, and social cohesion are examined in the case of Macedonia.

Institutionalization, Sustainability, and Timely Exits

Peacebuilding INGOs have significant stores of social power (van Ham, 2010: 8). They are constantly restructuring or adapting in response to development needs, strategic priorities, and funding opportunities. Amidst the multiple pressures of revenue generation and aid flight into new or emerging areas of conflict, peace-building INGOs must tackle organizational issues such as the restructuring of their physical presence (offices, staff, projects) in multiple geographies. The challenge of closing projects and programmes, or withdrawing operations from specific coun-tries following organizational restructuring, strategic redirection, or funding cuts from donors, is accompanied by the demand for 'building-up' the capacity of na-tional partners so that they can survive independently following the exodus of external players and without extended external support (Atkinson and Scurrah, 2009; Banks and Hulme, 2012; Hayman, 2015: 48–64).

Following the mixed record of peacebuilding success over the years (Reimann, 2005: 40; Carey and Richmond, 2005), critical peace studies scholars have probed the constraints, limitations, and sometimes contradictory results of INGO led peacebuilding. Criticism has been levied not only towards the externally driven agenda of INGOs, including the 'anarchy of their good intentions', (Goodhand and Lewer 1999: 81) and the limits of their role as 'a universalizing force' (Christie, 2012: 7). Some scholars also question the nature of INGO motivations and re-lationships with states and elites, highlighting their less than benign role in the design and implementation of projects (Gerstbauer, 2005: 24; Harrison, 2017). McMahon (2017) alludes to the games played by INGOs, and their local part-ner organizations (LNGOs) by highlighting how they often take advantage of aid monies and opportunities by playing along with donor rules and visions, often to the detriment of local relevance and capacity building.

Peacebuilding INGOs are subject to a lot of criticism when it comes to build-ing the capacity of their partners. This is because of the tendency to treat local partners in an instrumental way. Partnerships are often built around specific de-liverables, activities, and the management, and M&E of the same (Popplewell et al., 2016: 4). Southern NGOs are dependent on outside funding as they are not usually rooted in their own economies. This makes them vulnerable to outside influence, and to project-based development, as few donors provide core funding to these NGOs. Project funding is focused and finite, and does not cover overhead costs or core administrative costs, creating financial sustainability challenges for southern NGOs (Low and Davenport, 2002: 370; Gunnarson, 2001: 24).

Driven by top-down strategic and financial considerations, INGO operations can linger on for decades after they initially commence in any post-war context, gradually reducing their staff numbers and program breadth before the inevitable need to fold up operations arrives (Campbell, 2018). Withdrawal can take place due to high operating costs, poor value for money or poor cost effectiveness, unexpected funding shortfalls, and changes in the strategic direction of the or-ganization. Many peacebuilding INGOs develop principles on exit only after the decision to exit has been made (Ahmed et al., 2018). Discussions around exit and sustainability barely feature when partnerships are agreed, or at the point when capacity-building relationships are developed (Low and Davenport, 2002: 370; Gunnarson, 2001: 24). At the time preceding exit, even though local partners are consulted and informed about exit processes, very often the design and timing of exit is a top-down imperative from the headquarters that filters down to the country offices, rather than a mutually orchestrated process (Brehm, 2001: 57; Gardner et al., 2005). Developing responsible exit strategies early on in the project life-cycle can help peacebuilding INGOs overcome 'programme disconnect', characterized by the pursuit of ad hoc, issue-driven, and survival-oriented programming. In pursuing projects that are tied to shifting donor priorities, INGOs invest time and use valuable resources for implementing activities with weak local resonance. Losing norm resonance with local issues in pursuit of donor strategic priorities also creates a patchy and dispersed organizational legacy.

Knowing the right time to withdraw support involves monitoring exit processes carefully (Hayman, 2015: 48–9). Ideally speaking, an exit strategy should be built into every project design by incorporating capacity-building and preparing successor organizations within the life cycle of the project. In reality, the needs within projects evolve over time; partnerships and projects often have no clear exit strategy in place, even if they did, the strategy would often be irrelevant by the time the decisions on final exit are made because of the modifications in activities over time (Hayman, 2015: 48–9). Without access to rolling funds, the beneficial impacts of time-bound successful projects are often lost (Van Rooy, 1998: 5). The local ownership literature acknowledges the importance of upping capacity-building as donor funding shrinks. Developing successor organizations and training second generation leadership for local CSOs are critical factors for enhancing sustainability (Hayman and Lewis, 2018: 361–73). While in most cases, relationships with local CSO partners end after withdrawal, in limited cases, INGOs have retained formal or informal relationships with their former partners (Gerstbauer, 2010). This can include maintaining a small funding window to continue providing ad hoc support; shifting to an advocacy-based relationship; or formally joining the partner's advisory board. In other cases, informal relationships are maintained through INGO networks and alliances (Hayman, 2015: 56–7). The nature and timing of exit therefore can have important implications for the organization's overall legacy and footprint.

Apart from the considerations of timing, and the sustainability of local partners, exit is rarely accompanied by the institutionalization or the formal adoption of successful project models by national agencies. Institutionalization allows the transfer of knowledge and supports local ownership and capacity-building in the long term (Shinoda, 2008: 99–101). It also shifts the discourse around ownership from 'participation' and 'compliance' in international regimes to more tangible outcomes (Hayman and Lewis, 2018: 360–1). By co-designing and co-implementing projects with national government departments from the outset, INGOs can hand over their projects to national actors before exit. Certain types of programmes might be more amenable to institutionalization than others. Datzberger (2016: 326–27) identifies education reform projects as an area of development programming, that are typically easier to hand over to national governments. Chapter 3, where I discuss the *Mozaik* kindergarten model, which was adopted into the national pre-school system in Macedonia during 2011–2012, offers valuable insights for scholars and practitioners to gauge how institutionalization of donor-funded peacebuilding projects can strengthen local ownership, sustainability and enhance the direct legacy of an organization's multi-year operations.

Organizational Learning and Reflection

Herbert Kelman (1995: 19–27) notes that, if peacebuilding interventions are to make a difference, there needs to be a transfer of knowledge and resources to people beyond those directly participating in the project. Given the important role played by INGOs in implementing various peacebuilding projects, how they learn from, and reflect on the lessons from various M&E processes is an important area for understanding peacebuilding legacy from an organizational perspective. Due to the strong emphasis placed by donors on meeting specific targets within 12-, 18-, and 24-month intervals, peacebuilding is often reduced to the delivery of a sequence of activities, planned and delivered to a tight schedule. Learning for the most part remains mired in the immediate and the medium-term monitoring of project outputs (Anderson and Wallace, 2013: 2). This is because monitoring is an ongoing management function, intended to gather key data and indices that inform decisions in real-time, and is done by programme staff (Church and Rogers, 2006). Monitoring can only track progress towards change by measuring results in the short-term, against set goals; and by reviewing changes in a given context against the programme model. It is aimed to assure funders and implementers that programme implementation is on track, or going on as planned (Scharbatke-Church, 2011: 467). Evaluation, on the other hand, can be both *formative*, conducted in the midst of an ongoing project to identify progress and opportunities for improvement, and *summative*, conducted at the end of the project to understand the changes achieved (Scharbatke-Church, 2011: 467).

Another fundamental barrier to long-term measurement is donor policy and organizational approaches regarding the primary purpose of evaluation. Financial accountability upwards to donors for the resources used is frequently prioritized by both donors and implementing organizations. This is often at the expense of truly capturing or understanding the long-term nature of conflict transformation and peacebuilding (Bamat, 2012; Millar, 2014b). Upward accountability focuses on immediate results (Campbell, 2018), it does not encourage strategic thinking related to peacebuilding legacy. Moreover, theories of change underpinning peacebuilding projects are not theories in the strict academic sense; instead, they offer

loosely framed explanations of how and why a set of activities can promote specific goals. In many cases, theories of change or logical frameworks are not a key
part or a part at all of the programme-planning process (Brown et al., 2015: 5, 9,
14, 31 cited in Autesserre, 2017: 119). Weak or inflexible theories of change can
forfeit the leverage offered by having a strong M&E approach built into the project
life-cycle (de Coning, 2018). Scholars therefore urge the adoption of a 'revisionist
theory of change' approach during the life-cycle of the project itself, to enable the
process of 'monitoring as learning' (Lederach et al., 2007).

Designing evaluation practices that can support organizational learning over
the long-term therefore requires a 'process use' approach—one that interrogates
how peacebuilding is done, and what lessons arise from it. A process-driven approach to organizational learning is less about sifting information, it has to be
reflective, linking the performance of individual projects to assess 'cumulative effectiveness' and organizational legacy in a given context (Rogers, 2012). Learning
from reflection also entails taking corrective action to rectify any misalignment between an organization's aims; and the outcome of its activities in relation to those
aims (Argyris, 1992: 67; Campbell, 2008: 21). Even when programmes are ongoing, the practical issues, the logistical issues, and the resulting adaptations that are
seen and recorded in various interim reports are often omitted from organizational
learning loops. The reason for this learning lacunae is rooted in resource allocation
practices. In any given context, individual peacebuilding organizations do not find
it cost-effective to undertake controlled comparisons between areas that they operate in, with areas that are not covered by project funding (Lemon, 2017). Limited
resources for learning through comparison are reinforced by the limited sharing
of knowledge and know-how between different peacebuilding organizations due
to the competition for limited donor funds (Hewitt, 2017).

Peacebuilding cannot be a solo effort; to be effective it requires rigorous first-
level organizational learning before sharing and collaboration can take place. As
part of the vocabulary around integrated peacebuilding, individual organizations
are urged to see peacebuilding not only through the narrow lens of their own core
competencies, but in a more holistic way, that would consider the peacebuilding
needs within a context and, at the systemic level, in terms of how individual efforts
relate to those of others (Ricigliano, 2003: 446). Any thinking around long-term
effects must therefore include the processes of learning and reflection that shape
first-order learning, understood as 'the processes through which organizations
learn from interpretations of the past more than anticipations of the future' (Levitt
and March, 1988: 320). Routines and frames influence how far appropriate structures can be put in place to enable first-order organizational learning (Campbell,
2008: 95-7). Learning what works and what does not should be integrated into
organizational routines so that it can be replicated into future interventions in a
given context as second-order learning. Without this kind of 'double-loop learning', defined as the process whereby individuals within an organization openly

and honestly examine the underlying assumptions and behaviours that may have caused gaps between the intended and actual outcome of their actions, peacebuilding organizations cannot re-assess and adapt their theories of change to the context (Argyris, 1992: 68; Campbell, 2008: 20–1, 29).

Andrews, Pritchett, and Woolcock (2013: 307–8) describe this as a process of iterative incrementalism. Each stage can lead to learning about effectiveness in the short and medium term. It can inform adjustments in ways that enable programmes to become flexible or adaptive in achieving their goals, thereby responding to the local needs in ways that strengthen the organizational legacy. Diverse actors can use their individual expertise in political, social, and or structural peacebuilding in mutually reinforcing ways, and through an iterative process of learning and reflection (Ball, 1997: 8). Such an approach departs from the practices of large bureaucracies like the UN and bilateral donor agencies that can reproduce interventions to fit their routines (Barnett and Finnermore, 2004: 34; Campbell, 2008: 97). Instead of being adaptable and responsive, these international bureaucracies tend to reproduce themselves, resulting in tick-box rather than collaborative and reflexive second-order learning (Campbell, 2008). The overall result is ad hoc and unstructured learning from the implementation of different projects.

Concerted efforts are underway to remedy the barriers to inter-organizational learning. In 2017, three international peacebuilding organizations—Saferworld, Conciliation Resources and International Alert launched the Peace Research partnership. Funded by UK Aid, this three-year research programme aims to generate knowledge, lessons, and recommendations tailored to policymakers and practitioners working on peace and security issues (Saferworld, 2017). The focus is on the much-needed element of shared learning. Although a positive development in itself, deeper commitment to learning across the different levels of operations is still missing. How institutional memory is preserved or lost and what is retained informs organizational learning processes as well as the sustainability of peacebuilding work.

Institutional memory involves memories internal to a peacebuilding organization that provides facts and narratives about past organizational activity. Institutional memory consists of archival memory as preserved in the official records and paperwork, the human memory of the employees, and the electronic memory as held in websites and electronic documents. Some types are better preserved than others. Documentation and digital memory are the easiest to retain (Heideman, 2016: 467). Given the dynamic nature of the sector, which draws on the energy and commitment of a fluid aid worker population, staff retention is often challenging. Without efforts to capture the human memory and learning that staff take with them when they move on to new employment, there are few opportunities for future staff to draw on or build from past learning. This can lead to a loss of valuable practical or hands-on knowledge (Heideman, 2016: 467). Capturing the learning from individual experiences of project implementation can thereofre offer valuable opportunities for retaining learning from project related activities.

A lack of institutional memory also inhibits internal reflection and learning from projects after the withdrawal of donor funding (Swidler and Watkins, 2009). Donors are unmotivated to look at the effects of programmes years after projects have concluded (Cekan, 2016). Few organizations go back after they exit to study the effects of previously implemented projects, in ways that can inform learning and reflection processes within and between peacebuilding INGOs, and contribute to an understanding of the organizational legacies of peacebuilding. In short, few long-term results can be observed following multiple years of programming on specific themes. As a corrective to this gap, in recent years, there has been a growing interest in commissioning post-closure evaluations (PCE). These differ from an ex-post evaluation or other forms of end of project or end of programme evaluation in that they are commissioned or conducted by a funder after financial support has been formally withdrawn. They require revisiting a country, partner, or a project site. PCEs can be critical for examining and understanding in greater depth what the lasting effects (if any) of an intervention has been, and why (Kinsbergen and Plaisier, 2016). Through follow-up research with the beneficiaries and by collecting feedback about the changes (if any) across the structural, institutional, normative, and attitudinal realms, PCE can provide both donors and peacebuilding INGOs a more accurate understanding of whether their projects and programmes are really sustainable. For policymakers, PCEs can provide insights into what works and what does not, and can offer lessons for sustainable peace and for future project planning.

In Sri Lanka, Voluntary Services Overseas (VSO) closed its operation in March 2014, nearly 40 years after it began work on mental health, volunteerism, and active citizenship to support civil society development on the island. As part of its efforts to understand the long-term effects and influence of these projects, VSO commissioned a PCE to the International NGO Training and Research Centre (INTRAC), an Oxford-based research and training organization. The aim was to develop principles and a methodology for closing individual projects, country offices, and programmes in order to continue to grow the body of evidence on sustainable peacebuilding (Iles, 2015). In another recent example, following the transfer of its income and assets to national NGO partners, the INGO EveryChild commissioned a longitudinal evaluation of its exit from six countries in 2015. EveryChild was concerned with maintaining continuity so that institutional memory, contextual knowledge, and relationships of trust continued through the transition process (Morris, 2015). It also attempted a sustainable continuation of services and support for the children and beneficiary communities in the six countries from which exit had taken place about 15 months prior to the PCE being undertaken (Popplewell et al., 2016). Similarly, the Swedish INGO *Kvinna till Kvinna*, which withdrew from Croatia in 2006 after 13 years of operations, and

Plan International in the case of the Philippines, are further examples of peace-building organizations that have undertaken PCEs to assess the contribution of their projects to long-term change in the communities that they worked in for 10+ years (Kvinna till Kvinna. 2011; Hayman, 2015: 58; Lewis, 2016).

In a post-COVID 19 world, when precarity defines employment and global markets, further cuts in development assistance can be anticipated, with a heightened need to demonstrate 'value for money' and related issues of 'impact' or 'effective outcomes' (Menkhaus, 2004). Learning and reflection from peacebuilding work becomes imperative, as does the move towards long-term M&E of conflict transformation efforts. Creating organizational frameworks for long-term monitoring of outcomes and impacts beyond project life-cycles would require investing in PCEs, employing standardized indicators for monitoring cumulative effectiveness, and the development of staff capacities towards that end. It also demands a shift from dominant approaches to M&E that privilege international expertise, assuming it to be superior to local knowledge, to the use of indigenous monitoring and evaluation (IM&E) (Autesserre, 2017: 125). Indigenous capacities, systems, and skills to prevent overt violence between groups already exist in every society and are part of the socially resonant conflict management and monitoring processes. These practices offer the potential for tracking long-term changes and for encouraging post-exit learning and reflection. They are a cost-effect resource that is often overlooked by mainstream peacebuilding organizations (Millar and Podder, 2021).

The Transformative Potential of Technocratic Peacebuilding

Peacebuilding INGOs have become the de facto practitioner arm of the global peacebuilding community and their work contributes to the broader processes of change in post-war societies (Dibley, 2014). At the root of their efforts is a transformative agenda, namely, to transform societies from being conflict-affected to embracing peaceful tools for conflict resolution, to progress towards a more inclusive, conciliatory, and representative social relations (Berdal, 2014). In pursuit of their transformative agenda, peacebuilding INGOs design, and deliver 'thematic programming'. Designed as short-term projects lasting anywhere between six, nine, and twelve months in duration, thematic programmes are constructed on loosely conceived theories of change, that anticipate how and why a desired change is expected to occur in a particular context (Vogel, 2012: 26). In delivering these projects, peacebuilding INGOs must cater to multiple accountabilities, which are often at cross-purposes including upward financial accountability to donors, and downward accountability to beneficiaries or those indirectly impacted by their activities (Christensen and Ebrahim, 2006; Abouassi and Trent, 2016: 284). There is also horizontal accountability to peer organizations that are demonstrated

Transformational peacebuilding	Binaries	Technical peacebuilding
Timeframe	vs	Timeline
Long-term investment	vs	Short-term needs
Sustainability	vs	Activities
Intergenerational peace	vs	Empowerment
Affordability	vs	External financing
Institutions	vs	Temporary structures
Process	vs	Outputs
Legacy	vs	Achievements

Fig. 1.4 Binaries in transformational and technical peacebuilding

in self-regulation mechanisms, and knowledge sharing practices (Ebrahim, 2003; Schilleman, 2011; Ebrahim, 2016).

Efficiency in these areas entails recognition as a reliable partner and encourages donors to disburse more funding for projects that can have little resonance with local needs. Short-term project success can end up creating a drop in the ocean effect, becoming atomized examples of effectiveness amidst a patchwork of mixed performance. The current suite of M&E tools that are embedded in technocratic peacebuilding cater to measuring the performance of these atomized, standalone efforts. They contribute to an incomplete understanding of peacebuilding, with the ability to capture only some parts of 'impact' at a given time, rather than their cumulative effects (Figure 1.4). Technocratic peacebuilding leverages accountability to donors or formal peacebuilding accountability; it is committed to meeting bureaucratic clock time (Hutchings, 2007; Campbell, 2018), managing budgets and activities, and tick box learning (Mac Ginty, 2012a).

Transformative peacebuilding by contrast, requires flexibility, and reflection on the part of the implementing staff, so that the intended outcomes can be aligned with the local needs. Staff should be able to question their underlying assumptions; and adapt activities accordingly. To be truly accountable locally, it is important that peacebuilding does not end with short-term projects, it unfolds as a dynamic process not tied to the life-cycle of projects or to policy time. To engage with the legacy of peacebuilding, we must think beyond projects and engage with the peace writ large (Fisher and Zimina, 2009: 9). Methodologically, this is challenging. Long-term evaluation does not fit into the DNA of the peacebuilding industry. Longitudinal studies, or follow-up research with project participants years after a project closed, are a luxury that few peacebuilding organizations can afford. Amidst the constraints of time and resources, rarely is there the ability or willingness to turn attention inwards to capitalize on the cumulative knowledge stored in the institutional memory of the country office staff, and in the project documents of multiple peacebuilding organizations. Mapping this knowledge can help both donors and implementing agencies to learn about the legacies that they leave behind once country offices nationalize or shut down. It can foster more strategic and long-term approaches to peacebuilding (Podder, 2021).

On the part of donors, instead of treating project objectives as 'locked in,' once an agreed programme of work has been funded, they must allow for greater flexibility by building in the time for taking a pause, for reflecting on project designs, and for altering the designs if necessary during the programming life-cycle (Anderson et al., 2004). This would require a more open dialogue between donors and implementing partners. On the part of INGOs, instead of pursuing funding across different priority areas, opportunities for funding must be strategically linked to the objective of strengthening their organizational legacy in a country. Such an engaged learning approach demands strategic thinking around organizational direction from within, and from their leadership. To facilitate this, the commitment to learning and reflection must be internally guided rather than externally imposed or tied to donor specified M&E. It must become part of the 'moral compass' of peacebuilding actors within the field. In practical terms, this would require navigating the internal divisions within the peacebuilding field, overcoming the competition for resources and mistrust. If done well, sharing of knowledge through inter-organizational learning can contribute to encouraging transformational processes, while pursuing technocratic peacebuilding.

Continuity in programming would enable peacebuilding organizations to be more strategic in developing formal partnerships with government departments to encourage institutionalization of the project gains. Without institutionalization, structures like child protection committees, women's groups, and youth groups founded as part of the various peacebuilding projects disperse or simply become defunct amidst the pressures of everyday survival. By investing in building the capacity of a core group of local implementing partners, it would be possible to select and train successor organizations and their leadership. For donors, distributing funding in ways that allow the implementing partners to build deep and long-lasting relationships across a limited number of communities can support their long-term transformation. Continuity in programming both in terms of themes and geographic areas allows INGOs to be more adaptive. They are able to revise the theories of change of their projects in response to changing socio-political dynamics. Adaptation becomes a pro-active and pre-emptive part of programming. It can support the planning of a timely and responsible exit strategy.

Finally, the dissemination of international norms through peacebuilding programmes that align expectations of domestic governance and social attitudes to international standards or norms of governance and human rights also presents transformative potential from within the contours of technocratic peacebuilding

(Paris 2004). Normative shifts can be achieved by adjusting the focus from the one-way conduit of norm transmission from the Global North to the Global South (Chandler, 2013), to examining the resonance and retention of these norms in local contexts. When communities are sensitized to international norms around human rights and child protection, at a time when the national government is largely a trustee of international actors, it can generate a manufactured rather than an authentic peacebuilding process. Even when there is legal adoption of externally sponsored norms such as with the case of countries seeking accession to the EU, legal adoption into government policy does not create resonance or retention in the social milieu. Programmes catering to external norms are likely to generate superficial connections, norm contestation, non-participation, and non-adoption of norms. Without social resonance, and deeper internalization at the individual and group levels, values transmitted through peacebuilding projects are unlikely to be retained in the long-term, or lead to meaningful change in people's attitudes and behaviours.

The tendency to approach peacebuilding from ground zero implies that most organizations are oblivious to the endogenous capacity of both individuals and communities that remain resilient in the face of horrific, and at times never-ending cycles of violence. In particular, social learning during conflict, defined as the 'capacity and processes through which new values, ideas and practices are disseminated', (Pelling, 2003: 59) offers guiding principles for developing governance and institutions aligned with endogenous norms within post-war communities. Often times, peacebuilding actors fail to empower or work with the social learning and social capital that already exists or has been accumulated during the conflict years including pre-existing institutional capacity. By pursuing a patchwork of parallel projects and programmes that create friction and at times confusion in the minds of local communities (Björkdahl and Hoglund, 2013; Millar, 2016, the expectations generated by peacebuilding activities create 'minor utopias' (Winter, 2006). They introduce externally projected ideas, and socially alien norms about how individuals and communities should behave in order to transition to peaceful lives.

I argue that the straitjacket of technocratic peacebuilding at the normative transmission, institutional consolidation, and organizational learning levels has a powerful potential for transformative peace, if technical activity is incremental, in-depth, long-term, learning-oriented, and adaptive (Fisher and Zimina, 2009: 20). Technical and transformative peacebuilding need not be contradictory approaches; in fact, through the application of internal learning and reflection, peacebuilding organizations can adopt a greater awareness of contextual nuances and of the normative fit of change oriented programmes. This can allow peacebuilding actors to identify and build the capacity of successor organizations, and plan timely and responsible exits with local partners, early on in the programming life-cycle rather than exiting when convenient for them. By designing projects that integrate longitudinal evaluation processes through the use of IM&E tools, it can be possible to monitor effects even when projects are completed, and donor funding has ceased. This, together with the use of PCE, can create a strong commitment to observing and understanding long-term change.

The transformative and technocratic avatars of peacebuilding can cooperate to make peacebuilding sustainable. Technocratic peacebuilding must apply transformative principles to think strategically about the long-term and about peacebuilding legacy, while remaining grounded in local knowledge and capacities. In summary, effective peacebuilding requires flexibility, responsiveness, and creativity. It demands learning and reflection, the ability to pause and think internally, and in relation to the context in which projects are implemented. Understanding the endogenous structures and capacities, and supporting, rather than transplanting them with externally imported models, can become the most effective route to sustainable peace, and to stronger peacebuilding legacies.

2

Data and Methods

Introduction

The greatest challenge for peace and conflict studies scholars today is to find ways
to filter their scholarly knowledge and findings into peacebuilding policy and practice. Barriers to effective knowledge transfer of critical scholarly insights stem
from several factors (see also, Rapoport, 1970: 282; Mack, 2002, 516–20). These
include: a constant pressure for results among policymakers; the expectation of
linear knowledge utilization models on their part; the challenge of synthesis of
project outcomes; single case dismissal of generalized findings by academics; and
finally, the mismatch between the need for extensive time for academic research on
the one hand, combined with the limited time for reading and reflection on the part
of policymakers on the other (Millar, 2018c). To bridge the gap between academic
scholarship and peace practice, I pursued a knowledge production partnership
with a leading peacebuilding INGO based in Washington, D.C. Co-production
of research outcomes through collaborative partnerships between university academics, charities, business or industry, and the government has become part of
the research impact and public engagement agenda across the higher education
sector in the United Kingdom (Gibbons, 1994). The objective is to form alliances
for producing and transferring knowledge between different stakeholders to promote learning and innovation (Crewe and Young, 2002). This interest in research
collaboration is framed by an evidence-based logic, one that is tied to the growing
demand for demonstrating the real-world impact of academic scholarship, and of
the policy interventions that they study (Aniekwe et al., 2012: 3).

Partnership between INGOs and academics for advancing knowledge can take
different forms. INGOs can serve as research brokers, gatekeepers, and host institutions by lending formal affiliation to a researcher while in the field. They can
also engage researchers as evaluators for various projects, or act as implementers
of research activities like surveys and field experiments (Green, 2017). In post-
war countries, most research is conducted under less than optimal conditions.
Identifying research populations; mapping subjective perceptions on the conflict;
gaining familiarity with the needs, interests, and concerns of the human research
population; and assessing the quality of information received are some common
challenges faced by academic research scholars (Cohen and Arieli, 2011: 425).

Peacebuilding Legacy. Sukanya Podder, Oxford University Press.
© Sukanya Podder (2022). DOI: 10.1093/oso/9780192863980.003.0003

Secure access and the difficulties with developing trust amongst local populations who remain suspicious of outsiders encourage academic researchers to seek institutional affiliation with a range of peacebuilding organizations including INGOs. In effect, INGOs bring presence on the ground through their operations. Their local partners and networks of trust across rural communities offer invaluable access for primary data collection by researchers (Green, 2017).

Yet, like any partnership, there can be hidden perils. Some of the problems with relying on gatekeepers can affect the quality and representativeness of the data collected. For example, local staff in the field can have their own motivations and reasons for referring or not referring academic researchers to specific locations or potential respondents (Groger, Mayberry, and Straker, 1999). There is also the problem of attempting to sell an overly optimistic success story for reputational reasons. Goodhand (2000: 12) notes that research like any other form of intervention occurs within an intensely political environment. In the context of post-war reconstruction, INGOs act as conduits of donor aid, and are unlikely to be viewed by governments and local actors as neutral or altruistic. A field researcher must tread carefully; listen impartially and without judgement (Burgess, 2002). When conducting research in partnership with INGOs, researchers need to be vigilant and aware of the host of different identities that shape the dynamics of interaction with their research subjects, and with the knowledge production partner (Aniekwe et al., 2012; Fransman and Newman, 2019). For the researcher, it can be difficult to remain immune from one's prior experiences, as these can shape one's understanding and interpretation of events (Malejacq and Mukhopadhay, 2016). As an Indian origin female researcher based at a British university, I had to negotiate these multiple identities while maintaining objective neutrality and distance from the internal narrative of the partner organization and the study of peacebuilding legacy.

In this chapter, I discuss the context of my research on peacebuilding legacy using the cases of youth focused media and peace education efforts by the partner INGO in Sierra Leone and Macedonia. I first focus on the choice of cases and research techniques, discussing in particular the underappreciated value of meta-ethnographic synthesis for analysing the institutional memory of projects implemented by peacebuilding organizations over 15+ years. Second-order interpretations of the meta-data were used for capturing the transmission of peacebuilding norms via the different media and education projects. Through this process, I examine how far behaviours and attitudes of recipient audiences especially children and young people were shaped through these influences. Then, I discuss the challenges of conducting fieldwork in post-war environments, focusing on sampling; access, research fatigue, and trust issues. I further reflect on the ethical dilemmas that arise particularly with regard to researching children and young people. I discuss the fieldwork design and data gathered in Sierra Leone and Macedonia, reflecting on the process through specific examples and observations.

Lastly, I focus on the contributions and limitations of my meta-ethnographic synthesis approach and primary fieldwork, incorporating my observations on the research process. Specifically, I reflect on the field data; the secondary interpretations of the meta-data arising from the evaluative studies, and the measures used to triangulate my findings.

Research Design

The research design combined archival research and primary data collection. Archival ethnography of project proposals, periodic reports, evaluations, and internal staff communications allowed me to make the most of understudied meta-data found in the institutional memory stretching back over time. Archival research of organizational monitoring and evaluation processes was undertaken through a desk-based review of project documents and through phone and Skype based interviews with the partner INGO staff at the headquarters, and in the field. In using the institutional memory of the multi-year projects, I tried to synthesize and interpret the available longitudinal evidence for the learning and reflection purposes of the partner organization. Such a research design was selected to try and bridge the gap between the realms of policy, practice, and academia (Masefield et al., 2020). The archival data was synthesized through the application of Noblit and Hare's model of meta-ethnographic synthesis which I will discuss shortly. Primary data collection was carried out using interviews, focus group discussions (FGDs), and participatory methods such as timelines and mapping of the programming life-cycle with the country office staff, and with current and past project participants. The findings are relevant for the longitudinal analysis of a wide array of peace interventions. They can inform the broader peacebuilding community about these rarely studied long-term effects through the lens of peacebuilding legacy.

The research design relied on two country cases. While different, both cases elucidate the features of a broader population of post-Cold War civil conflicts and post-war liberal peacebuilding (Gerring, 2004). Sierra Leone is representative of a broader population of mostly African cases, such as Liberia, the Democratic Republic of Congo (DRC), and more recently South Sudan, where international involvement has followed a heavy footprint (Chandler, 2006; Lemay-Hébert, 2009). These countries present weak institutions and corrupt political systems where prolonged and intrusive statebuilding efforts have enhanced state weakness and dependency on external aid. Educational segregation and intergroup tensions in Macedonia present broad similarities across the Balkans, including in Kosovo and Bosnia and Herzegovina (BiH). Macedonia also links to cases such as Cyprus and Israel where ethnicized identities have promoted segregation in schools (McGlynn and Zembylas, 2009; Zembylas, 2010). The segregation debate in Macedonia, and the policies of integrated education and social cohesion advanced by external donors such as the EU, the Organization for Security and Cooperation in Europe (OSCE), and the OECD, speak to the broader challenges with promoting intercultural communication across deeply divided societies (Bush and Saltarelli, 2000).

Practical considerations around the availability of longitudinal evaluative data also determined the selection of cases. Youth focused peacebuilding programmes run by the partner INGO's country teams in Macedonia and Sierra Leone had run for over 15+ years allowing the study of longer-term effects. The Macedonia country programme addressed the intergroup dynamics of peacebuilding through the media and education projects concerning intercultural communication. The Sierra Leone country programme focused on intergenerational issues and the empowerment of children and youth as agents of peace through the use of radio and community outreach efforts. This variation enabled the study of two types of attitudinal shifts, i.e. intergroup and intergenerational, through an examination of the long-term effects of early years' education and media projects in Macedonia, and media and community outreach activities, especially youth focused radio in Sierra Leone. From a programmatic standpoint, Macedonia was 'sunsetting' in terms of donor interest at the time of fieldwork, and Sierra Leone was 'near sunsetting'. With the peacebuilding 'industry' moving on from these countries to other more urgent hotspots, they offered important historical aspects that enabled a study of norm transmission and institutionalization through the lens of peacebuilding legacy.

Case Study Research

Methodologically speaking, case studies can be atheoretical, interpretive, hypothesis-generating, theory-confirming, theory-informing, or deviant types (Lijphart, 1971: 691). Other prominent typologies include Eckstein's (1975: 96–123) categorization of configurative-idiographic, disciplined-configurative, heuristic, plausibility probe, and crucial types of cases (Gerring, 2007). Across these categories, the basic typology consists of case studies that aim to describe, explain, or interpret a particular 'case' by following either an inductive or theory guided approach. Inductive case studies are highly descriptive and lack an explicit theoretical framework to guide the empirical analysis (Yin, 2003). Theory-guided case studies are guided by a well-developed conceptual framework that focuses attention on some theoretically specified aspects of reality (Levy, 2008: 4). In this study, a theory guided diverse case method was selected. Whether peacebuilding legacy was strong or weak was linked to norm resonance and the degree of institutionalization. I followed the method of difference in which the two cases present different values on these dependent variables. In both cases there was weak norm resonance and variable institutionalization. A mixture of most similar and most different analysis along the spectrum of accidental to one of deliberate institutionalization was adopted (Seawright and Gerring, 2008: 300).

Meta-ethnographic Synthesis

In simple terms, meta-ethnography involves induction and interpretation, and the product of the synthesis is the translation of studies into one another. Meta-analysis has been a central part of the methodological canon of evidence-based medicine. It presents a qualitative method for synthesizing the results of qualitative studies which enable the researcher to understand and transfer ideas, concepts, and metaphors across the different studies. Like secondary analysis, qualitative synthesis could involve reinterpretation, but unlike secondary analysis, meta-analysis is based on published findings rather than on primary data (Britten et al., 2002: 209–10). A scarcity of dedicated time and resources on the part of university academics can limit the opportunity for long-term fieldwork beyond the doctoral project. This, together with research-fatigue among conflict-affected and post-war communities, demand that we look for ways to maximize the synthesis and interpretation from available information to triangulate our findings (Kakos and Fritzche, 2017: 130; Boesten and Henry, 2018: 572).

Combining data from multiple sources can take different forms. These include document analysis, narrative review, textual analysis, and systematic reviews (Fairclough, 2003; Akobeng, 2005; Bowen, 2009: 27). Here, I follow Noblit and Hare's (1988) seven-step process for conducting a meta-ethnography. I started by collecting the different archival documents, and evaluation reports, determining how the studies were related; translating the studies into one another; synthesizing translations; and expressing the synthesis, although these steps can overlap or occur in parallel (Britten et al., 2002: 209). There are three main differences in this method relative to other methods of qualitative synthesis. First, is the choice of purposive sampling including maximum variation sampling rather than random samples. Second, the interpretations of the storyline in each study is condensed into metaphors, themes or concepts, that allow systematic comparison while retaining the original meaning of each study. Third, comparison between studies involves a process of translation. While preserving the structure of relationships between concepts within any given study, the preservation of meaning is emphasized. The focus is on interpretations and not objective findings (Noblit, 2018: 36).

Meta-ethnography does not automatically yield new or 'third order interpretations' although it does constitute additional layers of interpretation (Ecker and Hulley, 1996). The aim is not to generalize the findings to a wider population but to specify the findings of the studies as a whole, and then dig deeper into the meanings evident across the studies (Hughes and Noblit, 2017). Meta-ethnography in the end is not simply an aggregation of interpretations already made in the studies being synthesized. Instead, the synthesis involves translation, of the whole storyline or interpretation into one another (Noblit, 2018: 36). Translating full storylines can be more complex than concept by concept interpretation. This is due to a tension between identifying the salient themes, concepts, or metaphors that can reduce the account to a manageable level and preserving the salient contexts in which these concepts apply.

Drawing an analogy between studies while retaining contextual nuance may require concepts to be applied in contextually specific ways (Turner, 1980: 53–6). There are three possible types of translation: reciprocal, refutational, and lines-of-argument, depending on how translations are synthesized (Noblit and Hare, 1988). Reciprocal translation involves studies that are about similar things that can be synthesized as direct translations through the comparison of metaphors. Refutational studies require more careful translations as the competing explanations and their implications need to be examined. Finally, lines-of-argument translation involve inferences about some larger issue, by first translating studies into each other and then constructing an interpretation of a line of argument, that can reveal hidden meaning in the individual studies. This can be achieved through the use of grounded theory techniques (Glaser and Straus, 1967). Through a detailed comparison of the differences and similarities among the studies included in the synthesis, a new interpretative scheme can be produced. The final stage of meta-ethnography is expressing the synthesis as a line of argument, as text, or presenting them in summary tables, diagrams, or models (Campbell et al., 2011: 10–11).

By capturing longitudinal developments, meta-ethnography allows researchers to capture the continuities and shifts, that cannot be discerned in any single project report. This means that the consecutive project archives are useful for explanatory and exploratory analysis. They also help us to reflect on the strategic direction of programming. In the two cases studies, details about the context, the setting, organizational culture, and implementation of each project as captured in the archival documents enriched the analysis. This enabled a more complete understanding of the long-term effects of the different projects implemented by the partner INGO. Meta-ethnography also offered a low-cost and flexible tool for capturing institutional responses and adaptions. It allowed me a 'rich qualitative insight into the interactions of the users, to retroactively reconstruct specific actions at a fine level of granularity' over time (Geiger and Ribes 2011: 1).

Reading and Translating the Studies

The research underpinning this book was conducted during January 2017 until March 2019 followed by the writing up of the results. Data collection and analysis took place in two phases. Primary documents and interview data from the field was analysed between January and August 2017 and written up between January and December 2018. Further interviews via Skype were completed between January and December 2019. I spent six months reading the studies and determining how the studies in each country case were related. The data from the evaluation reports and project documents were 'examined and interpreted in order to elicit meaning, gain understanding, and develop empirical knowledge' (Bowen, 2009: 27). By applying a meta-ethnographic approach, this 'patchy' evidence could be rigorously mapped. Atkinson and Coffey (1997: 47) refer to documents as 'social facts', which are produced, shared, and used in socially organized ways. Project documents contained text (words) and images that were recorded by external evaluators, interns, and country staff at different points in the programming cycle (Rapley, 2007; Corbin and Strauss, 2008). Programmatic documents are interrelated in their meaning and reflect evolution of priorities within a given context. Re-examining the evaluation data from previous studies also enabled a deeper contextual knowledge that had historical value (Kakos and Fritzsche, 2017: 130). Through the study of interconnectedness, a deeper interpretative approach into organizational learning during the life-cycle of the various projects was possible.

Interpretations and explanations in the original studies were treated as data and were translated across several studies to produce a synthesis (Britten et al., 2002: 210). The focus of the translation was on programme concepts that informed country office learning behaviour and learning concepts concerning norm transmission. This two-pronged focus allowed for a comparison between different studies, while preserving the structure of relationships between learning and programme concepts within any given document. The following steps were followed during the reading and translation of the evaluation reports. First, each evaluation report was coded for the following details: project type, the underlying theory of change, project outputs, objectives of the funder, the nature and timing of activities; existence of formal institutional links, timelines, number of participants, nature of the sample, and the role of different implementing partners. In the second stage, a synthesis table grid was drawn up, consisting of five categories: project details, project achievements, programme concepts, learning concepts, institutional links, and future recommendations (see Appendix 3 and 4). Through this process, the relationships between the programme concepts arising from the different studies were considered in each case.

Idiomatic translation was followed, the meaning of the text was preserved, interpretations and explanations in each report were treated as data and translated across the different studies to produce learning concepts from project implementation. Two categories of learning concepts were identified. The first category identified four types of organizational learning behaviour; these included: *creative* (enterprising and intuitive) *static* (tick box), *progressive* (future sustainability driven), and *adaptive* (flexible and responsive to criticism/recommendations)

Table 2.1 Country office learning behaviour

	Phase I: Jan. 1997– Aug. 2000	Phase II: Sep. 2000– Dec. 2002	Phase III: Jan. 2003– Dec. 2005	Phase IV: Jan. 2006– Dec. 2008	Phase V: Jan. 2009– Dec. 2012	Phase VI: Jan. 2013– Dec. 2015	Phase VII: Jan. 2016– Dec. 2019
Sierra Leone	–	Creative	Adaptive	Static	Adaptive	Static	Adaptive
Macedonia	Creative	Progressive	Adaptive	Adaptive	Progressive	Progressive	Creative

(see Table 2.1). The second category of learning concepts coded the norms transmitted through peacebuilding projects run by the partner INGO in each country. By identifying the key norms being advocated through specific projects, it was possible to code nine concepts on norm transmission for each country. The norm concepts were weighted according to how often each concept was mentioned in the text of each report. These were cross-checked with the overall recommendations of each report to ensure there was consistency in the weight attached to them. During the analysis and writing up stage, the data in the evaluation reports was taken to be first-order interpretations (Schütz, 1962: 51–9). Using the evaluation data and the findings from the meta-ethnographic synthesis, I inferred three further second-order interpretations from the nine norm concepts identified in each case study. These include 'intercultural communication', 'quality pre-school education', and 'citizenship and ethnic identity' in Macedonia. In Sierra Leone the second-order concepts inferred included 'access and acceptance', 'agency and behaviour', and 'citizenship and participation' (see Table 2.2).

Table 2.2 Norm concepts and second-order interpretations for norm transmission

Second-order interpretation	Norm concepts in Sierra Leone	Norm concepts in Macedonia	Second-order interpretation
Access & acceptance	Information	Minority language	Intercultural communication
	Sensitization	Intergroup contact	
	Empowerment	Socialization	
Agency & behaviour	Voice	Enrolment	Quality pre-school education
	Capacity	Institutionalization	
	Participation	Pedagogy	
Citizenship & participation	Governance	Segregation	Citizenship & ethnic identity
	Democracy	Integrated education	
	Elections	Social cohesion	

Reflections on the Process

Due to the explicit organizational commitment to learning from evaluation, the institutional memory of the projects in Macedonia and Sierra Leone had been systematically preserved over the years by the ILT based at the headquarters, the regional offices, and the country offices. I could access a combination of archival (paper archives), human, and electronic memory (files and databases). In both cases, archived digital files were the easiest to access. Staff turnover, organizational restructuring, and a gradual transition from international to local staffing meant that continuous human memory for each phase of programming was not always available. Personal communication such as memos, and internal communications such as electronic mails, could not be included in the synthesis due to privacy, and data protection regulations. In Macedonia, a total of 12 evaluative studies were included in the meta-ethnographic synthesis covering the period between 1998 and 2019. The documents reviewed comprised four final evaluations, one thematic evaluation, one baseline study, one mid-term evaluation, and two final narrative reports. Two further internal documents were analysed, including a logical framework of the *Mozaik* project for 2004–2006 and an organizational mapping document. These reports were either donor-funded external evaluations or internal evaluations undertaken by the country office staff, or external M&E consultants contracted by the country office. Learning evaluations independent of donor-funded programmes were missing in Macedonia. Internal evaluations collated at the end of the school year were not available for the meta-ethnographic synthesis due to data protection requirements. This limitation in the available evidence meant uncritical or overly positive outcome narratives in the evaluation reports had to be cross-checked with primary interviews, and with secondary sources such as Tankersley (2001), Shochat (2003), and Milcev (2013) among others.

A total of 18 evaluative studies were included in the meta-ethnographic synthesis for Sierra Leone covering a range of media and community outreach projects implemented between 2000 and 2019. These included ten external, six internal, and two learning evaluations. Drawing on the project reports, and in consultation with the radio production team, the different radio programmes were categorized according to their thematic and normative focus, i.e. the values or ideas that they promoted. These were cross-checked with the source of funding for each programme, the concerned donor's strategic priorities as advertised in the funding call, and the local relevance of the themes selected over time. Drawing up this timeline was aided by staff continuity. The senior media producer had been with the studio since 2000, making it possible to map the evolution of radio programmes and the different themes guiding the content, especially in terms of local versus donor input and influence on radio programming. The meta-ethnography of the different project documents and evaluations shared from the digital repository allowed me to determine how local social, cultural, economic, and normative ideas shaped the content of the radio shows. The evaluative data was triangulated using primary and secondary sources, such as published policy papers, donor reports, and primary interviews with community residents, project participants, evaluators, and country office staff. Such a research strategy enabled a more rounded perspective on the long-term effects of the various radio programmes, and community engagement activities on intergenerational relations, and youth attitudes to peace more broadly speaking.

Challenges of Fieldwork in Post-war Countries

Field research in post-war countries comes with some special challenges. These include problems with access, sampling, validity, trustworthiness, and bias. War-related trauma can inhibit the ability as well as the willingness of conflict-affected populations to communicate their experiences (Barakat et al., 2002: 992). For researchers, limited infrastructure, and physical insecurity can present safety concerns that are exacerbated depending on the race, gender, and nationality of the field researcher (Craig et al., 2000: 20). Quantitative researchers face data scarcity to ground their analysis. Databases such as census records can be missing and outdated, this together with the limited availability of comprehensive geographical maps can complicate the design and administration of large-scale survey research (Haer and Becher, 2012: 3–4). These practical issues are accentuated by the difficulty of establishing trust, often the most critical ingredient for successful field research by qualitative and ethnographic researchers. Bosk (2004: 418) sums it up: 'no trust, no access, no trust, no consent, no trust, no data'. While the grey zone between trust and distrust is a feature of field relationships in stable contexts too, in post-war contexts, the partial trust dynamic is further amplified (Chakravarty, 2012: 252–4).

During civil wars and in ethnic conflicts, civilians are wary of unfamiliar social interactions given the possibility of being targeted and attacked. This distrust lingers on in the post-war setting and creates segregation between groups (Menzel, 2015; Benzing, 2020: 101). For researchers in the field, trust becomes a multi-layered issue. On the one hand, researchers need to adopt fieldwork strategies to mitigate the vulnerabilities of research participants in post-war societies. On the other hand, trustworthiness of respondent accounts can be suspect, with the possibility of fabrication or what Zulaika and Douglass (1996) term 'fictionalization'. The complexity of human interactions introduces trust and distrust at the same time. Fujii (2010) suggests that when researchers find discrepancies in oral testimonies, they can use such accounts for the collection of meta-data to better understand the context. Trust therefore is a continuum and not a binary issue (Celestina, 2018).

To access populations, gatekeeper consent such as that of families, elders, or chiefs can become culturally appropriate (Clark, 2011). These factors create layers of complexity in how ethical research and reliable data can be collected and how trust is negotiated (Chiumento, 2016: 17). For this study, tracking down all the individuals who took part in the original evaluations was not possible. Little follow-up research had been conducted with project participants associated with the different projects. Strict data protection laws restricted the maintenance of up-to-date lists of former beneficiaries, which made tracing them impractical. Therefore, a snowball sampling method had to be used. As a purposive sampling technique, snowballing involves a deliberate choice of participants due to the qualities they possess. In this sampling strategy, a bond or link exists between the initial sample and others in the same target populations (Berg, 2004). It belongs to the wider set of link-tracing methodologies (Spreen, 1992). Snowball sampling can play a key role in locating, accessing, and interviewing hidden and hard to reach populations. Snowball sampling while useful comes with the potential pitfall of limiting the validity and reliability of research findings (Etikan et al., 2016). This is due to the reliance on referrals that can potentially exclude individuals outside of the specific networks of a research contact (Van Meter, 1990).

Ethical research demands a certain vigilance, openness, and flexibility about how the research process is negotiated and implemented. In this study, the knowledge production partnership with the partner INGO, demanded both an awareness and vigilance on my part of the potential pitfalls that relying on gatekeepers for negotiating research access could pose (Baaz and Utas, 2019: 157–78). I was well aware that on the one hand, the trust deficit was mitigated by accessing populations through the partner INGO's trusted networks. On the other hand, conflicts of interest can arise when using INGOs to access research populations. This is because reputational concerns can influence their decision to allow access to successful projects or to communities where their work has been positively received. Profound biases may be insurmountable if a researcher only interacts with those within the specific network being accessed (Cohen and Avieli, 2011: 428). This limitation is balanced by considerable advantages that weighed heavily on my mind when deciding on research access.

Practical realities like research fatigue, however, justify the reliance on intermediaries. The continual, repetitive research of particular communities or populations in conflict-affected countries has led to feelings of resentment, over-research, and research fatigue (Clark, 2008: 955). Exposure to multiple researchers and evaluation teams often asking the same questions can make communities reluctant to participate in, or become disengaged from the research process. Some target populations like ex-combatants can also start to look for tangible benefits like money for their participation. In other cases, research participants can feel used, or taken advantage of, in the name of research ethics that bar researchers from paying individuals for partaking in focus group discussions (FGDs) (Cronin-Fruman and Lake, 2018: 609). In her research in the DRC for example, Lake (2018) encountered many individuals who expressed hope that support would result from sharing their stories with researchers. D'Errico et al. (2013: 53) have also noted community frustrations with academic research that failed to deliver local benefits or desired changes.

Ethical Considerations

Conventionally, there are three conventional standards or 'canons' of research ethics (Cloke et al., 2000): informed consent for research participants; confidentiality; and do not harm. Ethical approval for the research was received from the university's research ethics committee. In addition to procedural ethics (Ellis, 2007: 4–5) this research took note of the situational and relational ethics involved. Researchers have moral and ethical responsibility in monitoring and responding to ethical issues during fieldwork (Davis, 1998; Eder and Corsaro, 1999; Fujii, 2012). Durham (2000) notes that research with young people requires us to pay close attention to the social landscape, the topology of power, rights, relationships, and social structures that youth are entangled with. Intergenerational differences between children and adults in a given context shape the power relations between the researcher and the child informant (Mayall, 2000). I adhered to ethical symmetry in this research. The ethical relationship between researcher and informant was viewed the same regardless of whether the interaction was with adults or with children (Christensen and Prout, 2002: 482). Taking account of the social and cultural positioning of children in their particular circumstances can help acknowledge biases in age or developmentally based assumptions about children's competencies, as these are likely to vary given the local cultural context. With children and young people, 'ethical considerations depend on the researchers' ability to understand, and respond to the feelings of the children they work with' (Davis, 1998: 329). While listening authentically to youthful voices (Carnevale, 2004; 2020), it was necessary for me to reflect on how these voices are produced, and what change their voices can precipitate.

I was also aware of feminist ethics and the ethics of care during the research (Christians, 2005). For women researchers, following feminist approaches, in which mutuality, kindness, respect, and connectedness between researcher and researched (including their communities) are valued (Swartz, 2011: 48) must be balanced with an awareness of the gendered dimensions of research with children and young people. When approaching children as social agents (Barker and Weller, 2003; Boyden and de Berry, 2004), or even as research co-participants, women must contend with ethical concerns around power imbalances and relationships between ourselves, the children who take part in the research, and the adults surrounding them. The onus of accountability on researchers is considerable, given that researchers have the power to transmit and potentially also

distort the thoughts of others (Peritore, 1990). This makes it all the more important that they remain objective throughout the data collection and data analysis
stages. It is also important to recognize our own positionality, biases, affiliations,
and perceptions.

Researchers require 'a radical consciousness of self' (Davis et al., 2000), and must
apply reflexivity in their fieldwork (McDowell, 1992). Reflexive examination of
our position as researchers is important as it is not possible to assume the role
of neutral observers whilst in the field (Barker and Smith, 2001: 146). Our position as researchers, and the relationship we develop with those we research, can
be linked to the reality of gendered social relations (Holmes, 1998; Davis et al.,
2000). I have found that gender and race can be particularly significant in the development or maintenance of field relationships. For example, male researchers
can face greater obstruction with accessing young children when compared with
women (Tooke, 2000). Women can be accorded a more intimate role of insider and
consequently I have been given greater access to children, women, and youth in my
previous research in Liberia and in Mindanao, Philippines (Podder 2012a; 2012b).
This was again the case in my research with primary school and kindergarten
staff, and children in Macedonia. As a man, I may have faced more challenges,
as men are perceived to be out of place in the feminized world of childcare (Barker
and Smith, 2001: 146). Invariably, this might have afforded me an undue advantage as a woman academic researching children and young people attitudes
towards peace.

Field Research in Sierra Leone

In Sierra Leone, data collection took place during March–April 2017 in Freetown,
Bo, and the Port Loko areas. I gathered a total of 25 semi-structured interviews
with current and former country office staff, youth reporters, project partner staff,
former evaluators, and national and local elites (government officials, chiefs, and
civil society leaders). I completed institutional memory mapping and timeline exercises with the country office staff in the field. I did further interviews via Skype
with former staff and various evaluation consultants during 2018. This research
design allowed the cross-checking of longitudinal data presented in the evaluative studies. It also enabled triangulation of findings from the meta-ethnographic
synthesis. In addition to interviews, I undertook community meetings in four locations: Sinjo and Bamba villages near the town of Pujehun, in Malen Chiefdom, Bo
district, and in Kemen and Maconteh villages near the town of Port Loko in Port
Loko district. I completed six FGDs (n = 56) with community members in these
locations (Table 2.3). The community meetings were organized through the country office staff and their local partner NGOs. I travelled to the community meetings
with one of the country office staff; a driver, and a research assistant. Languages

Table 2.3 Details of FGDs

FGD with community members	Location	Participants (by gender and age)	
FGD 1 with male and female residents	Sinjo	6	4
FGD 2 with women of mixed ages	Bamba	–	10
FGD 3 with males of mixed ages	Bamba	10	–
FGD 4 with elders	Kemen	5	5
FGD 5 with youth	Kemen	4	4
FGD 6 with youth	Maconteh	4	4

from which translation was required included Mende, Krio, and Temne. Translation was facilitated by the research assistant during the course of the meetings. Villagers were notified in advance of our visit. No monetary payments were made for their participation in the research. We provided biscuits and soft drinks during the FGDs as a token of appreciation. Individual consent was sought prior to the interviews, and an ethics related information brief was shared with all research participants prior to data collection.

Research with Child Reporters and Young People in Freetown

My research in the capital and the surrounding areas focused on children and young people and their sensitization through radio programmes produced by the partner INGO. In my interviews with the former child reporters working on radio programmes like Golden Kids News (GKN), I found that involvement in radio offered them access to CSO networks, but this access, experience, and training did not translate into sustainable employment opportunities. I found that exposure to liberal norms and civil society activism encouraged these child reporters and other young people in Freetown and the surrounding peri-urban areas to seek work with the local NGO sector, or to start their own NGOs. Entrepreneurship resulted in mixed outcomes. One of the former GKN reporters, Hassan,[1] used his contacts at the United Nations Mission in Sierra Leone (UNAMSIL) radio to design youth focused advocacy programmes, that became the seed for his local NGO.[2] Hassan began working with the communities in Kroo Bay, and in Central Freetown, looking at water issues. He found that children were prone to water borne diseases in these settlements, and faced security issues while fetching water. Based on this practical observation, Hassan prepared a project proposal for the treatment of stream water to ensure that it was safe for drinking. He was able to

[1] Names have been changed to conceal identity of the respondents.
[2] GKN reporter 1, Freetown, 8 April 2017.

secure small pots of donor funding and expanded this work on water issues to over 50 communities, covering 5,000 directly affected children. His organization expanded gradually, and undertook capacity-building work on various governance, education, and child protection issues. The NGO won the youth organization of the year title in 2014.[3]

Samuel, another former GKN anchor, also registered his own NGO to sensitize youth on elections, youth empowerment, skills development, and civic education in a range of technical and vocational education skills, such as carpentry and masonry. Samuel however found fundraising a challenge, and has struggled to secure donor funding to sustain his efforts. He found that advocacy work had some negative effects.[4] Elders found CSOs as disruptive of traditional social relations, turning children against adults, and encouraging them to demand rights and opportunities without meeting their own obligations and duties (Boersch-Supan, 2012). Financial management aspects of running a CSO also posed serious challenges. For both Hassan and Samuel, the recruitment and retention of staff, and funding overhead costs through short-term grants created anxiety. The government did not offer any support, in fact, the family support unit (FSU) of the Sierra Leone Police often asked Hassan to help with their child protection cases.[5] As a result, for the GKN reporters translating their peacebuilding training into practice proved challenging. These stories are representative of the mixed experiences of young people exposed to liberal peacebuilding, and the considerable structural barriers to realizing their creative agency.

For the other youth I met in the capital, similar to Hassan and Samuel, awareness of rights had empowered them to agitate around issues of transparency and responsive governance, although their capacity to implement these liberal ideas appeared to be mediated by the reality of their everyday challenges and the structural barriers to their socio-economic mobility. For many young people their life conditions were largely unchanged, even decades after post-war peacebuilding efforts started in Sierra Leone. In this sense, they were able to adjust to, or adopt the liberal norms instrumentally, while remaining cynical about the full applicability of these norms to their local context. Sometimes access to peacebuilding projects created 'haves' and 'have nots' across youthful populations in Freetown. One respondent noted that 'trainings can include the same youth as participants due to their familiarity across the CSO network'.[6] This created barriers for a wider youth population, who felt left out.

Civil society activists admitted that radio did encourage dialogue and a certain amount of reflection on different types of behaviours to allow communities to make considered choices on the issues of governance, electoral participation,

---

[3] Ibid.
[4] GKN reporter 2, Freetown, 10 April 2017.
[5] GKN reporter 1, Freetown, 8 April 2017.
[6] Marie, Election Monitor, Freetown, 9 April 2017.

and rights. However, the constant transmission of appropriate social behaviours through sensitization and advocacy programmes, was designed to encourage conformity rather than critical thinking.[7] Respondents felt that the sensitization programmes not only provided them with facts and information but also taught youth, about the choices they can have and what they should opt for.[8] Then, there was the challenge with perceptions. Respondents felt that it was difficult to overcome stereotypes for certain types of youth. For example, the *Okada* drivers continue to remain marginalized as they are associated with ex-combatants and 'at risk' youth, even when they were civilians and did not take part in the civil war.[9]

The ad hoc nature of engagement on the youth question by both the government and the international actors has led to inadequate, short-term investments with limited follow-up. Barring the repeated investments in elections related advocacy, most other projects with youth, have been one off, rather than cumulative. These short-term investments in training and capacity-building did not translate into sustainable livelihoods, creating weak institutional and normative legacies. The country office staff on their part were aware that the norms that resonated with the local audience may not always synchronize with donor strategic priorities. This meant that they had less control over the duration and content of radio programmes. For example, *Bush Wahala*, which was a highly successful radio programme that offered communities critical information around land issues, and a lively forum for discussion, lost funding from the Open Society Initiative for West Africa (OSIWA) in 2013.[10] Without donor support, the programme had to be scrapped, much against the wishes of the country team and their listeners. This explained the dwindling portfolio of radio programmes over time.

Land Conflicts and the Rural Hinterland

Research in the rural communities exposed me to some of the realities around tense intergenerational dynamics. It is well-recognized that rural communities in Sierra Leone face myriad problems with reconciliation, reintegration, livelihoods, underdevelopment, food insecurity, politicization, and crime. The combination of widespread nepotism, corrupt tendencies among the local elites, most prominently the Paramount Chief, and the national political elite's desire for development, have offered ideal conditions for various foreign investors to set up agrobusinesses such as palm oil plantations (Millar, 2016, 2017, 2018a; Ryan, 2018). It was important for me to recognize that land grabs were not the only trigger for conflicts in the

---

[7] Expert, Institute for Governance Reform, Freetown, 6 April 2017.
[8] John, former GKN reporter, staff with National Election Watch, 7 April 2017.
[9] Commonwealth Youth Caucus Sierra Leone Representative, and World Peace Prayer Society Peace representative.
[10] Country Director Sierra Leone, Freetown, 2 April 2017.

Fig. 2.1 Community meetings, Sinjo, Pujehun
(Photo courtesy of the author, March 2017).

rural hinterland. The social dynamics prior to the arrival of agrobusinesses were not always stable or peaceful. This was tied to how a particular area or chiefdom was affected by the war (1991–2002), whether the chiefdom benefited from infras-tructure development after the war, and the dynamics with regard to ex-combatant reintegration, and refugee resettlement as they played out in the post-war recon-struction phase (Peters, 2011a, 2011b; Peters and Richards, 2011). Community meetings around Pujehun and Port Loko areas (Figure 2.1) offered insights into the uncertain development benefits and systemic corruption behind the phenomenon of large-scale land grabs. To reverse the negative consequences of expulsion and dispossession, local and international peacebuilding organizations including the partner INGO have sensitized, informed, and supported local communities in their efforts to reclaim control over the use of land, forests, and waterbodies. This civil society activism on the one hand, aggravated pre-existing land tenure dispar-ities. On the other hand, it helped re-define the local governance space, the social relations of agrarian change, and the dynamics of intergenerational justice in the rural hinterland.

Customary land tenure systems vary across the country, as they are not ho-mogenous. Each ethnic group has their own rules regarding the governance of land, succession, and inheritance. Among the Mendes in the south, the rules are progressive, women own land and can be elected as Paramount Chiefs. In the east and the northern provinces amongst the Limba, Korankos, and the Temne groups, women and youth are treated as minors. They are viewed as lacking the capacity to manage land and all land-related issues are dealt with by older men as these are considered weighty or serious issues.[11] In these regions, women, and youth stand at a comparative disadvantage regarding land allocation, and the use of small holdings. Dispute settlement through formal legal action is of the last resort, as individuals that are taken to the police or the courts, become enemies for life.[12] To maintain social equilibrium, every effort is made to resolve disputes at the community level. Traditionally, conflict management whether at family, village, or chiefdom levels was the role of the customary elders and chiefs (Denney, 2013: 11; Millar, 2016). In the post-war period of empowerment around rights and governance, CSOs like Namati have used legal empowerment to encourage access to justice. They have trained community paralegals and the dispute mediation facilitated by paralegals has allowed the average citizen to defend their rights without taking matters to formal courts.[13]

Village chiefs I met in Sinjo lamented that conflict mediation by CSOs had 'undercut' tributes normally paid to town and quarter chiefs for dispute settlement.[14] In Sinjo and Bamba, community members were at loggerheads with the Paramount chief in Malen chiefdom, Pujehun, on account of his support for the Socfin Agricultural Company (SAC), a Belgian subsidiary in Sierra Leone. A lack of transparency and full informed consent in negotiating the terms of the land deal; disagreements over the regular distribution of land lease payments to all claimants; loss of employment and livelihoods; and limited corporate social responsibility (CSR) investments by SAC had fuelled bottom-up civic mobilization. The Malen Affected Land Owners and Users Association (MALOA) emerged during 2011/2012,[15] with support from CSOs like Green Scenery. Livelihood mapping studies revealed that in monetary terms, land owners and users in Malen had suffered an income loss through the leasing of farmlands. The consumption requirements of community residents outstripped the monies received from the SAC's surface rent payments.[16] MALOA was registered as a CSO and started their own advocacy campaign against SAC. This led to new intra-community dynamics. Tensions brewed between youth groups that continue to be employed by SAC, or are aligned with the Paramount Chief, and MALOA members, who have been sacked by the Company, and are identified as troublemakers by the SAC and the Paramount Chief.[17]

---

[11] Skype interview, Staff, Namati, 11 October 2020.
[12] Ibid.
[13] Ibid.
[14] Village chief, Sinjo, 10 April 2017.
[15] Skype interview, Staff, Green Scenery, 10 October 2020.
[16] Ibid.
[17] CSO activist, MALOA, 10 April 2017.

Fieldwork in Macedonia

In Macedonia, field data was collected during August–September 2017. The focus was on the experiences of three groups, (1) staff who worked directly with the bilingual immersion groups and media projects, including evaluators; (2) the beneficiaries, including children and youth; and (3) participants, including the teachers, trainers, and parents. The research was specifically interested in how these three groups understood and internalized the norms around intercultural communication, and what changes *Mozaik* values facilitated if at all, in their thinking and responses towards other ethnic communities in Macedonia. I completed a series of semi-structured interviews, FGDs, and classroom observations with teachers, parents, *Mozaik* alumni, and primary schoolchildren. Research was conducted in Skopje, Debar and Struga in the local languages with simultaneous translation into English. In terms of demographic trends, the capital Skopje is a mixed settlement with a majority Macedonian population. Struga, is also a mixed settlement, inhabited by Macedonians and Albanians, although these communities do not mix voluntarily. There are also divisions between rural and urban inhabitants in Struga and its outlying areas (Kelsi, 2013: 20). Debar is a majority Albanian settlement, on the border with Albania, and is close to the tourist hotspot of Lake Ohrid.

During my meetings, I was accompanied by a local translator (Albanian) and one of the INGO programme staff (Macedonian), to assist with translation in the two languages. The sample included eight teachers (five Macedonian and three Albanian), 12 parents (six Macedonian, five Albanian, and one Macedonian-Turkish); and 16 primary (eight), and secondary school (eight) children (ten girls, six boys). In Struga one FGD with *Mozaik* teachers and one FGD with parents were held. Meetings in Debar, included one FGD with the *Mozaik* parents and one FGD with the primary school teachers. I also ran FGDs with 15 *Mozaik* alumni. This included six alumni in Skopje and nine alumni in Debar. This sample included one boy and eight girls in Debar, and one boy and five girls in Skopje. I also undertook two primary school visits in Skopje and Debar. These visits involved one classroom observation of third-grade students in Skopje and one observation of the primary school teachers' common room in Debar.

Previous studies suggest that interviews are not suitable for use with preschoolers, because of children's limited language skills and dependence on the interpersonal relationships with their caregivers (Touliatos and Compton, 1983; Garbarino and Stott, 1989; Boehm and Weinberg, 1997). Children cannot read or fully understand written questionnaires even when they are read out loud to them. This makes participant observation and the audio-recording of children's naturally occurring talk most appropriate for data collection (McKechnie, 2000: 62). I used participant observation with primary schoolchildren in Skopje, and preschool children in the *Mozaik* groups in Struga and Debar. Unobtrusive participant observation, where the researcher stays apart while carefully observing interactions between children, can help mitigate the unequal status between the observer, and the observed, given the natural authority that adults have over children (Fine and Glassner, 1979; Fine and Sandstrom, 1988). Observation was particularly helpful in documenting children's non-verbal activities and cues (McKechnie, 2000: 66). With the primary schoolchildren in Skopje, open-ended conversations about their recall of *Mozaik* values were recorded in a notebook with the permission of, and in the presence of, their third-grade teacher (Rapley, 2001).

Observations from the *Mozaik* Groups in Struga, Debar, and Skopje

The *Mozaik* group in Struga was located in the centre of town. The day I visited in September 2017, there were around 14 children who were spread out across a large room, split into two sections. One section had dedicated play areas, with toys and books, and the other section had designated quiet areas for naps. There were two teachers in charge of this group, one Albanian and one Macedonian. It was the first day of kindergarten for a child; he kept crying inconsolably and kept calling for his mummy. The other children seemed calm and were well settled and played in small groups. A couple of children came up to the teachers after finishing a drawing. From what I could observe, all of them spoke mainly in Macedonian. This was understandable. The centre of Struga is predominantly Macedonian, while the rural areas are mostly Albanian. Settlements are largely mono-ethnic, encouraging people to relocate into unofficial territorial pockets. During lunch, the children lined up to move to the large dining hall. It was set up with small round tables and chairs. The children were supervised by a single lunchtime assistant who helped some of them with their lunch.

In the afternoon, I interviewed the teachers with the help of my translators. The teachers recalled their struggles around 2011, when both of them had worked without pay for a year to keep the group going. The teachers reflected on the qualitative changes that had followed from institutionalization, such as the dwindling resources and mounting workloads. They were more hesitant however to discuss about pedagogical issues and the local politics surrounding institutionalization. These appeared to be contentious topics with possible negative reputational fallouts and therefore avoided. I also met three *Mozaik* parents (two women and one man) in the late afternoon. They had been notified in advance of my interview request and had consented to take part in the research. The parents saw this interaction as an opportunity to voice their frustrations with the changes in the *Mozaik* groups. They lamented the reliance on donations for toys, books, and toiletries. Parents also contributed funds for improvements in the infrastructure; such as relaying the pavements in the outdoor play areas. They felt that the rising numbers affected the ability of teachers to offer personal attention to the children. At full capacity, there were nearly 30 students in each of the two *Mozaik* groups; and only two teachers to oversee the students in each group. The concerns over quality notwithstanding, demand for enrolment in *Mozaik* outstripped supply, with long waiting lists, making the *Mozaik* experience inaccessible to many children in Struga, and the surrounding areas.[18]

In Debar, the *Mozaik* group was located on the premises of the local primary school. I met with the head teacher in the morning, and the *Mozaik* teachers in the afternoon. The teachers in Debar reflected less on the 2011 struggles; they were focused more on the present state of affairs and voiced their concerns about the changes in the *Mozaik* model. Absorption into the national pre-school curriculum had forced upon them additional administrative tasks around writing reports and observations. With no budget available for external M&E, the teachers' workload had grown considerably in this regard.[19] This was in addition to the rising student numbers in each group. Parents that I met in Debar and Skopje noted behavioural improvements in the children after joining *Mozaik*. Parents were exposed to better parenting skills. The teachers supported the children by observing and noting their activities each day, and communicated regularly with the parents. The children in the groups, were encouraged to use polite words and parents were asked to teach and enforce social manners, and a daily routine with their child.[20] For children prone to hyperactivity, parents were encouraged to create a calm and structured environment at home similar to that in the *Mozaik* groups.[21]

In Skopje, the limited appeal of the pedagogical aspects was evident in my conversation with the *Mozaik* parents. There was little expectation attached to the bilingual aspects. As one parent noted, 'in the beginning we did know what to expect. Later, we realized that the children were learning about the other language and culture.'[22] For Macedonian parents in Skopje who did not ordinarily socialize with Albanians, an opportunity to connect with the Albanian parents through children's friendships in the *Mozaik* groups arose. Often these friendships did not last beyond the *Mozaik* years, and after the children moved into mono-lingual instruction from primary school onwards, contact waned. Most parents felt that the *Mozaik* model of bilingual immersion would not work during primary and secondary school. There was also an understanding of the limited transformative effects of *Mozaik*. 'Interventions like *Mozaik* are managing symptoms but not the real cause of the problem, which has to do with identity and education.'[23] Parents acknowledged that the history of each ethnicity, and how it is projected in the

[18] FGD *Mozaik* parents, Struga, 3 September 2017.
[19] Albanian teacher, *Mozaik* group, Debar, 5 September 2017.
[20] FGD *Mozaik* parents, Debar, 5 September 2017.
[21] Ibid.
[22] Parent interview, Macedonian Female, 48 years old, Skopje, 3 September 2017.
[23] Skype interview with Macedonian civil servant, 17 April 2020.

textbooks is problematic. Religion also plays a divisive role. Parents could choose if their child should study about the history of all religions or only one specific religion, taught by a priest or the imam. As one parent noted, 'every school in every municipality is different depending on the population dynamics. These practices reinforce segregation and biases.'[24]

Mozaik Alumni in Debar and Skopje

The alumni in Debar had a good recall of their *Mozaik* experience based on familiarity and regular socialization in the post-*Mozaik* years. This was partly due to their ability to recall collectively and piece together different elements of their experience during the FGDs. The alumni noted that they learnt a lot about each other's culture, religion, and language. Over the years, the Macedonian children admitted to have forgotten some of the Albanian words learnt during *Mozaik*, and social friendships had continued only if the parents remained friends. They did, however, recognize the importance of friendship and social ties across ethnic lines. 'Every time a new child joined, the older children would help the younger children, we would eat together and share the food, and play together, we learnt about creative work, learnt how to share our toys.'[25] The children thoroughly enjoyed the various creative pursuits learnt while at *Mozaik*, such as drawing, painting, art and craft, and storytelling. After being exposed to these experiential methods while at *Mozaik*, the alumni found primary schooling to be more about rote learning. The emphasis on creativity and games was lost. For example, if children got into a fight in *Mozaik*, they were asked to draw why they were angry. The alumni found these creative outlets for managing stress helpful and continued to practise them.[26] One of the alumni noted that, 'it makes a difference that we went to the *Mozaik* kindergartens, *Mozaik* taught us that there is no difference, everyone is equal, and is entitled to having an opinion. We learnt to respect everyone.'[27]

The alumni in Skopje that I met felt that these *Mozaik* values held strong in the first two years of primary school, after which children started to adapt to the segregated education system. The teaching style became more directed, with less room for openness and critical thinking. One of the alumni noted that 'the teachers did not like us being inquisitive…they told us to behave a certain way, they could sometimes hold prejudice about other groups.'[28] This was in stark contrast to the environment in *Mozaik*. 'In middle school and high school few teachers care about us, there are lots of subjects, many teachers, and lots of children in the classes.'[29]

---

[24] Skype interview with Macedonian civil servant, 17 April 2020.
[25] FGD with six *Mozaik* alumni, 5 girls, 1 boy, Debar, 3 September 2017.
[26] Ibid.
[27] Ibid.
[28] Ibid.
[29] Ibid.

The children felt that their opinions got lost, and it became more difficult for them to resist the outside pressures around segregation and difference. Issues that I discuss in greater detail in the Macedonia case study.

Potential Limitations and Biases

Interviews and observations conducted in conflict-affected and post-war contexts might present problems with validity and reliability due to the less than optimal conditions around access and trust. Problems with recruiting interviewees and cultural differences such as language barriers are some of the well-identified limitations which were also faced in this research (Fujii, 2010; Cohen and Arieli, 2011: 425–6). The choice of snowball sampling though effective, is likely to have given rise to a bias in the sample population. The issue of respondent recall and the trustworthiness of oral accounts were some of the other limitations faced. Using intermediaries for interpretation of local languages (Macedonian, Albanian, and Krio) into English may have given rise to translation bias. It is well known that during the translation of responses some nuance is likely to have been lost. Simultaneous translation into English, rather than recording interviews and transcribing later, did allow me to observe non-verbal cues that enriched my understanding of cultural appropriateness, and of the context.

Reliance on evaluative data for understanding peacebuilding legacy can present limitations as well. Most scholars would agree that evaluations of peacebuilding projects adopt an institutional rather than an experiential approach. They can involve a certain element of selling a success story or a positive performance narrative to donors (Mika, 2002). However, as Millar points out, the assumed impacts of institutional solutions are in reality social experiences (2014a: 506). How local people experience peacebuilding projects vary considerably and often in unpredictable and complex ways, and over time. These effects can be captured only partially in short-term evaluations around project impact.

It is also necessary to acknowledge the limitations of meta-ethnography as a research method. Due to the time-consuming nature of translation, the number of studies that can be included is often small. Too large a sample would lead to a reductionist analysis or context stripping, allowing researchers less time to immerse into the details of the studies being synthesized. The selection of studies included can also be subjective. Noblit and Hare's approach does not require researchers to formally appraise the quality of the studies included. This lack of vetting around the quality of the data can be a source of weakness. Further, in seeking an interpretation of interpretations, or secondary interpretation, the meta-ethnographic synthesis approach can be overly-relativist. To overcome these potential limitations, time and effort must be invested in the construction of metaphors. It is important to establish whether the studies address the same question or not before summarizing the findings and conclusion from each (Noblit and Hare, 1988, 119–22). In this research a clear set of rules was applied for determining the inclusion criteria, and all available evaluative studies were included, making the selection criteria less subjective. While weights can also be assigned to each study based on mathematical criteria specified in advance, so that findings can be synthesized across the studies and the method can be replicated later, this route was not adopted in this research (Borenstein et al., 2011: xxii–iii).

These factors lead us to consider the generalizability, trustworthiness, and the validity of the findings. In terms of generalizability, the results from this study present a partial rather than a comprehensive summary of long-term effects in the two cases. The theoretical framework on peacebuilding legacy, however, offers a guide for further studies on mapping legacy, as does the use of meta-ethnographic synthesis using evaluative data. However, gauging the full spectrum of social, cultural, economic, and normative effects of the media, education and community outreach efforts on both the direct participants and more dispersed audiences was not possible due to the time-lag between the various projects, and the difficulty of tracking down relevant respondents in both countries. Without follow-up research and live databases for the different project beneficiaries, tracking this sample can be impossible for research purposes. This limitation illuminates how the longitudinal study of programmatic effects is neglected not only by donors but also by the peacebuilding INGO staff themselves.

Efforts were made to overcome these shortcomings through the triangulation of the data and findings. The meta-ethnographic synthesis of evaluative data was used in combination with interviews, participant and non-participant observation for the cross-checking of facts (Denzin, 1970: 291). Wherever possible, results in archived reports were cross-checked with field interviews and with M&E experts, both internal and external to the organization. By drawing upon multiple (at least two) sources of evidence; it was possible to seek convergence and corroboration through the use of different data sources and methods (Bowen, 2009: 28). By triangulating the institutional memory with follow-up interviews across the various groups of respondents', efforts were made to identify the potential or actual bias both prior to fieldwork and during data analysis. Finally, in accepting that context refracts peacebuilding efforts, and cultural bearings can muddy attempts to measure and account for the direct causal flow and impact of particular interventions, this research did not seek to establish causation or attribution. Instead it tried to step beyond the immediate, technocratic, and short-term nature of programme evaluations to follow an interpretive approach—one that enabled deeper reflection on time, transformation, and intergenerational peace. It also helped gauge the role of norm resonance and retention, institutionalization and adaptation, and organizational learning and reflection in shaping peacebuilding legacy.

3

Peacebuilding through Pre-school Education and Media Programmes in Macedonia

Introduction

Beginning from a bifurcated idea of the state at independence (1991), one that was rooted in a privileged position for the ethnic Macedonians, a residual legacy of arrangements within the former Yugoslavia, observers would argue Macedonia has made visible progress towards multi-ethnic accommodation of minority demands since the 2001 conflict (Smith, 2010; Popovska and Zhanet, 2015; Georgieva and Shehu, 2017). Language rights were one of the main points of contention during the peace negotiations brokered by international actors like the NATO and the EU, with the ethnic Albanian elites demanding equal official status for their language and the ethnic Macedonian parties viewing it as a threat to national sovereignty (Meka, 2016). Guarantees for mother tongue and multilingual education became important instruments for transition out of conflict, as linguistic cleavages had become politically salient.

On paper, the Ohrid Framework Agreement (OFA) of August 2001 was an important and necessary step toward reducing interethnic tensions. In practice, while providing stronger protection for minority rights, through the recognition of language rights, and by introducing education in the mother tongue of the minorities, the OFA has contributed to an increase in interethnic separation (Bieber, 2005; Reka, 2008; Anger et al., 2010). This is enhanced through the policies of territorial decentralization, and administrative devolution of education to local municipalities (Myhrvold, 2005; Lyon, 2015). These policies together encourage physical separation of ethnic groups in ways that inhibit true social reconciliation (Clark, 2010: 345; Arraiza, 2014: 9). Amidst the reality of pronounced and increasing ethnic segregation, external players like the EU and NATO among others have invested in a range of education and media projects that emphasize the concepts of integrated education and social cohesion norms (Krstevska-Papic, and Zekolli, 2013).

Peacebuilding Legacy. Sukanya Podder, Oxford University Press.
© Sukanya Podder (2022). DOI: 10.1093/oso/9780192863980.003.0004

This backdrop sets the scene for the intercultural communication projects designed and implemented by the partner INGO's Macedonia office between 1997 and 2019. Children and young people were seen as a means for, as well as the targets of, educational, psychological, information, and entertainment-based interventions (Lemish, 2008: 283). Peace education focused bilingual immersion groups and a suite of media and theatre projects were aimed at fostering intercultural dialogue (Broome and Collier, 2012: 253). From a peacebuilding legacy perspective, the story of institutionalization of the bilingual immersion groups presents an important lesson for developing sustainable legacies that peace education initiatives offer relative to the ad hoc and unsustainable nature of youth focused media projects. In terms of normative legacy, the norms of social cohesion and integrated education were packaged in ways that encouraged local acquiescence with unfamiliar values, eliciting only mixed receptivity to them.

The trajectory of norm transmission, resonance, and retention in Macedonia presented a non-linear process, with variable adoption between national, subnational, and individual levels. Due to the low local resonance of the externally promoted values of intercultural communication and social cohesion, the intergroup exchanges facilitated through the peace education and media projects implemented by the Macedonia country office resulted in a 'non-authentic' or 'superficial' adoption of these norms. Legal adoption and policy implementation of these donor prescribed norms made little difference at the individual and the community levels, as the policies did not speak to everyday realities. As a result, the implementation of the *Mozaik* bilingual kindergarten groups and the related media and theatre projects such as the *Nashe Maalo* children's television series presented contradictory effects in terms of conflict transformation.

This is because, in deeply divided societies, collective beliefs about who is a victim and who is an aggressor are transmitted intergenerationally; they become unquestioned truths and can be highly resistant to change (Weick, 2001 cited in Kupermintz and Salomon, 2005: 294). These beliefs have encouraged 'epistemic rigidity' or a strong adherence to the narrative and position of one's group, and the rejection of information that may threaten the collectively held beliefs (Kruglanski, 2004a). The opportunities for transformative peace through better social relations and denser forms of intergroup interaction did not therefore materialize through these intercultural communication initiatives. Variation in intergroup interaction was based on local history and social capital dynamics rather than on the exposure to externally sponsored peace norms. A superficial adoption of these norms meant that they were not retained over time, and both the individual and the ethnic groups returned to earlier behaviours of mixed social distance and limited social interaction (Risse et al., 1999; Crawford, 1993 cited in Björkdahl, 2008: 136).

In a society characterized by commercialized, ethnically segregated, monolingual, and globalized media structures, mainstream media and post-primary monolingual education did not encourage affinitive ties of civic belonging. Rather,

Macedonian parents and adults and through their influence their children continued to harbour negative stereotypes and prejudices towards other ethnic communities, especially the Albanian community (Tankersley, 2001). The intergenerational transmission of ethnic essentialism remains a major inhibitor to peace. It requires healing the anxieties of the older generation to allow the younger generation to socialize freely across the interethnic divide (Schönpflug, 2001; Segall et al., 2015). Peacebuilding efforts in Macedonia need not only adopt a long-term and transformative peace lens; they must also embrace an intergenerational peace lens.

The chapter is organized as follows. I first discuss the national context of war, peace, and interethnic relations in Macedonia, tracing developments in the former Yugoslav state to identify key triggers for the 2001 conflict. I then show the segregating effects of the ORA and how it has exacerbated ethnic distance across early years education despite an explicit policy commitment in the OFA for encouraging integrated education. This is discussed alongside the various policy and practical developments relating to early years provisions in the third part. Analysis of the evolutionary trajectory of the *Mozaik* bilingual immersion groups is presented next. This analysis brings to light numerous adaptations, shocks, and areas of programmatic dilution that were necessary for the successful institutionalization of these groups into the national kindergarten system. With regard to norm transmission, resonance, and retention, I found that while the institutional legacy of *Mozaik* was strong, its normative legacy was mixed and was linked to the social capital dynamics and the local history of intergroup socialization. The suite of media projects that complemented the intercultural communication efforts are discussed next. These efforts present a weaker institutional legacy in comparison with the *Mozaik* groups, although their normative legacy is shaped by broader social capital dynamics as was the case with *Mozaik*. I summarize the main findings in the conclusion.

War, Peace, and Interethnic Relations in Macedonia

Macedonia was once considered to be unique in that it was the only former Yugoslav state to have seceded without violence and bloodshed in 1991. Macedonia was created as a nation-state of the Macedonian people, with other groups such as the Albanians, Serbians, and the Turkish, relegated to minority status. As a result, post-independence statebuilding lacked joint ownership of the idea of the state between the majority Macedonians and other minority groups, in particular the largest minority group—the Albanians. Ten years after independence, in February 2001, conflict broke out between ethnic Macedonians and Albanians, initiating eight months of unrest that brought the country to the brink of civil war. Violent clashes between the Macedonian armed forces, and ethnic Albanian insurgents of the National Liberation Army (NLA) ravaged the countryside (Koktsidis,

2019). The NLA claimed to be fighting for greater political and economic rights for ethnic Albanians, whilst the Macedonian government accused them of fomenting ethnic divisions with support from the ethnic Albanians in Kosovo and Albania (Pearson, 2002; Karajkov, 2008).

In many respects, these ethnic tensions trace their origins to the hierarchical and categorized nature of ethno-nations in the parent state, Yugoslavia. Macedonians as a Slavic-speaking group, who constituted the majority in one of the republics (Macedonia), were classified as a *narod*, or people, and as one of the constituent peoples of the federal republic by the 1974 constitution of the Socialist Federal Republic of Yugoslavia. The Albanians were divided between republics. They were perceived as having a 'kin-state' outside Yugoslavia, and were classed as *narodnost* or nationality (Brown, 2000: 128–30). The 1974 Constitution guaranteed the Albanians the same rights as the Macedonians, including proportional representation in the legislature. The Albanians could fly their national flags, and their language was considered of equal status to that of the Macedonians (Koinova, 2013: 34-35). Although some of the rights for the Macedonians were curtailed in 1981, the Albanians were never explicitly defined as a constituent element of the republic (Koinova, 2013: 2). Their rights were given individually to persons belonging to a nationality. Due to these categorizations, the Macedonian *narod* enjoyed a privileged position within the parent state, at the expense of others groups (Koinova, 2013: 135).

Several measures over the years led to intensified interethnic tensions. Koinova (2013: 2–5) writes that 'in July 1981, the syllabi for teaching Albanian was revised, and the hours of study for the Macedonian language increased. In 1983, a number of Albanian teachers were expelled from the League of Communists for not using Macedonian as required'. These measures were accompanied by a growing restriction on property ownership, religious teaching, and secondary education. Restrictions on educational freedoms triggered protests in the Albanian inhabited towns of Gostivar, and Kumanovo, often resulting in arrests, trials, and imprisonment. This trend of marginalization of the Albanian population and their rights continued after the collapse of Yugoslavia in 1991, when the Macedonian republic emerged as one of the successor states (Fontana, 2016b: 89).

In the lead up to independence, a clear-cut majoritarian electoral formula was adopted in 1990, at the founding election. Albanian nationalism was considered a potential threat in Macedonia. Authorities remained wary of the potential loss of western territory inhabited predominantly by the Albanians on account of their secessionist demands (Koinova, 2013: 44–53). After independence, Macedonia had struck a powersharing arrangement between the Macedonians and the Albanian elites (Fontana, 2016b: 35). By 1991, there was limited access in Parliament for Albanian parties demanding to be a constituent element of the state. The 1991 Constitutional Preamble reduced the status of the Albanian language to that of the Roma and the Vlach peoples who lacked nationality rights. The new constitution established Macedonian as the sole official language and recognized a special status for the Macedonian Orthodox Church. In 1992, a new citizenship law requiring 15 years of residence for naturalization stripped many Albanians who worked outside the country from citizenship rights (Spaskovska, 2012: 383–96).

Relations between the Albanians and Macedonian groups were marked by sporadic violence in the lead up to the 2001 conflict (Table 3.1). From 1995, all school teachers were required to be Macedonian citizens, and to pass a Macedonian language test. Albanian teachers who protested against this measure were dismissed and the Albanian teacher training college was closed. By 1993, the number of Albanian-language secondary schools had declined from ten in 1989, to only one (Pettifer, 2001: 137–47). Clandestine links between the Albanian officials and discontented leaders across the border during the Kosovo conflict (1998–1999) strengthened minority claims for autonomy (Koinova, 2008: 381). In 1995, Albanian demonstrators had confronted Macedonian police after opening an Albanian-language university. The establishment of the University of Tetovo that taught only in the Albanian language elicited resistance, protest, and political tensions. Although labelled as illegal, by 1999, the university had enrolled over 4,500 students. Most of the staff were graduates from the University of Prishtina, Kosovo, and there was heightened suspicion among Macedonian political elites

Table 3.1 Macedonia timeline: evolution of ethno-national violence, 1989–2001[1]

1989
Primarily non-violent channeling of interests.
1990–1991
Minority demonstrations, boycotts.
1992
Violent clash between minority and government forces.
1993
Tensions around the discovery of a paramilitary conspiracy.
1993–1994
Minority and governmental threats, constitutional boycott by the minority.
1994
Tensions around elections and in the parliament.
1995
Minority demonstrations crushed by the police.
1996
Tensions around the functioning of a semi-parallel university.
1997
Minority demonstrations crushed and leaders imprisoned.
1998
Tensions around the semi-parallel university.
1999–2000
Tensions related to the Kosovo crisis.
2001
Guerrilla clashes with government forces

---

[1] *Source*: Koinova, 2013: 31.

around the role of the parallel university in fomenting Albanian nationalism and secessionist demands (Fontana, 2016b: 100–1).

Accommodation of the rights of ethnic Albanians was one of the main grievances expressed by the rebels during the 2001 conflict (Hislope, 2004). Armed conflict lasted about seven months (February–August 2001). Different opportunity structures, ethno-spatial, operational, international, and state response factors accounted for the decision to use violence by the Albanian insurgency in Macedonia (Koktsidis, 2019: 2). The conflict involved both paramilitaries, and the state security forces. It led to 150–200 deaths and 650 wounded, with about 7% of the population displaced (Fontana, 2016b: 10). The Organization for Security Cooperation in Europe (OSCE), and the UN peacekeeping forces intervened early in Macedonia (Kaufman, 1996). Albania, as the kin state for the minority in Macedonia, refrained from active support for the secessionist movement. This was due to the pressure from the international community; and due to the hope of advancing Albania's own transition (Koinova, 2013; Koneska, 2016: 59–78).

Language Rights and the Demand for Education in the Mother Tongue

The OFA implemented legal reforms for establishing a power-sharing model (Aleksovska, 2015: 55). Brokered by the NATO, the OFA addressed Albanian concerns around the issues of national recognition, legitimate belonging, and recognized status by mandating targeted policies around language, identity, and status (Karajkov, 2008). In particular, the 'symbolic-psychological' drivers of interethnic conflict such as the desire for education in the mother tongue, the provision of quality pre-school education, and the *language* of instruction in school and university education proved both contentious (Bormann, et al., 2017). They remain a significant point of ethnic fracture in the years since the OFA (Fontana, 2016b). As Brubaker (2013: 5–6) puts it, language 'is an inescapable medium of public discourse, government, administration, law, court, education, media and public signage'. Identity is intricately bound up in ethnicity and religion: everyone knows who they are and by extension who others are (and are not).[1] The nature and intensity of tensions can be conceptualized as existing on a continuum ranging from peaceful yet strained co-existence.[2] Nearly 20 years since the 2001 conflict, these interethnic tensions continue to animate everyday existence and limit interactions between the Albanian and Macedonian communities. Their lives are lived in parallel. Interethnic marriage is rare, as is having friends who are not from the same ethnic group.[3]

---

[1] Interview with external evaluator of *Mozaik*, Skopje, 2 September 2017.
[2] Interview with two *Mozaik* parents. Macedonian mother, 48 years old, Skopje and 45-year-old mother Skopje.
[3] Ibid.

In primary education, resources devoted to minority students and minority language institutions is scarce, and the quality of instruction in minority languages is lower than in Macedonian (OECD, 2015). Educational performance outcomes, suggest that Albanian and Roma students have lower attainment and this affects their employment prospects and future socio-economic status (OECD, 2019: 50, 75). According to the latest World Bank data, while Albanians represent nearly 25% of the total population, they account for only 15.6% of secondary students and only 5.5% of tertiary enrolment (OECD, 2019: 76). Children from minority communities have less opportunities and remain confined to the territories inhabited by their co-ethnics, hindering efforts for a truly multi-ethnic state (Reka, 2008). In Macedonia's socio-economic reality, language and education are not just about identity, they are also about access to resources and government jobs, and therefore education has taken on a powerful symbolism for minority rights.

Before 2001, whilst Albanian was the language of instruction in primary and secondary schools for the Albanian minority, university-level education was undertaken almost exclusively in Macedonian. As a result, most Albanians could speak Macedonian, although the reverse did not apply. The demand for university education in the Albanian language became part of the broader push for legitimate cultural entitlement for them. The OFA addressed these underlying issues and attempted to close the gaps concerning language and representation as key drivers of conflict. It established the right to education in the language of ethnic communities representing 20% of the population (i.e. Albanian) (Koneska, 2012: 37–8). By guaranteeing primary and secondary education in children's native languages, the OFA states unequivocally that 'equal access to quality education is crucial for providing equal opportunities and a pre-requisite for other policies including the policy of equitable representation'. It also emphasizes that integrated education will contribute to social cohesion (OFA Review on Social Cohesion, 2015: 31). This brings us to explore how far the objective of integrated education has been realized in reality by examining the relevant conceptual, policy and practical dimensions involved.

Educational Segregation and Early Years' Provision: Integrated Education for Conflict Prevention

An education system is very important for the creation of social cohesion in divided societies, through the socialization of children (Novelli and Smith, 2011). Albert Bandura's social learning theory suggests that children observe the behaviour and attitudes of others, imitate this, and thereby model their own behaviours and attitudes (Bandura, 1977). By teaching a communal language, promoting multiculturalism, and addressing interethnic relations through education, schools and teachers can contribute to social cohesion (Heyneman and

Todoric-Bebic, 2000; Anger et al., 2010). Teachers are therefore an important so-cialization agent for children. In the communist tradition of former Yugoslavia, schools were a powerful instrument of socialist propaganda, education was highly centralized, and the primary mode of instruction was through teacher led trans-mission. This tradition continues across the Western Balkans, and Macedonia is no exception (Wertsch, 1991: 112). The way teachers present ethnic groups and whether they promote or oppose interethnic relations has a great influence on the ideas of children (Van Balkom and Beara, 2012).

In addition to a transmission mode of teaching, teachers from different ethnic groups may use discriminatory remarks based on their own personal prejudice or teach and reflect on issues of politics and history based on their own eth-nic group narrative. According to Grozdanovska (2007: para 26), 'most teachers believe they must fight for the ideals of their nationality'. This reinforces hate narra-tives and perpetuates a competitive form of nationalism that weakens the prospect of achieving a truly integrated education system, and through it more meaningful social cohesion. Schooling plays an intrinsic role in how identities, memories, and notions of citizenship and belonging are formed and transmitted. When schools do not promote positive attitudes towards other ethnic groups, there is a great risk of disintegration and interethnic conflicts (Du Pont, 2005). In Macedonia, it is one that encourages segregation and separation rather than integration and inclusion.

The School System and Monolingual Instruction

The education system is organized around four languages of instruction in pri-mary schools (Macedonian, Albanian, Turkish, and Serbian), and three languages of instruction in secondary education (Macedonian, Albanian, and Turkish) (Ministry of Education and Science, 2018: 14). 75% of primary and secondary schools are monoethnic. The language of instruction for each community is mono-lingual. Only in certain mixed localities, such as Kicevo and Tetovo, do students from Albanian and Macedonian ethnicities attend the same school. The result has been a proliferation of the 'two schools under one roof model' (Arraiza, 2014: 20). This means that there are limited opportunities for children from different ethnic groups to interact. Indeed, amongst children, language is seen as a major barrier to communication with other ethnic groups (Brusett and Otto, 2004: 54). Schools are run on a shift system, with different ethno-linguistic groups of children taught at different times throughout the school day. 'Albanian kids, Macedonian kids, Turkish kids, study in separate classrooms. They may be at the same school (and in the same physical space) but they have separate timetables.'[4] Lessons are shorter

---

[4] Interview with external evaluator of *Mozaik*, Skopje, 2 September 2017.

when students attend in shifts, and class sizes remain extremely large, with up to 40 pupils in Albanian language classes. This affects the quality of minority language education (Fontana, 2016a: 867). The reason for physical separation of the Macedonian and Albanian students in schools derives from post-war security concerns (Kavaja, 2017: 484).

In the years following the 2001 conflict, in some mixed schools, small-scale fights and brawls between the pupils during the class breaks and small-scale incidents of violence in previously mixed high schools were reported in Skopje, Struga, and Kicevo (Barbieri, Vrgova, and Bliznakovski, 2013: 5). The school administrators decided to arrest any escalation, by introducing a strict shift system with the different ethnic groups using the same school premises at different times of the day, including during the breaks, and during extra-curricular activities. Other factors encouraged this move. Protests against mixed classes, and shared education facilities took place in 2003, in the Albanian majority towns of Tetovo and Kumanovo (Kavaja, 2017: 486). Similar protests by Macedonian parents, pupils, and teachers took place in Bitola (2000–2003), when Albanian language classes were planned to open at the same school as the Macedonian children (Lyon, 2013: 503).

Apart from community-based divisions, political leaders did not cooperate across ethnic and party lines. Several cases of resistance to the opening of new Albanian-medium classes took place in the municipality of Struga. Classes approved by the Albanian deputy education minister were later declared illegal by the ethnic Macedonian education minister (Lyon, 2013: 496). Schools also faced various financial constraints. The process of decentralization that began in 2005 gave municipalities the responsibility to fund and run pre-school institutions, primary and secondary schools, in collaboration with central authorities (European Commission, 2020). The progressive transfer of power to municipalities, however, was not accompanied by a matching reallocation of funds in line with their new responsibilities (Fontana, 2016b).

Outside of education, there is little social interaction between different ethnic groups and little social cohesion. Indeed, residential segregation has increased since the 2001 conflict (Brusett and Otto, 2004: 35). For example, certain neighbourhoods are distinctively Albanian. Shops and restaurants in these areas use the Albanian language rather than Macedonian and, as respondents reported, 'will look at you differently' if you do not speak Albanian.[5] The different ethnic groups use specific epithets to describe one another. Some Macedonians may use offensive names for the Albanians, such as 'shqiptari' or 'shqipiteria.'[6] In other words, children grow up in a world of prejudicial vocabulary and amidst structures that justify

[5] FGD *Mozaik* parents, Struga, 3 September 2017.
[6] FGD *Mozaik* parents, Skopje, 1 September 2017.

'group thinking', and negative constructions of 'the other' group.[7] The sticky bonds of homogenous ethnic groupings mean that weak, bridging ties linking different communities are lacking. If children from different ethnicities do not communicate or interact with each other the possibility of developing close friendships becomes unlikely (Petroska-Beska and Najcevska, 2009). It leads to a situation in which negative stereotypes are reinforced through both home and school life, creating a social climate that is characterized by interethnic distrust, suspicion, and dislike (Gallagher, 2010a; 2010b). These have had a detrimental impact on social cohesion.

Policy and Practical Developments on Integrated Education

Following the signing of the OFA, organizations such as the EU, and the NATO, promised Macedonia paths to membership. This introduced greater international pressure to reform education policy, and to shift away from educational segregation and monolingual schools to a more integrated education model. As a concept, integrated education implies 'an educational system that allows for, fosters and supports inclusion and interaction of cultures among all actors' (Bakiu, Dimitrova, and Brava, 2016: 6). In a multiethnic society, integrated education can act as a means to promote mutual cooperation, and communication among the different ethnic communities (Krsterska-Papic and Zekolli, 2013: 135). It can help transcend 'superficial civility' as indicated in the case of everyday social actions in deeply divided societies (Mac Ginty, 2014). As a concept, integrated education is rooted in the ideas around social cohesion and intergroup contact. The idea of social cohesion draws on the assumption that differences among identities are homogeneous and collective (Green, Preston, and Sabates, 2003). It emphasizes the generation of shared values and identities. It implies that the minority groups must adjust to the majority's social and cultural norms so that the society becomes cohesive. Such a theoretical assumption tends to reinforce the status quo, rather than encouraging deep social transformation (Kirchberger and Niessen, 2011).

The National Strategy for Education released for the decade 2005–2015, did not promote the integrated education concept explicitly (Ministry of Education and Science, 2006). It was only after the Ministry of Education and Science (MoES), supported by the Organization for Security and Cooperation in Europe (OSCE) High Commissioner on Minorities, adopted the strategic document on *Steps towards Integrated Education in the Education System in the Republic of Macedonia* (2010) that concrete measures linked to integrated education became part of the official government policy (Ministry of Education and Science,

---

[7] Ibid.

2010). Aspects in which Macedonia has been lagging behind, such as 'democratic and decentralized school management; interesting and inclusive textbooks; extra-curricular activities and de-politicization of the curricula and the textbooks' (Petroska-Beska et al., 2009: 21), became the target of reform efforts. Actual timelines for implementation were not drawn and targeted funding for schools regarding physical infrastructure or capacity building that could support the principles of integration were also missing at this stage (Barbieri, Vrgova and Bliznakovski, 2013: 7–10).

Efforts to address educational separation via the Strategy for Integrated Education have been stymied by politicians concerned about the reaction within their ethnic constituencies (Koneska, 2012). From the perspective of the Albanian minority, the integration policy is resisted because of a fear of assimilation into a Macedonian culture and language. Albanian parties have protested against the proposed introduction of Macedonian language teaching in Albanian, Serbian, and Turkish medium classes. For example, in 2011, the MoES revised the study of Macedonian language from grade four to grade one of primary school. Albanian parties resisted the decision and it became highly unpopular with parents, students, and teachers from the Albanian, Serbian, and Turkish minorities. This decision was revoked by the Constitutional Court within months. At the same time, a shift from bilingualism to monolingualism, with children instructed in their mother tongue without gaining proficiency in the official language, can have negative implications for their employment prospects later (Fontana, 2016b: 210–11).

In the absence of political buy-in from ethnic minority groups, external donors, INGOs, and local CSOs have assumed primary responsibility for advancing educational integration. Since 2009, the UNICEF has supported programmes to help local authorities in Macedonia to develop mechanisms for enhancing interethnic relations through schools. In 2011, following the conclusion of the UNICEF project, USAID, working with the Center for Human Rights and Conflict Resolution (CHRCR) and the Macedonian Civic Education Center in Skopje, introduced the state-wide Interethnic Integration in Education Program (IIEP), which operated from December 2011 until March 2017 (Petroska-Beska, and Osmani, 2015). In the period 2012–2013, the MoES supported by the Norwegian Embassy, implemented the 'We Learn Together' project, focusing on the integration of pupils from different cultural backgrounds using extracurricular activities. Seventy schools in 25 municipalities were targeted through it. More recently in 2014, UNICEF in cooperation with the Macedonian Civic Education Center started the Inclusive Education programme in seven primary schools with more than 10% of Roma students (Aleksova, 2016: 5–6). During 2017–2022, the MoES has partnered with USAID to strengthen youth interethnic integration, by upgrading curricula and textbooks, renovating schools; and by supporting civic education skills and volunteering practices among youth (USAID, n.d.).

Early Years' Education

We turn our attention now to the policy on early years' education, which provides the context for the bilingual immersion groups run by the Macedonia country office. In terms of the institutional structure, curriculum development for pre-primary education is under the shared responsibility of the Ministry of Labour and Social Policy (MoLSP) and the MoES. Specialized bodies affiliated to the Ministry provide technical expertise and develop policies in specific areas. The State Education Inspectorate (SEI) conducts the external evaluation of school performance and undertakes ad hoc school inspections in response to written requests from teachers, parents, school principals, or the municipality. The Bureau for Development of Education (BDE) develops curricula and associated learning standards for all levels from pre-primary to secondary education (except for vocational education and training subjects). In addition, the BDE also provides teacher training and conducts education research (Ministry of Education and Science, 2018: 12).

The theoretical importance placed on early years education is part of Macedonia's national education policy. It is premised on the finding that the first five years are the most important for child development. 'At the age of three years, children start becoming aware of the differences around them. It is when the child forms their own values and ideas about the world around them ... the biggest part of child development wraps up by the age of seven [sic].'[8] Pre-school or kindergarten education is seen as a significant agent of early socialization. Educational orthodoxy holds that 'early childhood matters': the earlier children are taught pro-social skills and conflict resolution the better. The 'earlier the better' premise is centred on the notion that preschool interventions *can* alter the cognitive, emotional, social outcomes, and skills in very young children (Brooks-Gun 2004; Sylva et al., 2010).

In this respect, peace education initiatives can be used to change the nature of intergroup relations within society by specifically targeting its youngest members, the rationale being that young learners are more open to new ideas and information (Bar-Tal 2004: 262). Peace education is mainly concerned with changing the mindset, and with the promotion of a culture of peace (Danesh, 2006; Salomon and Nevo, 2002: 4). A culture of peace entails the integration of peace across diverse levels, such as families, communities, ethnic, and religious groups. It enables individuals and groups to manage their conflicts, productively, and cooperatively (Galtung, 1969). It has the goal of developing intercultural understanding and requires reorienting the learning and socialization processes that support the psychological leanings towards violence (Harris, 2002: 20). Betty Readon (1988), a well-known American peace educationist, categorizes the field of peace education into several specific topical areas. These include conflict resolution, cooperation,

---

[8] Interview with Councillor, Bureau for the Development of Education, 5 September 2017.

non-violence, multicultural understanding, human rights, social justice, world resources, and the global environment. Across the spectrum of these topics, peace education can promote either a cognitive or fact-oriented education about peace, or it can fulfil a broader approach premised on promoting 'education for peace' (Rosandić, 2000: 10).

Children at the age of three to six years are 'free from prejudices towards, and stereotypes of their peers' and are more likely to learn pro-social behaviours (Milcev 2013: 121). The UNESCO states that preschool education is 'one of the critical long-term answers to the problem of violence in society', since the patterns of violence and aggressive behaviour in adolescents and adults can be traced to behavioural and social problems in early childhood (UNESCO, 2002). At the preschool level, the central aim of introducing integrated education was to bring children from different ethno-linguistic backgrounds together so that they could 'learn to learn together' from a very young age (Lange and Dawson, 2010: 218–19). Two prominent donor funded projects have implemented the integrated education agenda at the kindergarten level. First, is the *Mozaik* bilingual immersion groups implemented by the partner INGO's Macedonia country office. Second, is the work of the Nansen Dialogue Centre (NDC) which has implemented a model of integration based on extra-curricular activities, training of teachers; and co-operation with parents in eight schools in Macedonia since 2008 (seven primary schools and one secondary).[9] In the following section, I examine how the *Mozaik* programme interacted with the wider context; and whether contextual differences between the different *Mozaik* groups in terms of geographic location shaped the transmission and retention of *Mozaik* values. In particular, I map the lifecycle of the programme to interrogate how the evolution of the *Mozaik* project contributed towards a weak normative legacy while generating a strong institutional legacy.

Evolution of the *Mozaik* Bilingual Immersion Groups: A Story of Shocks, Adaptation, and Institutionalization

Piloted in 1997, the *Mozaik* bilingual immersion groups attempted to teach children aged between three and six years to learn peaceful multicultural co-existence.[10] A novel bilingual approach was adopted to help bridge the gap created by pre-school segregation in public kindergartens (Milchev 2013: 127). By advocating a 'tolerance education perspective', *Mozaik* used structured interaction

---

[9] The schools are based in the following municipalities: Jegunovce, Strumica, Petrovec, Karbinci, Konche Cair, and Vinica. See http://www.nmie.org/index.php/en/our-schools (accessed 20 June 2019).

[10] Albanians are concentrated in the Western and north-western part of the country where Macedonia borders Albania, Kosovo, and Serbia. In cities like Tetovo, Debar, and Gostivar, Albanians form the majority. A significant number of Albanians also live in Kicevo, Struga, Kumanovo, with lesser numbers in Skopje. Based on discussion with external evaluator of *Mozaik*, Skopje, 3 September 2017.

in mixed kindergarten groups, to socialize children from different communities into becoming more accepting of their differences whether religious, cultural, or linguistic (Tomovska 2009: 93). The model drew on the findings of sociologists like Durkheim (2013), and Bobo and Licari (1989), in applying pre-school education to socialize children in ways that would promote mutual understanding and limit the possibility of ethnic violence. The objective of promoting a child-centred pedagogical model of pre-school education was based on Gordon Allport's (1954) contact hypothesis. The aim was to expose children from different ethnicities to other cultures, and to encourage them to communicate their feelings and resolve conflicts peacefully by learning key words in a peer language. The underlying theory of change, anticipated that after attending *Mozaik*, children, their parents, and the teachers would respond to individuals from diverse backgrounds with greater empathy and consideration. Since it was first piloted in 1997–98, the *Mozaik* kindergarten groups expanded from two pilot groups in Skopje and Kumanovo in 1997, to 13 pre-school locations across ten municipalities (up until 2017), with more than 2,000 alumni having attended these groups by 2021.[11] In October 2011, the Macedonian government took the decision to institutionalize the *Mozaik* programme as part of its integrated education efforts.[12] The *Mozaik* groups were adopted by the government in January 2012 as part of the state's kindergarten provision. Since 2012 the *Mozaik* teachers have been absorbed into the payroll of the MoLSP, making them permanent state employees. These practical wins in terms of institutionalization have not been without some important adaptations and shocks such as the conflict of 2001, financial cut backs, dwindling quality, and a progressive politicization on the issue of teacher's employment. I discuss each in turn.

The Conflict of 2001 and After

Four years after the *Mozaik* programme started, the conflict between the Macedonian and Albanian groups erupted, bringing the country to the brink of civil war. This despite ten years of relative peace after the fall of former Yugoslavia. The conflict of 2001 seriously deteriorated the already fragile interethnic relations in the cities of Gostivar, Tetovo, Struga, and Kumanovo. This initiated a growing tendency towards segregation rather than integration (Van Hal, 2004, 2005). Ethnic divisions in society, filtered into schools, with conflicts breaking out among pupils in Kumanovo in 2001 and Struga in 2004 (Koinova, 2013). These hostilities threatened the running of the *Mozaik* programme in certain areas of the country. For example, in Debar (an Albanian-majority area), Macedonian families evacuated

---

[11] Update provided by Country director, Macedonia country office, 19 July 2021.
[12] Institutional memory mapping of *Mozaik*, with Macedonia country office staff, 7 September 2017.

to take refuge elsewhere. The exodus resulted in empty classrooms and general insecurity. Remarkably, Debar's *Mozaik* programme survived by remaining open for the small numbers of children who continued to attend amidst the upheaval.[13]

While persevering, the *Mozaik* groups faced resistance as they attempted to expand into new areas. During 2004–2006, donor funding from the Swedish government was extended to fully integrate the *Mozaik* groups into the Macedonian public education system as well as to expand it to other ethno-linguistic communities such as the Serbian community in Kumanovo, and the Turkish community in Gostivar. There was resistance from some non-*Mozaik* teachers and directors in public kindergartens on account of the bilingual emphasis of the model.[14] Concerns that minority groups would not prioritize learning and speaking the Macedonian language because they could receive education in their mother tongue from the pre-primary stage were put forward (Reka, 2008). These pockets of resistance did not however undermine the growing demand for *Mozaik* enrolment in the post-OFA years.

Fig. 3.1 *Mozaik* kindergarten in Struga
(Photo courtesy of the author, 5 September, 2017)

[13] Ibid.
[14] Ibid.

Table 3.2 Timeline of *Mozaik's* development

Piloted as two bilingual immersion groups with Swiss funding in 1997.

Children aged three to six years taught peaceful multi-cultural co-existence through structured interaction in mixed kindergarten groups.

Bilingual instruction and intercultural communication.

Expanded to 13 *Mozaik* pre-schools across ten municipalities.

Mozaik has been adopted by the government in January 2012 as part of the state's kindergarten system.

Between 1997 and 2005, 510 children were educated through the *Mozaik* model.

As the timeline (Figure 3.2) illustrates, *Mozaik's* development occurred in several phases up to its formal adoption by the Macedonian government in 2012. These phases were funded by the different grants from the Swiss and Swedish governments up until 2010, amounting to approximately USD three million in funding.[15] During each phase of the programme, there were progressive financial cutbacks. The availability of toys, books, and learning aids to support children's development diminished.[16] Shrinking funding and resources took place alongside growing programmatic demands in terms of the physical expansion of the groups across different geographic locations, and the growth in pupil numbers.[17] Following two tranches of recurring grants between 2002–4 and 2004–6, funding from a mix of donors was sought on an ad hoc, piecemeal basis. By 2010–11, funding was not assured; rather donors requested the Macedonian government to take over the programming costs.[18]

During this time of financial uncertainty, a small grant from the Swiss government kept the programme going between 2009 and 2010. There was a one-year gap (2010–11) when the programme received no donor funding at all. It created an atmosphere of uncertainty for the teaching staff, the parents, and the children. The employment status of *Mozaik* teachers was a particularly contentious issue. Until 2008, their salaries had been funded by the Swiss government; but from 2008–10, as the institutionalization process evolved, teachers lobbied for employment with the local municipalities. It was only in 2011, that *Mozaik* teachers achieved recognition (and the desired status) as government employees, and were placed on the government payroll. During the critical period of 2010–11, there was simply not enough money for salaries, and as discussed above, teachers worked without

---

[15] Ibid.
[16] Ibid.
[17] Ibid.
[18] Ibid.

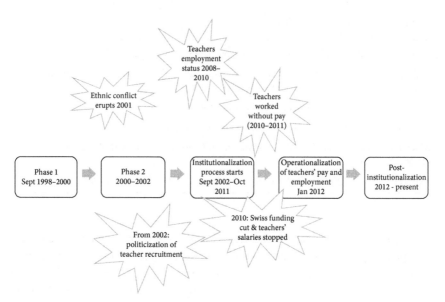

Fig. 3.2 *Mozaik* timeline: Financial shocks and adaptation

pay.[19] These financial constraints had a negative impact on teachers' morale and in turn affected the quality of educational provision. A mother whose three children attended *Mozaik* kindergarten in Skopje reported that the lack of money and related insecurity surrounding teachers' employment and wages meant that '*Mozaik* was not implemented fully … teachers were not happy [and] were talking to parents regarding their own employment issues rather than about the children's development'.[20]

Dwindling Resources and Quality

The quality of the programme also changed over its life-cycle. Several parents noted that process issues such as 'no nap time, better resources like toys and books compared with the public kindergarten groups were a major draw'.[21] The bilingual or intercultural communication aims of the project were secondary to child enrolment (Tankersley, 2001: 131). In Albanian majority areas like Kichevo, Albanian parents were drawn to instruction in their own language, this was also true of Serbian, Turkish and Roma parents when the groups expanded to offer their languages

---

[19] Ibid.
[20] Parent interview, Macedonian female, 48 years old, Skopje, 3 September 2017.
[21] Institutional memory mapping of *Mozaik*, with Macedonia country office staff, 7 September 2017.

later. Teachers joined on account of a range of incentives including: better pay, opportunities for professional development, and better learning resources.[22] However, with time, funding cuts resulted in a decline in available learning resources. Institutionalization efforts meant, increasing the affordability of the groups for the Macedonian government became a priority. As a result, a no-frills approach was adopted to narrow the differences in provision with the state pre-school groups (Naskova 2014b: 12). Dwindling resources and a sharp decline in quality did not augur well with the parents. Some complained that the *Mozaik* groups had become like the other state kindergarten groups, under-resourced and under-staffed.[23]

Standardization Measures

To enhance sustainability, the government pursued greater standardization of procedures to absorb the *Mozaik* groups into the state's kindergarten system. From 2002 onwards, when the process of institutionalization had started, the teacher–student ratio was reduced in order to make the model financially viable for the MoLSP. The original teacher to student ratio in the *Mozaik* groups, was 1:4. This ratio dwindled to 1:12 by 2015, with ever-expanding student numbers. In terms of the number of bilingual teachers in each group, the government reduced the numbers from four to two, while the student numbers increased from 16 to 24 per group, to make them more cost-effective.[24] Between 1997 and 2005, 510 children were educated through the *Mozaik* model. Another 500 students attended *Mozaik* between 2006 and 2017. Yet, during this time, only 18 new teaching positions were approved to meet the demands of rising student numbers.[25] As institutionalization progressed, parents were required to provide toiletries and pay for their children's meals. One parent in Skopje noted that she had experienced 'the best' of *Mozaik* with her two older daughters who attended between 2000–2 and 2003–6. However, her son attended *Mozaik* from 2010 to 2013, when it had become institutionalized as part of the state kindergartens. She felt that her third child had 'the worst type of *Mozaik* experience'.[26]

Training and Monitoring

Other reasons for dwindling quality were related to the irregular monitoring of the groups' performance. In the initial years (1998–2010) when donor funding

[22] Ibid.
[23] Interview with external evaluator of *Mozaik*, Skopje, 2 September 2017.
[24] Interview with Macedonia country office head, Skopje, 2 September 2017.
[25] Institutional memory mapping of *Mozaik*, with Macedonia country office staff, 7 September 2017.
[26] Parent interview, Macedonian female, 48 years old, Skopje, 3 September 2017.

was available, resources were allocated from the donor budget for the regular in-service training of the *Mozaik* teachers. SEI and the BDE advisors were trained regularly for monitoring the groups through periodic classroom observations, and for providing feedback on the programme goals.[27] In the post-institutionalization phase, this funding earmarked for training and monitoring was no longer available. The SEI inspectors did not visit classrooms or observe teachers every term. They only made annual visits to the kindergartens to examine the administrative aspects of the operations, such as finance, strategy, and planning.[28] As a result, the educational or pedagogical function of the kindergartens became progressively underdeveloped. The MoES and the MoLSP, and their agencies (BDE and SEI) did not invest in developing appropriate M&E tools (Naskova, 2014b: 3–4). Kindergarten staff simply followed the national step by step methodology for monitoring programme quality, which did not accommodate the bilingual and two-teacher model of *Mozaik* (Naskova, 2014b: 3–4).

Adjustments

Over time, aspects of the programme were tempered and adjusted in order to attract the government's interest, bureaucratic support, and eventual adoption. In other words, the success of institutionalization required compromise. Examination of the programme's adaptation process offers us important lessons for developing a sustainable institutional legacy that involves timely hand over to the national partners. For example, at inception, children started from three and half years of age and moved directly from *Mozaik* to primary school. In September 2008, primary education was transformed into a nine-year education programme with children being enrolled at the age of six instead of seven (OECD, 2019: 2). Reflecting this change, children as young as two or two and half years started attending the *Mozaik* groups if they were toilet trained. The lowering of the enrolment age had important pedagogical implications. It led to an increase in the *Mozaik* class sizes, weakened the bilingualism component, and resulted in an uneven distribution of carer attention.[29] One of the *Mozaik* teachers in Struga noted that 'the model of bilingual education works best with children between four-six years of age; when children are still developing their vocabulary, and speech abilities, while actively learning new words… Instead of supporting the older children with learning new words, we must spend more time caring for the younger children, who cannot even speak their own native language.'[30]

---

[27] Institutional memory mapping of *Mozaik*, with Macedonia country office staff, 7 September 2017.
[28] Ibid.
[29] FGD with *Mozaik* teachers, Struga, 3 September 2017.
[30] Interview with *Mozaik* teacher in Struga, 3 September 2017.

Lessons

The evolution of the *Mozaik* project offers us a few key takeaways. First, the success associated with institutionalization was largely tied to the ability of the project staff to adapt to a range of internal and external shocks. While creating a durable institutional legacy at the kindergarten stage, there was little reflection about the normative legacy of the *Mozaik* groups. As the next section will discuss, the ability of the *Mozaik* groups to change socialization behaviours of the children, their parents, and wider communities was weaker. To some extent this was again an institutional problem. The bilingual focus of *Mozaik* contrasted with the monolingual and segregated character of the state's school education provision from primary school onwards. This meant that there was a lack of continuity between the different stages of children's schooling and educational development. The gains made from the exposure to *Mozaik*'s intercultural communication values were rapidly dissipated once children move into the segregated and monolingual format of primary and secondary schooling. Second, although the integrated education policy has been embedded into the government's policy rhetoric since 2011, in reality, efforts to encourage intercultural communication remain stunted and donor driven at best. Most integrated education initiatives continue to be led by civil society actors and are funded by external donors. They are marginal to the mainstream Macedonian educational system. As a result, children unlearn the patterns of behaviour around tolerance and harmonious co-existence they are exposed to during *Mozaik* once they transition into mainstream education. Wider societal tendencies around segregation and in-group socialization further reinforce these trends. Through an in-depth examination of *Mozaik*'s role in norm transmission, the under-emphasized role of social capital and local history in norm retention, i.e. in preserving the values and friendships gained through *Mozaik* beyond the kindergarten years, became clear to me. I present these findings next.

Norm Transmission and Retention: Social Capital, Inter-regional Difference, and the Limits of Diffusion

The sociological and education literature emphasizes the importance of early years education as critical to pro-social moulding, simply put, pre-schooling transmits particular *norms* around socialization. As we saw in Chapter 1, norms are informal 'rules of behaviour' that are jointly held and sustained by various social groups (Elster, 1989; Krupka and Weber, 2013). In the norm diffusion literature, the morally persuasive characteristics inherent in the norm are emphasized. In essence, making norms resonate with a particular audience becomes the key to their adoption or acceptance (Acharya, 2004). Scholars like Björkdahl (2013:

324–5) suggest that while possessing 'prescriptive and proscriptive qualities', most norms stipulate conditions of appropriate behaviour. How far norm stipulated behaviour is appropriate or not in a given context, remains largely outside of the realm of norm promotion or norm transmission activities, especially in the context of peace and statebuilding processes. Adoption of externally promoted norms, such as that of integrated education or intercultural communication, takes root… 'as a political process, which is expected to spill over into … society' (Kappler and Lemay-Hebert, 2016: 8). Attachment to norms depends in part on how far the ideas transmitted appeal to, or resonate with, shared expectations about proper behaviour for an actor with a given (ethnic) identity.

In the post-institutionalization phase, the *Mozaik* groups received two EU grants (emergency EU grant 2011-12/13) for 18 months, and then from 2014 to 2015. The relationship between the EU and Macedonia in the field of education is not just related to the provision of economic support (Dobbins et al., 2008). It is also connected with the transmission and diffusion of prominent liberal values such as human rights and tolerance. As a norm maker, the financial support of the EU comes attached with certain standards of accountability, to be implemented through the application of international standards of evaluation and measurement. In this respect, *Mozaik*'s surveys and evaluation tools mirrored the requirements of the wider liberal peacebuilding technocracy, which endeavour to gauge the immediate and short-term outcomes (Mac Ginty, 2012a). In working 'within the framework of modernist, technical reason, manifested through various positivist, pragmatic, and functionalist views of knowledge', that pay scant attention to the social and cultural context, the *Mozaik* project reflected the main pitfalls of peace education efforts delivered within the framings of the liberal peace (Gur-Ze'ev, 2001: 316).

Recent work in the field of peace education has begun to critique coloniality and Eurocentrism, unmasking how these issues are implicated in the depoliticized and largely de-contextualized application of peace education projects (Bajaj and Brantmeier, 2011; Shirazi, 2011; Bajaj, 2015; Keet, 2015; Williams, 2017; Zakharia, 2017; Zembylas, 2017, 2018). Early childhood education interventions in established democracies such as the United Kingdom (UK) and the United States of America (USA), are evaluated not only in terms of direct programmatic effects, rather, the family and neighbourhood contexts are also taken into consideration, particularly in terms of poverty rates, and segregation in public housing (Jencks and Mayer 1990; Massey 1990; Jarrett 1997). Such factors are rarely acknowledged or incorporated in terms of evaluating educational interventions in post-war environments (McGlynn and Zembylas, 2009). M&E mechanisms are standardized and focus on participants and their immediate social networks: families and teachers for example in the case of *Mozaik*. This positivist approach fails to capture the complexity of human interactions and the role that existing local, cultural, and historical factors can play in shaping the legacy of peace education programmes.

The networked, longer-term dimensions of programmatic legacy is rarely assessed in terms of their impact on social capital or vice versa. In Macedonia, I explored how social capital shaped the programmatic outcomes of *Mozaik*, and through it, the transmission and retention of the project's values.

Mozaik Values and Behaviour Change over Time

As identified in its theory of change, the *Mozaik* groups offered opportunities for children and their parents to participate in training activities with their peers from other ethnic and cultural backgrounds. These targeted activities emphasized how to deal with cultural differences and the issues that arise from them (Naskova 2014a: 3–4). Exposure to the culture and beliefs of other groups it was anticipated would enhance cooperation and intergroup respect. A 2006 external evaluation funded by the Swedish government included a sample of 37 preschool children, their parents (93), and 18 teachers to examine shifts across the behavioural, emotional, and cognitive levels. It also examined the spill over effects of *Mozaik* norms into families and communities more broadly. In this evaluation, 75% of the parents reported that through having their children in *Mozaik* groups, they had undergone positive changes with respect to their own awareness of ethnic differences, and felt more capable of overcoming prejudices. They also reported feeling more accepting and respectful toward such ethnic differences (Euro-Balkan Institute, 2006: 85). At a behavioural level, 97% of the surveyed parents reported having friends from different ethnic communities, 67.7% reported that their children had friendships with children from other ethnic communities before entering *Mozaik*. Nearly 33% stated that the *Mozaik* groups had enabled their child to establish contacts with children from different ethnic groups for the first time indicating that *Mozaik* in itself had limited effects in fostering new intercultural friendships. 42% thought that because of *Mozaik* attendance, their child had learned more about the cultures of other ethnic groups. Most parents also noted increased self-confidence in their children, when making first contacts with children from other ethnic communities (Euro-Balkan Institute, 2006: 85–6).

A 2014 baseline study on the correlation between exposure to *Mozaik* values and inclusive or trusting interethnic behaviour continued to present positive indications. In the baseline study, 65% of the parents surveyed stated that they had noticed positive changes in their children following their enrolment in the *Mozaik* groups. These included becoming more sociable, better organized, able to resolve conflicts constructively, beginning to speak a second language, more independence, confidence, and responsibility, better personal hygiene habits, and enhanced creativity (Naskova, 2014a: 9). Through my field research with the *Mozaik* alumni, their parents and teachers, I probed whether these positive behavioural characteristics were enduring over time. I found that the benefits gained from

Mozaik socialization, namely exposure to a bilingual and multicultural education, were more readily lost if these values were not routinely reinforced by the family and the wider social or community environment. Variation in terms of the type of social capital prevalent in a given community, and its impact on how far *Mozaik* norms and values were retained by the children and their families, proved significant to an extent that was not originally anticipated by the project's initial theory of change. In short, the social capital dynamics across different regions became a major determinant of norm diffusion and their retention.

Social Capital and Norm Retention

Bourdieu (1980: 2) defined social capital as the resources inherent in more or less formalized relationships on their individual level. Coleman (1988: 409) understood social capital as a socio-structural resource that may have positive consequences for individuals and for society as a whole. Trustworthiness, information, and norms are further characteristics of social relations that may constitute resources for individuals (Coleman, 1988: 101–5). For Putnam (1995: 67), social capital constitutes 'features of social organization – network, norms, and trust', that enable participants to act together more effectively to pursue shared objectives (Putnam, 2000: 664–5). Based on Putnam and Bourdieu's differentiation between formal and informal relations, social capital might be differentiated into two forms: (1) network capital and (2) participatory capital. Network capital lies within informal relations with friends, neighbours, relatives, emotional aid, goods and services, information and a sense of belonging (Wellman et al., 2001: 437). Participatory capital is expressed through associational memberships that afford opportunities for people to bond and articulate their demands. In Macedonia, network capital was prominent.

Following conventional wisdom, network social capital can be categorized into three types. *Bonding social capital* (or exclusive) which suggests strong in-group cohesion or solidarity; *binding* (or inclusive) *social capital* which involves outward looking networks with distant friends, associates, and colleagues, and *linking social capital* generated from ties across different class, and political lines, where different groups access power and resources across the social strata (Begum, 2003). While in stable societies all three types of social capital help community cohesion; in deeply divided societies strengthening *linking social capital* is better than supporting exclusionary or bonding groups, because the norms restricting in-group entry and exit are more powerful, the boundaries less fluid, and the defining characteristics more easily identifiable (Bardhan, 1997).

Post-war contexts are frequently characterized by a lack of trust. Macedonia is no exception. Interethnic suspicion and distrust imply that Macedonia's ethnic communities have developed 'closed-networks' whereby individuals who share similar traits and experiences (including ethnicity) group together (Burt, 2005: 105). This creates dense, bonded connections based on network homophily or sameness. For many Macedonians and Albanians, these strong, 'sticky' bonds are centred on an exclusive, shared ethnicity. Such close, bonded relationships create networks based on familiarity, reciprocity, and trust, and are considered to provide a 'safety net for basic survival' (Colletta and Cullen, 2000: 6).

Yet such ties can lead to exclusive forms of solidarity. Ultimately, over-reliance on homogenized dense ties can lead to the exclusion (or expulsion) of other groups, and to intergroup conflict (Colletta and Cullen, 2000). Social network orthodoxy holds that if weak, bridging ties are fragile or absent, this can limit opportunities not only for individual advancement but also for societal cohesion (Bowd, 2008: 70). Weak bridging ties are considered important to post-conflict spaces, as they are more "… networked and associational, and connect people to the outside community … they can provide access to more strategic resources, and dissimilar individuals, that is unavailable in the immediate, primary network" (Colletta and Cullen, 2000: 6–7; Lin 2008: 50–69). The value of these kinds of re-lationships lies not in the fact that ties are weak or 'bridging links', rather that they are more likely to connect an individual to information and opportunities that are new or otherwise inaccessible (Lin, 2000). This dimension often bridges 'differences in kinship, ethnicity, and religion' (Colletta and Cullen, 2000: 6–7). Yet, bridging ties are frequently lacking in post-war contexts and depend largely on contextual and geographical factors that may well diminish the impact that educational programmes such as *Mozaik* might engender. I found that in areas where bridging capital was present, such as in Debar, norms transmitted through the *Mozaik* model endured more strongly than in Skopje and Struga, where more exclusionary, and bonded forms of capital dominated.

Blockages to Transformative Peace

The reason for this was due to the persistent misunderstandings that animate rela-tions between the two major ethnic communities. While some Macedonians view Albanian demands for greater recognition of language and rights as legitimate, further compromises to accommodate minority demands are viewed by many as leading to an inferior position of the Macedonians in their own state.[31] This po-sition is well-reflected in interparty debates; although local situations vary greatly (McEvoy, 2014). Interethnic relations in Struga and Kumanovo are considered as 'tense configurations' in contrast with the remarkably good interethnic rela-tions in Debar and Gostivar (Ragaru, 2008: 2–3). For example, the capital, Skopje

---

[31] Interview with external evaluator of *Mozaik*, Skopje, 2 September 2017.

had the most dispersed alumni network, despite having the highest concentration of *Mozaik* alumni. Parents I met felt that the pressures of living in the capital made young people 'distant, more rude, arrogant and cold'.[32] Ethnic communities were less integrated and often resided in exclusive pockets. Opportunities to socialize with other ethnic groups were more limited in the capital, due to the intermediating influence of 'politics, media, and the family'.[33] Although interethnic friendships are not entirely ruled out, these may exist at a superficial level, with lives of different ethnic communities lived in parallel. Intergroup interactions were more stereotyped, resulting in the prevalence of dense, bonded relationships based on specific ethnicities.[34] These created insular networks with weaker ties connecting children and their parents to 'other' communities in the capital.

Weak, bridging ties established during the *Mozaik* years withered rapidly because they were not reinforced institutionally and socially (i.e. through schooling, the family, and wider community contexts). Amongst children who attended the *Mozaik* programme in Skopje, 13% of parents surveyed in 2014 reported that their child brought home or invited a playmate from a different ethnic group (Naskova, 2014a: 8); 37% of the children surveyed reported living in areas that were ethnically mixed, compared to 47%, who said they lived in a community that was mostly monoethnic with a few families from a different group (Naskova, 2014a: 8). In Struga, a mixed settlement inhabited by communities of Macedonians, Albanians, Christians, and Muslims, voluntary intergroup mixing is limited. Parents reported spatial segregation between rural (Albanian), and urban (Macedonian) inhabitants in Struga and its outlying areas (Kelsi, 2013: 20). The lack of closely bonded social capital meant that in both Skopje and Struga, ethnic Macedonians feared marginalization at the expense of the Albanians, particularly in terms of political devolution, one of the OFA's key stipulations.[35]

For children who attended the *Mozaik* groups in Skopje and Struga, the friendship networks established during the kindergarten years fractured once the children started primary school. Parents in these locations felt that the teachers in the primary school did not have the time to talk to children, or to solve any of their problems.[36] During my interactions with third grade students in a Macedonian primary school in Skopje, the nuances of how *Mozaik* alumni experienced the transition to primary school became clearer. P., one of the six Macedonian children in the art class I was observing, had attended a *Mozaik* group in Skopje

---

[32] Parent interview, Macedonian female, 48 years old, Skopje, 3 September 2017.
[33] Interview with senior administrator, Debar primary school, 5 September 2017.
[34] Parent interview, Macedonian female, 45 years old, Skopje, 3 September 2017.
[35] Interview with external evaluator of *Mozaik*, Skopje, 2 September 2017.
[36] Parent interview, Macedonian female, 45 years old, Skopje, 3 September 2017; FGD1 and FGD2 with *Mozaik* parents and teachers, Struga, 3 September 2017.

for three years. P. recalled that 'They were good times [in *Mozaik*]'. 'My Albanian teacher was very nice, the other teacher (Macedonian) was not.' Among the *Mozaik* alumni that I met in the capital, *Mozaik* values were retained at best for a couple of years during primary school, after which the transition into monolingual, and segregated instruction limited the children's opportunity for using a second language, or to interact with children from other ethnic backgrounds. P. admitted that he had forgotten most of the words in Albanian. 'I remember some numbers, and some responses like "yes, please" and "thank you".' In Debar, by contrast, bilingual use was more common even after leaving *Mozaik*. K. a secondary school student, and a *Mozaik* alumni noted that when he meets his Albanian friends he uses Albanian rather than his native Macedonian language to communicate.

On the difference between teaching styles, P. noted that, ...'in [*Mozaik*] kindergarten, teachers [were] never shouting, they were very good. In [primary] school they are shouting... In the first grade we are not nice kids, we think we are in kindergarten. In kindergarten we play most of the time, if anything breaks nobody gets angry, but in school they will shout. Even in normal kindergarten, the teachers will shout if the kids don't sleep, or if the kids say I don't like this food, or if they don't eat the food. The teachers will say, "you cannot have what you like every day", but in our [*Mozaik*] group it wasn't like that.' On learning how to manage conflicts amongst friends during *Mozaik*, P. said, 'When I was in kindergarten, when we fight, I did not understand those things, now I understand them, I don't get mad at anything. We learn to say what we feel, instead of pushing or fighting. Some of my friends here in primary school are not from *Mozaik*, they can slap each other.' B. who had also attended *Mozaik* added, 'I will tell them not to do that, we are not gonna fight, don't just be mad, play stronger.'

Intergenerational Values

On the dissemination of *Mozaik* values from the children to the adults, in the 2014 survey, an overwhelming majority of parents in Skopje and Struga stated that interethnic integration in schools was important. 90% of the parents felt that, through attending *Mozaik*, their child had helped them understand and learn more about ethnic groups in their communities. This stated willingness to learn about other ethnic groups notwithstanding; in reality deep-seated changes in interethnic mixing were resisted. For example, while recognizing the importance of interethnic education, 69% of parents interviewed in 2014, felt that 'although it is good to be open-minded, it is better for people to stick to their own groups' (Naskova, 2014b: 11). In Debar, by contrast, demographic dominance of the Albanian community did not, however, inhibit friendships between the different groups. Interethnic ties were stronger, and different families across ethnic divides appeared to be more integrated than in Struga or Skopje.[37] In probing this variance in intergroup interactions, I found that in addition to social capital dynamics, local history played an important role in shaping the nature of interethnic interaction.

Macedonia's borders emerged from the partition of the territory of historic Macedonia (previously under Ottoman control), amongst Bulgaria, Serbia, and Greece during the First Balkan War (1912). Up until this time, the Albanians and Macedonians did not have adversarial relations. In fact, these communities cooperated against the Serbs during the Ohrid-Debar uprising (23 September–7 October 1913), organized by the Internal Macedonian Revolutionary Organization (IMRO) and the Albanians against the Serbian capture of the regions of Ohrid, Debar, and Struga (Todoroska, 2014: 262–3). After the Second World War, as we have seen, the state in Yugoslavia otherized the Albanians. The narrative of otherization became more pronounced after Macedonia was created as a republic in 1974, and even more so after the 2001 conflict. The historical cooperation between the two ethnic groups against the Serbian government was erased from the history textbooks, replaced by the myth of Macedonian victimhood (Todorov, 2016: 115–18).

In Debar, historical interethnic ties are preserved through strong familial connections. Partly due to the 'small town' character of Debar, families reported knowing each other well, and there was evidence of greater social cohesion. One Macedonian parent from Debar noted that these Albanian families in the area are 'old', 'they have culture, they have tradition, our ties are long-standing. These families are not like the Albanians in Gostivar and Tetovo (more recent settlers).'[38] *Mozaik* alumni had remained friends with one another years after they left the kindergarten. They admitted to meeting up sometimes and routinely greeting each other in passing. Students also maintained intermittent interaction with the *Mozaik* teachers. Some had siblings in the *Mozaik* group which helped keep the bonds alive. These ongoing interactions allowed the alumni to sustain their networks informally.[39] In Debar, enduring bonds were observed not only between the pupils and their teachers, but also between the teachers and the parents. The close-knit nature of social relations facilitated a more caring atmosphere among the alumni and their families (Davies and Talbot, 2008: 512).

During the FGDs in Debar, parents of the current *Mozaik* children reported that their children played with one another both in the *Mozaik* groups and outside of the kindergarten hours. The *Mozaik* alumni in the secondary school kept

---

[37] FGD with the parents of *Mozaik* alumni, Debar, 5 September 2017.
[38] Ibid.
[39] FGD with *Mozaik* alumni, Debar, 5 September 2017.

in touch with their teachers and visited each other regularly.[40] Structural factors facilitated this sustained interaction. Shifts in primary and secondary schools in Debar operate at the same time for the Macedonian and Albanian children, allowing them to play with one another despite the formally segregated setup. The limited numbers of children in the school meant *Mozaik* alumni were often found attending the same class, which facilitated the maintenance of friendships, years after they had left *Mozaik*.[41] These trends continued into high school, with classes for all children taking place in one shift. Indeed, alumni from Debar who were attending university in Skopje and Tetovo reported their continued reliance on friends and networks from Debar, regardless of their ethnicity, due to their strong bonds of friendship and trust.[42] These informal bonds had implications for the normative legacy of *Mozaik*. The values transmitted through the programme were not as readily lost amongst the alumni in Debar, to the extent observed in Skopje or Struga. Although the alumni recognized that without sustained efforts the bonds of friendship did have the potential to become weaker over time.[43]

Complementing *Mozaik* through Media and Theatre

In addition to *Mozaik*, the partner INGO's country office in Macedonia implemented a range of media and theatre projects to advance intercultural communication and exchanges in Macedonia and the wider Balkan region. To test the robustness of the role of social capital in norm retention across the different media projects, I reviewed the evaluative data on media messaging and behavioural change. Media interventions are known to produce mixed effects (Murrar and Brauer, 2018; Geber et al., 2016). As Bratić (2006:3) notes, 'some media might influence some people under some conditions some of the time'. This is because media programming, whether it be television drama or theatre, cannot and does not exist in a nebulous space devoid of political, social, cultural and economic influences (Bratić and Schirch, 2007). Here I discuss the programmatic dimensions of the media and theatre projects, and their overall normative and institutional legacy. Compared with *Mozaik*, television programmes and cultural productions were more difficult to institutionalize, and their norm transmission often had weak resonance due to the stark differences between the media representation of intergroup relations and the reality of social interactions. On the whole, the media projects implemented by the Macedonia country office generated a mixed normative and weaker institutional legacy compared with *Mozaik*.

[40] Ibid.
[41] Interview with senior administrator, Debar primary school, 5 September 2017.
[42] FGD with *Mozaik* alumni, Debar, 5 September 2017.
[43] FGD with *Mozaik* alumni, Debar, 5 September 2017.

Nashe Maalo

The media interventions began two years after *Mozaik* was piloted to complement its underlying messaging on intercultural communication. After the 2001 conflict, the OFA stipulated government encouragement for minority language media. The Macedonian Law on Broadcasting Services reflected this, encouraging public broadcasters to produce programmes in the languages of the dominant ethnic minorities. In response, Macedonian Television (MTV) Channel 1 continued to broadcast in the Macedonian language; MTV2 in the Albanian language and MTV3 were created in 2002 and began broadcasting in the Turkish, Roma, Vlach, and Serbian-Croatian languages. The popular private Macedonian-language broadcasters such as A1 and Sitel were also granted the right to broadcast in the languages of the minorities (Brussett and Otto, 2004: 36). The result was electronic media distribution that reflected the population settlements, and social capital dynamics. Like electronic media the print media are also monolingual, with nearly one thousand print media houses registered in Macedonia (Rusi and Spasovska, 2013). In many ways, the country's media space mirrored the segregation of the education sector. It was in this context of segregated media programming, that the Macedonia country office pioneered the children's edutainment space, by launching the first children's television programme *Nashe Maalo* (Our neighbourhood) that ran between 1999 and 2004.

Nashe Maalo was aimed at promoting intercultural understanding among children, encourage conflict prevention through increased cultural awareness, and the promotion of conflict resolution skills, to enable conflict transformation in a multicultural society. Produced as a 30-minute programme, the show followed the daily life of eight children from the Macedonian, Roma, Turkish, and Albanian ethnic groups, who lived together in an animated building with a voice, and in the same neighbourhood (Brussett and Otto, 2004: 4). Through this fictional storyline, the programme promoted the idea of shared spaces and interethnic cohabitation which in the aftermath of the 2001 conflict was inconsistent with local conditions and therefore presented weak contextual and normative resonance (Brussett and Otto, 2004: 7–8, 67–8). From a programming perspective however, the *Nashe Maalo* television series was a great success.

It put into motion a whole range of ancillary products. From producing magazines to music compact discs and audiocassettes in multiple languages, distributing a parent/teacher guide across schools, the television series was accompanied by a number of outreach projects that helped maximize and extend its impact (Brussett and Otto, 2004: 40–1). In April 2004, to coincide with the re-runs of *Nashe Maalo* on national television, a knowledge quiz show was started. Other outreach activities included an intended-outcome puppet show that targeted seven to nine year olds; and *Nashe Maalo* live theatre that targeted nine to eleven year-old schoolchildren. Drawing on formative research conducted among 400 children, the play was subsequently written and produced in collaboration with the Children's Theatre Centre (CTC), Skopje (Brussett and Otto, 2004: 44–5). The actors were drawn from different Macedonian ethno-linguistic communities. Beyond simple dramatic performances, this theatre involved direct communication between the audience and the cast (Brussett and Otto, 2004: 40–1).

Bridges for the New Balkans

The second media project was the Bridges for the New Balkans (BNB) (2000–4). It adopted a regional approach, and was funded by the Swedish government to complement *Mozaik*. BNB had a three-pronged focus; it used a combination of print, television, and radio messages to advance its intercultural communication agenda. The print component included the *Multi-Ethnic Forum* and the *Karavan* magazines distributed as a supplement in major daily newspapers across Macedonia like *Dnevnik, Utrinski Vesnik,* and *Fakti* in the Macedonian, Albanian and English languages respectively. Multi-ethnic editorial boards were drawn up, and all decisions regarding content were reached by consensus. The aim was to effect change at the attitudinal, cognitive, and emotional levels of the readers at large; as well as the direct beneficiaries, namely the participating journalists and editors (Euro-Balkan Institute, 2006: 13).

The television component included the Balkan Kaleidoscope, a series of documentary films broadcast in six Balkan countries: Macedonia, Albania, Bulgaria, Kosovo, Montenegro, and Serbia. The radio productions were broadcast in Macedonia by Life Radio, an independent bilingual radio station in Skopje. Other partners included Radio Bleta in Tetovo, Radio Vati in Skopje, Radio Ravel in Skopje, Radio Rumeli in Gostivar; Radio Kanal 77 in Shtip, and Super Radio in Ohrid. Three Macedonian language and two Albanian language independent, private local TV stations including TV ART in Tetovo, TV VIS in Strumica, TV IRIS in Shtip, TV KALTRINA in Struga, TV M in Ohrid, and Bitola TV cooperated as a networking group on joint productions and broadcast the programmes with subtitles in the language of the minority community in each location (Euro-Balkan Institute, 2006: 14).

The themes of the *Karavan* magazine addressed the perspectives and opinions of people from different ethnic and cultural backgrounds. Through the use of issue-oriented texts, stories, reflections, and analyses, the magazine tried to shed new light on issues underlying interethnic tensions and conflicts. In an external evaluation for the donor (2006), 66.9% of the 508 respondents surveyed[44] across nine

---

[44] The sample for the survey included Skopje (104 respondents); Bitola (58 respondents); Tetovo (48 respondent) Kumanovo (50 respondents); Prilep (54 respondents); Ohrid (50 respondents); Gostivar (50 respondents); Veles (54 respondents); Strumica (40 respondents).

sites in Macedonia, stated that they have never read the supplement. 23% stated that they read one or two issues, and 10% stated they read all of the issues. The profile of the respondents that reported the highest readership was men with a university degree in the age group of 35+ years. Of those who had read the supplement, 92.9% found them useful in changing their behaviour and attitudes towards other ethnic groups (Euro -Balkan Institute, 2006: 41–2). The biggest impact on the emotional and cognitive levels, was reported by respondents in ethnically mixed municipalities like Kumanovo and Tetovo, belonging to smaller ethnic groups like the Turkish and Serb communities, and in the age group of 55+ years, and with only primary education (Euro-Balkan Institute, 2006: 55). In terms of intergroup contacts, only 42.9% reported an actual increase in their contacts with members from other ethnic groups. The biggest increase was in ethnically mixed places such as Kumanovo (63.2%), where it was easier to establish contacts and friendships with members from other ethnic groups. Meeting new contacts was least possible in the ethnically compact towns, such as Veles, where respondents reported only a 20% increase in contacts (Euro-Balkan Institute, 2006: 50–1).

The Balkan Theatre Network

After several years of no further media projects, the Macedonia country office launched the Balkan Theatre Network (BTN) (2011–12) initiative, that focused on young people and youth leaders. Funded by the EU, the 23-month project was implemented at a time when the country office had transitioned to a fully national entity. The project involved partnerships with the Common Ground national NGO in Belgium, the Student Cultural Center Nish, Serbia, and the Center for Drama Education in BiH (Kelsi, 2013: 5). The aim was to increase youth participation in the production of interethnic, intended-outcome; and interactive theatre performances. Normatively, the project spoke to core EU values such as 'promoting tolerance, unity, and interethnic diversity among and within Balkan communities' (Kelsi, 2013: 9). The project's stated aim was 'to encourage the values of participatory democracy based on EU common values through the creation of new networks of cultural CSOs as the basis for sustainable intercultural dialogue and cooperation within the region and between the region and the EU' (Kelsi, 2013: 3). BTN had three target groups.

The primary target was six groups of youth leaders and drama educators from the three Balkan countries who were selected for their artistic talents and the ability to mobilize and empower youth in their communities. The secondary target groups were youth drama teams, individuals aged 15–19 years, who were selected to learn the necessary dramatic skills to produce theatre performances, and develop their knowledge of European values, the role of youth in participatory democracy, and the role of art in fostering intercultural dialogue. Lastly, there were the various audiences of the theatre performances created by the secondary target group. They were intended to benefit from the programme through their exposure to the contents of each drama, and the facilitated discussions and media documentary broadcast that followed (Kelsi, 2013: 37). The project tried to create, perform, and discuss dramas dealing with relevant social, historic, and interethnic issues. It chose theatre as a vehicle for cultural expression. Six new theatre plays, two per country (Serbia, BiH, and Macedonia) were produced and performed by the youth themselves, promoting regional cooperation based on common cultural values. At its completion, the BTN project had engaged 82 students in cultural activities by providing them with a platform to write, produce, and perform the new plays in the three countries.

Shortcomings of the Media Projects

There were several shortcomings with programme implementation, and the intended outcomes of BTN. The youth participants and the secondary school students who wrote and performed the drama productions became the primary target group contrary to the project's stated aim of primarily targeting youth leaders. This was due to the difficulty with accessing a large enough sample of youth leaders (Kelsi, 2013: 19). On the normative effects, BTN had little success in raising awareness of cultural activities across ethnic divides, amongst the youth, and youth leaders involved in the project. Many of the drama programs did not recruit an ethnically balanced mix of students; often there were only one or two minority students in each group.

The programme activities did not foster any significant growth of the network or the strengthening of ties between participating members. Tools designed to foster independent collaboration between participating organizations in the network were abandoned once the project closed. BTN did not continue to function as a structured, formalized network with regular meetings or interaction once the project concluded. A blog and a Facebook page created to foster the network's development became defunct once the project monies were spent. None of the CSOs made use of these platforms to remain connected (Kelsi, 2013: 9). The loss of local staff assigned to the project, made coordination between partners difficult after the project closed.[45]

Therefore, despite the success of *Nashe Maalo*, measured in terms of wide viewership and popularity, the *Nashe Maalo* values were not reinforced in a similar format until 2018, when the *New Heroes* television series was launched with funding from USAID (SfCG, 2019). Attempts to follow up with outreach and theatre productions for different age groups, while ensuring young people's continuing

---

[45] Institutional memory mapping of *Mozaik*, with Macedonia country office staff, 7 September 2017.

engagement with the *Nashe Maalo* characters, did not however cater to the evolving needs of the generation initially exposed to those values (Brusett and Otto, 2004: 59). Besides, *Nashe Maalo* represented a logic or a set of beliefs around intergroup and intercultural communication which did not resonate strongly with the local dynamics. There was little evidence of the adoption, or continuation of *Nashe Maalo* logic in real life or in related cultural productions, where a climate of depolarization, resignation, and powerlessness in interethnic relations has prevailed (Brusett and Otto, 2004: 61). According to the results of a youth study of 1,038 participants (50% male and 50% female and including a mix of all ethnicities conducted by researchers at the SS Cyril and Methodist University), 'Macedonian and Albanian citizens trust each other less in 2018, than they did in 2013' (Topuzovska et al., 2019:10, 45). Young people have greater trust in their immediate and extended family members and friends, and less towards non-ethnics (Cvetanova et al., 2016: 46). This growing lack of trust in persons considered to be from an 'out-group' and growing reliance on the 'in-group' does not augur positively for social capital dynamics, and the influence of media on them in terms of the time, transformation, and the intergenerational aspects of legacy.

Social Capital Dynamics and the Media Projects

The media projects implemented by the Macedonia country office did not exit in ways that could be integrated into the national media context. Unlike *Mozaik*, which was institutionalized into the national preschool educational provision, with the media programmes, there was little institutionalization or transfer of knowledge to local partners. Once the funding for each project ran out, there was little or no follow-up to reinforce the messages for the target audience. This was a lost opportunity to shape young people's attitudes to peace, as they transitioned from young children to young adults. As a result, strengthening the capacity-building work of local media organizations did not take place. In this way, the media programmes, though largely effective at the programming level, were not sustainable or locally owned in terms of their content, resulting in a weak institutional legacy. In terms of their normative legacy, the results were equally dispersed. In the case of the *Nashe Maalo* programme, studies conducted during its life-cycle to evaluate short term impacts including two viewership surveys (2000, 2004), presented mixed results in terms of effects. Initially, watching episodes of *Nashe Maalo* appeared to have a positive influence on children. After watching the show over a period of eight months, children showed improved attitudes and knowledge of other cultures. Stereotypes were less used when describing other ethnic groups, the willingness to interact increased, and the understanding of other languages improved (Brussett and Otto, 2004: 44–5).

However, by year three, children continued to exhibit strong negative stereo-types about other ethnic groups and about gender (Brussett and Otto, 2004: 44). The exposure to media and theatre-based messages did not help reduce the so-cial distance in their everyday lives. The *Nashe Maalo* values of intercultural exchange as defined in the curriculum document that guided the planning of the various episodes, did not reflect interethnic relations in society in an authentic manner. They remained fictional and aspirational, rather than reflecting reality. Group thinking was very common, and children were largely influenced by their family environment and the strong interethnic tension after the 2001 conflict. In-tended changes in terms of audience knowledge, attitude, and to a limited extent behaviour were largely superficial rather than meaningful and transformative.

The mainstream media programmes contained completely different and con-trasting narratives that weakened the resonance of the *Nashe Maalo* values. In the final evaluation of *Nashe Maalo*, 1,202 children, aged 8–15 years were surveyed about the intended outcomes (changes in attitudes, knowledge, and behaviour). A partial baseline conducted in 2000 was used for comparison. The survey results indicated that the show was most watched by members of the ethnic Macedonian and Serbian communities and least by the members of the ethnic Albanian and Turkish communities. By mapping the links between the project's outcomes (in-tended and unintended) and changes in social relations in Macedonia, the final evaluation found that the new social models presented through *Nashe Maalo* were often discussed with their family and in school; however, this did not translate into any substantial changes of behaviour towards children from other ethnic groups (Brusett and Otto, 2004: 22).

On the whole, the media and theatre projects could not reorient young peo-ple's attitudes towards more accommodating interethnic relations. Apart from language being a barrier to communication, social pressure to conform to parent's advice about socialization and the choice of friends was strong among younger children regardless of ethnicity.[46] Intergenerational transmission of ethnic essen-tialism, and how parents talk about other ethnicities is influential in the early years (Segall et al., 2015). Parents as the primary cultural agents for young children may de facto transmit essentialist beliefs about ethnicity in their young children (Schönpflug, 2001). Parents implicit attitudes or behaviours is known to shape children's racial attitudes (Pahlke et al., 2012 cited in Segall et al., 2014: 544, 553). In Macedonia, decision-making around socialization was determined by their close friends and parents. The Macedonian youth were more independent in their decision-making compared with the Albanian children, who were more tradi-tional and conformist to their parent's wishes.[47] In the evaluation studies, children

---

[46] FGD with *Mozaik* alumni, Skopje, 8 September 2017.
[47] FGD with *Mozaik* alumni, Debar, 5 September 2017.

reported some knowledge about the religious symbols and customs of other ethnic communities. The awareness of cultural similarities was much less compared
with the awareness of cultural differences. This outcome was largely contrary to the
project's theory of change which expected children to become resistant to stereotypes as a result of their exposure to the *Nashe Maalo* values. In reality, children
remained highly susceptible to the influence of their parents and friends, necessi-
tating families to be made the focus of the intended outcomes in place of children
(Bell, Hansson, and McCaffery, 2010). This result was consistent with my findings
from *Mozaik*, where families and social capital dynamics proved highly influential
in defining how far the values transmitted were retained over the longer term.

Conclusion

This chapter examined how far the normative push around integrated education
and social cohesion through the use of peace education and media projects have
succeeded in advancing the ideas around intercultural communication over the
long term. Donor-funded CSO activities and pressures from the EU, OECD, and
OSCE, and bilateral donors spurred a more systematic approach to introducing
integrated education in the school system across Macedonia following the OFA of
2001. The incorporation of the *Mozaik* groups into the state's kindergarten system
presents an important case for understanding sustainable institutional legacies of
peace education projects. Institutionalization was accompanied with some negative qualitative results. On the one hand, it triggered a decline in resources and
standards, including a dwindling teacher to student ratio; on the other hand, it
was these very changes that enhanced the affordability of the model by the government enhancing the model's sustainability. Normatively speaking, parents were
attracted to the *Mozaik* kindergartens because they provided more resources, more
individualized attention, better care, and highly trained and qualified teachers, and
a higher quality of education compared with the state kindergarten facilities. The
pedagogical emphasis on intercultural communication and bilingual instruction
was less influential in encouraging child enrolment.

The role played by local history, and social capital dynamics was a significant
finding in understanding the reasons for the mixed normative legacy of the *Mozaik*
programme and related media projects. Macedonia's ethnic communities socialize
within closed-networks, whereby individuals who share similar traits and experiences (including ethnicity) group more readily together. Such close, bonded,
in-group relationships have created networks based on familiarity, reciprocity,
and trust. As such, the OFA had minimal impact on reversing social segregation through its emphasis on integrated education and social cohesion. The hope
that children in deeply divided societies become more accepting of differences,
whether religious, cultural, or linguistic through their involvement in intercultural

communication efforts is offset by the growing ethnic segregation in the education system which is a key factor contributing to ethnic intolerance and distance among the youth. Stereotypes, prejudice, and distrust are ever-present among all ethnic groups and the weak economy in Macedonia creates even more resentment among the people. This is reinforced through the intergenerational transmission of ethnic essentialism.

Ethno-nationalist tensions in Macedonia are driven by historical, political, regional, national, and international dynamics that sustain incompatible world-views, competing constitutional rights claims, and a state that lacks robust democratic institutions to manage conflict. In deeply divided societies like Macedonia individuals identify most strongly with the in-group when salient group identities are threatened. Group stereotypes are endorsed by in-group members, and ethnic 'others' are depersonalized. Children learn prejudice, violence, and accept or learn behaviour patterns through the agents of formal and informal education including the media, the family, schools, and the community. These agents together support how children develop the capacity to act in social life through the application of critical understanding and moral judgement. Therefore, education for peace must occur on a continuing basis throughout a diversity of cultural sub-systems. The Macedonia case study offers important programming lessons for the sustainability and local ownership of peace education and media programmes with children and youth in contexts of interethnic and intergroup conflict. Peace education and media projects can produce a strong legacy if they focus on institutionalization and localization through the incorporation of local history and social capital dynamics. Through fostering the resonance of project values with local norms there can be longer-term retention of peace norms in ways that enable the meaningful transformation of intergroup interactions.

4

Children and Youth-Focused Radio in Sierra Leone

Introduction

Sierra Leone's brutal ten-year civil war in which the Revolutionary United Front (RUF) was pitted against the Civil Defence Forces (CDF) is often seen both as a symptom and a cause of intergenerational conflict. The civil war is characterized as a 'revolt of youth' against gerontocratic dominance, exploitation, and exclusionary patrimonial politics (Richards, 1996; Peters, 2011a). In the literature, several explanations are available for the extraordinary violence that was witnessed. The first is cultural. If culture is taken to be learned behaviour, then the youth sub-culture in West Africa was perceived as largely violent and negative. Robert Kaplan's (1994) sociological thesis, labelled as the New Barbarism thesis by detractors like Stathis Kalyvas (2001: 100), represented youth culture in Sierra Leone as nebulous 'loose molecules of society' that are predisposed towards violence. Other scholars such as Ibrahim Abdullah (1998) and Ismail Rashid (1997) used Marxist ideology (historical materialism) to equate youth culture with a lumpen philosophy (emerging from capitalist transformation), that was anti-social, anti-establishment, and revolutionary in orientation (Abdullah et al., 1997: 171–215).

Krijn Peters (2006) alludes to how the pre-war exploitation and control of rural youth through the manipulation of customary laws made them more amenable to join the RUF, and later the CDF, as the war progressed. The RUF was in addition to its numbers of child soldiers made up of politically and socially dislocated youths (Maclure and Denov, 2006; Denov, 2010). Many rural youths joined voluntarily to revolt against state predation; others were brutally coerced, unwilling participants, complying to survive. Coercive recruitment was prominent as the RUF's political revolutionary discourse did not attract wide support from ordinary Sierra Leoneans (Denov, 2010: 791–2). In Denov's research with child soldiers from both the RUF and the CDF, the majority self-reported that they had been abducted (Denov, 2010: 794). McIntyre, Aning, and Addo (2002) explain the rebellious orientation as a product of the breakdown in constructive social incentives, and a lack of social mobility. In many ways, violence during the civil war became a form of extreme political speech (Mitton 2008: 195).

Peacebuilding Legacy. Sukanya Podder, Oxford University Press.
© Sukanya Podder (2022). DOI: 10.1093/oso/9780192863980.003.0005

Background and Context Leading to the Civil War

To put these developments in context, it is worth considering the post-independence statebuilding process. When Sierra Leone achieved independence in 1961 under Sir Milton Margai and the Sierra Leone People's Party (SLPP), drawing its support from the Mende dominated south, the country had inherited a Westminster style parliamentary democracy. After the 1969 election, the All People's Congress (APC) led by Siaka Stevens came to power constitutionally. Stevens however focused on consolidating his personal power, turning the state into a highly centralized republic (Pham, 2007: 35–6). By 1978, Sierra Leone had transformed into a one-party state through a referendum delegitimating other political organizations. Drawing its support from the Temne-dominated north and the west, the APC, towed a line where political opponents were either co-opted or repressed (Truth and Reconciliation Commission, 2004: vol 2: 5, art. 11). Recruitment into the security services, the army, and the police, were based not on merit but on connections.

Members of the socialist-leaning APC youth league were also gleaned in the same ethos, and the privatization of wealth became prominent (Abdullah, 1998: 206; Addo, Aning, and McIntyre, 2002: 9–10). Leaders developed complex patronage networks through which resources were distributed to favoured supporters (Cubitt, 2012: 19). These networks supported the building of exclusive chains of authority that extended from the capital to aligned chiefdoms (Lawrence, 2014: 4). From farming concessions, to roads or infrastructure projects, allocation of resources was determined by this dynamic. Youth were embroiled in an intense competition for securing access to patrons. With closed patrimonial networks tightly guarded to non-insiders, the average Sierra Leonean youth had few routes to advancement or alternatives to progress (Abbink, 2005: 16). Party politics became the greatest obstacle to national cohesion and identity (Truth and Reconciliation Commission, 2004: Vol. 12, p. 5, art. 11).

During the period leading up to the 1991 civil war, youth culture and politics of the 1970s and 1980s were particularly turbulent (Abdullah et al., 1997: 171–215). Declining economic opportunities, together with a repressive and violent political regime, encouraged radical university students, and unemployed urban youth to forge an inchoate revolutionary discourse (Rashid, 2004: 66–89). College students formed reading and discussion groups based on pan-African and Marxist revolutionary discourses, with the ultimate aim of changing or overthrowing the repressive regime of the APC. They demanded inclusivity, openness, democratic decision-making, and fairer allocation of resources (Abdullah, 1998: 209–10). The economic mismanagement by the kleptocratic APC government left the country bankrupt following the fall in the price of iron ore and diamonds in the 1970s (Pham, 2007: 35–9). Economic recession and food shortages in the rural areas during the 1980s, and the early 1990s, were accompanied by growing political intolerance. The decline in public spending was symptomatic of the wider crisis of the patrimonial state (Pham, 2007: 37).

Conditions of structural violence and weakened social systems had severe consequences for children in particular. Amidst a growing economic crisis, food shortages escalated. Unpaid teachers and civil servants meant that the school system had begun collapsing, an important push factor for young children to join the RUF (Hirsch, 2001: 30; Peters, 2011b: 137). In the diamond mining areas of Kono, functional schooling had broken down long before the RUF arrived. Davies (1996: 13) notes that by 1987, less than 30% of secondary school age children were actually in school. Violent suppression of political opposition fomented considerable youth discontent in the 1980s. Student protests were routinely quelled through violent police action. Student activists demanded a return to pluralist rule and for revolution even (Zack-Williams, 1990: 22–31). The average youth felt left behind by the political system. They had little access to political opportunities, education, healthcare, and essential social services. The political elites were self-serving and corrupt, with little interest in the development of the young people.

Intergenerational Tensions and the Sierra Leone Civil War

In March 1991 the RUF, led by the former Sierra Leone Army (SLA) corporal Foday Sankoh and backed by the Liberian warlord Charles Taylor, invaded Sierra Leone from Liberia (Richards, 2001: 41; Adebajo and Keen, 2000: 8–10). The RUF claimed to be a political movement promoting liberation, democracy, and a new Sierra Leone with freedom, justice, and equal opportunity for all (Richards, 1996; Gberie, 2005: 44–5). Scholars are divided with regard to the nature of the RUF's recruitment and mobilization strategies. Scholars like Ibrahim Abdullah (1991, 1998) suggest that the RUF was driven by an inherently violent youth underclass, who were fighting for material profit, through the looting of alluvial diamonds. In a debate on youth culture and violence (Abdullah et al., 1997: 172–5), several African scholars, like Ibrahim Abdullah, Yusuf Bangura, Lansana Gberie, Cecil Blake, and Alfred Zack-Williams argue that the main combatants in the RUF were marginal, socially disconnected or lumpen youth who straddled both the urban and rural areas.[1] Paul Richards and Krijn Peters (2011), however, find Abdullah's lumpen youth hypothesis flawed. They argue that while the SLA recruits were from urban backgrounds, the RUF and CDF cadres were predominantly rural youth as demonstrated in the sampling of ex-combatants who took part in the post-war demobilization programme (Humphreys and Weinstein, 2007). Long-term socio-political neglect, fostered by a declining patrimonial system of governance, caused

---

[1] On the debate about the lumpen youth culture see Abdullah et al., 1997: 171–215.

grievances among the rural population, particularly youths. Traditionally agriculture has been unappealing for the rural labouring classes of youth from former slave backgrounds who felt exploited by the traditional laws that subjugated them. Local court cases, based on marriage disputes and seasonal labour demands on large upland rice farms owned by polygamously married village elders, were a major source of grievance that drove low status rural youth to join the RUF (Peters and Richards, 2011: 377–82). Those conscripted either voluntarily or by force during the early years of the civil war, came mainly from rural, semi-rural mining areas in eastern Sierra Leone like Kailahun, a hotbed of opposition to the policies of the Siaka Stevens government (Peters and Richards, 2011: 382–4).

Agrarian tensions and the nature of chiefly control over rural labour made matters worse. Rural youth were beholden to politicians and village chiefs, who had little interest in supporting them. Customary law disenfranchised youth from voting during the election of chiefs and Paramount Chiefs in the rural hinterland. One had to represent some 20 taxpayers to be deemed a tribal authority with the right to vote. With limited access to land and fixed assets, youth were seldom in a position to become tribal authorities. Their lives were beholden to institutions over which they had little influence (Peters, 2011b: 136). Marginalized rural youth rebelled against the existing gerontocratic social control and the inequitable power distribution (Hoffman, 2006). The rift that ensued resulted in large-scale mobilization of rural youth into the RUF. Paramount Chiefs were targeted for their complicity with the kleptocratic tendencies of the Freetown elite (Jackson, 2007: 95–6). In the countryside, the RUF replaced local chiefs with their own men (Keen, 2005 cited in Oswald, Sauter, Weber, and Williams, 2020: 4). The RUF attempted to develop a system of governance that regulated social life in areas under their control, following the motto, 'arms to the people, power to the people and wealth to the people' (Bangura, 2000; Mkandawire, 2002). In areas around Koidu and Rutile, looted goods were distributed to civilians, and hospitals were set up for the RUF fighters. Indeed, the civil war illustrated just what can happen when young people perceive their opportunities for social, economic and political mobility are stifled; and their frustration spills over into violence (Peters, 2011b: 130–3).

Post-war Liberal Peacebuilding and Youth Empowerment

Based on these arguments around intergenerational relations and the civil war, the crisis of youth explanation became the master narrative of post-war reconstruction, making youth empowerment the focal point of reconstruction and development efforts (Fanthorpe and Maconachie, 2010: 256; Boersch-Supan, 2012: 25–6; Podder, Prelis, and Sankaituah, 2021). While before the civil war, the crisis of youth alluded to the inability of young people to attain social adulthood (Peters, 2011b: 130). In the post-war period, because of the continuing gerontocratic and patrimonial control of resources, the structural barriers to social and economic mobility remained. Closed patronage networks can be conflict producing as they exclude large numbers of the youthful population. The SLPP and the APC continue to perpetuate clientelism and neo-patrimonial tendencies. Youth are seen as a threat to the political elite, unfit to lead, and predisposed to thuggery and violence (Peters, 2012: 879–88; Söderberg Kovacs and Bjarnesen, 2018). In addition to this projection, from time to time the threat of relapse into violence has been linked to the 'crisis of expectations', voiced initially by a large unemployed, disgruntled ex-combatant population with limited opportunities following their disarmament; and subsequently by the growing youthful population who 'can't eat the peace' to survive (Bangura, 2016: 37).

To arrest a reversal into conflict, Sierra Leone in many ways became the face of modern, liberal peacebuilding. Post-war reforms facilitated by the liberal peacebuilding project[2] involved a formulaic synthesis of Western-style democratization, good governance, human rights, the rule of law, and open markets (Mac Ginty and Richmond, 2007: 491). Sierra Leone was the first of two countries to fall within the UN Peacebuilding Comission's (UNPBC) mandate after its establishment in 2005[3] (Labonte, 2011: 90-1). The UN Country Team comprising a multitude of agencies, special programmes, and funds, invested nearly USD 381 million between 2009 and 2012 across four programmatic priorities: the economic integration of rural areas; youth economic and social integration; equitable and affordable access to health services; and accessible and credible public services (Labonte, 2011: 97). Much of the work done by international and national NGOs concentrated on transforming elite–non-elite relations. Non-elites were encouraged to demand good governance and accountability from traditional authority figures like the chiefs (Millar, 2015: 569–72). Nearly 25 INGOs, and 34 CSOs focused exclusively on the issue of children and youth, their rights and relationship with elders and the community (Datzberger, 2014: 196). Radio panel programmes and community and district level forums became the safe spaces for negotiating, and absorbing new ideas and practices.

Radio and Media in Promoting Peace and Reconciliation

In Africa, where a majority of the recent civil wars have transpired in the post-Cold War period, radio, and more recently mobile phones and the internet have emerged as a prominent source of public information and influence (Curtis, 2000; Kumar, 2006; Myers, 2009). While consumption of digital media is on the rise,

---

[2] For an overview of the liberal peace concept and its contradictory outcomes, see, in particular, Paris, 2004: 40–51; Duffield, 2001: 11; Richmond, 2006; MacGinty, 2010: 391–412.

[3] The other was Burundi. See UN Security Council, S/RES/1645 (20 December 2005); UN General Assembly, A/RES/60/180 (20 December 2005) cited in Labonte, 2011: 90.

low literacy rates, poverty, weak infrastructure, and low rural electrification mean, battery charged radios can be the easiest way for rural and remote populations to access information, news and opinion from across the globe (Aldrich, 2012: 35–8). In Sierra Leone, radio was first introduced under British colonialism to disseminate information on public administration following the recommendations of the Plymouth Committee (1937) (Head, 1979: 39). Radio programmes produced before the war, were broadcast in English, with the Sierra Leone Broadcasting Corporation (SLBC) being the only media player in the country (Cole, 1995). State monopoly over radio continued during the civil war years. During 1997–1998, the Armed Forces Revolutionary Council (AFRC) junta controlled FM99.9, run by the state broadcaster (Rogers, 2001).

When the civil war was drawing to a close around the year 2000, the airwaves began liberating, and there was scope to be both entrepreneurial and creative. The British government with funding from the Department for International Development (DfID) set up Radio Democracy FM 98.1 as the first alternative media station (Kabbah, 2010). The government of Sierra Leone's (GoSL) communications infrastructure also received substantial support. This included the upgrade and refurbishment of its studios and the supply of equipment across its facilities in Freetown, Bo, Makeni, Kenema, Kailahun, Magburaka, and Koidu (Sowa, 2013). In 2001, the UN Mission in Sierra Leone (UNAMSIL) established Radio UN FM 103.0 to support the ex-combatant reintegration process including that of the child soldiers. The Nightline show on UN radio hosted by DJ Base, was used alongside UN structures to rally young people to disarm.[4] Starting with these initial efforts, private stations like Kiss 104.0 FM was established in Bo; this was followed by a variety of community and religious oriented radio stations that supported the mediation and conflict resolution process. Radio Netherlands and the Open Society Initiative for West Africa (OSIWA) set up and equipped nearly 24 community radio stations allowing remote communities to take part in the national debates. As privatization progressed, the Independent Media Commission (IMC) was established by the government in 2000 to regulate the media sector. Soon, radio became a key tool for behavioural and social change programming (Sowa, 2013).

The partner INGO has used radio for conflict transformation in several postwar countries in Africa such as Angola, Burundi, Sierra Leone, Liberia, and the Democratic Republic of Congo (DRC) to name a few.[5] In West Africa, it started operations in Liberia in 1997 through a two-track approach: a multimedia production studio and a community services project. In Sierra Leone, this model was replicated, after the Abuja ceasefire (2000). The Sierra Leone operations were launched in April 2000, as an independent multimedia studio in the capital Freetown, which broadcast media productions alongside the grassroots work of

[4] Skype interview with the second country director of the Sierra Leone office, 9 May 2017.
[5] Skype interview with the first country director of the Sierra Leone office, 30 October 2019.

the Community Peacebuilding Unit (CPU).[6] Starting with its studio facilities in Freetown, additional offices and production studios were opened in the towns of Bo (2001), Makeni (2002), and Kailahun (2003). The CPU conducted community outreach activities by organizing meetings and discussions on key issues that were simultaneously addressed through their radio programmes (Konings and James, 2009: 249–50). These two interconnected parts used media and outreach as tools to disseminate public information, and promote public discussion on issues of both national and local interest. In addition to programmes targeting political and social issues, the studio used media and community engagement to deliver a range of children and youth focused peacebuilding projects.[7]

Studying Children and Youth Focused Radio and Its Legacy

The role of children and youth focused radio in Sierra Leone, and the resulting behavioural and structural changes are an understudied phenomenon, considering the scale of their use in the post-war years (Oatley and Thapa, 2012). Little scholarly attention has been paid to the normative and institutional legacies of children and youth focused radio—a gap I address in this chapter. I begin with a discussion around the post-war reconciliation initiatives organized by the partner INGO's country office in the initial years after the war and how these were grounded in local needs. To keep up with policy time, radio content shifted from an 'authentic' to a 'manufactured' peace. It became less resonant with the local context, and more aligned with donor priorities, expanding into areas like countering violent extremism (CVE) that had little relevance to the local context. A detailed examination of the key thematic areas across which radio programmes were produced reveals that some areas such as elections, governance, and accountability had greater continuity compared with areas like children's rights. I then examine the normative legacy of the radio programmes. Sierra Leone presents a case of mixed acceptance of external norms, with instrumental acceptance of the norms around child protection, gender, good governance, democratization, and human rights, amongst the previously disempowered in society. Empowerment of children, women, and young people, invited resistance from the traditional authority figures, who lost power following decentralization, and the post-2004 local governance reforms. Intergenerational peace attempted through radio-based deliberation was difficult to realize as the society does not transform radically. Improvements in the participation of women and youth in politics and local governance did not translate into their meaningful involvement on critical issues such as large-scale land acquisitions (LSLAs).

---

[6] Skype interview with the second country director of the Sierra Leone office, 9 May 2017.
[7] Skype interview with the first country director of the Sierra Leone office, 30 October 2019.

Women and youth were excluded from decision-making around the various land deals negotiated by the chiefs and the political elites in an era of liberal marketization. These decisions had wide-ranging negative effects on their livelihood prospects and on community food security. In other words, there was only rhetorical adoption of some of these liberal norms around youth and women's participation due to their weak resonance in the Sierra Leone context. After nearly 20 years of implementing multi-track media and community outreach projects, only a patchy and diffused institutional legacy follows. Without an explicit commitment to institutionalization, there has been a limited transfer of learning into the relevant government departments. This can be partly attributed to the reactive and issue-driven nature of radio programming, which is inherently difficult to institutionalize. The founding of community radio stations and the Independent Radio Network (IRN) offer some evidence of accidental institutionalization. These community radio stations hold the potential for supporting grassroots social action in the future.

Making Local Voices Count: Radio Led Reconciliation After the War

One of the first places the studio began producing live radio programmes was in Mile 91, a buffer zone between the government and the rebel held areas, host to a large internally displaced population (IDP). The studio collaborated with Radio Mankneh, to reach the local people, and to work with the IDPs.[8] Drawing on her previous work with the INGO Conciliation Resources, the first country director partnered with the Organization for Peace, Reconciliation, and Development (OPARD) to develop programmes on reconciliation issues.[9] The majority of its membership drew from young male ex-RUF living in Mile 91. While most organizations would be wary of collaborating with ex-combatants in the midst of ongoing tensions, the staff pooled resources to buy a motorcycle for the head of OPARD to reach out to other RUF combatants and encourage them to disarm. They involved the Council of Churches of Sierra Leone (CCSL) as a sort of 'moral guarantor' (Abdalla, Hussain, and Shepler, 2002: 80). OPARD played an important role in getting the RUF and the UN talking to each other, after some 500 UN peacekeepers were held hostage by the RUF in May 2000.[10] Working closely with contacts in the SLA, the studio's reporters were able to build a rapport with the RUF commanders in their stronghold around Kailahun. Armed with music cassettes and a letter

---

[8] *Radio Mankneh* was founded in 1994, in Mankneh village on the outskirts of Makeni city. It is the oldest community radio in Sierra Leone. During the conflict, the radio station was running from makeshift facilities near the IDP camps in Mile 91.

[9] Skype interview with the first country director of the Sierra Leone office, 30 October 2019.

[10] Interview with former UNAMSIL Force Commander, New Delhi, 30 April 2018.

from the popular musician Steady Bongo, messages in support of disarmament and demobilization were spread into rebel-held territory to encourage the RUF combatants to disarm.

Following these early successes of reaching out to the RUF, radio programmes like *Troway di gun* (Throw away the gun) encouraged societal reconciliation in novel ways. Local theatre and music outfits like the Freetown Players Group, and local musicians like Steady Bongo were involved in developing programming content. Most civil wars are about a breakdown in communication. In Sierra Leone, radio offered a forum, for the opposing sides to start talking, and to understand the miscommunication or gaps, encouraging what media scholars' term 'discursive civility'.[11] *Troway di gun* was hosted by Rashid Sandi of the RUF and Foday Sajuma of the CDF and produced in the local language, Krio.[12] By enabling the erstwhile warring groups to communicate their thoughts, it made ex-combatants from both sides feel heard and validated. Some of the other radio programmes such as *Common Ground News* (2000–8) focused on reconciliation, equality, and representation issues. *Home Sweet Home* (2001–6) encouraged repatriation for wartime refugees; while *Leh wi mek Salone* (2003–5) focused on ex-combatants and civilian reintegration more specifically (Figure 4.1).

At this time, the radio programmes were responsive to, and reflective of, contextual needs. Instead of presenting a cohesive national story, radio programmes like *Common Ground News*, tracked and reflected on developments from different parts of the country. By including the views of hard to access civilians from the remote towns of Makeni, Kono, and Kailahun, radio broadcasts presented ideas and voices, unheard on national radio before. Reporters would take current concerns from Kabala, and ask residents in Makeni or Port Loko about their views and perceptions. Soon it became clear that the local narratives around conflict and reconciliation were very different from the national concerns.[13] Radio ensured that the voices of the people from all sides were heard and considered during the peace process and that participants focused on accountability rather than revenge. Gradually the urban, male, anglicized discourse that dominated the pre-war media space shifted, becoming more representative of diversity. There was no language of war, nobody was called a rebel. These efforts allowed access to authentic and reliable information. The main emphasis was on developing radio content in an intuitive and grounded manner.[14]

Alongside the multimedia content produced by the studio, the CPU organized 'solidarity events' and 'peace festivals' to support the peace process. Local musicians wrote and performed songs during a cultural event that would bring people together, encouraging civilian cooperation with peace and disarmament (Konings

[11] Discussion with media studies expert, University of Sheffield, 30 March 2020.
[12] Skype interview with the first country director of the Sierra Leone office, 30 October 2019.
[13] Ibid.
[14] Ibid.

Radio Programme Timeline and Normative Focus

2000	2003	2005	2010	2015	2017
			Borderline 2010–2013: Democratic participation, equality, youth rights	**Salone mi Land** 2015–2016: democratic participation	
		Trait Tok 2005–2007: Children's rights/equality		**Accountability Now** 2015–2016: free speech, accountability, transparency	
	Mugondi Hindesia 2003–2006: Traditional justice, local conflict resolution practices, leadership (chiefs)	**Wi Yone Salone** 2005–2008: Accountability, transparency, democratic governance	**Uman for Uman** 2010–2013: Gender/equal rights, participation		
	Parliament Bol Hat 2003–2008: Political accountability & transparency		**Free well body business** 2010–2013: Gender		
		Nyu Barray 2007–2010: local governance, democracy promotion (elections & political representation), reponsible local leadership	**Bush Wahala** 2011–2016: Human rights & peaceful conflict resolution through formal political institutions/mechanisms		
Atunda Ayenda 2001–present: Youth/gender rights, reconciliation & justice					
Common Ground News Features 2000–2008: Reconciliation, equality, representation					
Golden Kids News 2001–2008: Children's rights/Human rights					
	Sisi Aminata 2003–2006: Children's rights, gender		**Lion Mountain** 2009–2012: Accountability, democracy/elections		
Salone Uman 2002–2008: Human rights/gender	**Leh Wi Mek salone** (formerly Troway di Gun) 2003–2006: Peace, reconciliation & conflict resolution				

Fig. 4.1 Radio programme timeline

and James, 2009). Getting these programmes off the ground were not without challenges, however. At the first solidarity event in Bo (2000), the main attraction was Jimmy B. a local musician who was the officially nominated 'peace ambassador'. The ex-combatants from the RUF, CDF, and the AFRC in the crowd rapidly turned violent, causing chaos and destroying the stage.

> They [ex-combatants] started shooting randomly, and wanted to destroy everything, including setting fire to the stage. Hell broke loose, there were stones and sticks flying in every direction.[15]

The disc jockey (DJ) used his local radio station contacts to organize a quick exit, barely managing to escape with the expensive sound system and musical instruments before they were burned down.

> The concert reconvened the very next day, with security cover provided by the Economic Community of West African States Monitoring Group (ECOMOG) forces. Jimmy B. spoke on radio urging peace. There was dancing in the whole of Bo town, the ex-combatants sang along, and were happy.[16]

From such a rocky start, these peace festivals became annual events in provincial capitals like Bo and Kabala. They gradually morphed into locally owned initiatives, organized by youth in collaboration with the local authorities and CSOs. Youth groups took joint responsibility alongside community elders to save and use the monies earned during the festivals for community projects, encouraging entrepreneurship and creativity among them.[17] In addition to the peace festivals, the CPU funnelled donor funding to local groups who wanted to start community radio stations. Between 2001 and 2003 five such stations, Radio Tombo, Radio Moa, Radio Gbafth, Radio Mankneh, Radio Bintumani opened successfully in Tombo, Kailahun, Mile 91, Makeni, and Kabala respectively with direct support from the studio. Once the community radio stations were operational, they became locally owned and managed by a board of directors elected by a coalition of community groups. Community members were involved as the producers, managers, and owners of media infrastructure.

Through the establishment of community radio stations, local and national media coalitions were formed. The Independent Radio Network (IRN), founded in 2002, brought ten broadcast media stakeholders under one umbrella organization. It worked closely with the studio to determine the training and capacity building needs of local and community radio stations. It also served as an independent oversight body for the community radio stations. Over time, the studio expanded its

---

[15] Interview with Studio Media Producer, Freetown, 30 March 2017.
[16] Ibid.
[17] Skype interview with the second country director of the Sierra Leone office, 9 May 2017.

outreach through formal MoU's with some 18–20 local radio stations.[18] Local radio partnerships helped the country office include community level issues into the content of its media programming. Another area of authentic and responsive radio programming was the studio's intervention in the conflicts between *okada* riders and the traffic police. In post-war Sierra Leone, *okada* or motorbikes offered an endogenous model for job creation in the informal sector for two or three young operators, with the riders taking turns. The exponential growth in motorcycle taxis created auxiliary jobs for a new generation of young mechanics and bike-washers (Peters, 2007a; Bürge, 2011). Due to limited exposure to traffic rules, growing tensions between bike riders and the traffic wardens over traffic violations created the space for an intervention. The studio supported the founding of various Transport Stakeholders Committees in Bo (July 2003), Makeni (September 2003), and in Kenema (November 2005) to manage the conflicts between the bike riders and the traffic wardens. The studio and its local partner NGO, the Centre for the Coordination of Youth Activities (CCYA) undertook trainings to organize and inform the riders on traffic regulations. These workshops were funded by DfiD. They also included the police, transport officers, and revenue officials. Radio programmes such as *Traffic Kotoku* and *On the Road* generated public awareness of the rights and duties of both riders and their civilian clientele. In terms of structures, the Bike Riders Association (BRA) was established, which later transformed into the Commercial Motor Bike Riders Union (BRU), a central monitoring body that allowed *okada* riders to find formal channels of representation as a recognized trade union (Sesay, 2006: 7–11). The BRU has 200,000 registered members making it the largest youth organization in Sierra Leone (Peters, 2007a: 21; Fortune, Ismail, and Stephen, 2015). This commitment to grounded and authentic reporting did not last, however. As donor agendas became more structured, a more formulaic programming focus emerged.

From an Authentic to a Manufactured Peace: Shifting to a Formulaic Narrative

During the war, Sierra Leone's civil sphere emerged as a political and humanitarian actor. Governance vacuums saw civilians take on governance responsibilities in the absence of chiefs who were killed or had fled (Peters, 2006: 139–42). Wartime shifts empowered marginalized groups such as women and youth to resist chiefly privileges, and to defend their human rights, a process described as the 'invention of human rights from below' by Archibald and Richards (2002: 340). Following the influx of multiple donors and CSOs, the external push on children's rights

---

[18] By 2015, the total number of community radio stations in Sierra Leone was 90, six of which were state owned. These stations broadcast on a range of issues, some are religious, some NGO funded, and some locally owned, See Grant et al., 2009; Kargobai, 2017: 15.

and gender sensitization overshadowed more primordial and localized forms of activism. The concept of 'rights from below' began interacting with the top-down concepts of human rights, advocated by the different peacebuilding actors (Boersch-Supan 2012: 47). Sierra Leone's vibrant and active civil society land-scape, which was responsive and reactive to local issues and needs both during and shortly after the war, became co-opted into donor agendas (Datzberger, 2015: 168).

CSOs were largely neutralized to serve and complement a national developmen-tal agenda that became co-steered by the international community. Liberal norms around human rights and the rights of women and children were transmitted through regular seminars and workshops. Rural youth were schooled about their rights, the role of the government, and the laws of the country. This imported dis-course on rights created its own friction(s) (Björkdahl and Höglund, 2013; Millar, 2013). Sensitization campaigns created incomplete and at times overlapping un-derstanding of processes such as transitional justice and reconciliation (Shaw, 2007; Millar, 2014a). The creation of a specific kind of civil society landscape and agenda-setting that fell in line with the externally led peacebuilding and develop-ment interventions shaped the type of norms that were transmitted through radio programmes on children and youth as well (Shepler, 2005: 197–8). Norms that resonated most strongly with the locals were overshadowed by liberal norms.

Mimicking these changes, the country office activities in Sierra Leone shifted from the post-war focus on social reconciliation towards the building of account-ability and good governance in support of the decentralization process (Everest, Williams, and Myers, 2004). This shift resulted in radio and community en-gagement efforts becoming structured across three priority themes: rights and participation of women, children, and youth; governance and anti-corruption; and democracy promotion and electoral participation. In opting to pursue thematic radio programmes, the primordial and organic flavour of programmes was lost. Radio based messages became more formulaic. They were designed to 'school' and 'manage' the civic public's expectations and behaviours in line with specific agen-das funded by the donors. Superimposed themes of empowerment, self-reliance, and participation, began masking authentic voices that were captured immedi-ately after the war. It created an artificial or manufactured peace rather than an authentic peace. I discuss each thematic category of radio programmes before analysing the implications of media-led peacebuilding for norm retention and for intergenerational peace.

Programming for Change? The Evolution of the Studio's Radio Programmes

Starting with the aim of producing programmes that could be heard by IDPs and ex-combatants, the content of radio programmes became progressively varied.

Radio became an important civic educational tool for sensitization around issues of children's rights, gender, sexual abuse, human rights, governance, and accountability. These topics were presented in myriad formats to inform and influence the listeners. Ranging from radio soaps to talk shows and phone-in programmes, a mix of presentation formats allowed individuals and groups to voice their thoughts and engage in healthy public debate. Radio and media-based peacebuilding efforts also became an important and easily accessible outlet for young people's cultural production. It allowed children a voice, largely suppressed prior to the war, and encouraged young people to negotiate a rightful place in society's decision-making processes. Radio became the main tool through which the post-war generation began to absorb new ideas and practices. Introduction and assimilation of the norms around rights, capacity, and participation had both positive and negative effects.

Mary Moran (2006: 23) notes that a logic of cultural otherness informs development policy. New ideas are gradually incorporated into the normal order of things, and become normalized both in the material and normative practices. While generating empowerment and enabling youth to be more assertive in local milieus, these new norms led to renewed tensions between elders and youth, reinvigorating intergenerational issues that have underpinned previous conflicts in Sierra Leone, and continue to define inclusion and exclusion of children and youth in the social and political realms.

Theme 1: Rights and Participation of Children, Women, and Youth

In introducing children and youth focused radio, produced by and for young people, programmes like GKN (2001–2008), *Atunda Ayenda* (2001-present), and *Trait Tok* (2005–7) prioritized the status of children in Sierra Leone, their access to education, and their relationships with parents and teachers. These radio programmes opened up new channels of learning and communication between youthful peers, and their adult carers (Shipler, 2006: 14). GKN was designed in the format of a human-interest magazine to allow children to discuss their aspirations and concerns. The opportunity to contribute stories and offer feedback gave youth a deep sense of ownership and first-hand experience in two-way communication. Children from mixed backgrounds from across the country were involved as actors, producers, and reporters. They undertook field-based research and engaged with youthful peers as well as the broader audience to develop the programme content. Bonano (2008: 5) found that through GKN, children could voice their own issues on radio, reflect on, and improve how society viewed and treated them. This lay the groundwork for child protection to become a widely publicized social norm with the Sierra Leone Child Rights Act (2007), providing a comprehensive protection framework for them.

Through GKN, a number of ex-combatants and street children got the opportunity to become a radio journalist. The child reporters felt empowered hearing their own voices on the radio. They influenced other children in the community positively and became inspirational role models. Samuel, a former GKN radio anchor, noted that:

> After the war, people did not know how to channel their grievances non-violently. Through the GKN program, we provided them the information on the proper means of communication that can reduce violence. Children and youth were encouraged to solve differences by engaging with the concerned parties. The GKN anchor would interview both parties to any issue, to provide a balanced view. As a result, education and information became a means to peace, and learning became freedom.[19]

Medium-term effects of GKN, on the knowledge, attitude, and behaviours of children aged 8–17 years with respect to children's rights, and child protection issues were assessed to be positive by a 2008 evaluation (Bonano, 2008: 8).[20] 'It helped both children and parents around issues of relationship management and the appropriate rules and norms could be transmitted.'[21] GKN also enhanced the child reporters' own understanding of child rights and child protection matters. Ernest, a former GKN presenter, realized that his rights had been violated during the war, when he was left to fend for himself on the streets. An adult (his parents or another caregiver) should have been there to take care of him. GKN was complemented by the radio drama *Atunda Ayenda* (Lost and Found) (2001–present), one of the longstanding successes associated with the studio. In 2020, *Atunda Ayenda* was broadcast on 21 radio stations, in addition to a partnership with BBC World Service, which broadcasts an English version of the *krio* production.[22] Tracing its origins to the USAID sponsored Youth Training and Education for Peace (YTREP) project (Fauth and Daniels, 2001), *Atunda Ayenda* started by memorializing the experiences of war-affected children and youth, intersecting stories of fictional characters, like *Makuta, Dragon, Jeneba, Salay, Rambo*, and *Demba* with real time concerns. Ismail Rashid (2006: 115–18) suggests that the show's popularity can be attributed to its novelty in the Sierra Leone context. Through free-flowing conversations about the war and wartime experiences, often narrated by a young person, *Atunda Ayenda* helped dispel myths about the war and the role of children and youth in it. The show attracted a loyal following among different age

---

[19] Interview with Samuel (name changed), former GKN reporter, Freetown, 20 March 2017.
[20] The evaluation by Bonano, included 201 respondents, representing both reporters and the audience. Data for evaluation was collected through FGDs, and interviews. 41 child reporters across Kailahun (10), Bo (10), and Mile 91 (21) were interviewed.
[21] Interview with Ernest (name changed), former GKN reporter, Freetown, 23 March 2017.
[22] Interview with Studio Media Producer, Freetown, 30 March 2017.

groups. Scriptwriters travelled to different parts of the country, including the re-motest areas such as *Kenema* and *Kailahun* to gather local stories, keeping the content current for the 15-minute-long episodes.[23]

Following the success of *Atunda Ayenda* and GKN, radio programmes like *Salone Uman* (2002–2008), *Uman for Uman* (2010–present), and *Free Well Body Business* (2010–2013) focused on health issues and gender-based violence (Figure 4.1). Subjects like sex with minors, child marriage, and polygamy were introduced into live discussions. Through the radio programme *Sisi Aminata*, children started talking about everyday sexual violence, such as teachers' rela-tions with young girls and sexual abuse in school. By applying a critical lens on these practices, various social taboos were busted. Rape victims spoke live on air, challenging long-held social stigmas concerning them. The health implica-tions of pursuing commercial sex work or taking up multiple sexual partners for material benefits were discussed openly.[24] *Sisi Aminata* exposed child abuse in domestic settings that prevented schooling. One of the reporters recalled, 'step-mothers would not allow a girl child to go to school, and made them do all the house work, while allowing her own children to go to school'.[25] *Atunda Ayenda*, *Trait Tok*, *Salone Uman*, encouraged school drop-outs to go back to school and un-derlined the importance of education, especially for girls.[26] The '*Pikin Verandah*' segment of GKN discussed the issues affecting teenage girls including menstru-ation, pregnancy, and sexual diseases. These discussions empowered minority Muslim girls to overcome traditional taboos concerning their school attendance, although social stigma around pregnant teenagers have continued, preventing them from attending regular school.[27]

These early advances notwithstanding, radio programmes, did not include an explicit focus on children's rights or protection related concerns between 2008 and 2014. Limited donor interest in pursuing child protection related media projects meant that the advocacy around child protection became a peripheral focus during radio discussions. It was not until 2014 that an 18-month project on 'Engag-ing youth as partners in preventing worst forms of violence against children' (WFOV) was funded by the EU. It was implemented in three countries: Liberia, Sierra Leone, and Guinea. The Ebola outbreak during 2014–16 resulted in financial and implementation related delays for the project, which took nearly 36 months to complete. Phase I of the project involved training and equipping youth re-searchers with the skills to identify the worst forms of violence against children and youth through primary data collection. Phase II presented research results

[23] Skype interview with the second country director of the Sierra Leone office, 9 May 2017.
[24] Interview with Marie (name changed) former reporter *Sisi Aminata*, Freetown, 30 March 2017.
[25] Ibid.
[26] Interview with Studio Media Producer, Freetown 30 March 2017.
[27] Interview with Maya (name changed) former GKN reporter, Freetown, 2 April 2017.

and recommendations for national policy. A guidance manual was completed and the research findings were disseminated through a series of events across schools, churches, and mosques, although policy uptake by formal child protection agencies was weak.[28] A radio listener survey was also conducted for evidence building purposes. 94.3% (200 of 212 respondents) admitted that child rights focused episodes on *Atunda Ayenda*, improved their knowledge and awareness of child protection issues, and encouraged them to take necessary action to stop violence against children (McGill and Zerla, 2017: 8–9).

Samuel, one of the youth researchers on the project recalled that 'there was a lot of fear and stigma linked to the Ebola outbreak at the time. As a result, geographic locations where the research could be physically conducted were limited.'[29] Youth who did take part in the research lamented the lack of targeted interventions to bring an end to the abuses of power and authority they faced in their family, and community relations. In Bo, for example, large numbers of youth engaged in sand-mining were caught up in a payment dispute. Although paid a decent wage by their employers, communal laws stipulated that the miners must collect their salaries from the chief. With the employers handing over salaries to the community leaders, delays with disbursement of payments, and at times deductions from their pay, became a point of contention between the elders and the youth.[30]

In Tombo, Freetown, Western Rural province, trafficking of children, and child labour was rampant. Relatives brought children from rural villages into Freetown, assuring parents of fair treatment and care. When the children arrived in the capital, they were made to work as fishmongers, missing out on schooling. They would collect fish from the trawlers and sell in the markets. Income generated by them was confiscated by the adults to pay for the child's food and lodging. In other cases, children were ill-treated by their own family. Some were physically abused, others were denied food, or schooling by a step parent.[31] These issues were discussed on *Atunda Ayenda*.[32] Two decades of post-war sensitization around child protection and children's rights, by international and local CSOs have only resulted in superficial changes in social attitudes (Bolten, 2018). This was due the weak norm resonance and the limited institutionalization of these efforts. They in turn raise questions about how far liberal values around rights and protection have truly been internalized and retained by the local populace? A discussion to which I return shortly.

---

[28] Skype interview with the second country director of the Sierra Leone office, 9 May 2017.
[29] Interview with a former youth researcher on the Worst Forms of Violence project, Freetown, 25 March 2017.
[30] Ibid.
[31] Ibid.
[32] Interview with Studio Media Producer, Freetown, 30 March 2017.

Theme 2: Governance and Anti-corruption

After the war, the international community was closely involved in reconstructing governance provision across Sierra Leone. The intergenerational tensions that instigated the large-scale violence during the civil war years became the target of donor-funded sensitization efforts, espousing the norms of good governance; accountability, and anti-corruption. Despite this, corruption and mismanagement of public funds was rampant under the SLPP government (1996–2007). Donor funds earmarked for poverty alleviation, education, health, and infrastructure development were siphoned off, with many members of parliament doubling up as contractors (Kandeh, 2008: 605–6). In the rural hinterland, local level reform commenced after the new District Councils were elected in May 2004 (Jackson, 2007: 95–6). The Local Governance Act (2004) entrusted on the councils the onus of service provision in the local communities and the function of tax collection to pay for these services alongside centrally disbursed funds. Three distinct groups of political actors—politicians (elected members of parliament); councillors or district administrators; and the chiefs—animated the local governance landscape, and conflict between them seemed inevitable (Jackson, 2005: 49–58). Amidst these reformist tendencies, the role of the chieftaincy, an integral part of local governance came under considerable scrutiny, not least, because chiefs had long been accused of kleptocratic tendencies (Fanthorpe, 2005: 27–30).

Although the chieftaincy was revived after 2000, the chiefs gained control of communal resources only after the chieftaincy elections in 2002. Radio programmes like *Mugondi Hidesia* (2003–6) and *Nyu Barray* (2007–10) focused on the accountability of the chiefs, chiefdom concerns, and local governance more broadly speaking. Following the decentralization of governance, the local councils were required by law to post their income and expenditure statements on a public notice board. Widespread illiteracy meant that few community members could read these statements, generating local disputes over financial spending. Radio programmes like *Accountability Now* stepped in to solve the issue. The reporters would interview the councillors and ask them to read out the expenditure statements on the radio for public knowledge (Everest, Williams, and Myers, 2004: 20–2). Amidst rising demand for more democratic and accountable leadership, chiefly decision-making became less infallible (Boersch-Supan, 2012). By working closely with the community based Civic Forums, radio programmes like *Accountability Now* simplified knowledge of the political process, and trained parliamentarians in public communication to engage with their constituents.[33] The studio also took up community concerns around corruption and exposed them on the radio. In 2007, the contractor in-charge of supplying blackboards across state schools was a youth leader of the SLPP, then the ruling political party. He

---

[33] Ibid.

was also a close confidante of the Vice President. Through investigative journalism, the reporters exposed the nepotism involved in awarding the supply contract in that instance (Everest, Williams, and Myers, 2004: 20–2).

Interpersonal conflict resolution skills imparted by the country office and other CSOs, reduced the demand for dispute resolution by the village chiefs (Millar, 2017: 299–300). 'Earlier, the chiefs would charge 50,000 Leones for dispute resolution to those who come to complain…now the money has dried out as there are few cases of interpersonal conflicts.'[34] This was symptomatic of the broader changes in the role and accountability of the chiefly elite. The demand for public accountability and a growing emphasis on public performance have weakened the role of heredity and tradition in consolidating chiefly power, creating a backlash from them.

> Earlier the Paramount Chief, the Town and Section Chiefs would determine disputes, and the Paramount Chief would sit in on important cases. Now, this is no longer required. Kangaroo court is against the law. Local government officials settle justice issues. Elections of sub-chiefs are now outside the authority of the Paramount Chief. If the Paramount Chief becomes powerful, the government will be weak.[35]
>
> The customary courts have lost power, the customary law officers are government appointed, and do not know local customs or traditions. They are interpreting customs and traditions differently. Earlier, the youth were shy in decision-making, today they are very active in taking decisions. Elders today have appreciation for the high levels of youth participation in governance. If there are tensions, these are with regard to the meaning of human rights and democracy.[36]

There are variable expectations of performance in the different regions of the country. Chiefs felt that, in the north, 'the traditional role is sufficient for respect'.[37] The local authorities are still powerful. They remain largely immune to the challenges posed by an empowered youth population.[38] In the south, however, 'traditional authority is not sufficient, there is a demand for performance. Once crowned chief, you will get the respect as a leader. However, people will continue to respect the chief based on how they work with the people.'[39] The demand for performance and

---

[34] Lady Town Chief, Pujehun district, Sinjo village Southern District, 2 April 2017.

[35] Paramount Chief 2, Parliament, Freetown. Chief 2 represented all the North and some eastern regions in Parliament.

[36] Paramount Chief 1, in Parliament, Freetown. He is a member of Parliament, representing the South and East regions.

[37] Ibid.

[38] Ibid.

[39] Lady Town Chief, Pujehun district, Sinjo village, Pujehun district, 4 April 2017.

accountability was growing in the north as well. In Port Loko district, the communities I met in Bureh, Kasseh, and Maconteh chiefdoms expressed disappointment with their elected representatives.

The Honorable (MP) makes no effort. The Paramount Chief and the traditional leaders are just the same. The Paramount Chief does not collect information from the communities. He spends more time in Port Loko and Freetown. Traditional leaders do not call for meetings, they have no time to discuss our woes. If you are a councillor, people expect much from you, but the councillor cannot do much (with the limited resources allocated by the government). In the next elections we will not re-elect them (the non-performing officials).[40]

Recent land conflicts have placed the accountability, trustworthiness, and the performance of the local elites at the forefront of community politics. It raises questions about whether the norms around accountability and transparency can contend with the reality of a neo-patrimonial society? These tensions are well evident in the context of the transfer of communal lands for private enterprise. Between 2014 and 2016, the studio implemented several projects for addressing land issues. With funding from the Open Society Initiative for West Africa (OSIWA), radio productions like *Bush Wahala* disseminated information on land rights in Bombali, Port Loko, and Pujehun districts, enhancing local political knowledge around the national land policy. 36 episodes of *Bush Wahala* were produced and broadcast twice every week on the IRN member stations (Baú, 2019: 377). Regular discussions around land rights were broadcast on *Atunda Ayenda*. A 29-minute film on land rights and land conflicts was produced in *Krio*, and 15 community forums were set up to encourage dialogue between citizens, traditional leaders, local authorities, media, and foreign companies (Bandabla, 2014: 7–9).

The USAID funded project 'Open for business: Promoting equitable land rights protection in Sierra Leone, Liberia and Guinea' (2016) extended the studio's work on land issues once the OSIWA funding ran out. The studio focused on engaging civil society actors, like Green Scenery and the Rural Agency for Community Action Programme (RACAP), and state actors like the Ministry of Land, Housing and Country Planning to promote equitable land rights. By raising awareness of the renegotiation clauses present in the different land lease agreements; aggrieved land owners and land users were informed of the possibility for revising the terms of the lease agreement every seven years.[41] Participatory theatre, mobile movie projection, radio broadcasting, and FGDs were used to sensitise and inform

[40] Male resident, 35 years, Kemen village, Port Loko, 6 April 2017.
[41] Skype interview with staff, Green Scenery, 11 October 2020.

the villagers in Pujehun district. Structures like land management committees were created for the purpose of defending land owners' rights (Basse, 2016: 5).

Sierra Leone's third Poverty Reduction Strategy Paper (PRSP) (2013–18) set the stage for a shift from post-war recovery to the development phase. The government's aim of becoming a middle-income country with 80% of its population above the poverty line by 2035, has triggered an opening up of the economy to foreign direct investments (FDI) (GoSL PRSP3, 2013: xiii). Linking of the under-developed economy to global markets has resulted in considerable social and economic shocks, re-igniting tensions around intergenerational and gender in-equalities (Millar, 2016, 2017; Ryan, 2018). Chiefdoms cover hundreds of villages and considerable land holdings. With no formal system of land titling in effect prior to the war, Paramount Chiefs have served as the repository of all land agree-ments and the final arbiter in land conflicts. Incentivized by private investors through salaried positions, they have been guilty of biased mediation, often advo-cating for the interests of the investors, rather than the local communities they sup-posedly represent (Millar, 2017: 298–302). The biased nature of their involvement has implicated Paramount Chiefs of corruption and fraud, in misrepresenting the interests of landowning families in various parts of the country.

In Sinjo and Bamba villages in Malen chiefdom, Pujehun district, this dy-namic was strongly at play. A stronghold of the SLPP, this part of the country is majority Mende, with some Temne, Fullah, and Vai people. The district is pre-dominantly Muslim with some Christian inhabitants. Since 2012, land acquisition by the Socfin Agricultural Company Ltd (SAC), one of the large-scale investors in oil palm plantation in Sierra Leone has triggered new conflicts, between elites and non-elites as well as between the company and the villagers. A subsidiary of the Belgian corporation Socfin, SAC has acquired 18,473 hectares (December 2017 figures) of arable land for rubber and oil palm plantations, with a total investment of USD 100 million in 2011 (Rahall and Schafter, 2011: 2). The deal had strong backing from the government including the Sierra Leone Investment and Export Promotion Agency (SLIEPA), which was created in 2007 by an act of Parliament. These investments were backed by the International Finance Corporation (IFC) of the World Bank Group to facilitate FDI and to improve the business climate in the country.[42]

In 2011, the Minister of Agriculture, Forestry and Food Security (MAFFS) signed a lease with the Paramount Chief and 28 landowners for the handover of 6,500 hectares of land in Malen chiefdom for a period of 50 years. This lease was renewable for an additional 25 years. The land was then sub-let by the Ministry to SAC. The company's operations have affected some 28,135 people in the chiefdoms of Malen, Bum, Lugbu, and Bagbo across Pujehun district.[43] During my FGDs

---

[42] Skype interview with staff, Namati Sierra Leone, 10 October 2020.
[43] Ibid.

with community members in Sinjo, residents complained that 'the landowners (villagers) rejected the plan to set up SAC, but the authorities – the Paramount Chief, the chiefdom speaker, and the section chiefs, signed the paperwork'.[44] This left the community residents feeling cheated and misled. It also acutely affected their livelihood options and food security. The youth felt that with the loss of land, the possibility of farming to sustain the families was also taken away, due to a lack of jobs in the Pujehun area.[45] Villagers who had been recruited to work on the palm plantations as part of SAC's local employment incentives, were swiftly dismissed for underperformance. Villagers who had been sacked felt hard done by. 'The task rate required by Socfin was too high. How can an old man and a young man do the same tasks?'[46] Efforts to raise their concerns over the unfair dismissals with the SAC Grievance Committee, and the Paramount Chief bore no results. 'The Paramount Chief is employed by, and receives a regular salary from SAC for managing local tensions.'[47] This had made him a biased mediator.

For those still employed with SAC, the pay for field hands was below the minimum wage, a mere 19,500 Sierra Leonean Leones or roughly USD 2.30 per day.[48] In neighbouring Bamba, the situation was even more dire. Cut off from aid, the village dwellings were visibly dilapidated, and there was no functioning water pump. The *Palaver* Hut (village meeting place) was in woeful disrepair. Due to the tensions between the Paramount Chief and the local councillor (his maternal cousin), residents did not feel safe, and lived in fear of being targeted by the police. The day before I visited Bamba (April 2017), a resident had been taken into custody by the police for stealing palm fruits at night. Illegal processing of palm for domestic consumption was being targeted by the SAC security staff, causing further grief to the locals. Amidst the ongoing tensions, corporate social responsibility (CSR) investments promised by SAC were unforthcoming. This added to the local grievances. In both Sinjo and Bamba, the villagers relied on NGO interventions to generate an income.[49] Unresponsiveness from the Paramount Chief towards their concerns made matters worse.

Sustaining the community is the main problem. There is no peace from the Paramount Chief downwards. The voices of the villagers are not heard, even when we make efforts to meet the Chief, we are told to come back to the village and sit down.[50]

---

[44] FGD1 with a group of ten male residents of different ages, Sinjo village, Pujehun district, 4 April 2017.

[45] Ibid.

[46] Ibid.

[47] Ibid.

[48] Ibid.

[49] FGD 2 with a group of ten women of different ages, Sinjo village, Pujehun district, 4 April 2017

[50] FGD1 with a group of ten male residents of different ages, Bamba village, Pujehun district, 4 April 2017.

The Councillor was more supportive and 'the only source of peace'.[51] When the villagers in Bamba wanted to get violent, or wanted to attack the SAC plantation to express the injustice they felt, the Councillor stabilized the situation by helping them to calm down. As a form of social mobilization, the affected villagers formed the Malen Affected Land Owners and Users Association (MALOA) around 2012. NGOs like Green Scenery helped them to register the organization.[52] Radio programmes like *Salone Mi Land*, *Atunda Ayenda* and *Bush Wahala*, opened a dialogue between citizens, traditional leaders, local authorities, media, and foreign companies. As a culmination of this process of stakeholder engagement, in March 2019, SAC made land lease payments of approximately 35 million Leones to land owners of Zone 'A' in Lower Malen, which covers 16,248.54 acres of land. Payment was made at the rate of USD 2.50 per acre.[53] SAC committed to making future payments through the banks, to ensure greater transparency, and accountability.

During 2019/2020, SAC has applied for the Roundtable on Sustainable Palm Oil (RSPO) standards for oil palm, to demonstrate commitment to the highest environmental; labour and CSR standards. Some informants alleged that the salary rates quoted to the RSPO inspectors were falsified by local youth to the inspectors, under pressure from the company.[54] The internal cohesion of MALOA is also crumbling. To weaken their resistance, police brutality, arbitrary arrests, and litigation has been used against MALOA members and their supporters.[55] The Councillor of Bamba, a key figure in the community mobilization against SAC, has reportedly reconciled differences with his maternal cousin, the Paramount Chief, in 2020. He was given a bike, and some money to leave MALOA.[56] New civic groups have emerged; some are supportive of SAC's operations like the Malen Youth Development Union (MAYoDU). Reports by Green Scenery in 2013 and 2019 regarding human rights abuses on the SAC plantation have triggered defamation lawsuits filed by the Company demanding compensation and a ban on publications considered to be defamatory.[57] Following a long-drawn-out legal battle, this defamation case was dismissed by the courts in December 2020.[58]

In Port Loko district, a LSLA by the Sierra Leone Agriculture (SLA) company triggered similar conflicts in the local communities. Like the SAC example, the SLA acquisition took place without proper negotiations and financial compensation for all interested stakeholders. In 2011, the land lease was resold for USD

---

[51] Ibid.
[52] Skype interview with staff, Green Scenery, 11 October 2020.
[53] Skype interview with staff, Namati Sierra Leone, 10 October 2020.
[54] Skype interview with representative, Green Scenery, 11 October 2020.
[55] Skype interview with representative, Green Scenery, 11 October 2020.
[56] Ibid.
[57] Factual background on SAC lawsuits, 17 March 2020. Online at https://www.business-humanrights.org/en/latest-news/socfin-lawsuits-re-defamation-by-green-scenery-sierra-leone/ (accessed 19 May 2021).
[58] Staff, Green Scenery, Skype interview, 10 October 2021.

five million to the Siva Group (Sesay and Sesay, 2017). The Siva Group cleared 7,114 hectares, an area roughly equivalent to 17,000 football fields to set up its operations, and in the process destroyed the communities' valuable wild palm, cashew trees, and other economic crops, without offering any compensation. It was soon clear that the Siva group did not have the capacity to develop the land leased, and it gradually started varying the terms of the agreement by unilaterally reducing the leased area for which surface rent was due. By 2017, surface rent was being paid for approximately only 5,000 hectares. This was done without formally returning the rest of the land to the communities. Although the company paid the rent arrears for 2016, it ignored all attempts by the communities and paralegals to renegotiate the terms of the lease.[59] Through community engagement meetings on land rights, video screenings, and participatory theatre, the studio became one of the mediators in this conflict.[60] Radio programmes like *Bush Wahala*, *Salone Mi Land*, and community meetings communities were used to inform communities about their rights. Namati, a legal empowerment organization explained the details of their lease agreements and made the affected villagers across the Bureh, Kasseh, and Bagbo chiefdoms aware of the 75-years' clause in the agreement at which point the terms of the lease could be renegotiated. Unlike in Malen, villagers I met in Kemen, Port Loko were more trusting of their Paramount Chief and felt that he was on their side.

> … after the landowners realized that their elected MP was a shareholder of the company, people went and attacked the Honorable's (MP's) house, and reported him to the President. SLA then came with the Deputy Speaker of Parliament, to represent the company, but the Paramount Chief did not agree to support the SLA.[61]

Armed with this information, and with the support of Namati, the affected villages took the Siva group to court in 2018. After several court sessions, in November 2018, the court ruled in favour of the communities, ordering the Siva group to return all of the lands to the Port Loko villages and to pay them USD 250,000 with 5% annual interest in unpaid rent, reversing the land grab by the company.[62] Although the communities got their land back, they did not receive money they were awarded in compensation. By the time the verdict was decided by the courts, the Siva group had already been declared bankrupt and the staff had left the country.[63]

More recently, the studio has undertaken the 'United for Greater Governance and Participation in Sierra Leone' project (2016–19) with funding from the EU.

[59] Staff, Namati, Skype interview, 10 October, 2020.
[60] Staff from United for Protection of Human Rights, Kemen village, 6 April 2017.
[61] Skype interview with staff, Green Scenery, 11 October 2020.
[62] Skype interview with staff, Namati Sierra Leone, 10 October 2020.
[63] Ibid.

The aim has been to strengthen local governance and accountability, and increased citizen participation in local decision making and governance in six rural districts (Port Loko, Kambia, Koinadugu, Moyamba, Pujehun, and Kono). 24 CSOs were trained in peer-to-peer civic sensitization; and were provided with small grants to implement peacebuilding activities with the local women and youth. The studio partnered with CCYA to improve community knowledge of local governance, and the inclusion of women and youth through peer-to-peer dialogue (Roy, 2018: 8–13). *Atunda Ayenda* were used to showcase the benefits of inclusion, by narrating the success stories of women and youth leaders. Live townhall meetings were held to sensitize citizens about their rights and responsibilities. Facebook and short message service (SMS) campaigns were also used for the public information campaigns.[64] Public sensitization encouraging the participation and inclusion of women and youth in governance issues have empowered communities to hold Paramount Chiefs and other authority figures accountable for their actions as evidenced in the examples from Sinjo and Kemen. However, this process has not been without hiccups. Pro-poor advocacy has made several CSOs including the studio unpopular with the political elites.

> In the Port Loko Chiefdom, when the elected MP colluded with the local traditional chiefs to interfere in the election of a particular Paramount Chief, the studio and its local implementing partner CCYA reported against the MP. The Honourable (MP) took offence to this action, and took the matter to court.[65]

Chiefs in particularly have resisted the push towards civic empowerment and political accountability.

> In Sierra Leone, the culture and tradition are different from the western norms, but the traditional norms are being changed forcibly. Unless change is a gradual process there will be tensions. Even with regard to land conflicts, the Paramount Chiefs are elected for life, they are the owner of the land, but today their decisions are being questioned.[66]

In reality, society does not change overnight. While radio-based sensitization has influenced the public, and to some extent spurred them into action, as witnessed with the efforts to enforce accountability and performance on local elites in Sinjo and Kemen, the liberal norms around good governance and accountability face significant structural barriers such as deep-seated corruption and neo-patrimonial

---

[64] Country Director Sierra Leone Country Office, Freetown, 28 March 2017.
[65] Staff from United for Protection of Human Rights, Kemen village, 6 April 2017.
[66] Discussion with Paramount Chiefs at the Parliament, Freetown, 28 March 2017.

politics. In the case of land conflicts, and governance issues more broadly speaking, the power and privileges of the rural elites remain intact. Many Paramount Chiefs double up as MPs, boosting their traditional influence with state power and national political backing, as was the case with the SAC land deal. The judicial pronouncements in favour of the communities in Port Loko suggest that recent CSO led advocacy; and sensitization on land rights have generated positive effects over the long-term. In the landmark judicial decision in Port Loko, the rights of rural communities have been protected from the abuses of power by investors, rural elites, and elected political leaders. These developments present a positive legacy, and augur well for the future of accountable governance in Sierra Leone.

Theme 3: Democracy Promotion and Electoral Participation

In post-war countries, democracy promotion is a cornerstone of the liberal peace. Two broad approaches exist. First, a political approach that focuses on the procedural aspects of democracy such as the conduct of free and fair elections, and the respect of political liberties. The second is a more developmental approach that takes a longer-term view of democracy; as a slow iterative process of interconnected political, economic, social, cultural, and attitudinal change (Zahar, 2012: 75). Democracy promotion 'favours incremental, long-term change in a wide range of political and socio-economic sectors, frequently emphasizing governance and the building of a well-functioning state' (Carothers, 2009: 5). In Sierra Leone, democracy promotion has been an institutional success, in that national presidential, and parliamentary elections have been held at regular intervals since 2002. In addition to this, local elections designed to stimulate the process of decentralization took place in 2004, 2008, 2012, and 2018.[67] Cumulative efforts around democracy promotion have started to show results. Afrobarometer survey data from 2015 suggests that 59% of the respondents preferred democracy to any other kind of government in Sierra Leone (See Figure 4.2). Nine out of ten Sierra Leoneans surveyed (92%) agreed that elections were the best way to choose political leaders (Thompson, 2016: 2). More parties have appeared on the scene. SLPP breakaway People's Movement for Democratic Change (PMDC), the APC offshoot, Alliance Democratic Party, the National Democratic Alliance (NDA), and the People's Democratic Party to name the prominent ones (Bertelsmann Stiftung's Transformation Index, 2018).

Radio has played an important role in enhancing voter knowledge about the electoral process. In the lead up to the first post-war election in 2002, the studio implemented the USAID funded Democracy and Governance project (2002–2005)

---

[67] Skype interview with the first country director of the Sierra Leone office, 30 October 2019.

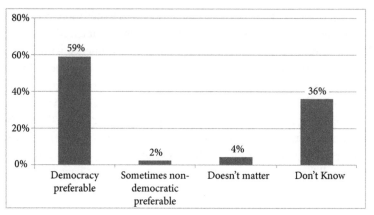

Fig. 4.2 Support for democracy in Sierra Leone (2015)
Source: Afrobarometer, see Thompson, 2016: 2.

(SfCG, 1998; 2004). This was a time, when voter apathy remained high, and youth often did not vote in the elections due to widespread discontentment.[68] To counter this apathy, the Westminster Foundation funded the studio to organize town hall meetings in which youth leaders from different villages were mobilized to rally young people to take part in the elections.[69] *Atunda Ayenda* sensitized them on the importance of voting; the value of democratic participation and its implication for accountable governance. Women's issues were discussed on *Salone Uman*, *Uman-to-Uman*, *Uman na Ose*, encouraging them to take part in public life, and to stand for elections.[70] Even in remote areas like Kailahun, several women candidates were successful in getting elected to local office in 2004. As the chair for the National Election Watch (NEW), a coalition of civil society groups and NGOs, the studio invested much energy for improving transparency and accountability of governance by holding briefings, encouraging radio-based discussions, and working closely with the government's decentralization secretariat.[71]

The studio became a member of the DfID's 'Promoting information and voice for transparency on elections' (PIVOT) strategy, supporting free and fair elections by improving citizens' ability to engage effectively with the electoral process (Taouti-Cherif, 2008: 5). Through the two national platforms, *Parliament Bol Hat* (2003–2008) and *Wi Yone Salone* (2005–8) citizens' access to information on the political reform process increased. Radio programmes like *Lion Mountain* (2009–2012), *Borderline* (2010–13), and *Accountability Now* (2015–16), focused

---

[68] Former Commonwealth Youth Caucus Sierra Leone Representative, and the World Peace Prayer Society peace representative, Freetown, 27 March 2017.

[69] Skype interview with the first country director of the Sierra Leone office, 30 October 2019.

[70] Interview with Studio Media Producer, Freetown, 30 March 2017.

[71] Skype interview with the second country director of the Sierra Leone office, 9 May 2017.

on elections, politics, and the Parliament.[72] People could phone in, and send text messages with their views after the radio discussions concluded. Radio-based debates tried to establish the real interests behind people's positions, deflecting disagreement, and encouraging mutually compatible views.[73] Radio shows were used for enforcing the accountability of political candidates and for enhancing voter knowledge. MPs and Paramount Chiefs were asked to explain their electoral mandate, and their plans for development.[74]

In the 2007 parliamentary and presidential elections, voter turnout was close to 75%, which gives some indication that young people did use their voting rights, however the election saw high levels of electoral violence (Peters, 2011b: 136). After the war, young people who had little or no access to land, and familiarity with violence, became willing to let their vote be bought. Some even let themselves be used as thugs by politicians to intimidate other voters as members of the political party electoral 'task force' (Christensen and Utas, 2008: 521–2). These vigilante groups were set up to handle security in the run up to the 2007 elections. Youth were involved in intimidating voters by breaking up opposition rallies, in exchange for promised benefits once their side (party or politician) won the elections (Fortune and Blah, 2012: 26–9; Enria, 2015: 648–56). Once the elections passed, promised benefits were unforthcoming, creating disappointment amongst youth who often risked their own lives for advancing the interests of their political patrons (Kovacs and Bangura, 2017: 192).

To arrest this trend, in the run up to the third post-war general elections in 2012, the National Election Commission (NEC) launched community engagement meetings, and trainings to engage youth so that they could manage grievances more peacefully during the elections. Nearly 300 community youth groups in the Freetown area alone were mobilized prior to the 2012 elections to resist politically motivated youth mobilization into electoral violence. The studio produced a short radio documentary about peaceful elections. Working closely with the NEC, CCYA, the National Democratic Institute (NDI) and various youth groups, cassettes were distributed to radio stations and youth groups.[75] The studio and the Westminster Foundation for Democracy also launched the Sierra Leone Elections Dialogue Series. It provided training and moderated debates between the political party candidates. In total, 14 debates were organized in 43 out of the 46 constituencies (Bidwell, Casey, and Glennerster, 2012: 1–2). Views from the young people were captured on the radio in the form of programme bulletins,

---

[72] Radio programming timeline provided by the Studio Media Producer.
[73] Skype interview with the second country director of the Sierra Leone office, 9 May 2017.
[74] Radio programming timeline provided by the Studio Media Producer.
[75] Skype interview with the second country director of the Sierra Leone office, 9 May 2017. See the documentary on 2012 Parliamentary Election Debate online at https://www.youtube.com/watch?v=Ritr1OHdWSg (accessed 12 July 2020).

amalgamating both public meetings and radio technology.[76] In the end, the 2012 elections were a very close race between the APC and the SLPP, with tensions mounting in various parts of the country including Freetown. President Koroma eventually received 58.7% of the votes, with SLPP's Maada Bio coming in second with 37.4% (Kovacs and Bangura, 2017: 182).

In the run up to the next elections in March 2018, the studio entered into a partnership with the Westminster Foundation for Democracy as part of the Standing Together for Democracy Consortium funded by DfiD (December 2016–June 2017). The consortium included seven Sierra Leonean organizations—IRN, NEW, Campaign for Good Governance, Institute for Governance Reform, and the 50/50 group, to inform individuals on democratic rights and responsibilities. The project aims were three-fold, (1) mobilizing youth to make their voices heard during the electoral process, (2) increasing the participation of women and youth, and, (3) building the national capacity for the conduct of peaceful, free and fair elections (Abess, Marcarthy, and Konneh, 2018: 7). As the consortium lead, the studio undertook 45 debates, 14 workshops, and 70 discussions on public issues (SfCG, 2018). Through media programming, young people were encouraged to shift their position from spoilers to becoming enablers and participants in democracy. Possible manipulation of youth into election-related violence was arrested through awareness generation around the disruptive effects of violence on the conduct of free and fair elections.[77]

In 2018, Innovation for Poverty Actions (IPA), and the Wellspring Philanthropic Fund sponsored the studio to organize 50 intra and inter-party town hall debates that were recorded and broadcast through radio; the studio ran surveys to analyse public perception of the debates and shared the results with the main political parties. The impact of media dissemination of these debates on the audience was also evaluated. The evaluation found that the debates were effective in increasing voters' political knowledge, but did not impact on their voting behaviour (Bidwell, Casey, and Glennerster, 2019: 2–3). The biggest value added of radio campaigns and community advocacy around democracy, elections, and non-violence campaigns lay in offering civic voter education and in encouraging young people to cast their vote (Bidwell, Casey, and Glennerster, 2019: 2–3). As a result of the multi-year projects in this area, there is a noticeable consolidation of democracy in Sierra Leone. At every election, political leaders are being held accountable. As one civil society activist noted, 'there is at least 65–70% turnover in the Parliament at every election.'[78] Another positive effect of the sensitization efforts is that youth are now less prone to mobilize into election related violence, and this resulted in the 2018 elections being relatively peaceful (Rosenblum-Kumar, and Denominator, 2018: 51–2).

---

[76] Skype interview with the second country director of the Sierra Leone office, 9 May 2017.
[77] Interview with Staff, CCYA, Freetown, 26 March 2017.
[78] Staff, Institute for Governance Reform, Freetown, 2 April 2017.

Radio Based Norm Transmission: Variable Resonance, and Inauthentic Norm Adoption

The life-cycle of the studio's varied projects present important lessons from a normative and institutional perspective. From a normative perspective, radio and community-based advocacy efforts assumed that liberal norms would operate positively, and in ways that allow local agency to manifest. In practice this was problematic. Attempts to modify the participation, and involvement of socially marginalized groups like women and youth, created tensions with the elders, who viewed Western norms around participation as undermining their power and authority in local settings. Human rights and legal standards advocated by NGOs were perceived by the chiefs as disruptive to traditional ways of life and as igniting conflict instead of fostering peace. Intergenerational peace is yet to be achieved. Following radio-based sensitization, a lot of young people began to question chiefs, and were willing to resist chiefly demands for seasonal communal labour like clearing roads (Boersch-Supan, 2012: 44). This refusal stemmed from an awareness of looking out for one's self-interests by adopting self-protective behaviours. Few however felt confident enough to question the government. Youth were readily bribed by token gifts, such as alcohol and small cash used by political leaders to win over their loyalties. Many youths continue to tow the political party line in exchange for political patronage. For example, during the Port Loko meeting of the APC Youth Wing in April 2017, the then President Ernest Bai Koroma was declared their 'Chairman for Life'.

For the most part, youth as a segment of society continue to be viewed as a threat, with suspicion and distrust, rather than as an asset for national development. Post-war efforts around empowerment was not inclusive of all youth; some had greater access to the resources of international peacebuilding than others, based on their proximity to gatekeepers in humanitarian organizations and their links with political patronage networks. Several groups, including those who are younger, young females, and strangers in community settings, i.e. migrants, ethnic minorities, and people from weak lineages have in fact been excluded from the benefits of changing norms (Manning, 2009: 20-1).

Norms around empowerment, participation, inclusion, ownership, and reconciliation, also resonated with youth in instrumental ways, i.e. only in so far as they could help them find jobs or complete their education. For example, vocational training linked to the DDR programmes focused on short-term training of ex-combatant youth in 'practical skills'. Donors and implementing CSOs expected youth to make use of the skills training creatively. The onus was placed on youth themselves to find sustainable livelihoods. Youth in Sierra Leone expected that by attending short-term trainings an immediate route to sustainable livelihoods would open up for them. This expectation was rarely met, given that the projects were never intended to offer long-term or formal employment opportunities. They were designed to enable youth to seek entrepreneurial routes to livelihoods in a post-war economy (Izzi, 2017: 103–5).

The target population of peacebuilding projects were also not equal in terms of their own ability to translate the training and ideas into practice. With the GKN child reporters, only a handful could convert their journalistic experience into a meaningful career in the civil society sector. Hassan, a former GKN anchor, noted that anchoring at a young age distracted him from his studies.[79] He dropped out from formal education rather early and did not attend university, believing he could make a long-term career out of radio. Although he gained practical experience in journalism, there was no formal training or certification to make these skills sellable later. Anchoring was not well-paid and at times he worked on a voluntary basis. To survive, most journalists rely on 'gombo', a practice where free meals, per diem payments, and transport facility are offered by political patrons to journalists in exchange for positive media coverage (Nyamjoh, 2005).

The misalignment of expectations, norms, and interventions fomented disappointment and frustration on the part of the youthful population. It also made them dependent on recurring donor funded projects for livelihoods support. Even when empowered in their thinking and actions, young people are disempowered by the structures in society that present barriers to their progress. Unemployment, idleness, and disappointment over unmet promises of economic development have created widespread bitterness. Most youth feel that the government and its international partners (donors) have raised youth expectations around livelihoods and access to public services. In reality, young people in Sierra Leone have few options when it comes to employment (Peters, 2011b: 140). Most youth still depend on the more resourceful in society that can support them materially and through political clout.[80] In the post-war period, dependence has shifted from elders and big men to INGOs as the latter are perceived as more resourceful. A 2009 study on youth vulnerability and exclusion in West Africa found that CSOs or NGOs were reported as the most important source of support for young people (Ismail et al., 2009). In some respects, the agenda around youth and peacebuilding has been defined for Sierra Leone rather than emerging organically from it. This resulted in a piecemeal, silo-esque approach to the complex, and multi-faceted nature of intergenerational peace.

In the rural hinterland, decentralization and local governance reforms opened up the political space, allowing women and youth to be more vocal, and to take part in local decision-making. Even in the remotest areas such as Kailahun, women in the local communities became thoroughly educated in issues such as early

---

[79] Hassan (name changed), former GKN reporter, Freetown, 1 April 2017.
[80] Staff, Institute for Governance Reform, Freetown, 2 April 2017.

marriage, and sexual and reproductive health (SRH).[81] Women were able to overcome cultural barriers towards working outside the home; taking on farming, and micro-credit businesses to earn livelihoods.[82] Yet as the land grabs in Sinjo and Kemen demonstrate, both women and youth were marginalized in the decision-making process around LSLAs indicating a non-authentic adoption of the norms around the inclusion of these groups in decision-making. Structural barriers to participation, economic inequalities, and deepening poverty following the loss of land have made youth disappointed or ambivalent about the gains of peace. As Bandura (2016: 39) notes, 'youth must be at peace in their daily lives, to be peaceful outside'. In such a context, radio programmes cannot and do not exist in a nebulous space devoid of political, social, cultural, and economic influences. Youth's ability to be transformative is linked to contextual possibilities, making the normative legacy of radio-led peacebuilding a diffused one at best.

Institutionalization of the Gains: Caught Between a Diffused and an Accidental Legacy

From an institutionalization perspective, the media programmes with children and youth did not always conclude in ways that could link them up with the state agencies such as the Ministry of Youth Affairs, the National Youth Commission or with future education, training, and employment opportunities. In terms of missed opportunities, the studio's plans around offering formal training to the child reporters could not be implemented due to a lack of donor support. As the first country director recalled,

> Radio was seen as a commercial activity. In reality, community radio is more like public radio and not a commercial enterprise. Fourah Bay College (FBC) was the only place to be trained as a journalist. We made efforts to organize a vocational training package along the lines of a community broadcasters' course through the Vocational and Educational Training Programme for the Organization of Islamic Cooperation (OIC) member countries (OIC-VET). The plan was to offer training via distance learning modules, and a week-long residential module in Bo, and Makeni. The plans to offer certifications and training to community broadcasters did not take off. Donors had a limited appetite for supporting the professionalization of the sector.[83]

Although Sierra Leone enjoys greater media freedom and diversity of ownership than other countries in the West African region, journalists have only rudimentary training in editorial standards and skills to produce radio programmes. The British

---

[81] Lady Town Chief, Pujehun district, Sinjo village, Pujehun district, 4 April 2017.
[82] Country Director Sierra Leone Country Office, Freetown, 28 March 2017.
[83] Skype interview with the first country director Sierra Leone country office, 30 October 2019.

Broadcasting Corporation (BBC) and its Media Action arm have held intermittent trainings with Star Radio in Sierra Leone. Freetown based mentors are trained by international trainers teach skills in impartial and accurate reporting to local reporters. While trainees are awarded a certificate of participation, it does not amount to any formal training.[84] Limited professionalization of the media sector feeds into a situation where information is used as a tool for political manipulation. Journalists facing financial precarity are increasingly susceptible to seeking political leaders for patronage (Betz, 2008).

The studio's collaboration with other key child protection organizations working on similar issues, like UNICEF, Save the Children, and the IRC were also piecemeal in nature, and did not result in enduring partnerships. The formal and informal protection structures that were created as part of community engagement on child protection had ad hoc links with the government departments such as the Ministry of Social Welfare (MSW). Links with structures like the family support unit (FSU) of the Sierra Leone Police, the judiciary, and the district magistrate, in locations like Kailahun, Makeni, and Bo, were also maintained for short periods only. No transition processes were put in place through which the various children and youth focused projects and their lessons could be absorbed or continued in some form by the government. This presented weak institutionalization of the gains from the advocacy around child rights and child protection. The studio's record of working with the government was similarly piecemeal in nature. Lower-level partnerships were more successful than with ministerial departments.

For example, in Makeni, the local police's efforts in rolling out a new community policing initiative was supported by it through the police community music festival (POLCOMMFEST).[85] Through the *Police Tok* radio programme, the local police in Kailahun successfully sensitized locals about community policing. In Mile 91, Radio Gbafth influenced reforms to the local court system by educating listeners about proper court procedures. Radio Moa in Kailahun district was used by the SLA soldiers to send messages to their families (Bonano, 2008). As part of its democracy promotion activities, the studio successfully struck an informal relationship with the Election Commission to organize electoral debates. While useful for the implementation of the election dialogue series, this interaction also did not develop into a more defined or formal relationship.

A Few Accidental Legacies: Community Radio, IRN, and the BRU

Two areas did, however, present an enduring albeit accidental institutional legacy, however imperfect. First, was the studio's support for community radio in Sierra

---

[84] Interview with Studio Media Producer, Freetown, 30 March 2017.
[85] Senior police officers interviewed in Makeni, Freetown, Kailahun cited in Bonano, 2008.

Leone and the founding of the IRN. Community radio stations offer a valuable foundation for civic engagement and discussion. Initially founded through donor funds, the sustainability of these structures remains challenging. Most community radio stations suffer from serious technical and structural deficiencies such as equipment shortages, power shortages, transportation, infrastructure, and resource gaps (Chi and Wright, 2009). Limited contributions from community members exacerbates their prolonged dependence on external support. Donor funding, though available for national issues like elections and Ebola, can be less forthcoming for the coverage of local everyday concerns, creating further financial constraints to their smooth functioning. Growing pressure from national bodies, like the Independent Media Commission (IMC) and the National Telecommunications Commission (NATCOM) for the payment of license fees and spectrum fees, have added further financial burdens. There is growing social pressure to register and pay core staff social security benefits (Chi and Wright, 2009: 16). There are also problems with political interference. For example, *Radio Wanjei* the only community radio station in the whole of Pujehun had political party representatives on its board prior to the 2018 elections, making it partisan (UNDP, 2018: 17). To stymie politicization, a Media Reform Coordination Group has been established to monitor community radio funding, over which the IRN maintains oversight.[86]

The second area of accidental institutionalization relates to the founding of the BRU. Similar to the community radio stations, the sustainability, independence, and financial viability of the various transport stakeholder committees and transport task forces remain precarious. Trainings offered by the studio and CCYA on conflict management and traffic regulations were ad hoc rather than annual exercises. These structures remain dependent on CSOs for funding, logistics, and technical support. There is the problem of politicization here as well. Seen initially as a potent counterweight to the pull of patrimonialism and a new model of youth solidarity outside of the state and formal politics, politicization of the BRU has been growing. The BRU leadership that controls the vote banks of the *okada* riders and allied trades (garages, mechanics, insurers, motorcycle retailers, and the like), are routinely courted by the political leaders to secure support from these vote banks (Peters, 2011b). Paramount Chiefs, who historically delivered votes for political leaders, are no longer able to influence the *okada* riders to show support for their preferred candidates. This has created new tensions between them and the Union leaders.[87]

---

[86] August 2018 consultative meeting on community radios in SL funded by UNDP SL in Makeni.
[87] Interview with Staff, CCYA, Freetown, 26 March 2017.

Conclusion

The Sierra Leone case study is astounding for the sheer breadth and outreach of its radio programmes. Radio transmitted specific norms around managing intergenerational relationships; it moulded civilian expectations around the accountability and performance of the political elites. Radio also provided a forum for social discussion and helped raise the consciousness of the population by drawing their attention to the myriad problems in society (Shepler, 2010: 627). During its lifecycle, and for nearly two decades, the studio disseminated information on human rights, democracy, and governance issues to different elite and non-elite audiences. Radio sensitization was accompanied by community-based peacebuilding and development related projects. Beginning with a grounded and locally resonant programming effort, over time the thematic focus of the radio programmes were more aligned with donor priorities, thereby losing some of their local resonance.

Improvements in the participation and the empowerment of women and youth, better enrolment rates for children, especially girls into primary schooling, decrease in domestic violence, and the ability to resist political manipulation during elections were some of the prominent wins of the radio sensitization efforts. They enhanced the critical thinking and the self-examination of behaviours and attitudes across all levels of society. The aim of encouraging dialogue and reflection on the different types of civic and political behaviours did not, however, translate into greater choices and change agentry for the youth. This was because radio not only provided relevant information, but also taught young people which choices were best for them. Prescriptive messaging overlooked the nuances involved with variable life outcomes creating youth disappointment with what peacebuilding and development could realistically deliver for them. At a group level, acquired values around rights did not empower beneficiary communities in ways that made them independent or self-sufficient. Compliance in an external narrative of development acutely enhanced their dependence on material support from donors, political patrons, and INGOs. It engendered weak local ownership.

The unprecedented involvement of children in radio programmes as researchers and presenters shaped the media content of various local radio stations. The founding of horizonal associations like the transport task forces, and the BRU and the creation of the IRN to oversee community radio stations, offered forums and structures for engagement and cooperation across generational divides. These normative and institutional legacies of the studio's media work, although mixed, do offer a genuine scope for radio to continue to give a voice to those who might otherwise remain silent. With donor flight setting in, there is an opportunity for local CSOs to move beyond agendas that are externally set. There is the potential to make a fresh start. In a period of low donor presence, both journalists and young people can choose to be innovative about the type of activism possible. They can re-own and reinvigorate an authentic peacebuilding narrative that addresses the needs of every generation.

Absence of an explicitly transformative remit for community radio stations offers further scope for innovation. Community members so far have rarely considered producing their own programmes or using their local radio stations to drive the agendas for public debate. In the period of post-donor radio programming, community radio can reclaim the media space through its support for grassroots led social change. The success of legal empowerment and land grab reversals, as evidenced in the Port Loko case, can offer powerful lessons for grassroots social action supported by local media in the future. By promoting ideas and issues that are important to local communities, and by promoting authentic, endogenous, and democratic communication, there is potential for ensuring norm resonance of radio programming in the future.

5

Learning and Reflection from Sierra Leone and Macedonia

Introduction

The urgency to produce results, can, and does undermine strategic thinking: it encourages an 'impatient' peace.

Country offices of peacebuilding INGOs can and often do exist for decades in a country recovering from conflict. During the different phases of their programming life-cycle, country offices must transform themselves across the relief to development phases of support. To remain relevant to the needs and preferences of the local context and to those of their beneficiaries (individuals and communities), the country office must adjust and readjust their aims and approaches over time, including revisiting the theory of change underpinning the various projects. This process of adaptation to the operating environment and coping with the contextual, political, financial, and staffing related 'shocks' offers critical yet remarkably less studied insights into how far learning and reflection or lack thereof can shape the overall footprint of peacebuilding legacy. This chapter focuses on the programming life-cycle of each country office to draw some comparative lessons regarding the organizational learning and reflection processes of peacebuilding INGOs.

Organizational learning can be defined as a process of developing new knowledge that changes an organization's behaviour to improve future performance (Garvin, 1993). Organizational learning theory in the context of the peacebuilding INGO community draws a distinction between the different levels of learning (Kolb, 1984). At the most superficial level there is the passive internalization of knowledge pre-developed by others. Tactical or second order learning takes place when people reflect on their practice. Such learning leads to adjustments within the margins of a given strategy. Experiential learning by contrast involves the testing of ideas and adaptation. The cyclical learning processes of theory, action, reflection, and adjustment may take place at different levels and at different points in time. In essence, organizational learning is about the process through which the knowledge of individuals who do the real work of peacebuilding in

Peacebuilding Legacy. Sukanya Podder, Oxford University Press.
© Sukanya Podder (2022). DOI: 10.1093/oso/9780192863980.003.0006

the field becomes that of the organization. What did organizational learning look like in Sierra Leone and Macedonia? In this chapter I use the data from the meta-ethnographic synthesis and my field interviews to analyse the learning and reflection trajectory of the two country offices over time.

The chapter proceeds as follows. I begin by discussing the recent push for adaptive and more agile peacebuilding approaches before reviewing the scholarship on learning from M&E. Such a review allows me to identify the barriers to learning that need to be overcome for studying the long-term legacy of peacebuilding work by INGOs. In the second part, the project specific learning derived from the meta-ethnographic synthesis of evaluative studies implemented by the two country offices is presented. The projects examined were implemented at various points during 1998–2019 in Macedonia and 2000–2019 in Sierra Leone. I analyse the nature and types of evaluations undertaken, the recommendations made, and ensuing corrective actions taken, if any. Through a combination of archival research and field interviews, rich qualitative insights into the learning behaviour of each country office can be discerned. The variation in learning behaviour between the two country offices is compared in the third part before summarizing the generalizable insights on furthering learning and reflection for stronger peacebuilding legacies in the concluding discussion.

The Push for Adaptive and Agile Peacebuilding

Over the past two decades international peacebuilding efforts have been grounded in the liberal peace (Paris 2004; Pugh 2005; Campbell, Chandler, and Sabaratnam 2011, Campbell, 2018). As the predominant model of post-war reconstruction, the liberal peace framework has become the only way of doing peace (Mac Ginty, 2007: 472). Its supporters emphasize the institutionalization before liberalization approach (Paris, 2004). One in which rebuilding a strong state, the rule of law, and free market economics take a top-down, externally guided dynamic (Doyle, 2005; Paris, 2010). The detractors of the liberal peace find that the heavy footprint of a top-down liberal peace can be counterintuitive to the need for a locally owned and sustainable peace (Campbell, Chandler, and Sabaratnam, 2011; Pugh, Cooper, and Turner, 2011; Mac Ginty and Richmond, 2013). Apart from the debate around the best approaches to building peace, the field also faces an evaluation problem. Within the liberal peace framework, the outcome is more or less guaranteed if the design is followed (Eriksen 2009: 662 cited in de Coning, 2018: 2). For the 'frameworkers', comprised of evaluation experts, the focus is on achieving pre-set outcomes. Their overall approach is embedded in technocratic and bureaucratic processes that are deterministic or linear in design (Eriksen, 2009). Concerned primarily with demonstrating short-term impact, the activities and outputs involved in technocratic peacebuilding are guided by logical frameworks (logframes) and theories of how change will manifest at the conclusion of

9–12-month project cycles (Benner, Binder, and Rotman, 2008: 43–62; Mac Ginty, 2012a: 287; Neufeldt, 2007: 10–11).

Logframes illustrate programme components that enable stakeholders to clearly identify inputs, outputs, activities, and outcomes (Funnel and Rogers, 2011). Theories of change explain the intended changes including how, why, and under which conditions (i.e. assumptions or factors) the outcomes leading to these changes will be achieved through the activities planned (Ober, 2012; Corlazzoli and White, 2013:6). These tools are linear in nature and therefore inherently incompatible with non-linear social change. Given the complexity and ambiguous nature of the task that is peacebuilding, the true impact of efforts cannot be captured in a neat causal chain (Leonhardt, 2003). Isolating the impact of specific interventions or projects from the complex political, economic, and social contexts in which they are implemented is next to impossible (Chigas, Church and Corlazzoli, 2014: 6; Millar, 2014a). This is because most projects suffer from the lack of a counterfactual. We do not know what would have happened without a specific intervention (Gaarder and Annan, 2013: 2). Impact evaluations continue to dominate the M&E processes used to study peacebuilding results at least in the short term (Rogers, 2008; Jones, 2011). There is, however, a growing recognition that both conceptually and methodologically short-term project evaluations *can* and *do* fall short of fully elucidating how and why moral values or norms that underpin social relationships are transformed over time (Roche, 1999).

This deterministic approach to building peace has been criticized by the opposing school, labelled as the 'circlers' by Neufeldt (2007). The latter are more 'pragmatic' in their approach. They encourage a shift away from understanding peacebuilding as programmatic and technical, to acknowledging its deeply political nature (Neufeldt and Fast, 2005; Campbell, 2011; Blum and Kawano-Chiu, 2012; de Coning, 2018). The 'circlers' argue that peacebuilding projects attempt to solve problems that are political rather than technical, and therefore a deterministic design based on linear cause–effect problem-solving cannot produce effective long-term results or strong legacies. Thinking pragmatically means switching from thinking about 'problems' and 'solutions', to thinking about the quality and sustainability of peacebuilding engagement (Richigliano, 2015). By being more relationship focused and responsive to each situation, the 'circlers' choose to monitor community-based organic processes that can enable lessons to emerge from specific cultural, geographic, and temporal contexts, without expecting them to be generalizable (Neufeldt, 2007: 8–12; Firchow and Mac Ginty, 2017: 6–8; Firchow, 2018). Tracking outcomes requires flexibility and reflection on the part of implementing staff so that the intended outcome can be aligned with the local needs.

In summary, a dichotomy lies at the heart of peacebuilding programming. On the one hand, long-term evaluation does not fit into the DNA of the peacebuilding industry. On the other, the United Nations' Sustainable Development Goals

(SDGs), particularly Goal 16 on peaceful and inclusive societies highlights the intertwined nature of peace and development, and the importance of sustaining peace (United Nations, 2015). In essence, the challenge lies in harnessing the potential for learning within technocratic peacebuilding for achieving transformative peace. The route to this lies in a more structured approach to learning and reflection. Creating a clear link between monitoring, evaluation, and learning requires approaching peacebuilding evaluation not merely as a form of assessment at the end of projects, but as a learning process involving continuous reflection, both during and beyond project implementation (Lederach et al., 2007: 2).

Mika (2002) notes that 'evaluation can be oriented to capturing the longer-term processes of a programme' by evaluating outcomes or results at the end of a funding cycle, or at the end of the programme itself. Final evaluation assessments at the end of a project is more common in the field, compared with post-closure evaluations, that take place following a complete exit. An adaptive and agile learning agenda requires strategic frameworks that commit implementers to timely exit strategies before the relevance and resonance of their projects start waning (Gready, 2013; Hayman et al., 2016). This recognition that resonance is highly significant if projects are to involve locals in any meaningful way requires reflexive practices that consider not only the immediate beneficiary or participant specific impact, but also look beyond the project's intended and actual outcomes. In practice, few peacebuilding INGOs undertake follow-up research with beneficiaries once they close down their missions (Levinger and McLeod, 2012). Donors are equally unmotivated to examine the effects of programmes years after projects have concluded. The overall result is ad hoc and unstructured learning from the implementation of the different projects (Denskus, 2012: 150; INTRAC, 2016).

Besides, peacebuilding INGOs that engage in multi-year programming undergo numerous adjustments and changes both at the operational level and at the strategic level as the country or the organization itself may undergo small and large transformations (Kamatsiko, 2014; Campbell, 2018). For most, the practical issues, the logistical issues, and the resulting adaptations that are seen and recorded in various interim reports can be overlooked or unwillingly omitted from organizational learning loops (Browne, 2013; Lemon, 2017). The reason for this learning lacunae is rooted in resource allocation practices. Most peacebuilding INGOs do not find it cost-effective or convenient to undertake controlled comparisons between areas they operate in, with areas that are not covered by their programmes (Lemon, 2017). 'Work that impacts behaviours, and relationships will by its nature have effects that extend beyond the immediate reach of an intervention's participants. These secondary effects need to be reflected upon [as well]' (Lemon and Pinet, 2018: 254).

The lack of resources for learning through comparison is reinforced by the limited sharing of knowledge and know-how between peacebuilding INGOs due to the competitive nature of bidding for donor funds (Hewitt, 2017). Efforts are underway to remedy these barriers. Slowly but surely, advances toward inter-organizational exchanges on 'learning from evaluative processes' are taking place. Initiatives by the Alliance for Peacebuilding, an association of several INGOs based in the United States, provides a space for dialogue between funders of evaluation and the project implementers (Kawano-Chiu, 2012). In 2010, it launched the Peacebuilding Evaluation Project in collaboration with the United States Institute for Peace (USIP). The goal of the project was to foster collaboration between funders, implementers, and policymakers in order to improve evaluation practice in the peacebuilding field. In other examples INGOs, such as CARE, SfCG, and Partners for Democratic Change, have agreed to synchronize their evaluative processes for their programmes dealing with women's empowerment and youth leadership development (Blum, 2011: 12; Denskus, 2012: 151–2).

The Peacebuilding and Evaluation Consortium (PEC) launched in 2013 and funded by the Carnegie Corporation of New York is another initiative to develop a community of practice. It brought together the Alliance for Peacebuilding, the Centre for Peacebuilding and Development (CPD), Mercy Corps, USIP, and SfCG for documenting, systematizing, and advancing the field of peacebuilding evaluation by sharing best practices and lessons from various cases of actual evaluation. In 2015, World Vision and the Massachusetts Institute of Technology Design Laboratory (MIT D-Lab) received USD five million funding over three years from USAID's US Global Development Lab to implement and evaluate the Lean Monitoring, Evaluation, Research and Learning (Lean MERL) initiative. This partnership including the partner INGO will develop, test, and evaluate new approaches for conducting baselines, evaluations, and programme monitoring processes. The aim is to pursue rigorous, streamlined, and beneficiary focused processes that can improve development outcomes.[1] In 2017, three further international peacebuilding organizations—Saferworld, Conciliation Resources, and International Alert launched the Peace Research partnership. Funded by UK Aid, this three-year research programme aims to generate knowledge, lessons, and recommendations tailored to policymakers and practitioners working on peace and security (Saferworld, 2017). The progress notwithstanding several barriers continues to inhibit learning from M&E.

Barriers to and the Limits of Learning from M&E

Peacebuilding evaluation as Blum defines it involves 'an evidence-based process designed to create accountability for, and learning from peacebuilding

---

[1] Interview with staff from the ILT, Washington D.C. 20 September 2017. See also, https://www.sfcg.org/search-joins-consortium-ilt/).

programmes' (Blum, 2011: 2). This emphasis is echoed in the OECD Development Assistance Committee (OECD-DAC) (2012) guideline document, *Evaluating Peacebuilding Activities in Settings of Conflict and Fragility*, widely used by peacebuilding practitioners. The 'learning behaviour' can be described as the ability to adjust to the evolving context, evaluate the relevance of a project's underpinning theory of change by collecting feedback from direct and indirect beneficiaries, and utilize mechanisms to process feedback in a responsive or non-defensive manner (Bush and Duggan, 2013: 12). Evaluations have become a central tool for funders to justify past expenditure, and for allocating future resources. The same financial accountability imperative has overshadowed the learning function from evaluation (Campbell, 2018). Accountability upwards to donors and to organization's headquarters is emphasized at the expense of linking feedback from beneficiaries into organizational learning, especially when programmes close (Martens et al., 2008). Amidst the pressures of delivering multiple targets to tight timelines, learning from evaluation is mostly 'tick box' learning rather than deep learning.

Most peacebuilding INGOs follow a 'recommended cycle of M&E activity' (Figure 5.1).[2] Such a formulaic approach to M&E has implications for creating a sustained programming cycle (Figure 5.1).

- Conduct a conflict and stakeholder analysis in the project area, or revisit and update an existing one.

- Consult with participants on the design of the intervention.

- Develop and articulate Theories of Change.

- Agree on indicators that the participants regard as meaningful.

- Implement the work while collecting data on the activities (outputs) and indicators (outcomes).

- Analyse the data, reflect on successes, failures, unexpected consequences, and broader impact of the programme.

- Redesign and repeat.

Fig. 5.1 Typical peacebuilding M&E activity flowchart
Source: See PeaceDirect, 2016.

---

[2] A Peace Direct project template is used here for illustration. See, 'Reflections on Peace Direct's Approach to Evaluating Local Peacebuilding Initiatives', online at https://www.peacedirect.org/wp-content/uploads/2016/11/Evaluation-paper.pdf (accessed 15 November 2020).

Capturing transformational processes across the life-cycle of disjointed programmes requires time and reflection to process feedback. Beneficiaries often do not fully understand the project design and the underlying theory of change, but are more likely to have a good understanding of how project activities impacted them, and their community (Barnett et al., 2007: 53). While beneficiary feedback is more readily incorporated for planning or informing NGO activity, it may not filter into immediate or future learning loops. This can create breaks in how far the feedback loop informs organizational learning from project implementation. Project evaluations tend to be timed to deliver financial and performance related accountability to donors. After fulfilling their immediate purpose, evaluation reports are relegated to the 'studies graveyard' (archived into digital or hard copy databases), with limited use made of the collective evaluation 'products' (Mika, 2002: 345–9). Learning evaluations are rare during project life-cycles, and if undertaken are often ad hoc or irregular in nature (Leonhardt, 2003: 56). Given the way in which M&E is structured during the programming life-cycle, several potential barriers to learning from evaluation can be identified. These can be categorized across four areas: (1) disciplinary disconnect, (2) technocratic dominance, (3) managing the institutional memory, (4) overcoming the fear of failure and the limited consequences of not learning.

Disciplinary Disconnect

Conceptually and theoretically there has been a notable disconnect between the field of peace and conflict studies (PCS) on the one hand, and Evaluation Research and Practice (ERP) on the other. Mainstream evaluation research is published in journals such as the *American Journal of Evaluation*, *New Directions for Evaluation*, and *Evaluation and Programme Planning* to name a few. Rarely are professional evaluators trained in peace and conflict studies or even when trained in the academic discipline or a cognate one (international development, post-war recovery, global governance, disaster management), they may not have the hands-on experience of programme design and implementation. From a practical standpoint however, the concept of M&E has become both anticipated and normalized into the organizational culture of peacebuilding INGOs. There may be times when evaluations can be feared or resisted by project staff due to the danger of exposing gaps in implementation. For the most part, however, evaluations are accepted as a necessary evil. They help explain the ways in which programmes are relevant and explore ways in which they might become more relevant (Bush and Duggan, 2013: 1–4).

Within the field of children and youth focused peacebuilding, most projects attempt abstract, intangible, and at times fluid or even reversible changes, such as improving 'children's rights', 'access to education', 'youth livelihoods', or 'youth's political participation'. Long-term change around individual attitudes or shifts in behaviour must translate abstract elements into concrete and measurable accomplishments. Quantifiable or observable indicators such as rise in voting turnout or decline in school dropout rates can be helpful in measuring outcomes (Chigas, Church, and Corlazzoli, 2014: iv). Participatory and ethnographic approaches can also be helpful, because they allow for a more nuanced understanding of the changes in the conflict contexts (Millar, 2014b: 2–3; Lottholz, 2018: 699; Millar, 2018b). These approaches allow the incorporation of both the 'inside out' (i.e. looking at the intervention's activities, outputs, outcomes and theory(ies) of change), as well as the 'outside in' (conflict analysis) perspectives (Chigas, Church, and Corlazzoli, 2014: iv). As of yet, ethnographic and participatory approaches are not mainstreamed into ERP because of time and resource constraints. This disciplinary disconnect between the tools used by mainstream ERP, the type of data collected, and the demands for long-term evaluation to understand the transformative outcomes of peacebuilding, poses an important barrier to meaningful learning from evaluation.

Technocratic Dominance

The demand for M&E across the peacebuilding sector has created a large mobile cadre of specialists and consultants. Roger Mac Ginty (2012a: 287) describes this trend as the growth of 'technocracy in peacebuilding', in which 'success' or 'failure' are measured through the application of specialist knowledge by a cadre of peace professionals whose expertise is neither local nor context-specific (Shapiro, 2005: 343). Instead, generic forms of knowledge around impact and evaluation that originate in Western liberal concepts of rationality are privileged (Mac Ginty, 2012: 296). Evaluation experts have become a specialist interest group that deploys specialist language regarding 'performance and effectiveness'. While appealing to the donor demand for efficiency and value for money, the language used by them may be exclusionary to non-speakers such as non-elites in local settings (Mika, 2002; Campbell, 2018). This technocratic dominance leads to the muting of experiential knowledge. As Denksus notes, 'organizational learning in conflict zones, is accompanied by a deliberate process of muting or ignoring the personal dimensions of local and international staff experiences in the field' (Caddell and Yanacopulos, 2006: 575–6, cited in Denksus, 2012: 150). Instead programme reports are composed in a technical and rational language. They apply management models and formulaic templates for the preparation of end of project results. These products constitute part of the 'performance' or what Grimes (2003: 35) terms as the 'showing of doing' in an anthropological sense. A certain commodification or reductionism follows (Bush, 2001).

Evaluation of multi-year programming requires longitudinal approaches and the collection of data at regular intervals. In the absence of long-term approaches to evaluation, short term engagement during the life-cycle of a project takes precedence. This can result in external evaluators 'parachuting' in, or drawing conclusions about project outcomes, without developing deep contextual knowledge; or an ongoing relationship with the project or its participants (Mika, 2002: 340; Denskus, 2012: 151). While distance is important for objective analysis, limited understanding of contextual and project specific nuances can result in overlooking the unintended effects, that is, the effects that fall outside of the logical framework or that go against the direction of the original theory of change (Lemon and Pinet, 2017). The dominance of technocratic and bureaucratic processes in M&E weaken the learning function within and between peacebuilding organizations (Campbell, 2018). The original aims of humanitarianism, sustainability, and reconciliation underpinning peacebuilding efforts become secondary to that of meeting targets and deliverables, and keeping budgets and spreadsheets; all elements fixated on the quantification of change (Denksus, 2012). In short, communicating positive outcomes to donors takes precedence over learning. A loss of autonomy and organizational unwillingness to engage in communicating about and learning from failure follows.

Fear of Failure and Limited Consequences of Not Learning

Few direct tangible consequences exist for organizations or individuals for not learning. A culture of caution ensures that only successes are reported, undercutting a fertile source of learning that failures can provide (Fisher and Zimina, 2009: 24). For donors, reporting takes precedence over reflection. As a result, amongst donors, 'institutional learning which is reflecting on the lessons learned from particular programmes, is undertaken on an irregular basis' (Leonhardt, 2003: 56). Honest reflection requires that both donors and implementing agencies value failure and become more proactive about learning from mistakes. Project managers need to rigorously document failures and revise their theory of change in response to the elements of programming that do and do not work (de Coning, 2018). By normalizing the reporting of poor performance, the fear of adverse consequences around future funding prospects and organizational reputation can be overcome (Salafsky, Margoluis, and Redford, 2001: 67–80). This shift in attitude towards learning from failure would allow peacebuilding INGOs to steer away from pursuing the peacebuilding agenda uncritically (Goodhand, Lewer, and Hulme, 1999).

In the context of limited learning, designing evaluation practices that can support organizational learning requires a 'process use' approach. Argyris and

Schon (1978) refer to learning loops that progress from following the rules (single loop), to changing the rules (double loop), to eventually learning about learning (triple loop learning). Critical reflection is essential to move between the loops: one that interrogates how peacebuilding is done and what lessons arise from it. A process-driven organizational learning is less about sifting information; it is reflective and requires corrective action to rectify any misalignment between an organization's aims and the outcome of its activities in relation to those aims (Campbell, 2008: 21; Argyris, 1992: 67; Benner, Binder, and Rotman, 2007: 41). It could also be about linking individual projects for 'cumulative effectiveness' (Woodrow and Chigas, 2009). Without any appropriate baseline assessment at the commencement of projects, learning from implementation requires innovative techniques. By comparing the theory of change and the main activities conducted with existing comparative data on what has and has not worked in similar projects, the outcome plausibility can be approximated. The results may require adaptation and may need to be 'translated', i.e. the findings between studies need to be organized into identifiable, analytical categories (Paffenholz et al., 2011: 3–10), yet the outcome plausibility evaluation approach can help overcome important gaps in learning due to a lack of data for meaningful comparison.

Managing the Institutional Memory

Institutional memory is defined here as the memories internal to a peacebuilding INGO. They provide facts and narratives about past organizational activity. A lack of institutional memory inhibits internal reflection and learning, after donor funding for projects cease (Swidler and Watkins, 2009). How far institutional memory is preserved, and what is retained or lost, determines the quality and depth of organizational learning processes, as well as the sustainability of peacebuilding work (Britton, 2005). Institutional memory consists of archival memory, as preserved in the official records (hard copy documents) concerning projects; the human memory of employees, and the electronic memory as held in websites, and electronic documents. Some types of institutional memory are better preserved than others. For example, archival memory can be tricky to preserve, documents can be misplaced, lost, or become inaccessible. Project documents are often shipped to remote locations and storage units near the head offices of INGOs. These paper archives are meant for internal memory, yet are rarely used for reflection or learning, due to the archiving and bulk storage practices (Heideman, 2016: 385). Human memory also has its limitations. It is subject to staff movements, the sunsetting of programmes, or the closure of local NGO partners due to insufficient funding. Local partner organizations and their staff are invaluable for preserving the institutional memory necessary for sustainable work in any given country (Heideman, 2016: 387). They are often the real gatekeepers of human memory. In practice, their memory and reflections on project implementation can often be underreported in the official reports (Denskus, 2012: 151).

The electronic memory, including basic information such as the lists of grants, names of projects, annual, and mid-term reports, unclassified correspondence, and e-mails can be more readily preserved. In recent years donors such as USAID have been active with maintaining digital archives of their project documents on a publicly available website (http://respond-project.org/archive/Digital-Archive. html). Electronic data management has become a routine feature of large peacebuilding organizations, and this was also the case with the partner INGO. Most of their evaluation reports have been digitized for public sharing, although data held on websites can be lost when the webpages are taken down. Maintaining beneficiary details, for tracking purposes after projects close is currently restricted by data privacy laws in Western democracies.[3] Therefore, local approaches are required for capturing the processes of change that take place beyond project timelines. By developing an experience-based theory that captures evolution over time, a reflective practice can support the study of peacebuilding legacy. The CDA Collaborative's 'reflecting on peace practice' concept (2016) is instructive here (Reimann, 2012). It urges practitioners to consider not only the immediate, beneficiary or participant specific impact, but to look beyond the project's intended and actual outcomes. Such an approach allows us to capture outcomes between different timelines, and across multiple projects (Lederach, Neufeldt, and Culbertson, 2007: 2). It can make learning constant, occurring both before, during, and after any project. This opens up the possibility for using methodologies that help analyse the meta-data. Meta-ethnographic synthesis used here can help synthesize and distill the lessons from project specific evaluations for organizational learning purposes.

Organizational Learning Practices of the Partner INGO

The knowledge production partner has an in-house institutional learning team (ILT) that was created in 2004, to provide a structured approach to learning from M & E processes.[4] The ILT is a global team, composed of ten full-time Design, Monitoring & Evaluation (DME) and thematic leads that work closely with

---

[3] Discussion with staff of DME for Peace, 18 June 2019.

[4] My research with the ILT concluded in 2018. It provided the time for data analysis, and the necessary distance from the organizational narrative. I was entrusted with insights into the organizational learning and reflection processes to highlight how learning from M&E was conceived, managed, and processed. The findings from the two case-studies are not in any way judgemental of organizational practices, effectiveness and performance of the partner INGO.

different country-based DME coordinators (Oatley, 2019). Some members of the ILT are active researchers with published research in the field of peacebuilding evaluation. The ILT also offers technical guidance for donors and international organizations like DfiD and UNICEF. They aim to use learning and reflection to enhance the effectiveness, accountability, and design of future projects. Learning practices include knowledge capture during the life-cycle of projects about what works and what does not. Through monthly 'What works' conversation series (web-based meetings), staff from different locations share lessons learnt and reflect on new problem-solving approaches. During 'Fail Fairs', staff are given the time and space to admit to and acknowledge things that did not go well with project implementation. Contextual lessons and generalizable findings are shared between the different regional learning teams (Asia Pacific, Africa, Middle East, and Europe). The findings from the final evaluation reports of completed projects are shared during the Evaluation Reflection Series events. Programme staff and implementing partners for each completed project, meet and discuss lessons in person or virtually. Following which, the ILT and concerned staff decide to redesign programme activities if and when necessary.[5]

In many respects, the partner INGO has been at the forefront of efforts for the sharing of knowledge and resources across the peacebuilding field, through its dedicated online resources like the DME for Peace portal. Post-exit evaluations however, were not part of the portfolio of M&E activities undertaken by the ILT at the time this research was undertaken. Through the meta-ethnographic synthesis, I could summarize the actions taken in response to the recommendations made in the various internal and external evaluations. An institutional mapping exercise with the staff was helpful in identifying the different phases of programming and the types of learning behaviour exhibited by each country office (Table 5.1). Based on the institutional mapping data, four types of organizational learning behaviour: *creative* (enterprising and intuitive) *static* (tick box), *progressive* (future sustainability driven), and *adaptive* (flexible and responsive to criticism/recommendation) were identified. In Macedonia, the distribution of these different types of learning behaviour was more even. In Sierra Leone, adaptive learning behaviours were more prominent. I analyse the learning trajectory of each country office next.

Macedonia Country Office Learning Trajectory

The Macedonia country office presented a resilient organizational trajectory, with effective programme management and implementation capabilities on the

---

[5] Based on discussions with three members of the partner INGO's ILT at headquarters and regional offices.

Table 5.1 Timeline and types of learning behaviour

–	Phase I: Sep. 2000– Dec 2002	Phase II: Jan. 2003– Dec. 2005	Phase III: Jan. 2006– Dec. 2008	Phase IV: Jan. 2009– Dec. 2012	Phase V: Jan. 2013– Dec. 2015	Phase VI: Jan. 2016– Dec. 2019
Sierra Leone	–	Creative	Adaptive	Adaptive	Static	Static	Adaptive

	Phase I: Jan. 1997– Aug. 2000	Phase II: Sep. 2000– Dec. 2002	Phase III: Jan. 2003– Dec. 2005	Phase IV: Jan. 2006– Dec. 2008	Phase V: Jan. 2009– Dec. 2012	Phase VI: Jan. 2013– Dec. 2015	Phase VII: Jan. 2016– Dec. 2019
Macedonia	Creative	Progressive	Static	Static	Static	Static	Progressive	Creative

one hand, and limited learning and reflection on the other (see, Appendix 1). Organizational resilience is understood here to be a 'deliberate effort aimed at strengthening an organization, and its effectiveness and sustainability in relation to its purpose and context' (Lipson and Warren, 2006: 2). The success stemming from the institutionalization of the *Mozaik* bilingual groups into the national pre-school education curriculum was tempered by the multiple internal and external shocks that diluted the quality, design, and pedagogical dimensions of the project itself. Efforts to shape the intercultural attitudes of different age groups through a variety of media and theatre projects were equally mixed and less sustainable compared with the *Mozaik* peace education initiative. I weave here the story of organizational learning by combining the institutional mapping data with the 'programming lessons' and then by comparing the recommendations made in various evaluation reports with the follow-up actions as collated from the evaluative data.

In Macedonia the programming timeline can be organized into seven phases, each demonstrating a specific type of learning behaviour. The first phase (January 1997–September 2000) marked the inauguration of three bilingual immersion groups in the public kindergartens in Skopje (2) and Kumanovo (1). The Swiss Agency for Development Cooperation (SADC) funded these pilot groups initially for one year. Funding was later extended for a further two years. This was a *creative* phase of organizational learning; with only limited reflection. Staff were focused on getting the bilingual groups off the ground and on developing media activities that complemented the focus on intercultural communication.[6] The country staff took enterprising decisions around where to open the groups and how best to design the bilingual model given the contextual realities of interethnic

---

[6] Institutional memory timeline with staff, 23 August 2017.

difference and segregated education. At the operational level, donor stipulated norms around integrated education were initially resisted by primary school teachers as non-authentic (Björkdahl, 2008: 136).

At the beginning, the *Mozaik* groups operated separately from the state kindergarten system. The teachers in the state kindergartens were sometimes resistant to the new model. There was also some evidence of weak ownership on the part of some school directors.[7]

Alongside the *Mozaik* groups, the *Nashe Maalo* children's television programme was aired between 1999 and 2004. As the first children's television series, the show became hugely popular due to its high-quality technical production. Children's viewing preferences permeated into the family environment, in that children discussed the characters with their family and peers. *Nashe Maalo* had a positive influence on children's attitudes and knowledge. After watching the series over a period of eight months, 'stereotypes were less frequently used when describing other ethnic groups. Children's willingness to interact with other ethnic groups increased, and their understanding of other languages improved' (Brusset and Otto, 2004: 44). During this phase, the *Mozaïk* model met its key objectives (Anger, Van Roo't, and Gestovska, 2010: 23). For the staff, the focus remained on expanding the provision of the bilingual model as part of the state kindergarten system, and on increasing enrolment.[8]

The second phase began around September 2000. New bilingual groups were opened in the ethnically mixed communities of Struga, Debar, and Gostivar. This phase (September 2000–December 2002) was marked by *progressive* learning tendencies. Six new *Mozaik* groups were added and 12 more teachers were recruited and trained while retaining the four teacher per group model.[9] To strengthen the internal M&E processes, a clinical psychologist was engaged to help teachers manage hyperactivity, and developmental problems faced by the three to six year olds. Three mentors (up from one in 1998) were involved for overseeing the programme. Regular monitoring involved psychometric tests for measuring group dynamics.[10] During this phase, the learning around the pedagogical aspects of the bilingual immersion groups was better structured. Efforts were made to involve two counsellors from the BDE on the advisory board.[11] The BDE mentors visited the *Mozaik* groups three times every year to produce quarterly reports on their progress and to run training sessions for the teachers. Internal evaluations were conducted by distributing questionnaires at the end of the seminar or the training session.[12]

---

[7] Interview with Country Director, Centre for Common Ground, 22 August 2017.
[8] Institutional memory timeline with staff, 23 August 2017.
[9] Institutional memory timeline with staff, 23 August 2017.
[10] Ibid.
[11] Ibid.
[12] Ibid.

2002 also marked the beginning of the institutionalization process for the *Mozaik* groups. In a major adaptation of its original design, the four-teacher model was changed to two teachers per group to make the model affordable for the MoLSP, while keeping the goals of intercultural communication intact. With this dilution in delivery, parents became concerned about the quality of the pro-gramme, although the demand for enrolment was still high.[13] On the media front, after the 2001 conflict, the OFA encouraged minority language media, which made the *Nashe Maalo* series highly relevant.[14] A study on 'Ethnic and Gender Stereo-types in Children in the Republic of Macedonia' (November 2001), showed that exposure to the *Nashe Maalo* series did not transform pre-existing attitudes. Chil-dren continued to harbour strong negative stereotypes about other ethnic groups and also gender stereotypes (Brusset and Otto, 2004: 44).

During the second phase, the first regional theatre project, the Bridges for the New Balkans (BNB), was launched with Swiss government funding. The initia-tive produced three theatre plays involving minority youth in the production of the dramas. While focusing on multi-ethnic exchanges, the project aimed at en-couraging cooperation among different media production houses in the Balkan countries (Euro-Balkan Institute, 2006: 36–7). In this, the project targeted journal-ists, youth, and the adult population in general. The theory of change underlying the project anticipated that by learning more about the other ethnic groups, and, by making oneself familiar with their identities, contacts, and communication would increase, and intolerance and prejudice would diminish (Euro-Balkan Institute, 2006: 36). Poll survey on the readership of the *Multi-Ethnic Forum* and *Karavan* magazine supplements suggested a weak general readership; as only 33% of the to-tal respondents reported reading them regularly (Euro-Balkan Institute, 2006: 41). Exposure to the culture and perceptions of other groups did not translate into an increase in interethnic contacts or friendships (Euro-Balkan Institute, 2006: 59). The limited influence that the project had on intercultural communication did not however, discourage the development of future media projects with a regional emphasis, suggesting both weak learning, and limited reflection regarding their normative resonance.

The third phase (January 2003–December 2005) marked a *static* period of learn-ing. At a time when Swiss government funding for mentors, trainers, and for the preparation of training material was being cut, a 'training of trainers' model was devised. Instead of hiring new teachers, trained teachers who had been made re-dundant due to funding cuts were recruited for the new Macedonia-Serbian and Macedonian-Turkish groups in Kumanovo and Gostivar.[15] Fresh funding from the Swedish government sourced through the Swedish International Development

---

[13] Interview with Country Director, Centre for Common Ground, 22 August 2017.
[14] Ibid.
[15] Interview with Country Director, Centre for Common Ground, 22 August 2017.

Agency (SIDA) supported the opening of these groups.[16] The policy of decentralization (2005) made it easier for municipalities to open new classes in primary schools in minority languages (Lyon, 2012: 80; Koneska, 2012: 28–50).[17] While the *Mozaik* groups conformed with national developments in education policy, local dynamics affected their operations indirectly (Fontana, 2016a: 867). In some state kindergartens, Macedonian sensitivity to the opening of new *Mozaik* groups offering Turkish and Serbian languages constrained the staff decisions regarding expansion.[18] On the media front, the final evaluation of *Nashe Maalo* (2004) found that, although hugely popular, the show's fictional narrative around intergroup interactions was unrelatable to everyday life. For intercultural communication norms to be retained, the evaluation found that families rather than children should have been the focus of the show (Brussett and Otto, 2004: 13). Follow-up actions to reinforce the *Nashe Maalo* values, such as the Knowledge Quiz Show and the *Nashe Maalo* Live Theatre, did not shift their focus to the families, indicating a *static* learning trajectory.

Phase IV (January 2006–December 2008) was dominated by organizational restructuring and *static* learning. During this phase, the country office in Macedonia started its transition towards establishing a local NGO identity. An external Board of Directors, a Statute, an Annual Plan, and all other documents required by the law were put in place for the transition by January 2006. The ex-patriate country director transferred managerial and financial responsibilities to the national staff. This transition was accompanied by financial cutbacks and staff redundancies. Operational and overhead costs were halved. A smaller office space was rented and staff salaries were adjusted to national levels. Overhead costs were waived by the regional office in Brussels and the headquarters in Washington, D.C.[19] During this phase of adjustment, an evaluation by the Euro-Balkan Institute (2006) offered evidence of language use disparity in the *Mozaik* groups. While Macedonian was spoken by the Turkish and Albanian children, the Macedonian children were often less inclined to use the minority languages. Acknowledgement of the lopsided classroom dynamics in the evaluation reports did not trigger a shift in the design and delivery of the *Mozaik* methodology. The issue of weak norm resonance was not adjusted as the *Mozaik* groups grew in numbers indicating a learning gap.

In September 2008, primary education was transformed into a nine-year programme with children being enrolled from the age of six years instead of seven (OECD, n.d.: 2). This change had a knock-on effect on the *Mozaik* groups, with younger children beginning to enrol if toilet trained.[20] Once younger children were allowed to join, the demand for childcare or nurse assistants grew

---

[16] Institutional memory timeline with staff, 23 August 2017.
[17] On the policy of decentralization see, Lyon, 2011, 2012, 2015; Kreci and Ymeri, 2010.
[18] Institutional memory timeline with staff, 23 August 2017.
[19] Institutional memory timeline with staff, 23 August 2017.
[20] Interview with *Mozaik* evaluator, Skopje, 18 August 2017.

(Naskova, 2014b: 19). The original pedagogical emphasis on bilinguality and intercultural communication was adversely affected as the younger children were less able to learn new words.[21] The country office staff had little control over this dynamic. Funding cuts made financial contributions from the local municipalities and the government for the bilingual groups more urgent. This also exposed the *Mozaik* groups to local political dynamics concerning teacher recruitment.[22]

During *Phase V* (January 2009—December 2012), significant progress made towards institutionalization was marred by *static* learning. When the funding from the Swiss government ceased in 2010, the payment of teachers' salaries became a contentious issue. In some *Mozaik* groups, teachers continued working without pay during that academic year. In other cases, teachers received salaries from the local municipality budgets. Under pressure from the teachers' lobby, the Macedonian government decided to include the *Mozaik* groups into the state kindergarten system from January 2012 onwards. *Mozaik* was recognized and included in the updated National Programme for Pre-school Education. All 18 *Mozaik* teachers became MoLSP employees. Policy developments at the national and local levels were supportive of this. The adoption of the 2010 strategic document on *Steps Towards Integrated Education* was accompanied by external agencies like UNICEF supporting local authorities to develop mechanisms for enhancing interethnic relations in the state schools (Aleksova, 2016: 5–6).

Working alongside the Center for Human Rights and Conflict Resolution (Northern Ireland) and the Macedonian Civic Education Center in Skopje, USAID introduced the state-wide Interethnic Integration in Education Program (IIEP) in December 2011 (Loader et al., 2018: 121). Similar to the results of *Mozaik* and the complementary media projects, these parallel efforts forged only superficial connections, suggesting weak societal resonance of the intercultural communication norm. A primary school teacher from Strumica recalled her experience of the IIEP project. 'It had involved a single visit to a village near Tetovo, some structured activities like games between Albanian and Macedonian children, and structured exchanges between teachers and students through social media networks like Facebook. These activities were sporadic one-off attempts for facilitating intergroup socialization, and did not address the deeper social tensions that inhibited meaningful interaction.'[23]

During this phase, the BTN project (2011–12) was launched using funds from the EU's Macedonia office. Normatively, the project, appealed to EU values such as tolerance, unity, and interethnic diversity. This was a time when concepts such as 'social cohesion' were being mainstreamed into the government's policy language.[24] In addition to launching a new network of cultural CSOs, the project

---

[21] Institutional memory timeline with staff, 23 August 2017.
[22] Ibid.
[23] Skype Interview with primary school teacher, Strumica, 19 April 2020.
[24] Interview with BDE official, Skopje, 23 August 2017.

produced six new theatre plays. These plays were produced and performed by the youth themselves and were aimed at promoting regional cooperation based on common cultural values (Kelsi, 2013: 5). There were several shortcomings with programme implementation and its intended outcomes. The project appeared to have little effect on the cultural awareness of the youth leaders, who were the main target of the planned activities. As for the CSO network, without any formal procedures put in place for regular meetings once the project concluded there was no foundation for sustainability (Kelsi, 2013: 17–19). In terms of learning, the country office, pursued the media projects to appeal to donor norms, and as part of its fund-raising strategy. There was limited reflection on the financial and long-term sustainability of these efforts or on their normative resonance.

This phase was characterized by a transient focus on building youth leadership in Kosovo. Funded by the European Commission, the Youth Democracy and Peacebuilding project was implemented in the three regions of Prishtina, Prizren, and Mitrovica of Kosovo. Five youth focused CSOs and 150 young people in the age range of 15–22 years were trained in mediation, dialogue, and reconciliation; 27 youth teams competed for ten small action grants to implement community-based projects around music, poetry, and sports. At the end of the project, 40% of the 150 participants felt that they were better equipped, having developed their leadership; conflict resolution skills and organizational management skills. They also improved their understanding of democracy and human rights. The unique experiences of developing project proposals and implementing small action grants were valuable for the youth involved. In terms of weaknesses, there were no concrete links made with any government organization or department, a major weakness of the project. In this sense, the project replicated previous initiatives implemented by other NGOs. Without developing joint activity with the municipalities, these projects had limited effects and their short-term impact soon fizzled out (REA Prishtina, 2011: 4–7).

During *Phase VI* (January 2013–December 2015), with new funding from the EU Macedonia office, three new groups were inaugurated (2 x Albanian-Macedonian, and 1 x Macedonian-Turkish). With this addition, the *Mozaik* groups had expanded from 16 in 1998 to 24 in 2015. This phase marked a *progressive* learning trajectory. The country office staff focused their efforts on the standardization of the *Mozaik* model and on the incorporation of the *Mozaik* methodology into the state kindergarten system. Through targeted training modules, 303 teachers working in the state kindergartens were trained in the intercultural communication methodology of *Mozaik*; 73 primary school teachers (grades one-three) were also trained by experienced *Mozaik* teachers across ten multi-ethnic municipalities (Naskova, 2014b: 10). This period witnessed a fillip in the efforts for building the capacity of the BDE advisors, SEI inspectors, and counsellors from the relevant government departments.[25] They were trained in evaluation methods to conduct

---

[25] Institutional memory timeline with staff, 23 August 2017.

internal M&E for maintaining the quality of preschool education (Naskova, 2014b: 8–9).

As part of a *progressive* learning trajectory, dedicated working groups were created. Representatives from the MoLSP and academic advisors from the Institute for Pedagogy in Skopje contributed to developing a monitoring protocol. Documents to standardize practices for the daily planning and monitoring of the groups approved by the MoLSP supported the institutionalization process (Naskova, 2014b: 8–10). The other area that witnessed investment was in strengthening links with the *Mozaik* alumni. Between 1998 and 2012, 1000+ children had attended the *Mozaik* groups. Up until that time, no formal links were maintained with the alumni once they left the kindergarten groups. In 2012, an alumni network was formally inaugurated with a dedicated Facebook page. Efforts to develop and maintain an alumni network were not sustained, however. Mounting funding pressures in the next few years resulted in the loss of support staff and the Facebook page soon became inactive.[26]

Phase VII (January 2016–December 2019) presented another *creative* period of learning for the country office. Monitoring of programme quality and maintaining pedagogical development of the *Mozaik* groups proved challenging after the EU grant closed in 2015. Slow pedagogical development became one of the pitfalls of institutionalization. The focus of staff efforts was on securing recognition from the MoES for the *Mozaik* curriculum, including the contents of the teachers' training module.[27] The country office secured USAID funding for a four-year project on 'Advancing social cohesion' (ASC) in June 2017. This new funding was used to train a broad range of stakeholders in the *Mozaik* methodology, including the state kindergarten teachers, pedagogical students, parents of the *Mozaik* children, education inspectors, and counsellors from the SEI and BDE.

Since 2019, a shift to online training in *Mozaik* methodology presented a more sustainability driven initiative on the part of the country office staff. By June 2019, 97 kindergarten teachers, and 304 parents across ten municipalities were trained across four groups of primary schools. 18 community outreach events to engage 1,141 school students were organized in collaboration with the Open Fun Football schools, a long-standing partner that has worked on various projects funded by SIDA, and the EU funded phase of the *Mozaik* project (CCG, 2019: 18–19). During this phase, negotiations were underway with the central and local government officials for the creation of up to four new *Mozaik* groups, and for using funds from the ASC project to support the training of new *Mozaik* teachers. Maintaining the quality of the integrated education model within a segregated education system remains a core challenge going forward. As a follow up to the *Nashe Maalo*

---

[26] Interview with Country Director, Centre for Common Ground, 24 August 2017.
[27] Ibid.

television series, 24 episodes of a new reality television series *New Heroes* involving youths from all ethnic communities (Macedonian, Albanian, Serbian, Turkish, and Roma) were planned (CCG, 2019: 6, 14). The 'family' was still not made the intended focus of intercultural media entertainment, as recommended in the final evaluation of *Nashe Maalo* (2004). This inability to revise the focus of media programming highlights a tendency on the part of the Macedonia country office to design projects that appealed to donors, rather than pursuing activities that would speak to the contextual realities.

Learning from Evaluation in Macedonia

A 'success' narrative founded on quantifying project outputs, was presented in several of the evaluation reports as captured in the meta-ethnographic synthesis (Appendix 3). For the Macedonia country office, commitment to high levels of local and donor accountability and the timely delivery of project activities overshadowed a more strategic approach. Management of local relationships and national government contacts were both demanding and time-consuming for the country staff, leaving little room for strategic thinking. For example, during the 12-year period, between 2002–2015, 15 different points of national government contact for the *Mozaik* project meant that the country office staff had to regularly establish and manage new working relationships with the MoLSP.[28] Considerable time was also invested in the planning and execution of various project activities and towards fund raising. As a result, reflection regarding the normative resonance of intercultural communication concepts; or the institutional and normative milieu within which these projects were executed was limited. There were fewer learning evaluations across the various education, media, and theatre projects in Macedonia. Recommendations made in the various mid-term and end of project evaluations elicited limited adjustments. For example, the problems with unequal language use, making the family the focus of media projects and addressing the superficial nature of interethnic contacts, demanded revisions to *Mozaik*'s theory of change that did not take place.

The country office engaged multiple research organizations and evaluation specialists for evaluating the different phases of the *Mozaik* project and the various media and theatre initiatives. The positive institutional legacy of the *Mozaik* project notwithstanding, there was little systematic effort to observe behaviour change over the long term, especially amongst the alumni. Follow-up research with this cohort was necessary to fully grasp the long-term implications of their exposure to intercultural communication initiatives. The evaluative studies at various points in time confirmed that time spent in the bilingual groups did not result

---

[28] Interview with Country Director, Centre for Common Ground, 24 August 2017.

in increased or long-lasting contacts with members of other ethnic groups outside of normal patterns of social interactions (Appendix 1; Appendix 3). The role of social capital in influencing the duration and density of social interactions was however overlooked. The multiple designs and expertise used for evaluating the different initiatives also meant that there was no control sample or longitudinal research design in place.

> No proper baseline was established (until 2013), nor a reference group of chil-
> dren organized for the different projects during the formative research phase of
> *Mozaik*. The determination of indicators at the beginning of the programme if
> checked regularly over the years, could have provided an excellent opportunity
> to measure effects over time.[29]

The use of varied methodologies and diverse respondent samples limited the scope for controlled comparison. Research with child soldiers in Mozambique and Sierra Leone offer examples of longitudinal studies that are not resource-intensive, involve follow-up research with the same sample of respondents, and allow the study of long-term effects. The child soldier life outcome study in Mozambique, for example, collected information on 39 male ex-child soldiers over a 16-year period between 1988 and 2004 at two intervals (Boothby et al., 2006: 87–107). In Sierra Leone, survey interviews were conducted at three time points (T1, 2002; T2, 2004; and T3, 2008) with 260 ex-RUF child soldiers; 47.3% of the original sample at baseline were re-interviewed at all three time points (Betancourt et al, 2010: 607). Similar data collection efforts could have been built into the different phases of the *Mozaik* project. Follow-up research with the *Mozaik* alumni was another important area of missed learning for the country office.

The Macedonia country office also exhibited limited engagement in inter-organizational learning. Apart from the USAID funded IIEP project, the Nansen Dialogue Centre (NDC) has implemented a model of integrated education since 2008. The model involves bilingual activities with two teachers from different ethnic backgrounds. The focus is on extra-curricular activities, training of teachers; and cooperation with parents across eight schools (seven primary schools; and one secondary).[30] The complementarity between the NDC and *Mozaik* models did not, however, encourage cross-fertilization of ideas or regular exchanges, barring occasional participation by the project staff in conferences like the 'Inter-Ethnic Education and Youth' workshop organized by the British Council, Skopje (24–25 February 2010) (Anger, van Roo't, Gestakovska, 2010: 8). Limited

---

[29] Interview with *Mozaik* external evaluator, Skopje, 18 August 2017.
[30] The schools are based in the following municipalities: Jegunovce, Strumica, Petrovec, Karbinci, Konche Cair, and Vinica.

inter-organizational learning has meant a possible sidelining of the *Mozaik* model in the context of the wider national and international efforts in Macedonia in the field of preschool education. As one of the evaluators noted, 'UNICEF is trying to develop a new education programme on pre-school education, but they are completely ignoring the *Mozaik* model. There is competition about who will get donor money, and which project will be regarded as the best program...'[31] This element of marginalization was not acknowledged by the country office staff during the institutional mapping exercise, indicating limited reflection about their organizational legacy and relevance in the future.

Sierra Leone Country Office Learning Trajectory

In the case of children and youth programmes implemented by the Sierra Leone country office, the focus was on reorienting intergenerational relations taken widely to have been at the root of the civil war (Boersch-Supan, 2012). Projects were designed to mend relationships disturbed by prejudice, predation, negative experiences, and a lack of clear and trustworthy communication. Consequently, building trust, enhancing human rights education, and fostering clear communication between conflict protagonists were considered a priority. Media programmes, especially radio, were used to facilitate this transformation alongside outreach and community-based projects. Here I discuss the results from the institutional mapping of the various radio programmes and the meta-ethnographic synthesis of the evaluative studies. Together they help charter how the different projects implemented since 2001 has informed organizational learning; the recommendations made in the evaluations for adapting the projects and the subsequent actions taken, if any.

In Sierra Leone, the programming timeline is clustered into six phases. The *first phase* between September 2000 and December 2002 was a *creative* one. The country team used music, drama, and local artists from the cultural milieu to appeal to the masses. By involving ex-combatants and children as radio presenters, marginal voices were empowered (Abdalla et al., 2002). This was a time when donor priorities were nebulous, enabling the staff to be responsive to and reflective of contextual needs. The studio produced radio programmes like *Trow Away di Gun* that highlighted the local narratives around conflict and reconciliation. These efforts allowed local populations access to authentic and reliable information. Radio programmes like *Common Ground News* and *Home Sweet Home* provided information on DDR and refugee repatriation. Important strides were made with regard to popularizing a child-rights framework though programmes like *GKN* (2001–2008) and *Atunda Ayenda* (2001–present). Gender issues were addressed

---

[31] Interview with *Mozaik* external evaluator, Skopje, 18 August 2017.

through *Salone Uman* (2002–2008). Social norms around corporal punishment in schools; and at home changed. Child marriage, rape of minors, and polygamy were made a punishable offence (Abdalla et al., 2002: 21–2).

Radio played an important role in enhancing voter knowledge of the electoral process in the lead up to the first post-war election of 2002. Four radio stations pooled their resources to provide independent coverage of the elections leading to the development of the IRN (Mullins, 2011). At this time, voter apathy remained high, and youth often did not vote due to widespread discontentment.[32] Through the Democracy and Governance project (2002–2005), the studio sensitized youth on the importance of non-violent democratic participation, and its implication for accountable governance. A 2002 baseline study surveyed central government officials on their knowledge of democratic reforms. 88% of the respondents (n = 400; age = 15–55 years) from the listener surveys taken in 2002 and in 2004 reported listening to the radio programmes and nearly 57% reported listening to *Atunda Ayenda* (SfCG, 2005:16–18). The first comprehensive evaluation in January 2002 made four prominent recommendations: (1) producing radio content in local dialects; (2) building alliances with local partner NGOs; (3) arresting youth mobilization into election related violence and (4) investing in the sustainability of community radio stations. The staff took remedial actions to adapt their projects in ways that addressed the first two recommendations. For example, radio programmes in *Mende*, *Temne*, and *Limba* languages were broadcast in the southern and the northern regions during 2002. This helped balance the existing media programmes that were mostly in English or Mende, and had created some resentment amongst the northern populations (Shepler et al., 2002: 96; Everett, Williams, and Myers, 2004: 4).

During *Phase II* (January 2003–December 2005), an *adaptive* learning trajectory developed. Donor priorities around good governance, democracy promotion, decentralization, and anti-corruption efforts filtered into the programming focus. The founding of the IRN enabled the studio to provide media coverage to the whole country. As part of the first post-war elections, the studio organized town hall meetings in which youth leaders from different villages were mobilized to rally young people to vote. Local governance reforms, accountability of public leaders, and chieftaincy issues were highlighted through radio programmes like *Atunda Ayenda* (2001–present), *Parliament Bol Hat* (2003), *Wi Yone Salone* (2005–2008), and *Mugondi Hidesia* (2003–2006). Children's rights and women's issues were addressed through new programmes like *Sisi Aminata* (2003–2006). This was launched in collaboration with the Ministry of Education, Science and Technology (MEST), UNICEF and the international NGO, CARE. *Sisi Aminata* was produced to increase knowledge and discussion around adolescent SRH issues.

---

[32] Interview with Former Commonwealth Youth Caucus Sierra Leone Representative, and World Peace Prayer Society peace representative, Freetown, 27 March 2017.

As part of the USAID's 'Democracy and Governance project', research was conducted in Kailahun, Kono, Kenema, and Koinadugu districts in 2005 (SfCG, 2005: 3). On average, 60 hours per week of discussion programmes created a real-time feedback loop for the general population to hold their political leaders accountable.[33] Shifting focus from locally driven issues to donor funded themes required that the radio programmes adapt from collecting local opinions to facilitating dialogue and discussion in local communities. A 2004 comprehensive evaluation recommended a gradual transition from ex-patriate to national staff; supporting IRN's development, and mentoring successor national organizations like the Media Peace Foundation as part of a well-considered exit strategy. These cues for early exit planning were ignored; instead, expansion and fundraising became the focus for the next decade (Everest, Williams, and Myers, 2004: 4). Learning from evaluation was therefore selective, and based on headquarters driven financial considerations around the profitability of the country programme.[34]

Phase III (January 2006–December 2008) presented a *static* learning curve. Weak professionalization of the media sector was highlighted in an internal evaluation of GKN. Although youth gained practical experience in journalism, there was no formal training or certification that enabled them to convert these skills into more sustainable livelihoods (Bonano, 2008: 33–4). Intergenerational communication, with a focus on parents listening to their children's concerns regarding their rights was also found to be weak. Evaluations during this time emphasized the strengthening of community-based protection structures for children; stronger monitoring; and follow up of the punitive aspects of formal child protection structures. These recommendations went unimplemented due to the ad hoc nature of engagement with formal and informal child protection agencies (Bonano, 2008: 33–4). The evaluation of *Sisi Aminata* (2007) found that the programme had a high listenership in Koinadugu and Bombali districts, and listeners (12–19 year olds) found the advice valuable. Parents and young people differed on whether sex education delayed or encouraged early sexual relations (SfCG, 2007: 5–7).

Recommendations for follow-up action to involve community leaders in SRH advocacy (2007) and broadcasting in local languages did not take place due to funding constraints.

During this phase, in addition to practical interventions in recurring conflicts between bike riders, the public, and traffic wardens (Sesay, 2006: 7–11), there was an enhanced focus on alliance building. The studio invested time and energy in developing a lasting coalition of partners, rather than establishing new partnerships by regularly collaborating with IRN, NEW, and CCYA on various

---

[33] Radio programming timeline provided by Studio Media Producer, Freetown.
[34] Skype interview with first country director partner INGO's office in Sierra Leone, 30 October 2019.

projects from 2008 onwards (Taouti-Cherif, 2008: 20). Alliance building came with its own complications. On the one hand, working with several partners as part of consortia arrangements allowed the pooling of diverse expertise in one place. On the other hand, consortia arrangements often gave rise to tensions between partners due to differences in management structures and workflow systems (Taouti-Cherif, 2008: 35–7). During this phase, improvements in democratic participation, reduction in electoral violence, and the ability of youth to resist political manipulation during elections were prominent wins of the sensitization efforts, in which community radio and the IRN played an important part. A 2008 internal evaluation of the election strategy found that strengthening the capacity of radio stations to produce quality programmes, conduct live reporting, and the improved ability of CSOs to manage funds and organize their staff, were unintended gains of the election focused programming (Taouti-Cherif, 2008: 4).

Phase IV (January 2009–December 2012) involved a *static* learning trajectory with some degree of continuity. Radio programmes like *Lion Mountain* (2009–2012) and *Borderline* (2010–2013), focused on elections, politics, and the Parliament. In the lead up to the November 2012 elections, the studio and the Westminster Foundation for Democracy launched the Sierra Leone Election Dialogue Series. The studio provided training and moderated debates between the political party candidates. Debates were organized in 43 out of the 46 constituencies. People could phone in and send text messages with their views after the radio discussions concluded. Views from young people were captured on the radio in the form of program bulletins, amalgamating both public meetings and radio technology.[35] The 2012 elections were generally peaceful, free, and fair. In previous elections, voting patterns had aligned largely with pre-existing party affiliations. However, during the 2012 elections, people voted against traditional party and ethnic affiliations in places where they had more information about candidates, for example, in the local council elections (Bidwell, Casey, and Glennerster, 2014: 2).

This was also a period when chieftaincy reform was underway. Issues of corruption, accountability, and discrimination against women in governance were the focus of different radio programmes like *Atunda Ayenda* and *Nyu Barray*. In responding to evaluation recommendations for closer engagement with formal agencies, the studio supported the PICOT alliance through media-based advocacy around chieftaincy reforms. PICOT was a coalition supported by Christian Aid. The coalition held meetings with the Ministry of Local Government on issues of community development (James, 2010: 2, 11). To raise public awareness among policymakers at the national and district levels, 14 radio episodes, each 30-minute long, were aired on 27 radio stations; 75 episodes of *Atunda Ayenda* also covered chieftaincy issues (James, 2010: 5, 11). Limited monitoring and follow up meant

---

[35] Interview with Studio Media Producer, Freetown, 30 March 2017.

that learning from evaluation around chieftaincy reform was severely limited (James, 2010: 14). Sustaining the CSO coalition was also challenging, due to coordination problems among the partners across the different locations. Evaluations found that the balance between the chiefs' services and loyalty to the government and their service to the community appeared to have shifted too far in favour of the government and national political parties (James, 2010: 2). During this phase, land conflicts were on the rise. The *Bush Wahala* (2011–16) series was used to inform communities about their land rights, farming, and livelihoods issues. When development processes became highly partisan, community radio made a major contribution to community cohesiveness (Grant, Ahalt Inks, and Wolff, 2009: 4, 17). Evaluations highlighted the need to support the technical and financial sustainability of community radio stations, and to include more women and youth in the radio debates (Grant, Ahalt Inks, and Wolff, 2009: 16) (see Appendix 2).

Phase V (January 2013–December 2015) was characterized by *static* learning amidst a flurry of projects on land conflicts. The studio implemented the three country USAID funded project 'Open for Business: Promoting Equitable Land Rights Protection in Sierra Leone, Liberia and Guinea' and the 'Equitable Land Rights Promotion' project funded by OSIWA (Lahai, 2016). The radio programme *Salone Mi Land* (2015–16) made information about land rights, farming, and livelihoods readily available for the aggrieved communities. 30 episodes of *Atunda Ayenda* focused specifically on land issues. 36 episodes of *Bush Wahala* were produced and broadcasted twice every week on IRN member stations. The studio also produced a 29-minute-long film in Krio on land rights and conflicts (Lahai, 2016: 44). 15 community forums were held to encourage dialogue between the citizens, traditional leaders, local authorities, media, and foreign companies (Basse, 2016: 19).

Working with communities in Bombali, Port Loko, and Pujehun districts, issues of corruption, human rights, governance, and education were addressed through radio. The baseline evaluation for the 'Equitable Land Rights Promotion' project recommended policymakers to use radio to gather feedback from their constituents (Bandabla, 2014: 10). The evaluation of these efforts highlighted several gaps. First, was the missing links with line ministries such as the Departments of Agriculture and Labor. Second, was the exclusion of women in the deliberations around land acquisitions. Third, was the limited involvement of legal practitioners to inform communities about land and property regulations; and finally, the need for supporting structures like land management committees (Lahai, 2016: 44). The weak link with formal agencies and problems with the long-term sustainability of local structures set up in connection with child rights focused projects had been flagged in the final evaluation of GKN (Bonano, 2008). The fact that these did not encourage adaptation on the part of the studio suggests a *static* learning curve.

Alongside land issues, the focus on democracy promotion and governance continued during this phase. Funding of USD four and half million from USAID was allocated for various activities in the lead up to the 2018 elections. They included: early warning systems for monitoring election-related violence; supporting female aspirants and political leaders to run for public office; and training of the media in elections policy dialogue (Gassan et al., 2018; Keita, 2018). The studio relied on its pre-existing networks to mobilize youth on various governance issues. Radio programmes like *Accountability Now* were used to enforce the accountability of political candidates; and for enhancing voter knowledge. MPs and Paramount Chiefs were asked to explain their electoral mandate, and to outline the plans for the development of their constituencies (Bidwell, Casey, and Glennerster, 2014).

During this phase there was a renewed focus on child rights issues. The three-country project on 'Engaging Children and Youth as Partners in Preventing Violence against Children in Liberia, Guinea, and Sierra Leone' was implemented with delays due to the Ebola outbreak. Research and data collection by trained youth researchers was interrupted. When the research was finally completed, a handbook on the worst forms of violence against children was published. There was, however, very little or no uptake at the policy level for this publication. Evaluative studies recommended follow-up studies; the provision of psychosocial support for youth researchers; and further opportunities for them in the form of informal affiliation with the studio. The recommendations did not elicit any follow up, suggesting weak learning in this area (McGill and Zerla, 2017: 11). In some respects, the limited learning and reflection from these projects is understandable. The Ebola crisis created considerable uncertainty for CSOs, accountability to donors in terms of delivering various project activities took precedence over learning and reflection.

Phase VI (January 2016–December 2019) was *adaptive* to the broader changes in the donor funding environment. There was a spike in project activity prior to the March 2018 elections. Voter education around democratic rights and responsibilities was implemented through a consortium made up of five national CSOs as part of the *Standing Together for Democracy Consortium* funded by DfID (December 2016–June 2017). Seven CSOs—IRN, National Election Watch, Campaign for Good Governance, Institute for Governance Reform, and the 50/50 group, implemented activities for mobilizing youth and women to participate in the 2018 elections. Similar to earlier efforts during 2012, the studio facilitated debates, workshops, and discussions on public issues. Some 35 radio stations received media training; and equipment support. A Disabilities Agenda, a Citizen Manifesto, and an Election Observers' reports were produced to develop policy guidance on these matters (Abess, Macarthy, and Konneh, 2018: 7–9, 11).

The studio also implemented a three-year EU funded project for strengthening local governance and accountability by empowering women and youth in the rural communities in partnership with CCYA. The focus was on making local council ward committees more functional in their role (Johnny, 2017: 5). 24 women and youth focused local CSOs in Koinadugu, Port Loko, Kono, Kambia, Pujehun, and Moyamba districts were trained in community based indigenous monitoring of local decision-making. Drawing on learning from previous projects, efforts were made to promote learning and sharing between the CSOs. District and budget oversight committees, school management, and community teachers' associations were involved in the monitoring of local governance services. This was accompanied by radio-based awareness raising campaigns through *Atunda Ayenda* and *Uman 4 Uman* (Roy, 2018: 7). The project's mid-term evaluation identified problems similar to those flagged in the previous projects. For example, weak links to formal agencies like the Ministry of Finance, the lack of necessary financial training to help build the sustainability and independence of the youth and women-led CSOs; and the limited opportunities for youth trained in journalism to secure more sustainable livelihood opportunities, highlighted consistent learning gaps (Roy, 2018: 8, 27).

Learning from Evaluation in Sierra Leone

The Sierra Leone country office was more learning oriented with regard to programmatic adjustments. The meta-ethnographic synthesis revealed greater responsiveness and the ability to effect concrete adjustments in response to the recommendations made in the evaluative studies (Appendix 2). For example, the recommendation around linguistic diversity (2002), encouraged the production of radio content in local languages. The recommendation for engaging more women through radio programmes, and including SRH issues were taken on board through the creation of the *Sisi Aminata* and *Uman 4 Uman* radio shows. Recommendations to counter youth mobilization into election related violence (2002), advancing decentralization of governance (2002), developing IRN (2004), and working with a core group of local CSO partners (2008) were implemented to positive effect, demonstrating adaptation and responsiveness on the part of the country office. In other areas, there was less willingness or capacity to adapt, resulting in static and tick-box learning. For example, donor funds for new or emergent areas of concern ranging from HIV/AIDS, gender, human rights, SRH, and child protection did not always reinforce one another, creating ad hoc and disjointed effects.

The scope and breadth of the media and community engagement activities in Sierra Leone were greater compared with that of the Macedonia country office. Implementing multiple and multi-track projects in parallel, left staff with little time for double loop learning.[36] Examining the underlying assumptions and reflecting on the gaps between the intended and actual outcomes of the various radio and community engagement activities was challenging. Staff were primarily invested in keeping pace with the evolving nature of public concerns, raising funds, building and managing local partnerships, and supporting community-based advocacy efforts. This made deep reflection on the lessons learnt from stand-alone projects less of a priority. Investments in periodic learning evaluations did not translate into a more structure reflection process. In fact, the trajectory of the Sierra Leone country office offers important lessons regarding how multiple years of in-country programming can obfuscate the larger question of peacebuilding legacy.

From an institutional legacy perspective, the studio's projects influenced the creation of various formal and informal structures within government departments. They included for example, the Gender and Children's Affairs unit within the Ministry of Social Welfare (MSW/GCA); the FSU within the Sierra Leone Police; and informal structures such as youth clubs, child welfare committees, land management committees, and women's empowerment centres. The latter were created during the span of specific projects and were consigned to fail, following the withdrawal of external funding, given the lack of sustainability and futures-oriented thinking. Even with community radio stations and the IRN, future problems with financial sustainability and technical capacity were flagged by the different evaluations (2002, 2004, 2009; see Appendix 2), urging greater national resources and investment. The short-term funding cycles and donor driven nature of the different projects made sustained investments to support these structures unavailable even when the intention and desire were there on behalf of the studio staff. The inability, and at times unwillingness, on the part of the government to step in to support local structures like community radio stations meant that they were left to their own devices to generate income and for managing finances. Low levels of literacy and financial training of rural residents meant that they fell back on prior ways of life, making project focused interventions transitional rather than transformational in their effects.

Variation in Country Office Learning Behaviour

The Sierra Leone and Macedonia country offices present different learning trajectories with some areas of similarity that offer important insights for the study of learning and reflection from M&E. The areas of similarity will be summarized first. The initial phase of operations was a *creative* learning phase with limited reflection in both cases. Staff exhibited an enterprising spirit and intuitive decision-making to get projects off the ground. The evaluative evidence suggests

---

[36] Interview with Country office M&E Specialist, Freetown, 30 March 2017.

that creative learning is more likely at the onset of post-war reconstruction efforts, when donors themselves are trying to understand the context. Agendas are loosely defined and there is more room for local implementers to remain 'authentic' or immersed in the local context and its needs. At the formative stage, the country office staff of multi-mandate INGOs can exercise greater agency by sidestepping bureaucratic formalities and the rigid cultural and normative constraints experienced by organizations like the UN or other large donor organizations (Campbell, 2018: 230). With time, however, the external hand of the international community begins to steer peace and statebuilding processes in the direction of a liberal peace, making donor funded peacebuilding efforts more structured, directed, and thematic (Chandler, 2006; Lemay-Hébert, 2011; Podder, 2013). This transition has a constraining effect on the agency of INGO staff, promoting a non-authentic or manufactured peace. Based on a comparative analysis of the learning trajectories in the two cases, four variables help explain the different types of learning behaviour exhibited by each country office during the phases studied. These include *staff continuity, national government buy-in, local partnerships, and donor rules.* I discuss each in turn, drawing on the findings from the meta-ethnographic synthesis (Appendices 3 and 4).

Staff Continuity

Staff continuity in Macedonia and a narrow focus on intercultural communication were a great enabler for institutionalization. Continuity in staffing allowed more time to be invested in developing working relationships with the relevant government agencies despite frequent changes in personnel within these departments. It contributed to higher levels of local ownership by the staff and the tenacity to overcome the internal and external shocks experienced during the life-cycle of the *Mozaik* project.[37] Without staff continuity, achieving the goal of institutionalizing the bilingual groups into the national preschool education system would have been difficult to realize. At the same time, too narrow a focus on institutionalization limited the staff's ability to reflect on the normative legacy of their projects. The theory of change underlying the intercultural communication projects was not adjusted over the years. Even after several evaluative studies had flagged the weak resonance of integrated education and social cohesion norms, there was a limited effort to radically alter the structure of the projects, partly on account of existential considerations. This explains the predominance of the *progressive* (sustainability oriented), and *static* approaches to learning with respect to the Macedonia country office.

---

[37] Institutional memory timeline with staff, Skopje, 23 August 2017.

In Sierra Leone, there was greater continuity in the first six years between 2000 and 2006 with regards to leadership. The country director was also the West Africa region director during 2002–2006 and later became the director of all operations in Africa between 2002 and 2006. As operations were on a larger-scale, movement of ex-patriate staff assigned to various projects was more frequent. Staff changes offered the opportunity to inject new energy and initiative into the operations; allowing staff to be more responsive to learning from evaluation in comparison with the Macedonia country office. Transition from international to national staffing in the post-2006 period created greater staff continuity across the radio production, finance, and M&E areas.

The multi-track nature of operations using radio and community engagement placed considerable demands on the staff, who had to manage multiple budget lines and were under pressure to deliver activities for projects that ran in parallel. Dedicated time for learning and reflection from M&E was often limited.[38] It was impressive to see that the staff undertook several internal learning evaluations and tried to adjust projects where possible. However, as discussed, the life-cycle of the Sierra Leone country office presented a far from organic evolution. There was pressure to engage in continuous fund raising to keep the various radio shows on air. The focus was on expansion, financial profit, and brand building. In pursuing donor determined agendas, there was limited critical reflection about the question of organizational legacy. Without deep thinking about the question of sustainability, formal institutional links and national handover to suitable successor organizations, short-term successes and adjustments could not be converted into formal institutional legacies.

National Government Buy-in

Media projects are issue-driven and ever-evolving in response to live controversies and debates in the public realm. For lasting effect, media-based sensitization efforts need to be linked into formal channels through cooperation with relevant government departments. In Sierra Leone, government officials were often unwilling to engage with civil society activities that were critical of their governance approaches.[39] Although cooperation with formal departments did exist from time to time, these were temporary arrangements rather than long-lasting in nature. For example, on the theme of elections and democracy promotion, the studio has supported the Election Commission during the last two elections (2012 and 2018) by hosting public debates with party candidates without establishing any formal partnership.

---

[38] Skype interview with second Country Director, Sierra Leone country office, 9 May 2017.
[39] Interview with then current Country Director, Sierra Leone country office, Freetown, 29 March 2017.

Without strategic partnerships with line ministries, the ability to establish sustained efforts for encouraging young people's non-violent participation in electoral politics was limited. The national government did not invest in continuing the influential advocacy work being done through donor funded media. Equally, professionalization of the media sector was left to external actors without government interest in developing the sector.[40] This explains the predominance of *static* learning in Sierra Leone in the area of institutional legacy. In Macedonia by contrast, improving the country's education system and adopting the normative push around integrated education and social cohesion remain a pre-condition for possible future accession to the EU and NATO. These political motivations created government buy-in through the legal adoption of these externally promoted norms. In practice, civil society actors have assumed the main responsibility for advancing intercultural communication and integrated education efforts supported by external funds. National policies on integrated education were tick box exercises for appeasing donors; they did not reflect the social reality of widening interethnic distrust and distance and therefore only led to a superficial adoption of norms at the societal level. Weak norm resonance at the societal level explains the *static* learning in the area of norm resonance and retention in Macedonia.

Local Partnerships

In Sierra Leone there was a focus on alliance-building, and developing a lasting coalition of partners rather than establishing new partnerships. Working with several partners as part of consortia arrangements allowed the pooling of diverse expertise in one place. It also helped strengthen community radio networks in Sierra Leone through the establishment of the IRN which has created a valuable institutional legacy, however imperfect. In building a core team of local collaborators including IRN, NEW, and CCYA, the Sierra Leone country office contributed to the capacity-building of local partner organizations. Such an alliance-building approach presented both advantages and limitations. On the one hand, alliances with IRN affiliated community radio stations enabled the studio to provide adequate media support and coverage. On the other hand, dependence on the multiple network partners created tensions due to divergent structures and workflow systems (Abess, Marcarthy, and Konneh, 2018).

In Macedonia, in order to encourage continuity and learning between the different media and theatre projects, the country office recruited professionals who were part of their initial theatre productions for later efforts. Youth participants trained in the first iteration of regional media and theatre projects such as Bridges for the New Balkans were recruited as local coordinators and supporters for the

---

[40] Skype interview with the first Country Director, Sierra Leone country office, 30 October 2019.

Balkan Theatre Network project (Stine, 2013). In the area of early years education, trainers for conducting workshops on *Mozaik* methodology were drawn from the pool of first-generation teachers, i.e. those who were involved with the *Mozaik* groups since 1997/1998.[41] There were other examples of building on established partnerships. The OFF schools, collaborated on various projects funded by SIDA and the EU (Naskova, 2014a; SfCG, 2019). In both cases, the willingness and ability to develop reliable and long-standing local partnership enhanced the creative and adaptive learning behaviours (Browne, 2013). In Sierra Leone, the partnership with OPARD, and in Macedonia, the partnership with the OFF schools are examples of creative partnerships that strengthened the ability to engage the desired target groups, i.e. ex-combatants and *Mozaik* alumni in innovative ways.

Donor Rules

The intercultural communication efforts in Macedonia, including the *Mozaik* kindergarten groups and allied media and theatre projects, received support from four main donors: Sweden (2004–2008), the Swiss government (2008–2010), the EU country office in Macedonia (2011–2013), and USAID (2017–2020). Sweden promoted the norm of conflict prevention in the EU as part of the development of the EU's common foreign and security policy. As a prominent norm advocate, Sweden pushed for the mainstreaming of conflict prevention efforts into the EU's policy discourse (Björkdahl, 2008: 135). Phased withdrawal of funding for the bilingual groups was rooted in the expectation that the Macedonian government would step in to fund these groups as part of their preschool educational provision. The donor rules around transition to national ownership set the stage for adaptive learning, and progressive institutionalization.

In Sierra Leone by contrast, donors assumed that skills training, human rights awareness, and democratic participation would produce positive effects. In practice, this was not always the case. Short-term training did not offer the certifications necessary to secure reliable future employment for the child reporters. When projects focused specifically on thematic advocacy such as child protection, child rights, and the training of children as journalists, efforts to involve them in the production of radio programmes are merely instrumental. The opportunity for professional development was not part of these short-term funded activities. There was little strategic thinking about the value added of training children as reporters apart from the novelty of their inclusion for project delivery. Donors and CSOs stepped in to fill the vacuum of weak governance and national institutions without creating the necessary linkages between short-term projects and national institutional development. This explains weak institutionalization

---

[41] Interview with Country Director, Centre for Common Ground, 24 August 2017.

and *static* learning around the sustainability of the media and conflict prevention efforts in Sierra Leone.

Conclusion

To summarize the findings from the meta-ethnographic synthesis, the Sierra Leone country office was more learning oriented. The Macedonia country office in contrast was less so. There was instead a more resilient approach to institutionalizing the *Mozaik* bilingual groups into the state preschool system. This element of sustainability was missing with the media and theatre projects in Macedonia, however. In Sierra Leone, the children and youth focused projects did not focus on sustainability and institutionalization. Therefore, the institutional legacy of the IRN in the area of community radio was by accident rather than by design. The BRU and the bike riders' associations were another example of accidental institutionalization. These emerged organically in response to the contextual needs of creating structure and organization for the bike riders. In other cases, structures set up as part of the different projects existed only so long as donor funding was available. This resulted in weak sustainability and institutionalization of project-based learning.

In both cases succession and handover issues were delayed. In Macedonia, nationalization and transition to a local NGO entity was linked to the withdrawal of donor funding for the *Mozaik* groups. This helped expedite the sourcing of national funds to support the project and strengthened the agency of the local staff. In Sierra Leone, the timing of the nationalization of operations, and the transition from ex-patriate to national staff, were part of a delayed exit strategy. Leadership decisions emanating from the headquarters in Washington, D.C. determined the timing of exit. Extending the programming life-cycle, weakened the norm resonance of the later projects focusing on issues such as on countering violent extremism.

In both countries, follow-up research with beneficiaries in the form of post-exit studies that can help build stronger organizational legacies was missing. At the country office level, the decisions around which programmes to pursue, when to change, or terminate them, and the criteria for normative relevance were tied to donor agendas with limited agency on the part of the staff. In Sierra Leone there were no concrete expectation of national handover and ownership with regard to the different projects funded by donors to the government departments, making sustainability and institutionalization secondary to the demand for fund raising, donor accountability, and timely project implementation.

6

Programming for Change

Media and Peace Education in Shaping Young People's
Attitudes to Peace

Introduction

The success of liberal peacebuilding lies in the dissemination, and ultimately the internalization and acceptance, of the values and norms underpinning the liberal peace. Various tools of social, attitudinal, and normative influence are employed as part of liberal remedies in countries recovering from conflict. How effective these tools are in securing long-term conflict transformation depends in part on the extent to which transmitted norms are successful in shifting attitudes towards more peaceful ones (Petty and Briñol, 2015: 268). In this chapter, I explore this question of attitude change. Through second-order interpretations of the meta-data, I analyse whether the processes of persuasion and norm transmission through the youth focused media and education projects contributed to attitude change; and how far the adopted norms and behaviours were retained over time. The results do not purport to offer scientific claims as to the views of the youthful population in the two countries as a whole, but rather seek to present the variety of young people's experiences following their exposure to the peace education and media persuasion initiatives studied.

The chapter is organized as follows. I begin by examining existing approaches to the study of young people's attitudes towards war and peace. Drawing on a range of disciplines, the process of attitude formation and the various environmental influences are debated, before examining the role of media and peace education in norm persuasion and attitude change. The literature on norm persuasion suggests that normative influence is often easier compared with attitudinal influence because individual's normative perceptions can be more malleable than their attitudes. Two prominent models of norm change—first, 'a social norms and group influence model' and second, 'the model of individual beliefs and learning'— guided the analysis for Sierra Leone and Macedonia respectively. Through the second-order interpretation of the evaluative data, I coded the norm concepts associated with the various projects in each case. These guide the analysis on whether

Peacebuilding Legacy. Sukanya Podder, Oxford University Press.
© Sukanya Podder (2022). DOI: 10.1093/oso/9780192863980.003.0007

the youth-focused media and education norms contributed to more peaceful attitudes and how far the adopted norms and learnt behaviours were retained over time. The main findings with regard to norm persuasion and attitude change are summarized in the final part. The concluding discussion highlights the limits of media and education-based norm persuasion in shaping young people's attitudes towards peace.

Children and Young People's Attitudes to War and Peace

In simple terms, an individual's attitude constitutes their beliefs or views towards different aspects of the world, and is the result of their own experiences and up-bringing (Crano and Prislin, 2006: 347). Attitudes present general and relatively enduring evaluations that people have of other people, objects, or ideas. These overall evaluations can be positive, negative, or neutral, and can vary over time, and in response to specific events (Petty, Wheeler, and Tormola, 2003: 354). Attitudes can be conceived along a continuum ranging from non-attitudes to strong attitudes (Converse, 1970). The latter influence thought and behaviour, are persistent over time, and are resistant to change (Krosnick and Petty, 1995). People act favourably towards things they have a positive attitude towards and negatively towards things they do not like (Petty, Wheeler, and Tormola, 2003: 354). In this, attitudes serve both symbolic and instrumental functions.

Attitudes serving symbolic functions are focused on what the object symbolizes or represents. Attitudes serving instrumental functions are focused on the intrinsic properties of the object, i.e., appraising the object in terms of their intrinsic attributes or consequences (O'Keefe, 2009: 271). Attitude formation is grounded in different types of information. These include cognitions or beliefs, affect or feelings, and actions or behaviour. Individuals are not always aware of the basis of their beliefs. Information that confirms previously held beliefs and attitudes is more readily accepted as valid (Ryffel et al., 2014: 402). Alternative information that is inconsistent with prior beliefs and attitudes is likely to be ignored, rejected, and/or simply misinterpreted (Kruglanski, 2004a, 2004b; Kunda, 1990). Highly heritable attitudes in particular have been found to be more resistant to change than less heritable attitudes (Petty, Wheeler, and Tormola, 2003: 354).

Young people's attitudes are of interest to peace and conflict researchers because they drive both violent and peaceful behaviours during and after conflict. Studies suggest that the meaningfulness and images of both war and peace shift in line with the developmental stages in children and young people, and become more profound with age (see Cooper, 1965; Alvik, 1968; Haavelsrud, 1970; Hall, 1993; Lernon, Ferguson, and Cairns, 1997; Maoz, 2000; McEvoy, 2000; Gillard, 2001; Kirpitchenko and Mansouri, 2014; King, 2018; Taylor, 2020; Warshel, 2021). For example, preschool children are known to internalize images of war and respond to them in morally relativist categories of 'good' or 'bad' due to their limited ability to verbalize their attitude (Rodd, 1985). Gender matters as well, with girls less interested in war and less attuned to viewing war as necessary or justifiable (Hall, 1993: 183–4).

Child behaviour and child development is nested in, and shaped by the context of the family, school, peer group, the community, and the larger society (Wessels, 1998; Wessels and Monteiro, 2004). Amy Jordan (2005), in her extension of Bronfenbrenner and Morris' (1998) ecological conception of child development, outlines the broader ecosystem of social relations that shape young people's attitudes. The ecosystem consists of (a) a macrosystem, i.e. the larger cultural context that shapes attitudes, beliefs, and behaviours; (b) the exo-system, i.e. the formal and informal social structures that indirectly influence children, such as the mass media; (c) the middle level of the family and the community, which constitutes the mesosystems; and finally (d) the individual level or the microsystem. Values and norms within these groups and the interactions between the different systems shape young people's behavioural development. Developmentally, children's peacebuilding potential is anticipated to increase as their agency grows (Taylor, 2020: 130). Adolescents and teenagers generally have greater autonomy in moving through their environments and may encounter more systems within their social ecologies compared with children. Because of their ability to exercise agency, they can potentially become influential agents and crucial partners for peace (McKeown and Taylor, 2017; Taylor et al., 2018; Taylor et al., 2019).

To be persuasive, media and education interventions must occur on a continuing basis throughout the diversity of these cultural subsystems and not just at the level of children and young people (Salomon, 2002: 4; Danesh, 2006; Messenger Davies, 2010). Without promoting change in the exo-, and macrosystem, without restructuring relevant institutions, simply targeting or influencing interpersonal (i.e., microsystem), or pro-social behaviours may not promote the necessary structural and cultural (i.e., exo- and macrosystem) changes that can support transformative effects (Bar-Tal and Halperin, 2009; Taylor, 2020: 132). To reorient the values, practices, norms, and beliefs around peace, reconciliation, and tolerance for future generations, the mindset of the older generation should also be targeted (Bandura and Walters, 1977). The agents of formal and informal education together support how or in what ways children develop the capacity to act in social life through exercising critical understanding and applying moral judgement (Friere, 1970; Lemish, 2008: 283). How far did the media and peace education efforts in Sierra Leone and Macedonia align with this logic of norm persuasion? I explore the persuasive appeals of these efforts and their long-term effects on attitudes next.

Media and Peace Education: Norms, Persuasion, and Attitude Change

Media and peace education efforts form part of a 'programming for change' approach. It involves changing young people's mental states as a precursor to changes in their behaviour through norm persuasion. While media does not directly inject specific behaviours, the effects of media are not negligible either (Katz and Lazarsfeld, 1955; Klapper, 1960; McQuail, 1987). In social psychology, persuasion is understood as a form of social influence, by which people are convinced to adopt a certain type of thinking or attitude, through information-sharing or educational entertainment formats (O'Donnell and Kable, 1982: 9). Persuasion refers to a favourable change in individual attitudes and behaviours based on receptive messaging from an influential source. Theories of attitude offer insights into the persuasion process. From the perspective of belief-based models of attitude, persuasion efforts either add some new salient beliefs about an object, change the evaluation of some existing beliefs, or change the strength or conviction with which some existing beliefs are held (O'Keefe, 2009: 269–70). Sometimes information about which beliefs are the most appropriate is also used to influence attitudes (Ryffel et al., 2014: 401). Field studies indicate that emotionally arousing messages are more effective in changing affect-based attitudes than cognition-based attitudes (Edwards and Von Hippel, 1995; Fabrigar and Petty, 1999; Mayer and Tormala, 2010). Persuasive appeals that match the pre-exisiting attitude base were more effective when attitudes were held with high certainty (Clarkson, Tormala, and Rucker, 2011). In contrast, attitudes held with low certainty were more open to mismatching persuasion (Ryffel et al., 2014: 398).

Most media and education focused peacebuilding projects seek to effect change across the individual, group, and structural levels. Their aim is to transform conflicts and encourage peaceful and non-violent behaviours (Lederach, 1995). These projects rarely act as a sole agent of change. They serve as a prominent influence factor in complex social systems that together can induce change (Severin and Tankard, 1992). How attitudes are structured and how they change, or resist change over time is understood through the study of various elaboration and validation processes. When people think carefully about a communication, their attitudes are influenced by their assessment of the substantive argument provided. When people are relatively unmotivated or unable to think, attitudes are influenced by simple cues in the persuasion setting that allow for a quick judgement (Petty and Briñol, 2015: 269). The amounts of consideration or deep thinking that is invested in the process determines not only the shift in attitudes but also their long-term retention (Petty and Krosnick, 1995). Differently put, the effectiveness of persuasive communication lies in the acceptance and internalization of the content and its messages. Acceptance is both a function of learning and retention (Hovland, Janis, and Kelley, 1953; Miller and Campbell, 1959; Watts and

McGuire, 1964; Greenwald, 1968; McGuire, 1968). Cognitive dissonance theory suggests that people will prefer to be exposed to information that is supportive or consistent with their current attitudes (Festinger 1957; Harmon-Jones, 2002). People might also seek out information that confirms with their prior beliefs. Conversely, people may seek out information that is non-supportive of prior beliefs if they are viewed as useful (O'Keefe, 2009).

In Macedonia, a 'building bridges theory' was at the heart of the programming focus around intercultural communication by the partner INGO. The media messages and peace education norms aimed at facilitating transformation in the attitudes held by children and young people across the ethnic divide (Salomon, 2011). Their aim was to build more frequent and positive intergroup interactions. In intergroup conflicts, changing attitudes can be challenging (Bar-Tal and Hameiri, 2020). Intergenerational trauma and personal as well as collective memory has a stronghold on the attitudes of the young (Bar-Tal, Diamond, and Nasie, 2017; Albarracin and Shavitt, 2018). In some respects, individual attitudes can become frozen and hard to reset.

In Sierra Leone, 'a shift in consciousness theory' was adopted by the country office to encourage a shift from violent to more peaceful behaviours at both the individual and the group levels (Allen Nan, 2010). High levels of violence witnessed during the civil war generated personal transformations for both civilian communities, and for the ex-combatants. People who share a significant experience like a civil war are known to develop a shared sense of social and political consciousness (Mannheim, 1988). Media messages around peace and reconciliation were intended to trigger a more collective transformation. Both individual attitudes and community attitudes were targeted through radio participation and open deliberation over the years. A collective consensus regarding peaceful behaviour was encouraged. How far were these efforts successful? Before examining this question, it is necessary to understand the differences between changes in norms and the shift in people's attitudes.

Norms and Attitude Change

Education and media-based sensitization, as part of attitude change campaigns that attempt to change individual feelings about specific behaviours, need to be distinguished from norm change campaigns that attempt to change the perceptions of others' feelings or behaviours (Tankard and Paluck, 2016: 187). Psychologists prioritize normative influence over attitudinal influence because individual's normative perceptions can be more malleable than their attitudes (Tankard and Paluck, 2016: 187–8). This is because individual attitudes are developed over a long period of time, and are closely linked to personal experiences or other well-developed religious or ideological beliefs. Attempts to counteract personal experience or longstanding beliefs can be more difficult and time consuming (Wicker, 1969).

Therefore, rather than attitude change, most post-war peace interventions seek to influence community members' perceptions of specific norms. Changing norms involves changing the normative belief ascribed to, and the motivation to comply with, existing referent objects (Tankard and Paluck, 2016). Adherence to a perceived norm is a more complex psychological phenomenon than simple observational learning (Bandura, 1971) or behavioural mimicry (Chartrand and Bargh, 1999).

Distinguishing attitude change from norm change can be critical for producing lasting peacebuilding legacies. Changed attitudes are not always reliable precursors of normative shifts. To change behaviour, perceptions of norms rather than the precursors of behaviour such as attitudes need to be targeted. Norm perception is a dynamic process. Social norms are standards of typical or desirable behaviour, and individuals' perceptions of these norms guide their personal behaviour. Therefore, influencing these perceptions is one way of creating social change (Chartrand and Bargh, 1999: 181). For the most part, individuals are motivated to understand what is normative in their home communities to create a sense of belonging; and to avoid social rejection (Blanton and Christie, 2003; Cialdini and Goldstein, 2004). Norms are not static rules of behaviour, learned once and internalized for posterity (Paluck and Shepherd, 2012).

Norm change interventions tend to target three key sources of norm perception, namely, individual behaviour, group summary information, and institutional signals. Individual perceptions of what is typical or desirable in their group encourage the tendency to conform with the existing social norms. Any deviation from group norms can elicit punitive results, whether in the form of social sanction, distancing, or other kinds of physical or material sanctions (Miller and Prentice, 1996). Individual behaviour is also shaped by the beliefs and choices of social influencers or social referents. Social referents can be both real and fictional, and can range from political and social leaders to fictional characters on radio and television (Paluck 2009a, 2010b).

Two general models of norm change are relevant here. First, 'a social norms model, and a group influence model' (Sherif and Sherif, 1953), and second, 'a model of individual beliefs and learning' (Hovland, Janis, and Kelley, 1953). A 'social norms model' recommends targeting the normative climate of relevant social models whereas, a 'learning and belief model' recommends targeting individuals' ingrained beliefs and values (Paluck, 2009b: 591). Because, attempts to counteract personal experiences or longstanding beliefs can be more difficult, and may also take more time (Tankard and Paluck, 2016: 183), peacebuilding radio often targets the normative climate within which individual beliefs are sustained. This was the case in Sierra Leone where a social norms model and a group influence model was applied. In Macedonia, by contrast, a learning and beliefs model targeted children's ingrained beliefs and values through the bilingual immersion groups. The power of group social norms in influencing intergroup relations was under-emphasized across the spectrum of peace education, media, and theatre projects implemented by the country office. This had implications for norm persuasion as elaborated later.

Media Persuasion and Peace Education for Norm Messaging

Weaving persuasive messages into the storylines of television dramas has been effective in shifting people's attitudes, beliefs, and intentions in several cases (see Schiappa, Gregg, and Hewes, 2006; Braddock and Dillard, 2016). Previous research shows that radio narratives can have a positive effect on the perceptions of social norms for intergroup interactions (Murrar and Brauer, 2019: 166). In postgenocide Rwanda, radio was found to have contributed to changes in individual behaviour, if not attitudes (Paluck and Green, 2009a). This was due to the dipping or elastic influence of media interventions. Their success in triggering norm change depends on various factors: first, the willingness of the audience to listen; second, their psychosocial response to the messages; third, the extent of mimicking of social influences and behaviours; and finally, the congruence between the new norms and the acceptable standards of behaviour (Singhal et al., 2006). Radio programmes in Sierra Leone presented 'bundles of ideas', wrapped up in advocacy packages. Through infotainment—drama, music, and live debates, fictional characters on *Atunda Ayen*da offered powerful social referents (Singhal and Rogers, 2002). They informed the audience members about the kinds of behaviours that were desirable, with varying degrees of persuasive influence.

Peace education interventions are known to differ in their effectiveness across different conflict contexts. Salomon (2006: 38–40) notes that individual's acquisition of conflict resolution skills through peace education can be more effective in ahistorical interpersonal conflicts, rather than in historically rooted collective conflicts. In the case of longstanding intergroup conflicts, peace education efforts must take account of the painful historical memories, and the collectively held beliefs about the 'other' ethnic group (Devine-Wright, 2001; Gunawardana, 2003). In Macedonia, without promoting changes in the exo- and macrosystems, without restructuring the relevant institutions, microsystem or interpersonal shifts encouraged through the introduction of prosocial behaviours generated superficial results. They could not promote changes in intergroup socialization. A broader transformation across the exo- and macrosystems was not realized (Bar-Tal and Halperin, 2009; Taylor, 2020: 132).

Second-Order Interpretations on Norm Persuasion and Attitude Change

Through second-order interpretations of the data, I analysed the ways in which the children and youth focused media and education norms contributed to more

Table 6.1 Second-order interpretation of norm concepts

Second-order interpretation	Norm concepts inSierra Leone	Norm concepts in Macedonia	Second-order interpretation
Access and acceptance	Information Sensitization Dependence	Language Intergroup contact Socialization	Intercultural communication
Agency and behaviour	Voice Capacity Participation	Enrolment Institutionalization Pedagogy	Quality pre-school education
Citizenship and democracy	Governance Accountability Elections	Segregation Integrated education Social cohesion	Citizenship and ethnic identity

peaceful attitudes and how far the adopted norms and learnt behaviours were re-tained over time. I coded the main themes emerging from the meta-ethnographic synthesis of the evaluation reports to identify nine learning concepts on norm transmission for each country (Table 6.1). I then combined these with the find-ings from the field interviews to analyse the reflections of young people about the effects of media persuasion and bilingual immersion on their attitudes to-wards peace. I followed Alfred Schütz's distinction between first-order constructs as reported in the interviews and evaluative data, and then applied second-order constructs based on my own interpretation and analysis of the data. As Schütz (1962: 59) puts it, 'the constructs of the social sciences are, so to speak, constructs of the second degree, that is, constructs of the constructs'. By applying Schutz's (1966: 116–32) strand of phenomenology, I interpreted the material in a way that offered me an understanding of the 'mental content of people's natural attitude' and possible shifts in response to the media and education-based norm persuasion efforts.

In the evaluative data, media-related persuasion was measured at various points through (1) radio listening surveys in Sierra Leone; (2) television audience surveys in Macedonia, and (3) behaviour changes during the different phases of bilin-gual immersion through the *Mozaik* groups. Given the lack of consistency in the methodology applied to capture the data in the evaluation reports, I focused on the prominent messages and themes delivered as part of the project aims. Scholars sug-gest that to elicit attitude change, the message source, target audience, and context of media-based persuasion should be accounted for (O'Keefe, 2009). In keeping with this approach, for the secondary analysis, I coded three elements: first, the normative arguments of the various projects; second, the basis for the arousal of specific discrete emotions; and third, the behavioural guidance advised by these productions. Once the prominent concepts emerging from the evaluative data across three categories in each case was identified, second-order interpretations were applied to organize them. The concepts included 'Intercultural Communication', 'Quality Pre-school Education', and 'Citizenship and Ethnic Identity' in Macedonia; and 'Access and Acceptance', 'Agency and Behaviour', and 'Citizenship and Participation' in Sierra Leone (Table 6.1). I discuss each norm concept in turn by analysing the persuasion effects at the level of the individual, and at the social or group level. I further examine their role in influencing young people's agency beyond the project timelines to assess cumulative effects and norm retention.

Macedonia

Intercultural Communication: Minority Language, Intergroup Contact, and Socialization

Exposure to conflict and violence can potentially enhance stereotypical thinking, elicit mistrust, and increase the political exclusion of the outgroup (Bar-Tal and Labin, 2001). Ethnic conflicts are deeply rooted in each side's collective narrative about their identity, aspirations, past and current history (Kupermintz and Salomon, 2005: 294). Time spent in the *Mozaik* groups had variable effects on improving intergroup contacts. In the initial years of primary school, alumni reported greater tolerance towards Albanian children. 'We lead separate lives, we don't mix, yet I feel differently from others in my high school. The other children have anger towards the Albanians.'[1] Over time, exposure to the monolingual instruction during the primary and secondary school years weakened these *Mozaik* values of tolerance. As a *Mozaik* alumni noted, 'when we were young, yes, there were differences with non-*Mozaik* children, as we grow older, there are not major differences, you would not be able to tell whether some children have been to *Mozaik* or not'.[2]

Socialized by grandparents, parents, teachers, and peers from an early age, Macedonian children learn to be wary of the other groups. 'The Albanians are untrustworthy and bad. They live and work here (in Macedonia), but they don't speak the language.'[3] Strong negative emotions, such as hatred, fear, and anger, interfere with the attempts to change attitudes (Eagly and Chaiken, 1993). They are transmitted intergenerationally through memories, experiences, and discursive interpretation of events by the older generation (Boulding, 1972). A teenage *Mozaik* alumni in Skopje who was born after the 2001 war noted that the 'Albanians for years have been trying to take away our country'.[4] It became

---

[1] FGD with *Mozaik* alumni, Debar, 5 September 2017.
[2] FGD with *Mozaik* alumni, Skopje, 8 September 2017.
[3] Primary school student, Skopje, 9 September 2017.
[4] FGD with *Mozaik* alumni, Skopje, 8 September 2017.

clear that the interethnic hatred and negative perceptions were less reflective of their own reality, but more a product of epistemic rigidity.

What then was the value added of the intercultural communication efforts? While contact interventions are known to be effective in reducing intergroup animosity in various post-war contexts, like in Rwanda (Paluck, Green, and Green, 2019), in Macedonia the results were less effective. At the individual level, exposure to the minority language and intergroup contact events increased basic awareness of the language, culture, and religious practices of the minority ethnicities. The dominant use of the Macedonian language in the groups by both teachers and the children created lopsided classroom dynamics. It reflected trends in intergroup interactions more broadly. At the group level, the ecological model of child development was not applied to the intercultural communication focused media and education projects (Jordan, 2005). Due to this, the *Mozaik* groups, and complementary media projects like *Nashe Maalo*, the Bridges for the New Balkans, and the Balkan Theatre Network had only limited persuasive effects on young people's attitudes and behaviours. Even when individual attitudes towards other ethnic groups shifted to more tolerant ones as a result of their exposure to the culture and perceptions of the minority ethnicities, they did not translate into an increase in interethnic contacts or friendships (Euro-Balkan Institute, 2006: 59).

The retention of edutainment messages on *Nashe Maalo* which targeted a wider audience was equally weak. This was due to the weak resonance and superficial adoption of the social cohesion norms that competed rather than conformed with existing beliefs. To be successful, intercultural communication efforts required the transfer of conflict resolution skills between collectives rather than between individuals (Coleman, 2003). Long-standing rifts between the ethnic communities weakened the persuasive appeal of media and education messaging. The anticipated negative social consequences arising from the adoption of new beliefs of intercultural tolerance dissuaded young people from adopting these values in the long-run. Young people conformed to the powerful norms of group social control in both the Macedonian and the Albanian communities. In fact, recent studies suggest that intercultural tolerance has waned (Topuzovska et al., 2019: 10; 45). Legal adoption of social cohesion and integrated education norms by the government were not reflected in the societal acceptance of these norms. Peace education and media projects were limited in their ability to persuade a shift in young people's attitudes towards more positive intergroup relations.

Quality Pre-school Education: Enrolment, Institutionalization, and Pedagogy

As one of the earliest projects on bilingual immersion, *Mozaik*'s appeal was rooted in the provision of quality preschool education, including a high teacher:student ratio, and high-quality teaching and learning resources. Pedagogical aspects around bilingual instruction were secondary considerations with regards to enrolment (Tankersley, 2001: 113). Therefore, the willingness of Macedonian parents to cross interethnic lines to enrol their children in *Mozaik* was not indicative of a newly found openness to the norms of intercultural communication or reflective of a positive shift in intergroup attitudes.[5] Following the institutionalization of the *Mozaik* groups into the state kindergarten system, the original emphasis on bilinguality and intercultural communication began to be diluted. Quality control of an integrated model of education within a segregated education system created further challenges. Compliance with national procedures, digital record keeping, and standardization did not account for *Mozaik*'s specificities such as the intercultural element. Teachers noted that 'institutionalization brought its own set of challenges... There was more administration, and more work with the increasing numbers of children. We had to observe the children, it was time-consuming and it complicated our work. We had to appease the state, and its bureaucracy.'[6]

The politicization of teachers' employment, particularly new recruitment, during the academic year 2010–11, reinforced intergroup schisms rather than transforming attitudes towards more peaceful relations. In Macedonia, state employment is politicized. State jobs are used as a carrot or a reward for political loyalty and candidates must enjoy the support of local political parties and government officials. Kindergarten teacher jobs represent secure government employment. They are highly coveted and accessed through ethnicized networks of political (and social) patronage. Recruitment decisions are not guided by criteria such as qualifications, experience, or expertise. Teacher recruitment can become subject to the whims of the local government, and to interethnic political competition. For example, if the local government is Albanian, then Macedonian candidates are not hired as teachers in the government schools.[7] For a programme such as *Mozaik* that was attempting to develop a model of bilingual, multicultural education, the question of teacher recruitment amplified interethnic schisms. It intensified competitive rather than peaceful attitudes.

Institutionalization weakened the pedagogical aspects as well. After the government made 100 days of pre-school attendance compulsory in 2012, children less than three years old were allowed to enroll if they were toilet trained. Younger children were less fluent in their mother tongue, and had a limited ability to learn a second language.[8] Little effort was made to extend the bilingual and dual teacher model of the *Mozaik* groups into the linguistically segregated state kindergarten system, creating inequalities in preschool education standards. These discrepancies in provision led to a further dilution of *Mozaik*'s norms and its persuasion

---

[5] Interview with external evaluator of *Mozaik*, Skopje, 2 September 2017.
[6] FGD with *Mozaik* teachers, Struga, 3 September 2017.
[7] Interview with external evaluator of *Mozaik*, Skopje, 2 September 2017.
[8] Interview with Macedonian teacher, Mozaik group, Struga, 3 September 2017.

effects. According to a 2010 OSCE report, only 26% of children in primary education, and 37% in secondary education interacted with non-ethnics in the school environment (OSCE, 2010, cited in Kavaja, 2017: 485). Without healing deep-rooted social schisms, integrated education initiatives like *Mozaik* can become technocratic processes that attempt to place the proverbial band-aid solution to deeply divided social configurations. Finally, long-term sustainability of a bilingual model requires continuous training for the kindergarten teachers. Pedagogical training when dependent on external funding can create gaps in the training provision (Baseline Survey, 2013). A shift to online training from 2019 onwards has opened up the possibility of a more sustainable and cost-effective model for the government (CCG, 2019). The long-term effects of the pedagogical aspects of the government's pre-school curriculum are yet to be ascertained.

Citizenship and Ethnic Identity: Segregation, Integrated Education, and Social Cohesion

In a multi-ethnic society, integrated education can act as a means to promote mutual cooperation and communication among the different ethnic communities, and help transcend 'superficial civility' (Krsterska-Papic and Zekolli, 2013: 135; Mac Ginty, 2014). Harmonious interethnic relations and trust among citizens are distinctive features of social cohesion (Green, Preston, and Sabates, 2003; Heyneman and Todoric-Bebic, 2000; Anger et al., 2010). My own research and the available scholarship suggest that the OFA was dualistic in its long-term effects. On the one hand, it provided greater protection for minority rights through its emphasis on education in the mother tongue; on the other hand, it also contributed to a deeper segregation of the educational system (Reka, 2008; Anger et al., 2010). At the policy level, the push for integrated education, intercultural communication, and social cohesion norms were reflective of the desire to conform to donor conditionalities. Improving the country's education system is seen as one of the pre-requisites for possible future accession to the EU and potentially to the NATO. While both ethnic Macedonians and ethnic Albanian elites have this interest in common, the contradictions in their respective nation-building projects have given rise to continuous political tension in the post-OFA period (Fontana, 2016b).

Deep-seated stereotypes, prejudice, and mistrust are difficult to resolve through the legal adoption of externally prescribed norms. Educational policies and practices around integrated education emphasize the integration of the minority group into the majority's social and cultural norms (Kirchberger and Niessen, 2011). Such a policy does not take account of how identities are understood and constructed in relation to matters of memory and citizenship, or how they evolve over time as the idea of the state is refined (Rothstein, 2005, cited in Aleksova, 2015: 60).

For example, in 2019, a new language law extends the official use of the Albanian language to the judicial system with the possibility of reversing judicial verdicts, if there is a lack of translation and interpretation facilities available during court proceedings. The law is opposed by the former ruling party, the Internal Macedonian Revolutionary Organization/Democratic Party of Macedonian National Unity (VMRO-DPMNE), the United Macedonia party, and the Left party. These parties and their vote banks adhere to the narratives from the communist era connected with the piecemeal accommodation of multiple identities with the state.[9] They stand at loggerheads with the policies of integrated education and social cohesion. While interethnic tensions have declined in terms of reported incidents of violence, a conflicted language segregation debate is reflective of the reality of social distance (Zembylas and Bekerman, 2013: 404). Such an approach only reinforces the status quo rather than encouraging societal transformation regarding interethnic attitudes. This is reflected in the educational segregation from primary school onwards that does not support or sustain the internalization of intercultural communication norms introduced through *Mozaik* and the complementary media projects.

Strained socialization dynamics across the ecosystem of children's social relations does not support a long-term shift in young people's attitudes towards harmonious interethnic relations. Children observe the behaviour and attitudes of elders and peers, imitate this, and thereby model their own behaviours and attitudes (Bandura, 1977). Whether the meso-system of teachers, parents, grandparents, and peers promote or oppose amicable interethnic relations can have a major influence on the ideas of children and young people (Van Balkom and Beara, 2012). In the post-2001 period, classroom separation has promoted social and cultural alienation instead of greater interethnic contact (Allport, 1959). Educational segregation and monolingual instruction continue to create negative lived experiences for children, which official policies on integrated education and social cohesion cannot mitigate (Deenen, 2015: 10). These frictions create the potential for further freezing the interethnic conflicts instead of supporting a positive transformation of intergroup relations (Du Pont, 2005).

Sierra Leone

Access and Acceptance: Information, Sensitization, and Dependence

In post-war Sierra Leone, peacebuilding efforts targeted young people through different projects offering vocational training, education, and leadership skills. These projects aimed at developing the capacity and skills of young people with the aim

---

[9] Skype interview with senior military officer from Macedonia, 17 April 2020.

of empowering them. The broad advocacy efforts notwithstanding, only a small percentage of young people had access to the training and capacity building efforts in real terms.[10] Those well-networked into the civil society sector would receive regular invitations to attend different workshops and training events. 'The same youth began to shop around between projects…this created a saturated bubble of some youth with greater access to peace projects than others.'[11] Exposure and access to advocacy and activism encouraged them to embrace a developmental culture. It led them to become citizen activists; others used their contacts to start their own local organizations where their entrepreneurial skills were tested.[12]

Radio presented lower barriers to access. Through a continuous and interactive process, audiences were persuaded to adopt a change in their attitudes and behaviours on a variety of issues. The main drawback with radio-based sensitization was the information provided; radio also told young people what choices were best for them. Prescriptive messaging brushed aside the nuances involved with life outcomes. Similar choices may not lead to the same outcome in every case, fomenting disappointment with what peacebuilding and development could realistically deliver in young people's everyday lives (Bangura, 2016). Peacebuilding norms created new expectations about how youth should be treated. They led to the desire amongst youth to be less marginalized and more central to decision-making. Improvement in their social status was less readily forthcoming, however. In applying a critical lens to social practices like child labour, radio-based sensitization did not take stock of the material and lineal interdependence in which generational responsibility and relations are embedded. Without changes in young people's access to resources such as land, and merit-based employment opportunities in the formal sector, the norms on rights and participation generated mixed acceptance.

At the individual level, acceptance was directly linked to the utility rather than the resonance with prior beliefs. This led to the instrumentalization of rights-based discourses amongst formerly marginal populations like youth and women, and resistance amongst elders and the traditionally powerful in society. Young people's attitudes to peace became tactical and ambivalent. The discourse on rights was invoked when relevant to furthering their interests. Youth chose conformity with the elders when compliance presented better livelihood opportunities as seen in the Pujehun example. Human rights-based approaches were irreconcilable with social control mechanisms that are culturally significant (Dixon, 2021: 35). Due to this resistance, radio sensitization could not persuade long-lasting change in the group norms. The diffusion of rights-based discourses created new forms of intergenerational tensions.[13] Youth and women's empowerment were seen as

---

[10] Interview with Country Director Sierra Leone Country Office, Freetown, 28 March 2017.

[11] Interview with National Youth Parliament Representative, Freetown, 22 March 2017.

[12] Interview with civil society activist, Freetown, 25 March 2017.

[13] Interview with female staff at local NGO established by a former GKN presenter, Freetown, 25 March 2017.

inimical to, and erosive of, established social norms around reciprocity, obligations, and hierarchy by the older generation. Community elders and chiefs perceived peacebuilding NGOs as socially disruptive. They were seen as pitting children against adults in the name of rights and empowerment, encouraging them to demand rights and opportunities from adults as a given, while denouncing the importance of traditional values and communal duties.[14]

Compliance in an external narrative of development acutely enhanced the dependence of rural communities on material support from donors, political patrons, and INGOs. 'Communities are not interested in how much funding is available, or the duration of project support, at the core of their expectation is some form of benefit, the insistence that interveners must help them.'[15] With patron–client relationships shifting to INGOs, a skewed relationship between the state and society developed. 'If a community requires textbooks for school, or tube-wells for safe drinking water they will go to ActionAid, rather than to the under-resourced local councillor or the inaccessible member of Parliament.'[16] This outcome was rooted in a deep-seated culture of dependency, of seeking help from the more resourceful in society. 'If one is successful, there is an expectation that you will need to give back to the community in the form of material support.'[17] When NGOs become the primary go to for support, they assume the role of caretakers instead of families, thus weakening the existing social capital. While intending to help, NGOs inadvertently caused harm. They cannot offer sustained support given their transient presence (Dolan, 2009; Branch, 2011). With the family and elders replaced by civil society actors as the primary providers of social care and support, additional layers of complexity were added to the pre-existing fissures in intergenerational relations.

Agency and Behaviour: Voice, Capacity, and Participation

The norms around *voice, capacity,* and *participation* transmitted through the radio programmes encouraged youth agency or the capacity to think and act independently, to make choices, and operationalize those choices in their everyday lives. Youth agency interacted with radio-based persuasion and community-based norm change campaigns to determine attitudes.[18] Previous studies on radio-based sensitization have found that if listeners think that the behaviours modelled in the radio dramas would not be effective in producing social change in their own context, they might not endorse these messages (Bilali and Vollhardt, 2015: 614).

---

[14] Ibid.

[15] Interview with a former GKN presenter who runs a local youth focused NGO, Freetown, 25 March 2017.

[16] Interview with staff, Institute for Governance Reform, 26 March 2017.

[17] Interview with a former GKN presenter who runs a local youth focused NGO, Freetown, 25 March 2017.

[18] For studies that examine how youth agency is framed and understood, see McEvoy-Levy, 2001, 2006; Del Felice and Wisler, 2007; Drummond-Mundal and Cave, 2007; Podder, 2015.

The second-order interpretation of the evaluative data confirmed this. Youth in Sierra Leone were fearful of adopting non-conformist attitudes particularly in rural settings where social control was stronger due to interdependent structures of family and kin relations. Corruption and neo-patrimonial control over resources like land by rural elites determined youth behaviour and capacity in ways that limited their ability to exercise agency. The other finding was that youth focused radio, while targeting a wide audience, did not address the priorities of the different youth constituencies and was therefore limited in terms of persuading economic, social, and cultural empowerment.

The scope of socio-political, economic, and cultural agency exercised by young people in the post-war period further determined the link between agency and behaviour. With regard to socio-political agency, local governance reforms opened up the political space, allowing youth to take an active part in public life. Through their participation in radio and community advocacy, children, and youth achieved a sense of inclusion, respect, and improved status in their communities. GKN encouraged more positive assessments of children's roles and talents' (SfCG, 2008/9: 1). Radio-based sensitization and community advocacy did not however persuade deep changes in post-war social relations around governance and participation. As we saw, women and youth were rarely included in deliberations around the land deals (Daley and Pallas, 2014; Millar, 2015). Their status as land users engaged in subsistence farming was subject to the landowner's willingness to provide them with access to the land (Marfurt, Käser, and Lustenberger, 2016: 290, 293).

LSLAs disempowered youth. Loss of arable land led to an out-migration of young men and women from rural communities to use land in adjoining chiefdoms. This created added burdens for their aging parents, spouses, and children.[19] Edutainment programmes like *Bush Wahala*, increased the knowledge of the rural communities regarding land ownership; it enabled non-violent mediation, by proposing dialogue as an alternative to conflict, thereby contributing to a shift in overt behaviour such as violent attacks (Baú, 2019: 383). In terms of the broader internalization of accountability norms regarding land acquisition, NGOs like Green Scenery and legal groups like Namati played an important role through dialogue, legal action, and the legitimate representation of local grievances. The knowledge gained through radio programmes, and the success of legal action to reverse land grabs as seen in the Port Loko example, had direct and persuasive effects on young people's approach to political violence. The use of judicial processes has encouraged a shift from violent to non-violent youth agency in the socio-political sphere.

In terms of economic agency, in the post-war period many youths were systematically disadvantaged or discriminated against on the basis of their role during the conflict. With limited access to education and formal jobs, large numbers of ex-combatants took to bike riding. The traffic police would arrest them or seize

---

[19] Skype interview with staff, Namati, 9 October, 2020.

their bikes for non-compliance with the traffic regulations. As the riders were largely uneducated, they turned to wartime social networks and support from their military commanders to understand and comply with the traffic rules. The conflict between the bike riders and the police wardens was resolved through donor funded conflict resolution trainings. Radio programmes such as *Traffic Kotoku* and *On the Road* generated public awareness of the rights and duties of both riders and their civilian clientele. The BRU and its leadership initially seen as a counterweight to patrimonial politics have been co-opted into the national political dynamics due to the large vote bank they represent. The BRAs have developed links to the chiefs, and to political and commercial elites as their patrons. In important ways the functioning of these associations is guided by the mutual obligations between these patrons and their youthful clients (Fanthorpe and Maconachie, 2010). Political interference in the national delegate elections including police arrests of candidates in December 2018 point to the growing politicization and a return to neo-patrimonial control (Sierra Network Salone, 2018).

Political party loyalism has eaten deeply into student life as well. Clashes between youth and the police in the towns of Kabala (2016), Kono (2012, 2013), Tonkilili (2012), and Bo (2017) are indicative of this trend.[20] In terms of cultural production, up until the 2007 elections, locally produced music on politics enjoyed great popularity. Pop songs such as 'Corruption' by Daddy Saj, 'Wake up' by Steady Bongo, and 'The System' by Jungle, appealed to a wide audience. Radio programmes were developed along similar themes, *Accountability Now* being an example of this trend. Protest music served as a powerful informal opposition, ushering political change in 2007 (Kandeh, 2008: 627; Shepler, 2010: 627–8; Stastik, 2016: 215–20). Once in power, the APC, which had effectively used protest music to win the 2007 elections against the SLPP, clamped down on its production (Stastik, 2012: 100–5). Politicized music abruptly dropped in popularity, as the political climate and tolerance for protest music waned, creating new controls on youth's cultural production.

Citizenship and Democracy: Governance, Accountability, and Elections

In Sierra Leone, politics and youth mobilization into violence have a closely intertwined history. Urban youth have been instrumental for the political elite, as thugs for the ruling party, and as political labour for decades before the civil war (Abdullah, 2002: 24–5). Socialization into violent party politics often became a route to upward mobility in a rigidly hierarchical social system (Christensen and Utas, 2008: 518). Relations of reciprocity and dependence between 'big' and 'small' people meant youth mobilization into the conflict, and in post-civil war politics

---

[20] Interview with Former Commonwealth Youth Caucus Sierra Leone Representative, and World Peace Prayer Society peace representative, Freetown, 27 March 2017.

had deep structural continuity. Youth participation in elections was less attuned to their citizenship and the exercise democratic rights and more about employment and social mobility (Hoffman, 2011; Enria, 2015). Donor assistance for democracy promotion was prominent from the 2007 elections onwards. Donors supported the National Election Commission and underwrote 70% of the cost of the elections. The Sierra Leone country office and its partners received funding to support voter education, voter registration, and to sensitize youth towards non-violent participation. Community radios proved quite effective in publicizing locally relevant information, neutralizing the effects of rumours and hearsay, reducing the chance of riots and public violence as a result (Sesay and Hughes, 2004: 136). Youth noted that they would take the money or alcohol offered by the politicians, but would not engage in violence on their behalf.[21]

From 2004onwards when decentralization and local governance reforms were afoot, voter apathy among the youth was very high. Informing young people about the importance of peaceful participation in elections and the judicious application of their political franchise was a major focus of community engagement and training efforts. Radio persuasion has played an important role in enhancing voter knowledge about the electoral process, and about the right to demand effective governance. Over the years, Sierra Leone has had regular national and local elections, with declining rates of electoral violence. Every election since 2004 has been used by the voters to hold their leaders accountable. Political turnover is high, with a reported 65–70% turnover in Parliament (2017).[22] This ability to raise questions and reflect on the performance of elected elites was a direct result of radio-based sensitization (SfCG, 1998; Shepler, 2010: 627; Taouti-Cherif, 2008). High political turnover has prompted a shift in the composition of the political elite. A new class of elected MPs from the civil society sector and the diaspora have started replacing Paramount chiefs as the traditional political class. This trend has been accompanied by a growing demand for accountability and transparency around electoral mandates. The evidence suggests a positive shift in young people's attitudes towards peaceful democratic politics and meaningful electoral participation. Although such a shift has not been able to reform the political culture. Lack of clear intergenerational transition of political power means that youth continue to rely on political party affiliation and political leaders for access to resources, reinforcing some of the neo-patrimonial trends around dependence that fuelled the civil war.

The Limits of Persuasion and Young People's Attitudes to Peace

From this analysis, we can conclude that attitudes are formed through both direct and observational experience. Social factors and social learning are important

---

[21] Interview with male local NGO staff, Freetown, 26 March 2017.
[22] Interview with staff, Institute for Governance Reform, 26 March 2017.

variables in determining prior beliefs (Slovak, Carlson, and Helm, 2007; Choe, Zimmerman, and Devnarain 2012). Existing norms affect how any new or emergent norm may be interpreted and evaluated. To be sustainable, new norms must fit coherently with existing norms and become embedded in the normative structure of the specific web of beliefs and social institutions (Florini, 1996: 376). When new norms are at loggerheads with social control mechanisms, they are unlikely to be adopted in any meaningful way. If norms resonate strongly with prior beliefs or if they are seen as beneficial in advancing the rights and voices of young people in local settings, they are more likely to be adopted. Once institutionalized in the public discourses and policies, norms only become powerful if they introduce practices to induce new patterns of behaviour and not just attitudes. Low resonance means norms may not be institutionalized as pockets of resistance, rejection, or alternative ideas are possible. Institutionalization is complete when there is both high norm resonance and the internalization of norms, not only at the individual, but also at the societal or group level.

In Sierra Leone, behaviour change communication focused heavily on targeted messaging. Radio triggered an instrumental adoption of the norms around issues of human rights, education, gender, and governance by women and youth, because these norms proved empowering for them. The older generation were less receptive to adopting the recommended behaviours concerning child abuse, child labour, and various SRH practices as these were seen to be at loggerheads with domestic social norms and practices. This was also the case with equitable access to land resources. Rural chiefs rarely consulted women and youth during land deal negotiations that affected their lives and livelihoods adversely. Obedience, subordination, and respect for the community's authority structures, and dependence on the part of youthful clients were valued over youth's independence and agency. In the case of elections and youth participation in electoral violence, the relevance, frequency, and consistency of messaging led to greater internalization, norm retention, and transformative behaviours. Through IRN and their network of community radio partners, messages around elections and electoral behaviours were effectively linked between the national and local media levels. Through meet-the-candidate events and district-level electoral debates, advocacy was combined with grassroots participation and reflection. By promoting a collective shift in societal norms around peaceful electoral participation, individual behaviour could be enforced more effectively.

In Macedonia, attempts to create intergroup trust through structured contact had limited long-term effects. Changes in young people's behaviours are linked to both contact quality and contact quantity (Binder et al., 2009). Structured contact through *Mozaik* and complementary intercultural communication programmes like the NDC and USAID funded IIEP projects involved a mix of virtual contact (social media), para-social contact (positive media portrayals of intergroup relationships), and extended contact (through friendships or positive relationships with an outgroup member) (Berger et al., 2016: 2). The contact initiatives were mostly ad hoc or short-term in nature with little follow-up. They emphasized more on virtual and para-social contact than on extended contact. The emphasis on assessing individual-level transformations overlooked the connection between the outcomes for individuals at the micro-level, and the outcomes that influence the consolidation of peace at the macro-level (Gürkaynak et al., 2008). Families were only indirect targets of the media and peace education-based persuasion efforts. In a society where the agency and capacity of young people to adopt norms were constrained by familial values and interactions, retention of norms took place at a rhetorical or superficial level, even when legal adoption of externally promoted concepts such as integrated education and social cohesion followed. Norm change and implementation across society was restricted to weak internalization and low resonance, and only a superficial adoption of these norms.

In conclusion, media and education programmes alone may not bring about more peaceful attitudes among children and young people. They must incorporate an ecological model of child development, targeting different actors at different levels through multilevel programming if they are to foster attitude change across society. In more closed societies, characterized by exclusive forms of social capital such as Macedonia, media and peace education were less influential in eliciting conformist attitudes (Salomon, 2004; Tropp et al, 2008; Romer et al, 2009; Taylor et al, 2019b). To effect long-term norm change, the peace education and complementary media and theatre projects needed to target group perceptions on intercultural interaction, rather than targeting other precursors to behaviours such as shifting social attitudes through increased intergroup contact (Paluck, 2009b: 594–600). Radio and media related work were more influential in shaping citizens' perceptions and attitudes to new ideas around rights, participation, democracy, and governance in societies with lower resistance to external norms such as Sierra Leone (McCombs and Shaw, 2017). From an attitude change and norm persuasion perspective, Sierra Leone presents a case of mixed acceptance of external norms, with high acceptance amongst children, youth, and women of the norms around human rights, accountability, and good governance that helped empower their position in society. These same norms fomented resistance from elders and traditional authority figures, who lost power following decentralization and local government reforms in the post-2004 period.

Finding ways to sustain the ripple effects of peacebuilding programmes requires dedicated, long-term, and institutionalized support for young people (Helsing et al., 2006: 196). In Macedonia, without capitalizing on the ripple effects emanating from individual or micro-level transformations in attitudes and beliefs, it was challenging to ascertain how far the norms that influence individual attitudes can reach others who did not participate in these programmes. Recent studies on the multiplier effects of peace education projects have shown that when alumni engage in further peacebuilding activities in their communities (see, Lazarus, 2011;

Ross and Lazarus, 2015; Ross, 2017; Cromwell, 2019: 62), the meso-level of the community acts as a bridge between the micro and the macro levels. Links with *Mozaik* alumni for scaling up and sustaining effects were not tapped until much later in the project life-cycle. Follow-up with the participants in the media and theatre projects was also limited or piecemeal at best. This did not allow multiplier effects that could strengthen the norm retention process to be generated (d'Estrée et al., 2001: 108). Given these dynamics, media and peace education programmes can only be as strong as the social institutions and the legal, political, and economic processes that assist in transforming conflicts (Bratić, 2008: 501). Without adequate follow-up, supportive national institutions, and normative resonance with the prevailing societal systems, the values and norms transmitted through peace projects often become obscure or lost over time. As a result, the persuasion effects of media and peace education in shaping young people's attitudes towards peace can often be transient or limited rather than enduring and transformative.

Conclusion
Transforming Peacebuilding
for Transformative Peace

The long-term effects of peacebuilding are often unpredictable. With children and young people, this is more the case because of the transitional nature of their experiences. As Deborah Durham (2000: 113) notes, being young is less about a specific age group: youth are social shifters; their experiences are not just relational and contextual, they are linked to the structural barriers that enable or withhold their access. I vividly remember my interview with the Minister of Youth and Sports in Liberia in 2009. She had served as the Country Director of World Vision in Liberia, prior to taking up the post of Minister. Several years of peacebuilding experience had exposed her to some hard truths about the ins and outs of post-war peacebuilding. During 2009, the reintegration of the residual caseload of ex-combatants was underway. Keeping ex-combatants and at-risk youth off the street through stop-gap training, animated the worldview of donors and policymakers (Jennings, 2008; McMullin, 2013). Yet as the Minister admitted, those attempting to target specific caseloads were well-aware that societal needs in a post-war society cannot be disaggregated. All young people in Liberia who have lived through the civil wars faced similar problems. They all had psychosocial needs, had missed normal social institutions like schooling, and few had meaningful livelihood prospects. Therefore, in a sense, they were all war-affected, whether they could take part in the formal processes of reintegration through DDRR or not.

The Minister admitted candidly that good intentions may not always translate into effective outcomes. Peacebuilding activities that try to build a young person's capacity and employability through a nine-month-long skills training intervention falter when young people are faced with the harsh socio-economic realities. 'A young man (ex-combatant) is trained in masonry, and after nine months he feels confidence in himself and goes out there (to work), but finds there is no job for him. Who is going to trust him and say come and fix my fence? So, the next thing he does, is to sell the tools, and you will find him sitting in the streets jacking people. The people in this country do not trust the young people, they prefer

Peacebuilding Legacy. Sukanya Podder, Oxford University Press.
© Sukanya Podder (2022). DOI: 10.1093/oso/9780192863980.003.0008

giving their jobs to older people who they have known for many years.'[1] Powerful words, which I did not fully grasp at the time. My study of peacebuilding legacy has made this observation far more meaningful today. I understand more clearly that peacebuilding remains effectively a patchwork of projects that create friction, and at times confusion for local communities (Millar, 2013). The expectations generated by peacebuilding activities encourage unrealistic ideas about how individuals and communities will move forward in their lives. Peacebuilding programmes create the hope for fresh opportunities, access to services, and sustainable livelihoods even when the state is indebted to donors and remains mired in corruption and incapacity (Bangura, 2016). The disappointment that follows reminds us of what historian Jay Winter (2006) describes as 'minor utopias'. Peacebuilding need not be utopian however. As this book has demonstrated, pursuing transformative peacebuilding through technocratic peacebuilding can be possible if technical activity is incremental, long-term, and committed to a change in both norms and attitudes, individually and intergenerationally.

Effective peacebuilding requires flexibility, responsiveness, adaptation, and creativity. It demands the ability to pause and think. Local agency, institutional capacity, and resilience are enablers for peace. Equally important is the understanding of how the local norms and practices shape individual and group attitudes. Ensuring norm resonance of projects and supporting local values and structures, rather than replacing them with externally imported models, can become the most effective route to sustainable peace. In 2017, the UN Secretary General Ban Ki-Moon advanced 'inclusivity' as a peacebuilding priority. Some would say, to be inclusive, peacebuilding practice must make use of local knowledge in reshaping and reconstituting peacebuilding (Danielsson, 2020: 1087). Peacebuilding must be dynamic, emergent, co-constituted, responsive. International peacebuilders must move away from being the providers or the imposers of external knowledge, to themselves becoming more open to epistemic transformation.

Shifting peacebuilding from an externally guided activity that imports Western norms and structures to one that is locally produced, requires the blending of international and local knowledge and practices including the institutions and norms that resonate with the local populations (Donais, 2012; Paffenholz, 2016). Such a shift would provide a more contextually relevant remedy. Timely exits can be planned through a rigorous commitment to internal learning and reflection, which help peacebuilding INGOs to develop their strategic thinking around handover and succession; and through the adoption of long-term and indigenous monitoring tools that assess the effects of peacebuilding efforts, even after donor funding for projects has ceased. Such an approach will allow both continuation and sustainability of project learning for the national partners. Planning

---

[1] Author interview with the former country director of World Vision Liberia and Minister of Youth and Sports during 2009.

transitions responsibly with indigenous monitoring and feedback mechanisms in place is critical for developing strong legacies.

In this concluding chapter, I revisit the main arguments of the book by examining the logics of institutional, normative, and organizational legacy operative across the suite of children and youth focused media and peace education projects in Sierra Leone and Macedonia. This sets up the discussion for exploring how far these logics present broader conceptual, methodological, and analytical value for peacebuilding practice. Relying on the book's theoretical and empirical insights, larger debates around the need for youth inclusion in peacebuilding are debated. The findings urge a shift from instrumental to transformative participation of young people as part of peacebuilding programmes. In terms of practical implications, the findings encourage greater vertical and horizontal integration of young people's participation in peacebuilding; a stronger engagement with the formal sphere; intergenerational responsibility; repairing state–citizen relations; and adopting an ecological model of peace.

The Study of Peacebuilding Legacy: Conceptual and Analytical Dimensions

This book set out to explore the potential within technocratic peacebuilding for a more transformative peace. The intrinsic tension between the short-termism that plagues how peacebuilding is designed, executed, and evaluated; and the long-term and evolutionary nature of conflict transformation led me to ask how do we go about understanding the legacy of peacebuilding efforts? To answer this, the book first developed the concept of peacebuilding legacy. By identifying the binaries between the technocratic and transformational dimensions of peacebuilding through the lens of time, transformation, and intergenerational peace, I explored the conceptual dimensions of legacy.

First was the concept of time in peacebuilding. Time in transformational peacebuilding is flexible and non-defined, while technocratic peacebuilding is time-bound, crafted into the straitjacket of six, nine, and twelve-month project cycles. The latter aligns with the bureaucratic clock time adopted by donors and implementing partners. It privileges policy time through periodic financial reporting upwards towards donors in place of local accountability to the very people that peacebuilding seeks to benefit. Much of the time of doing peacebuilding then is about performance. It is about the showing of doing. Peacebuilding INGOs spend considerable energy documenting different activities and meeting budgetary reporting and M&E requirements. They are engaged in doing peace as an impatient peace. Rarely is there the time to look back, to follow up, to try and understand how the lives of their project participants and beneficiary communities were transformed, if at all.

The second concept for conceptualizing peacebuilding legacy was conflict transformation. Reeler (2007) stresses that transformation is embedded in shifting relationships and change that affects society at a more systemic level. Most peacebuilding projects are about 'programming for change'; they seek change in instrumental ways, as projected in the theory of change underlying a specific project effort. The aim is to achieve a particular outcome rather than to think about the sequencing, timing, or the cumulative effects of the different projects. Without repeated interventions, the transformative effects are limited. Any short-term changes dissipate once project funding runs out, and beneficiaries tend to fall back on their basic social learning. So fundamentally there is a misalignment between what the principles and priorities are in terms of how donors are funding peacebuilding versus how the implementers can actually try and effect a transformational or long-term change.

Finally, there is the concept of intergenerational peace. In many of the intractable conflicts of our time, for example in Afghanistan, Palestine, Kashmir, and South Sudan among others, the conflicts have changed over time and across generations because they are so long drawn out. Peacebuilding efforts, while targeting the younger generation, can often overlook the important socialization roles played by the older generation in shaping their perspectives on peace and conflict. To be effective, peacebuilding efforts have to respond to the different generational needs for peace. Conflict transformation demands a long-term commitment to youth led and adult supported processes that emphasize youth inclusion and not simply donor facilitated participation in short-term projects (Prelis, Shelper, and Sankaituah, 2012: 4; UNOY Peacebuilders, 2018). As seen in the examples from Sinjo and Bamba, a lack of trust in the political elites, and public institutions meant that many young people choose to distance themselves from the government and from formal agencies, which can be self-defeating in the long run. Without establishing a two-way communication between the young people and the adults, and without repairing state–citizen relations, the gains of short-term technocratic peacebuilding will not be transformative or long-lasting (Von Kalteborn-Stachau, 2008: 2).

To measure legacy, I relied on three qualitative cues; together they offered a heuristic analytical framework for examining the long-term effects of peacebuilding in terms of norms, institutions, and organizational practices. The first cue was norm transmission: resonance and retention. I argued that how far the norms introduced by peacebuilding projects actually resonate in the local setting determines whether they are retained by the beneficiaries and by the communities of intervention. Missing resonance can become a major constraint to norm adoption both at an individual and at the group level. As we saw, early years bilingual immersion programmes in Macedonia resulted in only partial and at times transitory improvements in intercultural communication. When intergroup relations are strained due to structural problems concerning history, power-sharing, and identity politics, young people's involvement in structured intergroup interactions without addressing the deeper issues amounted to delivering band-aid solutions. In Sierra Leone, post-war development of civil society emphasized bottom-up advocacy and participation of marginalized groups like women and youth in politics and governance. While well-intended, these efforts were largely confined to the informal sphere and did not link into the formal sphere. The tendency to 'instrumentalize' or even 'programmatize' youth's political participation without any meaningful youth involvement in the formal institutions of policy-making had negative consequences for young people's peaceful attitudes. Youth focused programming did not translate into a meaningful transformation of young people's lives and livelihoods over the long-term (Altiok and Grizelj, 2019). It is important therefore to contextualize youth-focused programming to seek transformative participation and structural changes through young people's meaningful inclusion and involvement.

The second cue was the institutionalization and adaptation of project models through their successful handover to national agencies, whether government departments or successor NGOs. While capacity-building of local partners is often part and parcel of peacebuilding delivery, rarely do implementing agencies commit to the institutionalization of peacebuilding gains. Unless the learning from various projects is adapted into national systems, programmatic continuity and the sustainability of efforts will be lost. For institutionalization to succeed, proper investment of time and resources is necessary. Domestic actors need time to adapt projects and structures into their national systems, and in line with national normative frameworks. Handover or transition to national actors can also enhance the local ownership and resonance of these efforts. Institutionalization as a goal was absent in Sierra Leone, but present in Macedonia where the *Mozaik* model was adopted by the government into its national preschool curriculum. A narrow programming focus—namely preschool bilingual immersion groups—meant that there was a cumulative momentum, and continuity, which ultimately resulted in the incorporation of these groups into the national kindergarten system. The third cue was organizational learning and reflection from the M&E of peacebuilding projects. The cumulative evidence available in the institutional memory, including the human memory of staff, offers valuable evidence accumulated over multiple years of operations in a particular country.

Without an explicit organizational commitment to learning, valuable lessons can be lost. Capturing the long-term effects at an organizational level would require follow-up research with the beneficiaries of the various peacebuilding projects. It would also require committing resources for undertaking longitudinal studies. The findings suggest that peacebuilding INGOs and their local partners can often confuse information with wisdom, i.e. the raw material that enters the learning system, with the systematic filtering and analysis of this information for effective comparison or generalization (Edwards, 1994). To ensure that information does not disappear into organizational blackholes or remain lodged in the head of one or two individuals, appropriate methodologies such as meta-ethnographic synthesis for analysing the data is needed. Learning collaborations with academics can help combine the power of field presence and grassroots work with detailed analysis and rigorous enquiry (Schön, 1987; Edwards, 1997: 248). These collaborations can push INGO learning from experiential or learning-by-doing to more reflection-in-action focused approaches.

Operationalizing the Logics of Legacy for Peacebuilding Practice

How far do the logics for conceptualizing and measuring peacebuilding legacy have broader conceptual, methodological, and analytical value for peacebuilding practice? I examine the implications by structuring the discussion around the institutional, normative, and organizational aspects of peacebuilding legacy.

The Institutional Aspects of Peacebuilding Legacy

The legacy of the peacebuilding interventions stemming from the multi-year children and youth focused media and education projects in Sierra Leone and Macedonia presented different trajectories and influences on the behaviours relating to conflict resolution and peacebuilding between individuals and groups. The media projects in both countries presented a more dispersed legacy. In Sierra Leone, the development of IRN and the community radio infrastructure which has played an important role in electoral advocacy presents an important although unintended institutional legacy for the domestic media landscape. The prominence of *okada* riding in the post-war years has seen organization of the bike riders into various structures including the BRU, offering another example of an accidental institutional legacy. In Macedonia, the commitment to institutionalization held the key to building a stronger institutional legacy for the *Mozaik* bilingual immersion groups. This was not the case with its media and theatre projects however. Having the clear objective of some kind of handover to the government or a successor, local organization encourages local ownership. It helps in sustaining project-related gains. Two areas require future investment by peacebuilding actors. First is linking informal advocacy with formal systems; and second is ensuring both the material and non-material resonance of their projects.

Linking Informal Advocacy with Formal Systems

Much of the work of INGOs in local communities is weakly integrated into national systems. Most projects focus on social peacebuilding through advocacy, sensitization, training, and intergroup dialogue (Schirch, 2008). While advocacy and sensitization are important for introducing new ideas, these emphasize the normative rather than the institutional dimension of long-term change. There is an over-reliance on temporary institution-building as part of social peacebuilding. Structures like youth groups, women's groups, microcredit associations, and child welfare committees last only as long as project funding lasts. Unless successful peacebuilding models and temporary structures created during the lifecycle of peacebuilding projects are transferred or adopted into formal systems, the micro successes cannot be formally linked into macro-level change (Smith, 2004). This may require thinking about institutional links into the formal realm early in the life-cycle of peacebuilding programming. By building in the involvement of government departments into the project design at the inception stage, an invested peace constituency becomes an involved actor (Lederach, 1997: 96). This involvement can evolve into the phased handover of the project learning or the project model to national actors, whether government departments or local successor organizations in the civil society sector prior to exit.

Material and Non-material Resonance

Successful institutionalization requires adjusting and balancing prescriptive and elicitive models with locally resonant ones at both the material and non-material levels (Funk, 2012). Material aspects include developing viable funding strategies through government investments to support the transition of peacebuilding projects into national systems. Non-material aspects include resonance of the project design with the local culture and context. As we have seen, donors and their implementing partners can take the good intentions of their programmes as self-evident without seriously considering the degree to which these resonate with the history, culture, and norms of the local actors (Donais, 2009: 20; Autesserre, 2014). We have also seen that unless exogenous concepts relate to, or resonate with local values and norms they are likely to demonstrate weak retention. Their ability to trigger transformative effects with regard to young people's values and attitudes towards peace will be limited at best. Given this reality, the findings underline the importance of considering both the material and non-material aspects of institutionalization for a more sustainable peace (Lewis, 2003: 3).

The Normative Aspects of Peacebuilding Legacy

Through second-order interpretation of the meta-data, I examined attitude change in terms of how far the norms that were transmitted through the media and peace education projects led to a substantive change in terms of young people's attitudes towards peace. I found when norms resonated strongly with local settings and did not contradict local value systems, they were more likely to be retained and adopted in ways that contributed towards a stronger peacebuilding legacy. Once institutionalized in public discourses and policies, norms become even more powerful, in so far as they can induce or introduce new patterns of behaviour and not just attitudes. This is likely when there is high norm resonance and internalization of norms not only at the individual, but also at the societal or group level. In Macedonia the bilingual immersion groups with their emphasis on integrated education and intercultural communication attracted a lot of attention from parents because there was a real gap in terms of quality preschool education at the time the *Mozaik* groups were introduced.

The normative emphasis on bilingual instruction and intercultural communication was of secondary importance for children's enrolment into these groups. At the policy level, the external push from the EU and the OSCE among other donors for adopting integrated education and social cohesion concepts at the policy level meant that integrated education became an explicit part of the national education policy. At the societal level, however, the norms around social cohesion and intercultural communication had weak norm resonance. This gap between the normative purpose of the *Mozaik* groups, the motivation of the parents for enrolling their children, the policy rhetoric on integrated education, and the reality of limited intergroup socialization led to a degree of normative dissonance. Structured intergroup contact through peace education programmes was only partially helpful in reducing prejudice and biases. In identity-based conflicts characterized by interethnic difference, existing values and norms can hinder peaceful relations between groups. Children's choices remain embedded in their family context.

Enhancing trust and empathy through structured intergroup contact had limited long-term effects in transforming intercultural communication. Even when there was legal adoption into government policy, there was limited internalization or retention of these norms. In most cases, intergroup socialization dynamics mimicked the local social capital dynamics. In areas like Debar, children continued to socialize after the *Mozaik* years, due to the close family relations and the historical nature of amicable Macedonian–Albanian relations. In Skopje and Struga, once children entered monolingual instruction from the primary school onwards, they became socially distant and lived separate lives. Due to the limited opportunities for intercultural socialization between the families, the norms around intercultural communication introduced in the *Mozaik* kindergartens weakened more rapidly.

Unlike the peace education project in Macedonia, media programming in both Macedonia and Sierra Leone presented more dispersed results with regard to norm retention and attitude change. Radio and media can be powerful in shaping citizens' perceptions and in influencing their attitudes in societies with lower resistance to external norms. Radio-based sensitization was very effective regarding the advocacy around human rights, accountability, and electoral participation in Sierra Leone. Youth's participation during elections was an area that demonstrated consistent advocacy and discernible progress in terms of more peaceful attitudes. Because of the intergenerational nature of the conflict, youth and women who have traditionally been marginalized in society readily adopted the discourse on human rights, and related behaviours that helped them come forward and voice their concerns. In this sense, there was an instrumental adoption of those norms that favoured or furthered their status in society. Norms that were prescriptive or inconsistent with local values, such as the ban on child labour and the school attendance of pregnant teenagers, did not elicit any discernible change in group attitudes.

Media-based persuasion was less effective in generating attitude change in Macedonia, where the society is characterized by exclusive forms of social capital. The media projects like *Nashe Maalo*, the Bridges for the New Balkans, and the Balkan Theatre Network, had low norm resonance and did not fully reflect the reality of segregated social relations. Even when individual attitudes towards other ethnic groups improved through structured exposure to the culture and perceptions of the minority ethnicities, these did not translate into an increase in interethnic contacts or friendships (Euro-Balkan Institute, 2006: 59). Group social norms were more dominant in Macedonia. Children to a large extent conformed with what was normative in their communities. Their social interactions with other ethnicities were influenced or shaped by the views and values of their families. For media-based persuasion to be more effective, an ecological conception of child development was necessary (Jordan, 2005). In terms of the lessons for broader peacebuilding practice, the findings around the normative elements of peacebuilding legacy offer two prominent recommendations.

Norms Transmission, Resonance, and Retention is Intergenerational

Genuine and transformative shifts in social attitudes take time and must address the question of intergenerational peace. The sociologist Mannheim (1988) argued that people who share a significant experience like a civil war develop a shared sense of social and political consciousness. The vision for social change is therefore generational. Each generation develops distinct attitudes and values to issues such as building sustainable peace. Young people's peacebuilding experiences are situated within a social landscape of power, rights, expectations, and perceptions. Without adopting an ecological model of child development, peacebuilding norms can have limited influence. Without triggering a shift in broader social attitudes, and without securing the buy-in of the older generation, young people's ideas around social transformation will remain resistant to, rather than aligned with, an adult supported vision of change.

Policy Articulation is Not the Same as Norm Internalization

Top-down shifts in national policies based on donor agendas present elite acceptance of peace norms that can be superficial and transient. A specific political party
or leader can align their policies and pronouncements with external expectations
around donor promoted norms. Changes in the leadership or in political dynamics
can weaken the transformative power of norms as articulated in national policies.
Peacebuilding actors need to engage with the norm resonance and internalization
dynamics. A more bottom-up and locally resonant agenda around peace norms
is necessary for an incremental, gradual, and substantive shift in young people's
attitudes towards peace.

The Organizational Aspects of Peacebuilding Legacy

With regard to the organizational aspects of peacebuilding legacy, several important takeaways arise. First, it is anticipated that organizations that prioritize
advocacy and international linkages with the goal of becoming a movement for
change will present a very different learning profile compared with organizations
that maintain a focus on operational work and internal management of information requirements (Edwards, 1997: 246). In a similar vein, when an organization is
learning-oriented and is concerned about the legacy and sustainability of its programmes, it will pursue a different trajectory of exit and handover compared with
a more 'practice-' or goal-oriented organization that is rooted in the present and
committed to short-term goal seeking. In the case of the partner INGO, an explicit
commitment to learning at an institutional level did not however translate into an
equal commitment at the country office level. The evidence suggests variable levels
of commitment to learning and reflection between the two country offices. In some
respects this is understandable. The pressure of delivering on activities and outputs
in a time-bound fashion means that the more reflective elements of learning from
doing, such as revisiting theories of change and following up with beneficiaries,
became secondary or simply overlooked. Between the two case studies, the Macedonia country office presented a more committed approach to institutionalization
and high levels of staff continuity. The Sierra Leone country office presented a
more learning-oriented approach; it was more willing to adapt in response to various recommendations made by internal and external evaluations. In both cases,
exit planning was delayed and succession elements less structured than would be
necessary for building a strong organizational legacy.

   Second, across the sector, there is a tendency to prolong country operations,
to seek funding reactively in response to evolving donor themes. Such a reactive
fundraising strategy can lead to an ad hoc or scattered programming timeline.
Peacebuilders need to make the short-term positive effects of their projects last.
Lund (2003: 3) notes that, "when energies are dispersed in hundreds of different

directions... myriad of activities ...not guided by [an] overall strategy," it results in an inchoate legacy. Even when specific projects are successful in their immediate and short-term objectives, these micro gains may not be reflected in terms of systemic or macro-level change (Ricigiliano, 2015: 8). Peacebuilding INGOs need to think about legacy early by dedicating resources to PCEs, and through the development of successor organizations. Planned exits can strengthen the organizational legacy of peacebuilding CSOs in important ways. Timely exit strategies aid in terminating projects before they start waning (Hayman et al., 2016). They help take stock of not only the immediate impact of a project, but also both its intended and unintended outcomes. It can encourage the sharing of knowledge and know-how between peacebuilding organizations, and a more explicit and prolonged commitment to the development of local partners. Without timely exits and planned succession, communities tend to fall back on their basic social learning and this can result in a lost opportunity, of not quite harnessing the potential within technocratic peacebuilding for transformative peace.

Third, learning and reflection has different meanings depending on the location of the civil society actors. While there is an upward trend in both interest and investments, to encourage organizational learning in the Global North, learning practices among Global South partners to foster transformative and systemic change continue to play catch-up (Buchy and Ahmed, 2007: 360, 371). For transformative effects to take place, learning is not simply about producing and collating new knowledge by the Global North organizations; it is also about knowing and interpreting the knowledge in ways that enhance local awareness of peacebuilding legacy (Wood, 2020). Reflective practice allows peacebuilding INGOs in the Global North to think through the immediate and more long-term effects of their activities and choices. It also helps interrogate their thought processes, values, prejudices, and habitual action, in ways that can enhance sustainability and transfer of their learning to Global South partners (Bolton, 2005: 7). How can this process of knowledge transfer be strengthened and decolonized? (See Ndlovu-Gatsheni, 2021.) From this research, I would argue that INGOs and their local partners can create learning links between the communities and national and external stakeholders in several ways. This includes (1) documenting field level processes through learning diaries, to develop the habit of documenting change on the part of the field staff (Buchy and Ahmed, 2007: 366–8), and (2) maintaining continuity with local partnerships to contribute towards their long-term capacity building for possible handover or succession.

Documenting Field Level Changes

For organizations to learn, the learning from the field level needs to be fed back into the strategic and policy level actions. This process is not without its own complexities. Field staff are not a homogenous category (Denskus, 2007a). They can include both country office staff posted across various field offices and staff affiliated with partner NGOs in the country of operations. Local partner NGOs can be nascent entities with limited experience (McMahon, 2017). As a result, their internal management systems, and information systems management processes can be weak. These factors create important hurdles for systematic documentation of field level changes in a consistent manner. Further hurdles include the predominance of oral traditions that can make documenting field experiences less appealing for the field staff. However, if learning takes place mainly through interpersonal interaction, it allows tacit knowledge, memories, and experiences to be shared only in passing, rather than captured more systematically (ALNAP, 2003: 58).

Even when field staff are in a position to serve as the best conduit for information and impressions from the beneficiaries to upper management levels, they may be selectively hearing and interpreting what is communicated from the communities without reflecting on their own biases (Edwards, 1997; 237). Critical reflection can be developed in two ways. First, by encouraging staff to question and to reflect on the social and field processes they observe, and second, by encouraging local partner NGOs to document field level observations amongst their own staff, and amongst the local communities where they implement projects (Brehm, 2001; Kurian and Kester, 2019). Learning diaries can allow learning to be made into an explicit objective of peacebuilding work for staff across the local, national, and international levels (Smillie, Hailey, and Hailey, 2001: 71).

While critics would dismiss journaling as anecdotal, unscientific, and invalid, the limited educational attainment, and the considerable resource and time constraints faced by the field staff, would suggest that on balance learning diaries can offer a cost-effective way for capturing the developments on the ground (Verkoren, 2010: 805). Through the adoption of simple, more locally grounded measurement indices, local staff and the beneficiary groups, can think through, reflect on, and make sense of their experiences without the requirement of learning new or complex measurement systems (Firchow, 2018). To facilitate a higher order of learning, simple processes of coding events in the short-term such as timelines and ranking exercises can also be linked into the evaluation efforts over time to measure long-term changes (McDaniels and Gregory, 2004).

Continuity in Local Partnerships

Peacebuilding INGOs are often unable to sustain the short-term positive impacts of their projects because they overlook the importance of creating links between their grassroots work (through advocacy, activism, community engagement), and the larger socio-political systems (patronage, party politics, ethnicity), and institutional structures (formal and informal) in which they are embedded (Edwards and Hulme, 1992). Local NGO partners can become important intermediaries, bridging, or support organizations (Brown, 1991; Caroll, 1992; Brown and Kalegaonkar, 2002), that offer the necessary links between local actors and global actors through learning or feedback loops (Sanyal, 2006: 67). Consistent and meaningful knowledge transfer between the local and the global, however, requires continuity with local partnerships and steadfastness of purpose. By shifting from a project approach to a programme approach, peacebuilding INGOs must seek greater coherence in their activities (both locally and thematically). Finally, peacebuilding INGOs from the Global North must not only support capacity development of the Global South partners, but also invest in joint activities by developing shared programming objectives with the partner (OECD, 2010: 10).

The Sierra Leone country office invested in developing a core group of local partners like IRN, NEW, and CCYA, as part of various funding and consortia arrangements. This allowed the pooling of diverse expertise and the establishment of long-term collaborations. Through these enduring relationships, the country office contributed to the capacity-building of its local partner organizations over multiple years. In Macedonia, continuity and knowledge transfer was created through the involvement of teachers, professionals, and trained participants for earlier efforts into the later *Mozaik* groups, and the different media and theatre productions. The partnership with the OFF schools for community outreach activities with the *Mozaik* alumni was another area of partnership continuity. The willingness and ability to develop reliable and long-standing local partnerships enhanced both the creative and adaptive learning behaviours. They contributed towards strengthening the organizational legacy of multi-year programming efforts, even when explicit succession and exit plans were not in place.

The above reflections on the concept and logics of peacebuilding legacy, and their wider practical implications, lead me to arrive at a number of intriguing and noteworthy conclusions for peacebuilding programming with children and young people. Organized around four discussion points, this final part identifies areas for future innovation across both policy and practice.

Peacebuilding with Children and Young People: From Instrumental to Transformative Participation

1. Youth as Partners Rather than Targets

First, I would like to emphasize a necessary rethink around the targeting of young people through peacebuilding efforts in post-war societies. In both Sierra Leone and Macedonia, children and young people were the recipients of support, and the targets of various peace projects, rather than the authors of the liberal peace. In Sierra Leone, radio programmes provided youth with a platform to voice their concerns in an authentic manner. However, as we saw, including youth voices was only the first step towards their inclusion in politics and society. In many respects, their inclusion in peacebuilding projects led to instrumental rather than transformative participation (Becker, 2012: 7). This is because targeted support has some serious limitations with access, scope, and scalability that inhibit long-term change. In terms of access, the reliance on local NGOs to select participants for a youth programme, while beneficial in terms of tapping into existing networks, can exclude potential participants who are not part of the third party's networks. This was the case with the children and youth focused projects in Sierra Leone.

Then there is the question of scope. In Macedonia for example, the *Mozaik* project since its inception in 1998 has been attended by over 2,000 alumni. This is a fraction of the youthful population in a country with a 2.08 million strong population (Judah, 2020). From a programmatic standpoint, during its life-cycle, the *Mozaik* programme expanded its provision to include Macedonian, Albanian, Serbian, Roma, and Turkish children making the groups more representative of ethnic diversity. Although a well thought through step in terms of project expansion, the target of 2,000 children was still a very small number, given the large numbers of children requiring similar support. Therefore, even if programmes like *Mozaik* continue for a long time, unless they are replicated across the entire spectrum of pre-school educational provision, they can only reach a limited number of children and their families. This limited access would mean a large majority would continue to be left out of any direct exposure to the norms around intercultural communication. Therefore, the inadequate scale or the inability to scale and sustain scaled efforts is an important limitation of targeted support. Without grounding peacebuilding processes in young people's realities as a whole; without including different categories of youth in the design of projects so that their varied needs are met, peacebuilding cannot offer a more sustainable solution (De Houwer et al., 2013; Ebenezer-Abiola and Moore, 2020: 12).

When funders prefer partnering with larger, more established CSOs and national governments to secure their buy-in, they further diminish youth participation in peacebuilding (Ebenezer-Abiola and Moore, 2020: 4). This is because rarely is the direct mobilization of youth through centralized youth focused structures like National Youth Commissions considered by donors and their implementing partners. Youth-led organizations are also frequently overlooked. The grassroots entrepreneurship of young volunteers and youth start-ups are stymied by their limited access to resources and donor funding streams (Okumu, 2019). Youth as partners in peacebuilding would require donors to invest into small-scale, locally run programmes over longer timelines. For INGOs that focus on youth issues, instead of targeting them, they need to funnel donor funding to support the development of youth-led and youth serving initiatives in a consistent manner to create stronger peacebuilding legacies.

2. Youth as Agents of Change

Donor-funded projects enhance youth dependence on transient humanitarian aid networks, while weakening the role of more permanent caregivers like the family and the community. Dependency on aid enhances laziness or the perceptions of laziness instead of young people's productivity. It encourages a focus on acquiring skills and knowledge that are disconnected with the social context and that have little sustainability in terms of livelihood generation (Sakue-Collins, 2021; Dixon, 2021). Simply documenting youth experiences or involving children and youth in media production and delivery does not translate into transformative social and educational capital or create sustainable livelihoods (Soep, 2006a, 2006b; Hauge, 2014: 471). Normatively, projects can promote values that are often at loggerheads with the cultural knowledge and associational behaviour held by the older generation. Then there is the question of inclusion. Woodman and Bennett (2016) emphasize the transience of youth, the diversity of youth perspectives and experiences, arguing for broader conceptual and practical frameworks when engaging young people (McEvoy-Levy, 2006; Sommers, 2015). In practice, individual youth, youth groups, and communities will not experience inclusion in the same way because of the intersection of other potential power inequalities in society such as race, class, gender, culture, and language (Jennings et al., 2006: 50–3; Berents and Mollica, 2021).

Peacebuilding efforts do not automatically lead to a change in the locus of control and the distribution of power in society (Denskus, 2007a). Without identifying and addressing power asymmetries and abuses we cannot have transformative peacebuilding outcomes. If peacebuilding is conceptualized in terms of rebuilding a social contract and strengthening state–society relations, then larger structural questions concerning how power is exercised, allocated, and controlled cannot be separated from, and indeed can become central to, wider peacebuilding challenges (McCandless et al., 2015: 3–5). Thania Paffenholz (2015: 89), argues that what matters is meaningful inclusion, which in important ways is also about true citizenship. Roger Hart's (1997) ladder of participation which ranks participation from decorative to more meaningful ones can be instructive here. The peace education and radio programmes examined in this book fall within the lower rungs of Hart's ladder of participation. What we need are higher levels of partnership that allow youth groups and organizations to become co-implementers of peacebuilding efforts. Such an approach squarely puts youth in a leadership role, and encourages active youth participation beyond project lifecycles. Such high levels of participation depend to some extent on how youth are integrated across the vertical and horizontal socio-political realms.

Vertical integration implies youth engagement in governance through their participation in decision-making processes at the community and national levels.

Vertical integration is an inherently political project. It involves an intentional rebalancing of power, by strategically leveraging, and or limiting the power of higher-level actors, facilitating inclusivity, and or working iteratively towards these purposes (McCandless et al., 2015: 5). Horizontal integration includes supportive friendships, peer socialization, and the membership of various associations. Studies have found that a denser associational life among youth could enhance both horizontal and vertical social capital (Maclay and Özerdem, 2010: 348). The assumption that young people who take part in peacebuilding activities can become empowered as constructive change agents in society through civic engagement is to a large extent misplaced (Chirot and McCauley, 2006; Chaskin et al., 2018).

Given their short-term and stop-gap nature, most peacebuilding projects end up appropriating youth to serve the agenda of neoliberal interests by ensuring diverse participation without delivering long-term solutions to intergroup and intergenerational differences, or generating more sustainable forms of support. In this sense, peace projects can contribute towards remarginalizing youth (Sukarieh and Tannoch, 2008: 301; Hilker and Fraser, 2009: 9; Enria, 2015; 2018). Therefore, from a policy perspective, what is necessary is not simply inclusion; rather enabling youth's change agentry by supporting youth actions that can trigger changes in organizational, institutional, and societal structures and politics (Hart and Tyrer, 2006: 8; Drummond-Mundal and Cave, 2007: 65). Unless youth experience positive individual outcomes incrementally through participation and success in community change efforts, persuasion through media and advocacy will have limited long-term effects on their attitudes towards peace (Jennings et al., 2006: 36–46).

For peacebuilding practice, this would mean a shift away from merely investing in training youth in peacebuilding and conflict resolution behaviours, through implicit engagement. What is needed is explicit engagement, an incremental model whereby the training is utilized and applied in the everyday. In simple terms, while training youth in peacebuilding is important, training without opportunities to practise the skills learnt is not so helpful. Training young people in conflict management or mediation skills for example is a start. Supporting them as young mediators is the next step, and ensuring they have a role to play in local communities as community-mediators can further strengthen their role. Community youth mediation networks if recognized by formal organizations like the Ministry of Justice as legitimate sources for managing local grievances, can help reduce the caseloads for the formal courts system. This type of systematic thinking and long-term vision of linking the formal and the informal is how we can bank on peacebuilding interventions to promote further development in society and in governance (Podder, Prelis, and Sankaituah, 2021). This is how young people, instead of becoming instrumental agents for peacebuilding rhetoric, can become the agents of peace themselves.

3. Integrating Youth Activism into the Formal Sphere

Informal ambiguous forms of youth agency such as brokering between communities and local state actors, protesting dysfunctional state institutions, and providing community security through vigilante groups, may consolidate peace at a local level but for the most part youth activism in the informal sphere keeps them at the margins of society (Jeffrey and Dyson, 2014). Similarly, democratic rights and participation can in theory be empowering for youth in post-war societies; practising democracy through learned behaviours however takes time, as does the willingness, opportunity, and confidence to engage with formal processes (Sukarieh and Tannock, 2008; Kurtenbach and Pawelz, 2015). The relationship between the state and youth is often characterized by tension and distrust. Formal mechanisms and institutions like national youth councils, youth parliaments, and youth commissions can be tokenistic, exclusive, or politically aligned. There is also widespread prejudice or biases expressed by the formal institutions and authorities about youth's involvement in the civic space. Youth subcultures whether music groups, sports associations or street gangs, thrive at the margins of mainstream society. They create spaces for youth to apply their subaltern agency (Maira and Soep, 2005; Podder, 2015). Circumventing the formal sphere by forming associations that allow youth to operate independently or exclusively in the informal realm can result in either marginalization or the eventual co-optation in neo-patrimonial societies. This was exemplified with the BRU in Sierra Leone.

The route of avoidance or rejection of the formal sphere does not however support the goal of sustainable peace. Vivek Maru, the founder of Namati, the legal empowerment organization behind the successful land grab reversal in Port Loko, notes that, even when the political system is corrupt and the leaders cannot be trusted, it is important not to abandon the formal political institutions including the justice system. People can be empowered to transform those institutions to make them fair, more accountable, and more democratic (Maru, 2019). In that same vein, youth must interact with, and adapt to post-war politics in ways that allow them to survive and potentially thrive. On the part of the formal institutions, there is a need to examine the attitudes, ideas, and actions related to power-sharing. Adults need to share power with youth in ways that shift the assumptions about adult privilege, superiority, and wisdom (West, 2007). Instead, adults need to encourage and allow young people's creativity, energy, and responsibility to manifest fully by drawing on adult experiences and mentorship (Wheeler, 2003: 7). Intergenerational responsibility is important for addressing structural barriers to youth inclusion and their ability to exercise agency in the formal sphere. From restricted access to land use and land ownership as seen in the case of Sierra Leone, to stifled political change and limited political turnover in Macedonia, young people face structural barriers to their full economic, political, and social participation and deep-seated inequalities over the distribution and access to public resources (Finn and Oldfield, 2015: 29–31).

By enhancing intergenerational responsibility and thinking forward about youth futures, donors, INGOs, and national governments must allow young people to have uninterrupted rather than ad hoc access to mentorship, capacity-building, and technical support. This requires a mutually constituted process of trust based partnering between the adults and the youth. Some degree of receptiveness to young people's self-identified needs and mutual understanding is necessary for collaboration to happen across generations (Oosterom, 2018: 23). Adults must be willing to facilitate and enable youth inclusion by adopting a critical lens towards the visible and invisible structures and processes that can exclude the youth from important social institutions and practices (Purdey et al., 1994: 330). This shift in adult attitudes will help foster youth's positive contributions to community development, socio-political change, and encourage a critical citizenry where youth feel valued, respected, encouraged, and supported.

4. Adopting an Ecological Model of Peace

Last, but by no means least, youth experiences of conflict and peace are embedded in the different ecosystems that influence and socialize them. These include the family, the community, schools, and peers. For transformative peace to take effect, supporting the social ecology of the family and the community and their traditions rather than transplanting them is important. Thorsen (2013: 206) suggests that households are sites of both joint and separate interests. They are also the safe place for the expression and articulation of politics (Azmi et al., 2013). An ecological model of peace identifies parents, peer groups, schools, and the media as the primary transmitters of social norms, and political orientations, as well as of prejudicial attitudes. When teaching and learning processes reproduce socio-economic, cultural, and political inequalities, peace education projects like *Mozaik* end up facilitating superficial interactions rather than transforming the structural issues that maintain intergroup distance (Keddie, 2012). For more sustainable outcomes, peace education efforts must address the issues of representation and reconciliation in deeply divided societies (Green, Preston, and Sabates, 2003; Novelli, Cardozo, and Smith, 2015: 4). They must adopt an ecological model of child development, one that addresses the peacebuilding needs of both the older and the younger generations.

An ecological model also requires strategic commitment, and an understanding of the complexity and long-term nature of peacebuilding. In post-war societies, young people experience the adult generation as a major obstruction to enjoying full citizenship and making the transition to adulthood. This is due to a discrepancy between what leaders might feel is best for youth, versus what the youth actually feel they need (Nordstrom, 2006; Otterbein, 2009; Borer et al.,

2006: 7). Therefore, the consideration of the needs of the youth raises predicaments, tensions, and contrasting ideas connected to identity, membership, mobility, and inclusion (Bayart, 1993; Donnelly, 1996; Bailey, 2005: 76; Collison et al., 2017: 224). In Macedonia, divisive educational and ethno-nationalist politics have created structural and intergenerational barriers to transforming young people's attitudes towards intergroup relations. In Sierra Leone, youth's inability to access basic resources to become independent adults prolongs their waithood. This condition of being stuck does not arise from their own failure to transition successfully into adulthood. It rather stems from the nature of the socio-economic systems that inhibit rather than facilitate their development into fully fledged citizens (Sommers, 2012: Honwana, 2014: 30).

Without removing structural violence and encouraging social justice, a transformative, sustainable, or what Johan Galtung terms as 'positive' peace cannot be achieved (Novelli and Smith, 2011: 12–13). This would require strengthening social capital connected to social networks, civic norms, social integration, community structures, and civic participation (Nicholson and Hoye, 2008). It would also require spatial inclusion: through the closing of social and economic distance; social inclusion through relational belonging and acceptance; and functional inclusion: through the enhancement of knowledge, skills, and understanding of peace norms, and of course political inclusion (Collison et al., 2017: 224). National youth councils, youth parliaments, sector-specific consultations, and the inclusion of youth representatives in formal peace processes, and local government structures are typical examples of state-led formal political mechanisms (Kester, 2010; Oosterom, 2018). Within these mechanisms, youth participation is often narrowed down to youth being consulted as the users of key services rather than having a more influential, political voice (Checkoway and Gutierrez, 2006; Percy-Smith, 2010).

Youth's political citizenship can allow young people to have a real influence to shape or produce a favourable outcome in society (Checkoway, 2011: 341). Azmi et al. (2013) argue that young people's political agency needs to be seen in relation to the possibilities they find when civic space is restricted due to violence or state repression, as confrontational tactics may not work. Intergenerational dynamics are part of the power dynamics that shape local state–society relations. In Sierra Leone, some youth have challenged clientelism in the post-war years, yet many youths are also aware of the necessity of being part of the political patronage dynamics to secure their own interests. They must compete to have their share of the patronage linked benefits (Pratten, 2006: 720). Given these structural realities, changes in the attitudes of children and young people towards peace are triggered not by pursuing a programming for change strategy. Rather, when there is tangible social, economic, and political change, access to formal channels of participation, meaningful inclusion, and the ability to access sustainable livelihoods, a more substantive change in young people's attitudes towards peace takes root. It requires adult commitment to change and a striving for intergenerational peace. It requires thinking about the long-term effects of peacebuilding and its legacy.

Bibliography

Abbink, G. J. 2005. Being young in Africa: The politics of despair and renewal. In: Abbink, G. J. and van Kessel, I. (eds), *Vanguard or Vandals: Youth, Politics and Conflict in Africa*. Boston: Brill Academic Publishers, pp. 1–34.

Abbink, G. J. and van Kessel, I. (eds), 2005. *Vanguard or Vandals: Youth, Politics and Conflict in Africa*. Boston: Brill Academic Publishers.

Abdalla, A., Shepler, S., and Hussein, S. 2002. Evaluation of Talking Drum Studio – Sierra Leone. online at https://www.sfcg.org/wp-content/uploads/2014/08/sierra.pdf (17 January 2021).

Abdullah, I. 1991. The Colonial State, Mining Capital and Wage Labor in Sierra Leone, 1884–1945. *PhD diss.*, University of Toronto.

Abdullah, I. 1998. Bush path to destruction: The origin and character of the revolutionary United Front/Sierra Leone, *Journal of Modern African Studies 36*(2), pp. 203–35.

Abdullah, I. 2002. Youth culture and rebellion: Understanding Sierra Leone's wasted decade. *Critical Arts 16*(2), pp. 19–37.

Abdullah, I., Bangura, Y., Blake, C., Gberie, L., Johnson, L., Kallon, K., Kemokai, S., Muana, P. K., Rashid, I., and Zack-Williams, A. 1997. Lumpen youth culture and political violence: Sierra Leoneans debate the RUF and the civil war. *Africa Development 22*(3/4), pp. 171–215.

Abess, G., Marcarthy, J., and Konneh, A. 2018. *End of Project Evaluation. Standing Together for Free, Fair and Peaceful Elections in Sierra Leone*. September. Freetown: SfCG.

Abou Assi, K. and Trent, D. L. 2016. NGO accountability from an NGO perspective: Perceptions, strategies, and practices. *Public Administration and Development 36*(4), pp. 283–96.

Acharya, A. 2004. How ideas spread: Whose norms matter? Norm localisation and institutional change in Asian regionalism. *International Organisation 58*(2), pp. 239–75.

Acharya, A. 2011. Norm subsidiarity and regional orders: Sovereignty, regionalism, and rule-making in the third world. *International Studies Quarterly 55* (1), pp. 95–123.

Acharya, A. 2013. From the Boomerang to the Banyan: The diffusion of human rights norms reconsidered. Paper prepared for the Conference on Human Rights Futures. New York: Columbia University, 15 November.

Acharya, A. 2014a. Who are the norm makers? The Asian-African Conference in Bandung and the evolution of norms. *Global Governance: A Review of Multilateralism and International Organisations 20*(3), pp. 405–17.

Acharya, A. 2014b. Transnational civil society as agents of norm diffusion. In: Hall, R. B. (ed.), *Reducing Armed Violence with NGO Governance*. Abingdon: Routledge, pp. 97–113.

Active Learning Network for Accountability and Performance in Humanitarian Action (ALNAP). 2003. *ALNAP Review of Humanitarian Action 2003: Field Level Learning*. London: Overseas Development Institute.

Adam, B. 1990. *Time and Social Theory*. Cambridge: Polity Press.

Adam, B. 2004. *Time*. Cambridge: Polity.

Adebajo, A. and Keen, D. 2000. Banquet for warlords. *The World Today 56*(7), pp. 8–10.

Ahmed, F., Dillan, H., and Robinson, J. 2018. Planning for success from start to exit. On-line at https://www.peacedirect.org/us/wp-content/uploads/sites/2/2018/09/Planning-for-success-FINAL.pdf (accessed 28 January 2021).

Akobeng, A. K. 2005. Understanding randomised controlled trials. *Archives of Disease in Childhood 90*(8), pp. 840–4.

Albarracin, D. and Shavitt, S. 2018. Attitudes and attitude change. *Annual review of Psychology 69*, pp. 299–327.

Aldrich, D. P., 2012. Radio as the voice of God: Peace and tolerance radio programming's impact on norms. *Perspectives on Terrorism 6*(6), pp. 34–60.

Aleksova, A. 2016. Strengthening teaching and learning practices to support Roma students in Macedonia. Skopje: Macedonian Civic Education Center (MCEC) at http://www.edupolicy.net/wp-content/uploads/2016/10/MCEC_Anica_Aleksova.pdf (accessed 12 June 2020).

Aleksovska, M. 2015. Trust in changing institutions: The Ohrid framework agreement and institutional trust in Macedonia. *East European Quarterly 43*(1), pp. 55–84.

Allen Nan, S. 2010. Theories of change and indicator development in conflict management and mitigation. United States Agency for International Development. http://pdf.usaid.gov/pdf_docs/PNADS460.pdf.

Allport, G. W. 1954 *The Nature of Prejudice*. Reading, MA: Addison-Wesley.

Allport, G. W. 1959. Religion and prejudice. *Crane Review 2*, pp.1–10.

Altiok, A. and Grizelj, I. 2019. We are here: An integrated approach to youth-inclusive peace processes. New York: Office of the Secretary General's Envoy on Youth, April, available at https://www.un.org/youthenvoy/wp-content/uploads/2019/07/Global-Policy-Paper-Youth-Participation-in-Peace-Processes.pdf (accessed 9 November 2020).

Alvik, T. 1968. The development of views on conflict, war, and peace among school children: A Norwegian case study. *Journal of Peace Research 2*, 171–95.

Anderson, M. B. 1996. Humanitarian NGOs in conflict intervention. In: Crocker, C.A., Hampson, F. O., with Aall, P. (eds), *Managing Global Chaos: Sources of and Responses to International Conflict*. Washington, DC: USIP Press, pp. 343–54.

Anderson, M. B. 2004. Experiences with impact assessment: Can we know what good we do? In: Bloomfield, D, Fischer, M., and Schmelzle, B. (eds), *Berghof Handbook for Conflict Transformation*. Berlin: Berghof Research Centre, pp. 193–206.

Anderson, M. B. and Wallace, M. 2013. *Opting Out of War: Strategies to Prevent Violent Conflict*. Boulder, CO: Lynne Rienner Publishers.

Anderson, M. B., Chigas, D., Olson, L., and Woodrow, P. 2004. *Reflecting on Peace Practice Handbook*. Cambridge, MA: Collaborative for Development Action. Online at https://www.cdacollaborative.org/wp-content/uploads/2017/01/Reflecting-on-Peace-Practice-RPP-Basics-A-Resource-Manual.pdf (accessed 16 January 2021).

Andrews, M., Pritchett, L., and Woolcock, M. 2013. Escaping capability traps through problem driven iterative adaptation (PDIA). *World Development 51*, pp. 234–44.

Anger, J., van't Rood, R. A. and Gestakovska, Z., 2010. Learning study on the achievements and experiences of projects on inter-ethnic education and youth work in Macedonia. *Sida Review*. Online at https://www.sida.se/contentassets/65e16b53d4a94b36a677501d5f525 41d/14995.pdf (30 January 2021).

Aniekwe, C. C., Hayman, R., Mdee, A., with Akuni, J., Lall, P., and Stevens, D. 2012. Academic-NGO collaboration in international development research: A reflection on the issues. DSA sponsored working paper. Online at https://www.intrac.org/wpcms/wp-content/uploads/2016/09/Academic-NGO-Collaboration-in-International-Development_September-2012.pdf (accessed 3 February 2021).

Archer, C. 1994. Conflict prevention in Europe: The case of the Nordic states and Macedonia. *Cooperation and Conflict 29*(4), pp. 367–86.

Archibald, S. and Richards, P. 2002. Seeds and rights: New approaches to post–war agricultural rehabilitation in Sierra Leone. *Disasters 26*(4), pp. 356–67.

Argyris, C. 1992. *On Organisational Learning*, Cambridge: Blackwell Publishers.

Argyris, C. and Schon, D. 1978. *Organisational Learning: A Theory of Action Perspective*, Reading, MA: Addison-Wesley Publishing.

Arraiza, J. 2014. Language education policies in Bosnia and Herzegovina, Macedonia and Kosovo. Different path towards separate roads: The language education policies resulting from the Dayton, Ohrid and Ahtisaari comprehensive agreements. *European Journal for Minority Questions 1*, pp. 8–19.

Atallah, D. G. 2017. A community-based qualitative study of intergenerational resilience with Palestinian refugee families facing structural violence and historical trauma. *Transcultural Psychiatry 54*(3), pp. 357–83.

Atkinson, J. and Scurrah, M. 2009. *Globalizing Social Justice: The Role of Non-government Organisations in Bringing about Social Change*. London: Springer.

Atkinson, P. A. and Coffey, A. 1997. Analysing documentary realities. In D. Silverman (ed.), *Qualitative research: Theory, method and practice*. London: Sage, pp. 45-62.

Autesserre, S. 2014. *Peaceland: Conflict Resolution and the Everyday Politics of International Intervention*. Cambridge: Cambridge University Press.

Autesserre, S. 2017. International peacebuilding and local success: Assumptions and effectiveness. *International Studies Review 19*(1), pp. 114–32.

Auyero, J., 2011. Patients of the state: An ethnographic account of poor people's waiting. *Latin American Research Review* pp. 5–29.

Axelrod, R. 2006. *The Evolution of Cooperation*. New York: Perseus.

Azmi, F., Brun, C., and Lund, R. 2013. Young people's everyday politics in post-conflict Sri Lanka. *Space and Polity 17*(1), pp. 106–22.

Baaz, M. E. and Utas, M. 2019. Exploring the backstage: Methodological and ethical issues surrounding the role of research brokers in insecure zones. *Civil Wars 21*(2), pp. 157–78.

Bächtold, S., 2021. Donor Love Will Tear Us Apart: How Complexity and Learning Marginalize Accountability in Peacebuilding Interventions. *International Political Sociology 15*(4), pp. 504–521.

Bah, A. B. 2013. The contours of new humanitarianism: War and peacebuilding in Sierra Leone. *Africa Today 60*(1), pp. 3–26.

Bailey, R. 2005. Evaluating the relationship between physical education, sport and social inclusion. *Educational Review 57*(1), 71–90.

Bajaj, M. 2015. 'Pedagogies of resistance' and critical peace education praxis. *Journal of Peace Education 12*(2), pp. 154–66.

Bajaj, M. and Brantmeier, E. J. 2011. The politics, praxis, and possibilities of critical peace education. *Journal of Peace Education 8*(3), pp. 221–4.

Bakiu, B., Dimitrova, M., and Brava, A. 2016. How to achieve a truly integrated education in the Republic of Macedonia. Skopje: EPI. Available online at https://epi.org.mk/docs/D4V_Social%20cohesion_eng.pdf (accessed 22 Jan 2021).

Bakonyi, J., 2018. Seeing like bureaucracies: Rearranging knowledge and ignorance in Somalia. *International Political Sociology 12*(3), pp. 256–273.

Ball, N. 1997. Rebuilding war-torn societies. In: Crocker, C. A., Hampson, F. O., and AalI, P. (eds), *Managing Global Chaos: Sources of the Responses to International Conflict*. Washington, DC: USIP, pp. 614–15.

Bamat, T. 2012. Reflecting on peacebuilding evaluation. DM&E for peace. Online at https://vimeo.com/44251645 (accessed 18 September 2020).

Bandabla, S. 2014. Equitable land rights promotion in three districts of Sierra Leone: Baseline Evaluation Report. March. SfCG West and Central Africa.

Bandura, A. 1971. *Social Learning Theory*. Morristown, NJ: General Learning Press.

Bandura, A. 1977. Self-efficacy: Toward a unifying theory of behavioural change. *Psychological Review 84*(2), pp. 191–215.

Bandura, A. 1986. *Social Foundations of Thought and Action*. Englewood Cliffs, NJ.

Bandura, A. and Walters, R. H. 1977. *Social Learning Theory*. Vol. 1. Englewood Cliffs, NJ: Prentice-Hall.

Bangura, I. 2016. We can't eat peace: Youth, sustainable livelihoods and the peacebuilding process in Sierra Leone. *Journal of Peacebuilding & Development 11*(2), 37–50.

Bangura, I. and Kovacs, M. S. 2017. Shape shifters in the struggle for survival: Warlord democrats in Sierra Leone. In: Themnér, A. (ed.), *Warlord Democrats in Africa: Ex-military Leaders and Electoral Politics*. London: Zed Books Ltd, pp. 177–98.

Bangura, Y., 2000. Strategic policy failure and governance in Sierra Leone. *The Journal of Modern African Studies 38*(4), pp. 551–577.

Banks, N. and Hulme, D. 2012. The role of NGOs and civil society in development and poverty reduction. *Brooks World Poverty Institute Working Paper* (171).

Bar-Tal, D. 2004. Nature, rationale, and effectiveness of education for coexistence. *Journal of Social Issues 60*(2), pp. 253–71.

Bar-Tal, D. and Halperin, E., 2009. Overcoming psychological barriers to peacemaking: The influence of beliefs about losses. In Mikulincer, M. and Shaver, P.R. eds., *Prosocial motives, emotions and behavior: The better angels of our nature*, Washington, DC: American Psychological Association, pp. 431–448.

Bar-Tal, D. and Hameiri, B. 2020. Interventions to change well-anchored attitudes in the context of intergroup conflict. *Social and Personality Psychology Compass 14*(7). https://doi.org/10.1111/spc3.12534.

Bar-Tal, D. and Labin, D. 2001. The effect of a major event on stereotyping: Terrorist attacks in Israel and Israeli adolescents' perceptions of Palestinians, Jordanians and Arabs. *European Journal of Social Psychology 31*(3), pp. 265–80.

Bar-Tal, D., Diamond, A. H., and Nasie, M. 2017. Political socialization of young children in intractable conflicts: Conception and evidence. *International Journal of Behavioral Development 41*(3), pp. 415–25.

Barakat, S., Chard, M., Jacoby, T., and Lume, W. 2002. The composite approach: Research design in the context of war and armed conflict. *Third World Quarterly 23*(5), pp. 991–1003.

Barbieri, S., Bliznakovski, J., and Vrgova, R. 2013. *Overcoming Ethnic-Based Segregation: How to Integrate Public Schools in Macedonia and Bosnia and Herzegovina*. Skopje and Sarajevo.

Bardhan, P. 1997. Method in the madness? A political-economy analysis of the ethnic conflicts in less developed countries. *World Development 25*(9), pp. 1381–98.

Bargh, J. A. and Chartrand, T. L. 1999. The unbearable automaticity of being. *American Psychologist, 54*(7), pp. 462–79.

Barker, J. and Smith, F. 2001. Power, positionality and practicality: Carrying out fieldwork with children. *Ethics, Place & Environment 4*(2), pp. 142–7.

Barker, J. and Weller, S. 2003. 'Is it fun?' Developing children centred research methods. *International Journal of Sociology and Social Policy 23*(1), pp. 33–58.

Barnett, M. and Finnemore, M. 2004. *Rules for the World: International Organisations in Global Politics*. Ithaca: NY: Cornell University Press.

Barnett, M., Fang, S., and Zürcher, C. 2014. Compromised peacebuilding. *International Studies Quarterly 58*(3), pp. 608–20.

Barnett, M., Kim, H., O'Donnell, M. and Sitea, L. 2007. Peacebuilding: What Is in a Name? *Global Governance: A Review of Multilateralism and International Organisations* 13(1), pp. 35–58.

Basse, Y. O. 2016. 'Open for business': Promoting equitable land rights protection in Sierra Leone, Liberia and Guinea: Final Evaluation. October, Washington, DC: SfCG.

Bastian, M. 2014. Time and community: A scoping study. *Time & Society* 23(2), pp. 137–66.

Baú, V. 2019. Radio, conflict and land grabbing in Sierra Leone: Communicating rights and preventing violence through drama. *Media, War & Conflict* 12(4), pp. 373–91.

Bayart, J. F. 1993. *The State in Africa: The Politics of the Belly.* London: Longman.

Becker, J. 2012. *Campaigning for Justice: Human Rights Advocacy in Practice.* Stanford: Stanford University Press.

Begum, H. 2003. *Social Capital in Action: Adding Up Local Connections and Networks: A Pilot Study in London.* National Council for Voluntary Organisations. Online at http://eprints.lse.ac.uk/29402/1/Social_Capital_in_Action.pdf (accessed 12 January 2021).

Bekerman, Z. and Horenczyk, G. 2004. Arab-Jewish bilingual coeducation in Israel: A long-term approach to intergroup conflict resolution. *Journal of Social Issues* 60(2), pp. 389–404.

Bekerman, Z. and McGlynn, C. (eds). 2007. *Addressing Ethnic Conflict through Peace Education: International Perspectives.* London: Springer.

Bell, J., Hansson, U. and McCaffery, N., 2010. *The Troubles Aren't History Yet: Young People's Understanding of the Past.* Northern Ireland Community Relations Council.

Belloni, R. 2012. Hybrid peace governance: Its emergence and significance. *Global Governance: A Review of Multilateralism and International Organisations* 18(1), pp. 21–38.

Bellows, J. and Miguel, E. 2006. War and institutions: New evidence from Sierra Leone, *African Economic Development* 96(2), pp. 394–9.

Benner, T. and Rotmann, P. 2008. Learning to learn? UN peacebuilding and the challenges of building a learning organisation. *Journal of Intervention and Statebuilding* 2(1), pp. 43–62.

Benner, T., Binder, A., and Rotmann, P. 2007. Learning to build peace? United Nations peacebuilding and organizational learning: Developing a research framework. Online at http://edoc.vifapol.de/opus/volltexte/2008/662/pdf/berichtbenner.pdf (accessed 30 January 2021).

Benner, T., Mergenthaler, S., and Rotman, P. 2007. International bureaucracies: The contours of a (re) emerging research agenda. Paper presented at the German Political Science Association (DVPW) IR section conference. Darmstadt, 14 July. Online at http://citeseerx.ist.psu.edu/viewdoc/download?doi=10.1.1.614.2406&rep=rep1&type=pdf (accessed 12 January 2021).

Benzing, B. 2020. Whom you don't know, you don't trust: Vernacular security, distrust, and its exclusionary effects in post-conflict societies. *Journal of Global Security Studies* 5(1), pp. 97–109.

Berdal, M. 2014. Peacebuilding and development. In: Currie-Alder, B., Kanbur, R., Malone, D. M., and Medhora, R. (eds), *International Development: Ideas, Experience, and Prospects.* Oxford: Oxford University Press, pp. 362–78.

Berents, H. and Mollica, C. 2021. Reciprocal institutional visibility: Youth, peace and security and 'inclusive' agendas at the United Nations. *Cooperation and Conflict*, online first: 00108367211007873 (6 April 2021).

Berg, B. L. 2004. *Qualitative Research Methods for the Social Sciences.* Boston: Pearson Education.

Berger, R., Benatov, J., Abu-Raiya, H., and Tadmor, C. T. 2016. Reducing prejudice and promoting positive intergroup attitudes among elementary-school children in the context of the Israeli–Palestinian conflict. *Journal of School Psychology 57* (August), pp. 53–72.

Bergmann, W. 1992. The problem of time in sociology: An overview of the literature on the state of theory and research on the sociology of time, 1900–82. *Time & Society 1*(1), pp. 81–134.

Bertelsmann Stiftung's Transformation Index. 2018. Country Report Sierra Leone. pp. 1–37.

Betancourt, T. S. 2012. The social ecology of resilience in war-affected youth: A longitudinal study from Sierra Leone. In Ungar, M. (ed.), *The Social Ecology of Resilience: A Handbook of Theory and Practice*. London: Springer, pp. 347–357.

Betancourt, T. S., Borisova, I. I., Williams, T. P., Brennan, R. T., Whitfield, T. H., De La Soudiere, M., Williamson, J., and Gilman, S. E. 2010. Sierra Leone's former child soldiers: A follow-up study of psychosocial adjustment and community reintegration. *Child Development 81*(4), pp. 1077–95.

Betz, M. 2008. Media Sustainability Index. Sierra Leone. Online at https://www.irex.org/sites/default/files/pdf/media-sustainability-index-africa-2008-sierra-leone.pdf (accessed 12 January 2021).

Bidwell, K., Casey, K., and Glennerster, R. 2014. The impact of voter knowledge initiatives in Sierra Leone. Online at https://www.theigc.org/wp-content/uploads/2015/04/Bidwell-Et-Al-2014-Policy-Brief.pdf (accessed 12 November 2020).

Bieber, F. 2005. Partial implementation, partial success: The case of Macedonia. In: Russell, D. and O'Flynn I. (eds), *New Challenges for Power-Sharing: Institutional and Social Reform in Divided Societies*. London: Pluto Press, pp. 107–22.

Bilali, R. and Vollhardt, J. R. 2015. Do mass media interventions effectively promote peace in contexts of ongoing violence? Evidence from Eastern Democratic Republic of Congo. *Peace and Conflict: Journal of Peace Psychology 21*(4), pp. 604–20.

Binder, J., Zagefka, H., Brown, R., Funke, F., Kessler, T., Mummendey, A., Maquil, A., Demoulin, S., and Leyens, J. P. 2009. Does contact reduce prejudice or does prejudice reduce contact? A longitudinal test of the contact hypothesis among majority and minority groups in three European countries. *Journal of Personality and Social Psychology 96*(4), pp. 843–56.

Björkdahl, A. 2002a. Comparing conflict prevention mainstreaming in multilateral organisations – what lessons can be learned for the EU? In: van der Goor, L. and Huber, M. (eds), *Mainstreaming Conflict Prevention. Concept and Practice, Conflict Prevention Network Yearbook 2000/2001*. Baden-Baden: Nomos Verlagsge-sellschaft, pp. 105–26.

Björkdahl, A. 2002b. Norms in international relations: Some conceptual and methodological reflections. *Cambridge Review of International Affairs 15*(1), pp. 9–23.

Björkdahl, A. 2005. Norm-maker and norm-taker. Exploring the normative influence of the EU in Macedonia, *European Journal of Foreign Affairs Review 10*(2), pp. 257–78.

Björkdahl, A. 2008. Norm advocacy: A small state strategy to influence the EU. *Journal of European Public Policy 15*(1), pp. 135–54.

Björkdahl, A. 2013. Ideas and norms in Swedish peace policy. *Swiss Political Science Review 19*(3), pp. 322–37.

Björkdahl, A. and Gusic, I. 2015. 'Global' norms and 'local' agency: Frictional peacebuilding in Kosovo. *Journal of International Relations and Development 18*(3), pp. 265–87.

Blanton, H. and Christie, C. 2003. Deviance regulation: A theory of action and identity. *Review of General Psychology 7*(2), pp. 115–49.

Blattman, C. and Annan, J. 2011. *Reintegrating and Employing High Risk Youth in Liberia: Lessons from a Randomised Evaluation of a Landmine Action an Agricultural Training Program for Ex-combatants*. New Haven, CT: Innovations for Poverty Action.

Blattman, C., Hartman, A. and Blair, R. 2011. *Can We Teach Peace and Conflict Resolution?: Results from a Randomised Evaluation of the Community Empowerment Program (CEP) in Liberia: A Program to Build Peace, Human Rights, and Civic Participation*. New Haven, CT: Innovations for Poverty Action.

Blum, A. 2011. *Improving Peacebuilding Evaluation: A Whole-of-Field Approach*. Washington, DC: United States Institute of Peace.

Blum, A. and Kawano-Chiu, M. 2012. *Proof of Concept – Learning from Nine Examples of Peacebuilding Evaluation*. Washington, DC: United States Institute of Peace and Alliance for Peacebuilding.

Bøås, M. 2013. Youth agency in the 'violent life-worlds' of Kono District (Sierra Leone), Voinjama (Liberia) and Northern Mali: 'Tactics' and imaginaries'. *Conflict, Security & Development* 13(5), pp. 611–30.

Bøås, M. and Tom, P. 2016. International interventions and local agency in peacebuilding in Sierra Leone. In: Richmond, O. P. (ed.), *Post-Liberal Peace Transitions: Between Peace Formation and State Formation*. Edinburgh: Edinburgh University Press, pp. 143–59.

Bobo, L. and Licari, F. C. 1989. Education and political tolerance: Testing the effects of cognitive sophistication and target group affect. *Public Opinion Quarterly* 53(3), pp. 285–308.

Boehm, A. E. and Weinberg, R. A. 1997. *The Classroom Observer: Developing Observation Skills in Early Childhood Settings* (3rd edn). New York: Teachers College Press.

Boersch-Supan, J. 2012. The generational contract in flux: intergenerational tensions in post-conflict Sierra Leone. *The Journal of Modern African Studies* 50(1), pp. 25–51.

Boesten, J. and Henry, M. 2018. Between fatigue and silence: The challenges of conducting research on sexual violence in conflict. *Social Politics: International Studies in Gender, State & Society* 25(4), pp. 568–88.

Bolten, C. 2012. 'We have been sensitised': Ex-combatants, marginalisation, and youth in postwar Sierra Leone. *American Anthropologist* 114(3), pp. 496–508.

Bolten, C. 2014. Social networks, resources, and international NGOs in postwar Sierra Leone. *African Conflict and Peace Building Review* 4(1), pp. 33–59.

Bolten, C. 2018. Productive work and subjected labor: Children's pursuits and child rights in northern Sierra Leone. *Journal of Human Rights* 17(2), pp. 199–214.

Bolton, G. 2005. *Reflective Practice: Writing and Professional Development*. London: Sage.

Bonano, E. 2008. *Golden Kids News Evaluation Report*. Washington, DC: SfCG.

Boothby, N., Crawford, J., and Halperin, J. 2006. Mozambique child soldier life outcome study: Lessons learned in rehabilitation and reintegration efforts. *Global Public Health* 1(1), pp. 87–107.

Borenstein, M., Hedges, L. V., Higgins, J. P., and Rothstein, H. R. 2011. *Introduction to Meta-analysis*. New York: John Wiley & Sons.

Borer, T. A., Darby, J., and McEvoy-Levy, S. (eds). 2006. *Peacebuilding After Peace Accords: The Challenges of Violence, Truth and Youth*. Notre Dame, IN: Notre Dame University Press.

Bormann, N. C., Cederman, L. E., and Vogt, M. 2017. Language, religion, and ethnic civil war. *Journal of Conflict Resolution* 61(4), pp. 744–71.

Bosk, C. 2004. The ethnographer and the IRB: comment on Kevin D. Haggerty, Ethics creep: governing social science research in the name of ethics. *Qualitative Sociology* 27(4), pp. 417–20.

Boulding, E. 1967. Summary and challenges for future research. *The Journal of Social Issues* (special issue on Conflict and Community in the International System), XII, pp. 144–58.

Boulding, E. 1972. The family as an agent of social change. *The Futurist* 6, pp. 363–78.

Boulding, K. E. 1966. The economics of knowledge and the knowledge of economics. *The American Economic Review* 56(1/2), pp. 1–13.

Bourdieu, P. 1980. Le capital social: notes provisoires. *Actes de la recherche en sciences sociales 31*(1), pp. 29–34.

Bourdieu, P. 2000. *Pascalian Meditations*. Stanford: Stanford University Press.

Boutros-Ghali, B. 1992. *An Agenda for Peace: Preventive Diplomacy, Peacemaking and Peacekeeping. Report of the UN Secretary-General Pursuant to the Statement Adopted by the Summit Meeting of the Security Council on January 31.* New York: United Nations.

Bowd, R. 2008. From Combatant to Civilian: The Social Reintegration of Ex-combatants in Rwanda and the Implications for Social Capital and Reconciliation. Doctoral dissertation, University of York.

Bowen, G. A. 2009. Document analysis as a qualitative research method. *Qualitative Research Journal* 9(2), pp. 27–40.

Boyden, J. and De Berry, J. eds. 2004. *Children and Youth on the Front Line: Ethnography, Armed Conflict and Displacement* (Vol. 14). Oxford: Berghahn Books.

Brabant, K. V. 2010. *Peacebuilding How? Broad Local Ownership*. Geneva: Interpeace.

Braddock, K. and Dillard, J. P. 2016. Meta-analytic evidence for the persuasive effect of narratives on beliefs, attitudes, intentions, and behaviors. *Communication Monographs* 83(4), pp. 446–67.

Branch, A. 2011. *Displacing Human Rights: War and Intervention in Northern Uganda.* Oxford: Oxford University Press.

Bratić, V. 2006. Media effects during violent conflict: Evaluating media contributions to peace building. *Conflict & Communication 5*(1), pp. 1–11.

Bratić, V. 2008. Examining peace-oriented media in areas of violent conflict. *International Communication Gazette 70*(6), pp. 487–503.

Bratić, V. and Schirch, L. 2007. Why and when to use the media for conflict prevention and peacebuilding (Issue Paper 6). The Hague: European Centre for Conflict Prevention.

Bräuchler, B. 2018. Contextualizing ethnographic peace research. In: Millar, G. (ed.), 2017. *Ethnographic Peace Research: Approaches and Tensions*. London: Springer, pp. 21–42.

Brehm, V. M. 2001. *Promoting Effective North-South NGO Partnerships: A Comparative Study of 10 European NGOs*. Oxford, UK: INTRAC.

Britten, N., Campbell, R., Pope, C., Donovan, J., Morgan, M., and Pill, R., 2002. Using meta ethnography to synthesise qualitative research: a worked example. *Journal of Health Services Research & Policy 7*(4), pp. 209–15.

Britton, B. 2005. *Organisational Learning in NGOs: Creating the Motive, Means and Opportunity*. Praxis Paper No. 3. Oxford, UK: The International NGO Training and Research Centre (INTRAC).

Bronfenbrenner, U. and Morris, P. A. 1998. The ecology of developmental processes. In: Damon, W. and Lerner, R. M. (eds), *Handbook of Child Psychology: Theoretical Models of Human Development*. Hoboken, New Jersey: John Wiley & Sons Inc., pp. 993–1028.

Brooks-Gunn, J. 2004. Intervention and policy as change agents for young children. In: P. L.Chase-Lansdale, K. Kiernan, and R. J.Friedman (eds), *Human Development across Lives and Generations: The Potential for Change*. New York: Cambridge University Press, pp. 293–340.

Broome, B. J. and Collier, M. J. 2012. Culture, communication, and peacebuilding: A reflexive multi-dimensional contextual framework. *Journal of International and Intercultural Communication 5*(4), pp. 245–69.

Brown, A., McCollister, F., Cameron, D., and Ludwig, J. 2015. The current state of peace-building programming and evidence. 3ie Scoping Paper 2. New Delhi: International Initiative for Impact Evaluation (3ie).

Brown, K. S. 2000. In the realm of the double-headed eagle: Para-politics in Macedonia, 1994–9. In: Cowan, J. K. (ed.), *Macedonia: The Politics of Identity and Difference*. London: Pluto Press, pp. 122–39.

Brown, L. D. 1991. Bridging organizations and sustainable development. *Human Relations* 44(8), pp. 807–31.

Brown, L. D. and Kalegaonkar, A. 2002. Support organizations and the evolution of the NGO sector. *Nonprofit and Voluntary Sector Quarterly* 31(2), pp. 231–58.

Browne, E. 2013. *Monitoring and Evaluating Civil Society Partnerships*. GSDRC Helpdesk Research Report, GSDRC Applied Knowledge Services.

Brubaker, R. 2013. Language, religion and the politics of difference. *Nations and Nationalism* 19(1), pp. 1–20.

Brunnbauer, U. 2004. Fertility, families and ethnic conflict: Macedonians and Albanians in the Republic of Macedonia, 1944–2002. *Nationalities Papers* 32(3), pp. 565–98.

Brusett, E. and Otto, R. 2004. *Evaluation of Nashe Maalo: Design, Implementation, and Outcomes Social Transformation Through the Media, on Behalf of Search for Common Ground*. Channel Research. Belgium.

Brusset, E., De Coning, C., and Hughes, B. (eds). 2016. *Complexity Thinking for Peacebuilding Practice and Evaluation*. London: Springer.

Buchy, M. and Ahmed, S. 2007. Social Learning, Academics and NGOs: Can the Collaborative Formula Work?. *Action Research* 5(4): 358–77.

Bürge, M. 2011. Riding the narrow tracks of moral life: Commercial motorbike riders in Makeni, Sierra Leone. *Africa Today* 58(2), pp. 59–95.

Burgess, R. G., 2002. *In the Field: An Introduction to Field Research*. Abingdon: Routledge.

Burt, Ronald S. 2005. *Brokerage and Closure: An Introduction to Social Capital*. Oxford: Oxford University Press.

Bush, K. and Duggan, C. (eds). 2015. *Evaluation in the Extreme: Research, Impact and Politics in Violently Divided Societies*. London: Sage.

Bush, K. and Duggan, C. 2013. Evaluation in conflict zones: Methodological and ethical challenges. *Journal of Peacebuilding & Development* 8(2), pp. 5–25.

Bush, K. D. 1996. Beyond bungee cord humanitarianism: Towards a developmental agenda for peacebuilding. *Canadian Journal of Development Studies* 17(4), pp. 75–92.

Bush, K. D. 1998. A measure of peace: Peace and conflict impact assessment (PCIA) of development projects in conflict zones. Working Paper, 1. Ottawa: The Peace-Building and Reconstruction Program Initiative and the Evaluation Unit, IDRC.

Bush, K. D. 2001. Peace and conflict impact assessment (PCIA) five years on: The commodification of an idea. *Berghof Handbook Dialogue 1*, Berlin: Berghof Research Center, pp. 37–51.

Bush, K. D. and Saltarelli, D. 2000. *The Two Faces of Education in Ethnic Conflict: Towards a Peacebuilding Education for Children*. Florence: UNICEF Innocenti Research Centre.

Caddell, M. and Yanacopulos, H. 2006. Knowing but not knowing: Conflict, development and denial: Analysis. *Conflict, Security & Development* 6(4), pp. 557–79.

Call, C. T. 2008. Building states to build peace? A critical analysis. *Journal of Peacebuilding & Development* 4(2), pp. 60–74.

Campbell, R., Pound, P., Morgan, M., Daker-White, G., Britten, N., Pill, R., Yardley, L., Pope, C., and Donovan, J. 2011. Evaluating meta ethnography: systematic analysis and synthesis of qualitative research. *Health Technology Assessment* 15(43). Online at https://ore.exeter.ac.uk/repository/bitstream/handle/10871/13681/Evaluating%20meta-ethnography.pdf?sequence=2&isAllowed=y (accessed 8 January 2021).

Campbell, S. P. 2007. *What is Successful Peacebuilding? A Report Prepared for Catholic Relief Services*. Online at http://www.susannacampbell.com (accessed 19 January 2021).

Campbell, S. P. 2008. When process matters: The potential implications of organisational learning for peacebuilding success. *Journal of Peacebuilding & Development* 4(2), pp. 20–32.

Campbell, S. P. 2011. Routine learning? How peacebuilding organisations prevent liberal peace. In: Campbell, S., Chandler, D., and Sabaratnam, M. (eds), *A Liberal Peace: The Problems and Practices of Peacebuilding*. London: Zed Books Ltd, pp. 89–105.

Campbell, S. P., 2018. *Global Governance and Local Peace: Accountability and Performance in International Peacebuilding*. Cambridge: Cambridge University Press.

Campbell, S. P., Findley, M. G., and Welch, J. 2014. *Technology and Peacebuilding Learning and Evaluation*. Build Peace White Paper, April. Online at http://lyvoices.org/wp-content/uploads/2014/04/BP14-Panel-evaluation.pdf (accessed 18 January 2021).

Carey, H. F. 2017. *Subcontracting Peace: The Challenges of NGO Peacebuilding*. New York: Routledge.

Carnevale, F. A. 2004. Listening authentically to youthful voices: A conception of the moral agency of children. *Toward a Moral Horizon: Nursing Ethics for Leadership and Practice*. Toronto: Pearson Prentice Hall, pp. 396–413.

Carnevale, F. A. 2020. A 'Thick' conception of children's voices: A hermeneutical framework for childhood research. *International Journal of Qualitative Methods*. Online at https://doi.org/10.1177/1609406920933767 (accessed 12 August 2021).

Caroll, T. 1992. *Intermediary NGOs: The Supporting Link in Grassroots Development*. West Hartford: Kumarian Press.

Carothers, T. 2009. Democracy assistance: political vs. developmental? *Journal of Democracy* 20(1), pp. 5–19.

Carpenter, R.C., 2000. Surfacing children: Limitations of genocidal rape discourse. *Hum. Rts. Q. 22*, p. 428–477.

Carpenter, R. C. 2010. *Forgetting Children Born of War: Setting the Human Rights Agenda in Bosnia and Beyond*. New York: Columbia University Press.

Castañeda, C. 2009. How liberal peacebuilding may be failing Sierra Leone. *Review of African Political Economy* 36(120), pp. 235–51.

Cekan, J. 2016. How to foster sustainability. *Global Policy* 7(2), pp. 293–5.

Celestina, M. 2018. Between trust and distrust in research with participants in conflict context. *International Journal of Social Research Methodology* 21(3), pp. 373–83.

Centre for Common Ground (CCG). 2019. Mid-term Review of the Advancing Social Cohesion Project. Skopje. June.

Chakravarty, A. 2012. Partially trusting field relationships opportunities and constraints of fieldwork in Rwanda's post-conflict setting. *Field Methods* 24(3), pp. 251–71.

Chambers, C. 2006. Anthropology as cultural translation: Amitav Ghosh's in an antique land. *Postcolonial Text*, pp. 1–19.

Chandler, D. 1999. The limits of peacebuilding: International regulation and civil society development in Bosnia. *International Peacekeeping* 6(1), pp. 109–25.

Chandler, D. 2006. *Empire in Denial: The Politics of State-Building*. London: Pluto Press.

Chandler, D. 2013. Promoting democratic norms? Social constructivism and the 'subjective' limits to liberalism. *Democratisation* 20(2), pp. 215–39.

Chartrand, T. L. and Bargh, J. A. 1999. The chameleon effect: the perception–behavior link and social interaction. *Journal of Personality and Social Psychology* 76(6), pp. 893–910.

Chaskin, R. J., McGregor, C., and Brady, B. 2018. *Supporting Youth Civic and Political Engagement: Supranational and National Policy Frameworks in Comparative Perspectives. UNESCO, EU Horizon 2020 Project.* Available at http://www.childandfamilyresearch. ie/media/unescochildandfamilyresearchcentre/J4445—58606-NUI-Engaging-Urban-Youth-Policy-Report_v6.pdf (accessed 15 May 2019).

Checkel, J. T. 1999. Norms, institutions, and national identity in contemporary Europe. *International Studies Quarterly 43*(1), pp. 83–114.

Checkoway, B. N. 2011. What is youth participation?. *Children and Youth Services Review 33*(2), pp. 340–5.

Checkoway, B. N. and Gutierrez, L. M. 2006. Youth Participation and Community Change. *Journal of Community Practice 14*(1–2), pp. 1–9.

Chi, D. and Wright, R. 2009. *An Assessment of the Role of Community Radio in Peacebuilding and Development: Case Studies in Liberia and Sierra Leone.* Washington, DC: SfCG.

Chigas, D., Church, M., and Corlazzoli, V. 2014. *Evaluating Impacts of Peace Building Interventions.* London: DFID.

Chirot, D. and McCauley, C. 2006. *Why Not Kill Them All?: The Logic and Prevention of Mass Political Murder.* Princeton, NJ: Princeton University Press.

Chiumento, A., Khan, M. N., Rahman, A., and Frith, L. 2016. Managing ethical challenges to mental health research in post-conflict settings. *Developing World Bioethics 16*(1), pp. 15–28.

Choe, D. E., Zimmerman, M. A., and Devnarain, B. 2012. Youth violence in South Africa: exposure, attitudes, and resilience in Zulu adolescents. *Violence and Victims 27*(2), pp. 166–81.

Christensen, M. M. and Utas, M. 2008. Mercenaries of democracy: The 'Politricks' of remobilized combatants in the 2007 general elections, Sierra Leone. *African Affairs 107*(429), pp. 515–39.

Christensen, P. and Prout, A. 2002. Working with ethical symmetry in social research with children. *Childhood 9*(4), pp. 477–97.

Christensen, R. A. and Ebrahim, A. 2006. How does accountability affect mission? The case of a non-profit serving immigrants and refugees. *Nonprofit Management and Leadership 17*(2), pp. 195–209.

Christians, C. G. 2005. Ethical theory in communications research. *Journalism Studies 6*(1), pp. 3–14.

Christie, R. 2012. *Peacebuilding and NGOs: State-Civil Society Interactions.* Abingdon: Routledge.

Christie, R. and Algar-Faria, G. 2020. Timely interventions: Temporality and peacebuilding. *European Journal of International Security 5*(2), pp. 155–78.

Church, C. and Rogers, M. 2006. *Designing for Results: Integrating Monitoring and Evaluation in Conflict Transformation Programs Manual.* Washington, DC: Search for Common Ground, United States Institute for Peace, and Alliance for Peacebuilding. Washington, DC: SfCG. Online at www.sfcg.org/programmes/ilr/ilt_manualpage.html (accessed 30 January 2021).

Church, C. and Shouldice, J. 2003. *The Evaluation of Conflict Resolution Interventions: Part II: Emerging Practice & Theory.* Ulster University: INCORE.

Cialdini, R. B. and Goldstein, N. J. 2004. Social influence: Compliance and conformity. *Annu. Rev. Psychol. 55*, pp. 591–621.

Clark, J. N. 2010. Education in Bosnia-Hercegovina: The case for root-and-branch reform, *Journal of Human Rights 9*, pp. 344–62.

Clark, T. 2008. We're over-researched here! Exploring accounts of research fatigue within qualitative research engagements. *Sociology 42*(5), pp. 953–70.

Clark, T. 2011. Gaining and maintaining access: Exploring the mechanisms that support and challenge the relationship between gatekeepers and researchers. *Qualitative Social Work* 10(4), pp. 485–502.

Clarkson, J. J., Tormala, Z. L., and Rucker, D. D. 2011. Cognitive and affective matching effects in persuasion: An amplification perspective. *Personality and Social Psychology Bulletin* 37(11), pp. 1415–27.

Clastres, P. 1974. De l'ethnocide. *l'Homme*, pp. 101–10.

Cloke, P., Cooke, P., Cursons, J., Milbourne, P., and Widdowfield, R. 2000. Ethics, reflexivity and research: Encounters with homeless people. *Ethics, Place & Environment* 3(2), pp. 133–54.

Cohen, N. and Arieli, T. 2011. Field research in conflict environments: Methodological challenges and snowball sampling. *Journal of Peace Research* 48(4), pp. 423–35.

Cohn, B. S. 1996. *Colonialism and Its Forms of Knowledge: The British in India*. Princeton University Press.

Cole, B. 1995. *Mass Media, Freedom and Democracy in Sierra Leone*, Premier. Freetown: Publishing House.

Coleman, J.S., 1988. Social capital in the creation of human capital. *American journal of sociology* 94, pp. S95–S120.

Coleman, P. T. 2003. Characteristics of protracted, intractable conflict: Toward the development of a metaframework-I. *Peace and Conflict: Journal of Peace Psychology* 9(1), pp. 1–37.

Colletta, N. J. and Cullen, M. L. 2000. *Violent Conflict and the Transformation of Social Capital: Lessons from Cambodia, Rwanda, Guatemala, and Somalia* (Vol. 795). World Bank Publication.

Collison, H., Darnell, S., Giulianotti, R., and Howe, P. D. 2017. The inclusion conundrum: A critical account of youth and gender issues within and beyond sport for development and peace interventions. *Social Inclusion* 5(2), pp. 223–31.

Converse, P. E. 1970. Attitudes and non-attitudes: Continuation of a dialogue. In: Tufte, E. R. (ed.), *The Quantitative Analysis of Social Problems*. Reading, MA: Addison-Wesley, pp. 168–89.

Cooper, N., Turner, M., and Pugh, M. 2011. The end of history and the last liberal peacebuilder: A reply to Roland Paris. *Review of International Studies* 37(4), pp. 1995–2007.

Cooper, P., 1965. The development of the concept of war. *Journal of Peace Research* 2(1), pp. 1–16.

Corbin, J. and Strauss, A. 2008. *Basics of Qualitative Research: Techniques and Procedures for Developing Grounded Theory*. London: Sage.

Corlazzoli, V. and White, J. 2013b. *Measuring the Un-measurable: Solutions to Measurement Challenges in Fragile and Conflict-Affected Environments*. Search for Common Ground/UK DfiD.

Cortell, A. P. and Davis Jr, J. W. 2000. Understanding the domestic impact of international norms: A research agenda. *International Studies Review* 2(1), pp. 65–87.

Cox, R. W., 1981. Social forces, states and world orders: Beyond international relations theory. *Millennium* 10(2), pp. 126–55.

Craig, G., Corden, A., and Thornton, P. 2000. *Safety in Social Research* (Social Research Update 29). Guildford: University of Surrey, pp. 68–72.

Crano, W. D. and Prislin, R. 2006. Attitudes and persuasion. *Annu. Rev. Psychol.* 57, pp. 345–74.

Crawford, N. 1993. Decolonisation as an international norm: The evolution of practice, arguments and beliefs. In Reed, L.W. and Kaysen, C. (eds), *Emerging Norms of Justified*

Intervention. A Collection of Essays, Cambridge, MA: American Arts and Sciences, pp. 37–61.

Crewe, E. and Young, J. 2002. *Bridging Research and Policy: Context, Evidence and Links.* ODI Working Paper 173. London: Overseas Development Institute.

Cromwell, A., 2019. How peace education motivates youth peacebuilding: Examples from Pakistan. *International Journal of Educational Development 66*, pp. 62–9.

Cronin-Furman, K. and Lake, M. 2018. Ethics abroad: Fieldwork in fragile and violent contexts. *PS: Political Science & Politics 51*(3), pp. 607–14.

Cubitt, C. 2012. Political youth: Finding alternatives to violence in Sierra Leone. In: Maina, G. (ed.), *Opportunity or Threat: The Engagement of Youth in African Societies*, Africa Dialogue, Monologue series 1/2012, Umhlanga Rocks: ACCORD, pp. 15–54.

Curle, A. 1971. *Making Peace*. London: Tavistock Publications.

Curle, A. 1994. New challenges for citizen peace-making. *Medicine, Conflict and Survival 10*(2), pp. 96–105.

Curran, D. and Woodhouse, T. 2007. Cosmopolitan peacekeeping and peacebuilding in Sierra Leone: What can Africa contribute? *International Affairs 83*(6), pp. 1055–70.

Curtis, D. E., 2000. Broadcasting peace: An analysis of local media post-conflict peace-building projects in Rwanda and Bosnia. *Canadian Journal of Development Studies 21*(1), pp. 141–66.

Cvetanova, G. (ed.). 2016. *The Identities of the Student Population in the Republic of Macedonia*, Skopje: Institute for Sociological, Political and Juridical Research.

D'Costa, B. and Glanville, L., 2019. *Children and the Responsibility to Protect.* Brill.

D'Errico, N. C., Kalala, T., Nzigire, L. B., Maisha, F., and Malemo Kalisya, L. 2013. You say rape, I say hospitals. But whose voice is louder?: Health, aid and decision-making in the Democratic Republic of Congo. *Review of African Political Economy 40*(135), pp. 51–66.

Daley, E. and S. Pallas. 2014. Women and land deals in Africa and Asia: Weighing the implications and changing the game. *Feminist Economics 20*(1), pp. 178–201.

Danesh, H. B. 2006. Towards an integrative theory of peace education. *Journal of Peace Education 3*(1), pp. 55–78.

Danieli, Y. ed. 1998. *International Handbook of Multigenerational Legacies of Trauma.* London: Springer Science & Business Media.

Danielsson, A. 2020. Transcending binaries in critical peacebuilding scholarship to address 'inclusivity'projects. *Third World Quarterly 41*(7), pp. 1085–1102.

Datzberger, S. 2014. Peacebuilding and the depoliticisation of civil society: Sierra Leone [2002 – 2013]. PhD thesis, London School of Economics and Political Science. University of London.

Datzberger, S. 2015. Peace building and the depoliticisation of civil society: Sierra Leone 2002–13. *Third World Quarterly 36*(8), pp. 1592–1609.

Datzberger, S. 2016. Civil society as a postcolonial project: Challenging normative notions in post-conflict Sub-Saharan Africa. In: Dhawan, N., Leinius, J., Mageza-Barthel, R., and Fink, E. (eds), *Negotiating Normativity*. London: Springer, pp. 79–93.

Davies, C. A. 2008. *Reflexive Ethnography: A Guide to Researching Selves and Others.* London: Routledge.

Davies, L. and Talbot, C. 2008. Learning in conflict and post-conflict contexts. *Comparative Education Review 52*(4), pp. 509–17.

Davies, R. 1996. *The Sierra Leone situation: The Spill-over of the Liberian Civil War into Sierra Leone: Peace-making and peace-keeping possibilities.* UN Institute for Training and Research and International Peace Academy, May.

Davies, R. and Dart, J., 2005. The 'most significant change'(MSC) technique. *A guide to its use.*

Davis, J. M. 1998. Understanding the meanings of children: A reflexive process. *Children & Society 12*(5), pp. 325–35.

Davis, J., Watson, N., and Cunningham-Bailey, S. 2000. Learning the lives of disabled children: Developing a reflexive approach. In: Christensen, P. and James, A. (eds), *Research with Children: Perspectives and Practices*, London: Falmer, pp. 201–24.

De Coning, C. 2010. *Clarity, Coherence and Context – Three Priorities for Sustainable Peacebuilding*. Oslo: NUPI.

De Coning, C. 2013. *Understanding Peacebuilding as Essentially Local*. Oslo: NUPI.

De Coning, C., 2018. Adaptive peacebuilding. *International Affairs 94*(2), pp. 301–17.

De Houwer, J., Barnes-Holmes, D., and Moors, A. 2013. What is learning? On the nature and merits of a functional definition of learning. *Psychonomic Bulletin & Review 20*(4), pp. 631–42.

Deenen, H. A. J. H. 2015. *Fostering Inter-ethnic Relations in Macedonia, the Importance of Pre-service Teacher Training*. Unpublished Master's thesis, Utrecht University.

Del Felice, M. C. and Wisler, A. 2007. The unexplored power and potential of youth as peace-builder. Online at https://repository.ubn.ru.nl/bitstream/handle/2066/56049/56049.pdf?sequence=1&isAllowed=y (accessed 10 May 2021).

Denney, L. 2013. Liberal chiefs or illiberal development? The challenge of engaging chiefs in DFID's security sector reform programme in Sierra Leone. *Development Policy Review 31*(1), pp. 5–25.

Denov, M. 2010. *Child Soldiers: Sierra Leone's Revolutionary United Front*. Cambridge University Press.

Denov, M. 2015. Children born of wartime rape: The intergenerational realities of sexual violence and abuse. *Ethics, Medicine and Public Health 1*(1), pp. 61–8.

Denov, M. and Lakor, A. A. 2017. When war is better than peace: The post-conflict realities of children born of wartime rape in northern Uganda. *Child Abuse & Neglect 65* (March), pp. 255–65.

Denov, M., Fennig, M., Rabiau, M. A., and Shevell, M. C. 2019. Intergenerational resilience in families affected by war, displacement, and migration: 'It runs in the family'. *Journal of Family Social Work 22*(1), pp. 17–45.

Denskus, T. 2007a. Peacebuilding does not build peace. *Development in Practice 17*(4–5), pp. 656–62.

Denskus, T. 2007b. What are all these people doing in their offices all day? The challenges of writing-up stories from 'post-conflict' Kathmandu. *Journal of Peace Conflict & Development*, 11 (November). online at https://www.bradford.ac.uk/library/find-materials/journal-of-peace-conflict-and-development/PCD-ISSUE-11-FIELD-WORK-REPORT_-KATHMANDU_Tobias-Denskus.pdf (accessed 19 January 2021).

Denskus, T. 2012. Challenging the international peacebuilding evaluation discourse with qualitative methodologies. *Evaluation and Program Planning 35*(1), pp. 148–53.

Denzin, N. 1970. Strategies of multiple triangulation. In: Denzin, N. (ed.), *The Research Act in Sociology: A Theoretical Introduction to Sociological Method*. Englewood Cliffs, NJ: Prentice Hall, pp. 235–47.

Denzin, N. K. and Lincoln, Y. S. 2008. *Collecting and Interpreting Qualitative Materials* (Vol. 3). London: Sage.

Devine-Wright, P. 2001. History and identity in Northern Ireland: An exploratory investigation of the role of historical commemorations in contexts of intergroup conflict. *Peace and Conflict: Journal of Peace Psychology 7*(4), pp. 297–315.

Diamond, L. and McDonald, J. W. 1996. *Multi-track Diplomacy: A Systems Approach to Peace*. Boulder: Lynne Rienner.

Dibley, T. 2014. *Partnerships, Power and Peacebuilding: NGOs as Agents of Peace in Aceh and Timor-Leste*. London: Springer.

Dietrich, Wolfgang. 2013. *Elicitive Conflict Transformation and the Transnational Shift in Peace Politics*. London: Springer.

Dimova, R. 2006. 'Modern' masculinities: Ethnicity, education, and gender in Macedonia. *Nationalities Papers 34*(3), pp. 305–20.

Dirksmeier, P. and Helbrecht, I. 2008. Time, non-representational theory and the 'performative turn'—Towards a new methodology in qualitative social research. *Forum Qualitative Sozialforschung/Forum: Qualitative Social Research 9*(2). Online at https://www.geographie.hu-berlin.de/de/Members/helbrecht_ilse/downloadsenglish/performativemethodology (accessed 10 January 2021).

Dixon, A. 2021. Post-conflict initiatives and the exclusion of conflict-affected young people in northern Uganda. *The Journal of Modern African Studies 59*(1), pp. 21–39.

Dobbins, J., Jones, S.G., Crane, K., Chivvis, C. S., Radin, A., Larrabee, F. S., Bensahel, N., Stearns, B.K., and Goldsmith, B.W. (eds). 2008. Chapter 4 Macedonia, In: *Europe's Role in Nation-Building: From the Balkans to the Congo*, Santa Monica, California: RAND Corporation, pp. 49–72.

Dolan, C. 2009. *Social Torture: The Case of Northern Uganda, 1986–2006* (Vol. 4). Oxford: Berghahn Books.

Dolowitz, D. and Marsh, D. 1996. Who learns what from whom: a review of the policy transfer literature. *Political Studies 44*(2), pp. 343–57.

Donais, T. 2009. Empowerment or imposition? Dilemmas of local ownership in post-conflict peacebuilding processes. *Peace & Change 34*(1), pp. 3–26.

Donais, T. 2012. *Peacebuilding and Local Ownership: Post-Conflict Consensus-Building*. New York: Routledge.

Donais, T. 2015. Bringing the local back in: Haiti, local governance and the dynamics of vertically integrated peacebuilding. *Journal of Peacebuilding & Development 10*(1), pp. 40–55.

Donnelly, C. 2008. The integrated school in a conflict society: A comparative analysis of two integrated primary schools in Northern Ireland. *Cambridge Journal of Education 38*(2), pp. 187–98.

Donnelly, P. 1996. Approaches to social inequality in the sociology of sport. *Quest 48*(2), pp. 221–42.

Douglass, D., Zulaika, J., Douglass, W. A., and Douglass, W. 1996. *Terror and Taboo: The Follies, Fables, and Faces of Terrorism*. Hove, East Sussex: Psychology Press.

Doyle, M. W. 2005. Three pillars of the liberal peace. *American Political Science Review 99*(3), pp. 463–66.

Doyle, M. W. 2007. The John W. Holmes Lecture: Building Peace. *Global Governance 13*(1), pp. 1–15.

Doyle, M. W. and Sambanis, N. 2006. *Making War and Building Peace: United Nations Peace Operations*. Princeton, NJ: Princeton University Press.

Drew, E. and Ramsbotham, A. 2012. *Work Not War: Youth Transformation in Liberia and Sierra Leone*. London: Conciliation Resources.

Drummond-Mundal, L. and Cave, G. 2007. Young peacebuilders: exploring youth engagement with conflict and social change. *Journal of Peacebuilding & Development 3*(3), pp. 63–76.

du Pont, Y. 2005. A new priority for the OSCE: Education reform in South-East Europe. *Helsinki Monitor 16*(1), pp. 68–77.

Duckworth, C. L. 2016. Is peacebuilding donor-driven? Inside the dynamics and impacts of funding peace. *Journal of Peacebuilding and Development 11*(2), pp. 5–9.

Duffield, M., 2001. Governing the borderlands: Decoding the power of aid. *Disasters 25*(4), pp. 308–320.

Duffield, M., 2007. Development, territories, and people: consolidating the external sovereign frontier. *Alternatives 32*(2), pp. 225–246.

Duggan, C. and Bush, K. 2014. The ethical tipping points of evaluators in conflict zones. *American Journal of Evaluation 35*(4), pp. 485–506.

Durham, D. 2000. Youth and the social imagination in Africa: Introduction to parts 1 and 2. *Anthropological Quarterly 73*(3), pp. 113–20.

Durkheim, E. 2013. *The Evolution of Educational Thought: Lectures on the Formation and Development of Secondary Education in France.* Abingdon: Routledge.

Eagly, A. H. and Chaiken, S., 1993. *The Psychology of Attitudes.* Harcourt Brace Jovanovich College Publishers.

Ebenezer-Abiola, R. and Moore, J. 2020. *What Works in Youth Projects? Lessons for the Youth, Peace, and Security Field.* United States Institute of Peace.

Ebrahim, A. 2003. Accountability in practice: Mechanisms for NGOs. *World Development 31*(5), pp. 813–29.

Ebrahim, A. 2016. The many faces of non-profit accountability. In: Renz, D. O. and Herman, R. D. (eds), *The Jossey-Bass Handbook of Nonprofit Leadership and Management,* John Wiley Publishers, pp. 102–26.

Ecker, B. and Hulley, L. 1996. *Depth-Oriented Brief Therapy: How to Be Brief When You Were Trained to Be Deep—and Vice Versa.* San Francisco, California: Jossey-Bass.

Eckstein, H. 1975. Case studies and theory in political science. In: Greenstein, F. I. and Polsby, N. W. (eds), *Handbook of Political Science. Political Science: Scope and Theory* (Vol. 7, pp. 94–137). Reading, MA: Addison-Wesley.

Eder, D. and Corsaro, W. 1999. Ethnographic studies of children and youth: Theoretical and ethical issues. *Journal of Contemporary Ethnography 28*(5), pp. 520–31.

Edwards, K. and Von Hippel, W. 1995. Hearts and minds: The priority of affective versus cognitive factors in person perception. *Personality and Social Psychology Bulletin 21*(10), pp. 996–1011.

Edwards, M. 1994. NGOs in the Age of Information. *IDS Bulletin 25,* 117–24.

Edwards, M. 1997. Organizational learning in non-governmental organizations: What have we learned? *Public Administration and Development: The International Journal of Management Research and Practice 17*(2), pp. 235–50.

Edwards, M. and Hulme, D. 1992. Scaling up NGO impact on development: Learning from experience. *Development in Practice 2*(2), pp. 77–91.

Ellis, C. 2007. Telling secrets, revealing lives: Relational ethics in research with intimate others. *Qualitative Inquiry 13*(1), pp. 3–29.

Elster, J. 1989. *The Cement of Society: A Survey of Social Order.* Cambridge: Cambridge University Press.

Enria, L. 2012. Employing the youth to build peace: The limitations of United Nations statebuilding in Sierra Leone. *Human Welfare 1*(1), pp. 42–56.

Enria, L. 2015. Love and betrayal: The political economy of youth violence in post-war Sierra Leone. *The Journal of Modern African Studies 53*(4), pp. 637–60.

Eriksen, S. L. 2009. The liberal peace is neither: Peacebuilding, state building and the re-production of conflict in the Democratic Republic of Congo. *International Peacekeeping 16*(5), pp. 652–66.

Escobar, A. 2004. Beyond the Third World: Imperial globality, global coloniality and anti-globalisation social movements. *Third World Quarterly 25*(1), pp. 207–30.

Etikan, I., Musa, S. A., and Alkassim, R. S. 2016. Comparison of convenience sampling and purposive sampling. *American Journal of Theoretical and Applied Statistics 5*(1), pp. 1–4.

Euro-Balkan Institute. 2006. Thematic Evaluation of the Impact of Four Projects: Bridges for the New Balkans, *Mozaik* Bilingual Kindergartens, Safe Schools in Communities at Risk and Children, Theater, Education on the Inter-Ethnic Relations and Dialogue in Macedonia, prepared for the Swiss Agency for Development and Cooperation, 15 April–30 July 2006. Skopje: Macedonia.

European Commission. 2020. *Republic of North Macedonia: Overall National Education Strategy and Key Objectives.* March. Online at https://eacea.ec.europa.eu/national-policies/eurydice(2 October, 2020).

Evans-Campbell, T. 2008. Historical trauma in American Indian/Native Alaska communities: A multilevel framework for exploring impacts on individuals, families, and communities. *Journal of interpersonal violence 23*(3), pp. 316–38.

Everett, P, Williams, T., and Myers, M. 2004. *Evaluation of Search for Common Ground activities in Sierra Leone.* Washington, DC: SfCG.

Fabrigar, L. R. and Petty, R. E. 1999. The role of the affective and cognitive bases of attitudes in susceptibility to affectively and cognitively based persuasion. *Personality and Social Psychology Bulletin 25*(3), pp. 363–81.

Fairclough, N. 2003. *Analysing Discourse: Textual Analysis for Social Research.* Hove: East Sussex: Psychology Press.

Fanthorpe, R. 2005. On the limits of liberal peace: Chiefs and democratic decentralisation in post-war Sierra Leone, *African Affairs 105*(418), pp. 27–49.

Fanthorpe, R. and Maconachie, R. 2010. Beyond the 'crisis of youth'? Mining, farming, and civil society in post-war Sierra Leone. *African Affairs 109*(435), pp. 251–72.

Fargas-Malet, M. and Dillenburger, K. 2016. Intergenerational transmission of conflict-related trauma in Northern Ireland: a behavior analytic approach. *Journal of Aggression, Maltreatment & Trauma 25*(4), pp. 436–54.

Fast, L.A. and Neufeldt, R. C. 2005. Envisioning success: Building blocks for strategic and comprehensive peacebuilding impact evaluation. *Journal of Peacebuilding & Development 2*(2), pp. 24–41.

Fauth, G. and Daniels, B. 2001. Youth Reintegration Training and Education for Peace (YRTEP) Program: Sierra Leone, 2000–2001. Impact Evaluation. Online at https://files.eric.ed.gov/fulltext/ED466970.pdf (accessed 21 June 2021).

Festinger, L. 1957. *A Theory of Cognitive Dissonance.* Evanstone, IL: Row, Peterson.

Fetherston, A.B. 2000. From Conflict Resolution to Transformative Peacebuilding: Reflections from Croatia. Bradford, Centre for Conflict Resolution, Department of Peace Studies, University of Bradford. CCR Working Papers: No. 4.

Fine, G. A. and Glassner, B. 1979. Participant observation with children: Promise and problems. *Urban Life 8*(2), pp. 153–74.

Fine, G. A. and Sandstrom, K. L. 1988. *Knowing Children: Participant Observation with Minors.* Newbury Park, CA: Sage.

Finn, B. and Oldfield, S. 2015. Straining: Young men working through waithood in Freetown, Sierra Leone. *Africa Spectrum 50*(3), pp. 29–48.

Finn, C. and Scharf, T., 2012. Intergenerational Programmes in Ireland: An Initial Overview. Irish Center for Social Gerontology, National University of Ireland Galway.

Finnemore, M. and Sikkink, K. 1998. International norm dynamics and political change, *International Organisation 52*(4), pp. 887–917.

Firchow, P. 2018. *Reclaiming Everyday Peace: Local Voices in Measurement and Evaluation After War*. Cambridge University Press.

Firchow, P. and Ginty, R. M. 2017. Measuring peace: Comparability, commensurability, and complementarity using bottom-up indicators. *International Studies Review 19*(1), pp. 6–27.

Fisher, S. and Zimina, L. O. 2009. *Just Wasting Our Time?: Provocative Thoughts for Peacebuilders*. Berlin: Berghof Research Center for Constructive Conflict Management. Online at http://www.konfliktbearbeitung.net/downloads/file1042.pdf (accessed 10 November 2020).

Florini, A.1996. The evolution of international norms, *International Studies Quarterly 40*(4): 363–89.

Fontana, G. 2016a. Educational decentralisation in post-conflict societies: Approaches and constraints. *Third World Thematics: A TWQ Journal 1*(6), pp. 857–78.

Fontana, G. 2016b. *Education Policy and Power-Sharing in Post-"Conflict Societies: Lebanon, Northern Ireland, and Macedonia*. London: Springer.

Fortune, F. and Blah, O. 2012. Electing for peace in Liberia and Sierra Leone. *ACCORD* 23 (March), pp. 26–9.

Fortune, F., Ismail, O., and Stephen, M. 2015. *Rethinking Youth, Livelihoods, and Fragility in West Africa*. Washington, DC: World Bank. Online at https://openknowledge. worldbank.org/bitstream/handle/10986/22517/Rethinking0you0ize0doesn0t0fit0all. pdf?sequence=1 (accessed 10 May 2021).

Francis, D. J. 2000. Torturous path to peace: The Lomé Accord and postwar peacebuilding in Sierra Leone. *Security Dialogue 31*(3), pp. 357–73.

Fransman, J. and Newman, K. 2019. Rethinking research partnerships: Evidence and the politics of participation in research partnerships for international development. *Journal of International Development 31*(7), pp. 523–44.

Friere, P. 1970. *Pedagogy of the Oppressed*. New York: Herder & Herder.

Fujii, L. A. 2010. Shades of truth and lies: Interpreting testimonies of war and violence. *Journal of Peace Research 47*(2), pp. 231–41.

Funk, N. C. 2012. Building on what's already there: Valuing the local in international peacebuilding. *International Journal 67*(2), pp. 391–408.

Funnell, S. and Rogers, P. 2011. *Purposeful Programme Theory. Effective Use of Theories of Change and Logic Models*. San Francisco: Jossey-Bass.

Gaarder, M. and Annan, J. 2013. Impact evaluation of conflict prevention and peacebuilding interventions. Washington, DC: The World Bank.

Galama, A. and van Tongeren, P. (eds). 2002. *Towards Better Peacebuilding Practice: On Lessons Learned, Evaluation Practices and Aid & Conflict*. Netherlands: International Books.

Gallagher, T. 2010a. *Building a Shared Future from a Divided Past: Promoting Peace through Education in Northern Ireland*. In: Salomon, G. and Cairns, E. (eds), *Handbook on Peace Education*. Hove, East Sussex: Psychology Press, pp. 241–51.

Gallagher, T. 2010b. Key issues in coexistence and education. Coexistence International Brandeis University. Online at https://www.qub.ac.uk/Research/GRI/mitchell-institute/ FileStore/Filetoupload,756523,en.pdf (accessed 12 January 2021).

Galtung, J. 1969. Violence, peace, and peace research. *Journal of Peace Research 6*(3), pp. 167–91.

Galtung, J. 1976. *Peace, War and Defense*. Copenhagen: Christian Ejlers.

Galtung, J. 2000. *Conflict Transformation by Peaceful Means: A Participants' and Trainers' Manual*. Geneva: UNDP.

Garbarino, J. and Stott, F. M. 1989. *What Children Can Tell Us: Eliciting, Interpreting and Evaluating Information from Children.* San Francisco, CA: Jossey-Bass.

Gardner, A., Greemblott, K., and Joubert, E. 2005. *What We Know about Exit Strategies – Practical Guidance for Developing Exit Strategies in the Field. C-Safe Regional Learning Spaces Initiative.* Online at http://pdf.usaid.gov/pdf_docs/PNADE671.pdf (accessed 12 October 2020).

Garvin, D., A. 1993. Building a learning organization. *Harvard Business Review 71*(4), pp. 378–391.

Gassan, A., Marcarthy, J., and Konneh, A. 2018. *End of Project Evaluation. Standing Together for Free, Fair and Peaceful Elections in Sierra Leone.* September. Freetown: SfCG.

Gberie, L. 2005. *A Dirty War in West Africa: The RUF and the Destruction of Sierra Leone.* Bloomington, Indiana: Indiana University Press.

Geber, S., Scherer, H., and Hefner, D. 2016. Social capital in media societies: The impact of media use and media structures on social capital. *International Communication Gazette 78*(6), pp. 493–513.

Geiger, R. S. and Ribes, D. 2011. Trace ethnography: Following coordination through documentary practices. Paper presented at the *44th Hawaii International Conference on System Sciences* (HICSS).

Georgieva, G. D. and Shehu, F. 2017. Multicultural and intercultural raising and education for the children of preschool age in Republic of Macedonia. *Research in Physical Education, Sport & Health 6*(2), pp. 27–9.

Gerbner, G., Gross, L., Morgan, M., and Signorielli, N. 1986. Living with television: The dynamics of the cultivation process. In: Bryant, J. and Zillmann, D. (eds), *Perspectives on Media Effects.* Mahwah, NJ: Lawrence Erlbaum Associates, pp. 17–40

Gerring, J. 2004. What is a case study and what is it good for? *American Political Science Review,* pp. 341–54.

Gerring, J. 2007. Is there a (viable) crucial-case method? *Comparative Political Studies 40*(3), pp. 231–53.

Gerstbauer, L. C. 2010. The whole story of NGO mandate change: The peacebuilding work of World Vision, Catholic Relief Services, and Mennonite Central Committee. *Nonprofit and Voluntary Sector Quarterly 39*(5), pp. 844–65.

Gerstbauer, L.C., 2005. The New Conflict Managers: Peacebuilding NGOs and State Agendas. In: Krahmann, E. (eds.) New Threats and New Actors in International Security. New York: Palgrave Macmillan, pp. 23–43.

Gibbons, M. (ed.), 1994. *The New Production of Knowledge: The Dynamics of Science and Research in Contemporary Societies.* London: Sage.

Gillard, S., 2001. Winning the peace: Youth, identity and peacebuilding in Bosnia and Herzegovina. *International Peacekeeping 8*(1), pp. 77–98.

Glaser, B.G. and Straus, A. L., 1967. The discovery of grounded theory: strategies for qualitative research. New York: Aldine.

Gledhill, J. 2020. The pieces kept after peace is kept: Assessing the (post-exit) legacies of peace operations. *International Peacekeeping 27*(1), pp. 1–11.

Glennerster, R., Casey, K., and Bidwell, K. 2012. *The Impact of Information on Voter Knowledge and Engagement: Evidence from the 2012 Elections in Sierra Leone.* Online at https://assets.publishing.service.gov.uk/media/57a08a93ed915d3cfd00082e/Glennerster-Et-Al-2012-Policy-Brief.pdf (accessed 12 November 2020).

Glennerster, R., Casey, K., and Bidwell, K. 2019. Debates: Voting and expenditure responses to political communication. Draft Paper, March. Online at https://www.gsb.stanford.edu/gsb-cmis/gsb-cmis-download-auth/362906?pid= (accessed 12 November 2020).

Global Peace Index. 2017. Online at http://visionofhumanity.org/app/uploads/2017/06/GPI-2017-Report-1.pdf (accessed 19 January 2021).

Godelier M, Strathern M, eds. 1991. *Big Men and Great Men: Personifications of Power in Melanesia*. Cambridge: Cambridge University Press.

Goetschel, L. and Hagmann, T. 2009. Civilian peacebuilding: peace by bureaucratic means? Analysis. *Conflict, Security & Development 9*(1), pp. 55–73.

Goetze, C. and Guzina, D. 2008. Peacebuilding, Statebuilding, Nationbuilding: Turtles All the Way Down?, *Civil Wars 10*(4), pp. 319–347.

Goodhand, J. 1999. Sri Lanka: NGOs and peace-building in complex political emergencies. *Third World Quarterly 20*(1), pp. 69–87.

Goodhand, J. 2000. Research in conflict zones: Ethics and accountability. *Forced Migration Review 8*(4), pp. 12–16.

Goodhand, J., Hulme, D., and Lewer, N. 1999. *NGOs and Peacebuilding in Complex Political Emergencies: A Case Study of Sri Lanka*. University of Manchester, Institute for Development Policy and Management.

Gracy, K. F. 2004. Documenting communities of practice: Making the case for archival ethnography. *Archival Science 4*(3–4), pp. 335–65.

Grant, S., Ahalt, C., Inks, L., and Wolff, I. 2009. *Community Radio and Development in Sierra Leone and Liberia*. Washington DC: SfCG.

Gready, P. 2013. Organizational theories of change in the era of organizational cosmopolitanism: Lessons from ActionAid's human rights-based approach. *Third World Quarterly 34*(8), pp. 1339–60.

Green, A., Preston, J., and Sabates, R. 2003. Education, equality and social cohesion: A distributional approach. *Compare: A Journal of Comparative and International Education 33*(4), pp. 453–70.

Green, D. 2017. The NGO-Academia Interface: Realising the shared potential. Online at https://www.theimpactinitiative.net/impact-lab/collection/ngo-academia-interface (accessed 12 November 2020).

Greenwald, A. G. 1968. Cognitive learning, cognitive response to persuasion, and attitude change. In: Greenwald, A., Brock, T., and Ostrom, T. (eds), *Psychological Foundations of Attitudes*. New York: Academic Press, pp. 148–70.

Grimes, R. L. 2003. Ritual theory and the environment. *The Sociological Review 51*(2), pp. 31–45.

Grizelj, I. 2019. Engaging the next generation: A field perspective of youth inclusion in Myanmar's peace negotiations. *International Negotiation 24*(1), pp. 164–88.

Groff, L. and Smoker, P. 1997. Peace: An evolving idea: Implications for future generations. *Future Generations Journal 23*, pp. 4–9.

Groger, L., Mayberry, P. S., and Straker, J. K. 1999. What we didn't learn because of who would not talk to us. *Qualitative Health Research 9*(6), pp. 829–35.

Groß, L. 2015. The journey from global to local: Norm promotion, contestation and localisation in post-war Kosovo. *Journal of International Relations and Development 18*(3), pp. 311–36.

Grozdanovska, L. 2007. Class Struggle. *Transitions Online*. Available at www.tol.org/client/article/19030-class-struggle.html (accessed 11 October 2020).

Gunawardana, R. H. 2003. Roots of the ethnic conflict in Sri Lanka. *Journal of Buddhist Ethics 10*. Online at http://jbe.gold.ac.uk/10/gunawar-sri-lanka-conf.html (accessed 12 May 2021).

Gürkaynak, E. Ç., Dayton, B., and Paffenholz, T. 2008. Evaluation in conflict resolution and peacebuilding. In: Sandole, D.J., Byrne, S., Sandole-Staroste, I. and Senehi, J. (eds), *Handbook of Conflict Analysis and Resolution*. New York: Routledge, pp. 295–8.

Gvirsman, S. D., Huesmann, L. R., Dubow, E. F., Landau, S. F., Boxer, P., and Shikaki, K. 2016. The longitudinal effects of chronic mediated exposure to political violence on ideological beliefs about political conflicts among youths. *Political Communication 33*(1), pp. 98–117.

Haavelsrud, M. 1970. Views on war and peace among students in West Berlin public schools. *Journal of Peace Research 7*(2), pp. 99–120.

Haer, R. and Becher, I. 2012. A methodological note on quantitative field research in conflict zones: Get your hands dirty. *International Journal of Social Research Methodology 15*(1), pp. 1–13.

Hall, R. 1993. How children think and feel about war and peace: An Australian study. *Journal of Peace Research 30*(2), pp. 181–96.

Hanlon, J. 2005. *Is the International Community Helping to Recreate the Pre-conditions for War in Sierra Leone?* Finland: United Nations University (UNU).

Hanlon, J. 2005. Roots of civil war: Tick all of the above. In: Yanacopulos, H., and Hanlon, J. (eds), Yanacopulos, H. and Hanlon, J. (eds), *Civil War, Civil Peace*. Oxford, UK: James Currey, pp. 72–94.

Harmon-Jones, E. and Harmon-Jones, C. 2002. Testing the action-based model of cognitive dissonance: The effect of action orientation on post-decisional attitudes. *Personality and Social Psychology Bulletin 28*(6), pp. 711–23.

Harms, E. 2013. Eviction time in the new Saigon: Temporalities of displacement in the rubble of development. *Cultural Anthropology 28*(2), pp. 344–68.

Harris, I. 2002. Conceptual underpinnings of peace education, in: G. Salomon & B. Nevo (Eds) *Peace education: the concept, principles, and practices around the world* (New York, Lawrence Erlbaum), pp. 15–26.

Harrison, T. 2017. NGOs and personal politics: The relationship between NGOs and political leaders in West Bengal, India. *World Development 98* (October), pp. 485–96.

Hart, J. and Tyrer, B. 2006. *Research with Children Living in Situations of Armed Conflict: Concepts, Ethics and Methods*. Refugee Studies Centre, Oxford: University of Oxford.

Hart, R. A. 1997. *Children's Participation: The Theory and Practice of Involving Young Citizens in Community Development and Environmental Care*. London: EarthScan.

Hauge, C. 2014. Youth media and agency. *Discourse: Studies in the Cultural Politics of Education 35*(4), pp. 471–84.

Hayes, B. C. and McAllister, I. 2009. Education as a mechanism for conflict resolution in Northern Ireland. *Oxford Review of Education 35*(4), pp. 437–50.

Hayman, R. 2015. NGOs, aid withdrawal and exit strategies, *Journal für Entwicklungspolitik 31*(1), pp. 48–64.

Hayman, R. 2016. Unpacking civil society sustainability: Looking back, broader, deeper, forward. *Development in Practice 26*(5), pp. 670–80.

Hayman, R. and Lewis, S. 2018. INTRAC's experience of working with international NGOs on aid withdrawal and exit strategies from 2011 to 2016. *VOLUNTAS: International Journal of Voluntary and Nonprofit Organisations 29*(2), pp. 361–72.

Hayman, R., James, R., Popplewell, R., and Lewis, S. 2016. Exit strategies and sustainability: Lessons for practitioners. INTRAC, Special Series Paper No. 1. Online at https://www.intrac.org/wpcms/wp-content/uploads/2016/11/Exit-strategies-and-sustainability.-Lessons-for-practitioners.-November-2016.pdf (accessed 15 November 2020).

Head, S. W. 1979. British colonial broadcasting policies: The case of the Gold Coast. *African Studies Review 22*(2), pp. 39–47.

Heideman, L. J. 2016, June. Institutional amnesia: Sustainability and peacebuilding in Croatia. *Sociological Forum 31*(2), pp. 377–96.

Hewitt, J. 2017. *Building the Programs That Can Better Build the Peace, Experts Offer Ways to Ensure the Impact of Programs to Halt Violent Conflicts.* USIP: Washington, DC. Online at https://www.usip.org/events/building-programs-can-better-build-peace (accessed 13 March 2020).

Heyneman, S. P. and Todoric-Bebic, S. 2000. A renewed sense for the purposes of schooling: the challenges of education and social cohesion in Asia, Africa, Latin America, Europe and Central Asia. *Prospects 30*(2), pp. 145–66.

Hicks, D. and Holden, C. 1995. *Visions of the Future: Why We Need to Teach for Tomorrow.* Stoke-on-Trent: Trentham Books Ltd.

Hilker, L. M. and Fraser, E. 2009. Youth exclusion, violence, conflict and fragile states. Report prepared for DFID's Equity and Rights Team. Online at http://www.dmeforpeace. org/peacexchange/wp-content/uploads/2015/12/youth-exclusion-violence-conflict-and-fragile-states.pdf (accessed 11 January 2021).

Hirsch, J. L. 2001. War in Sierra Leone. *Survival 43*(3), pp. 145–62.

Hislope, R. 2004. Crime and honor in a weak state: Paramilitary forces and violence in Macedonia. *Problems of Post-Communism 51*(3), pp. 18–26.

Hoffman, D. 2011. Violence, just in time: War and work in contemporary West Africa. *Cultural Anthropology 26*(1), pp. 34–57.

Hoffman, D., 2006. Disagreement: dissent politics and the war in Sierra Leone. *Africa Today 52*(3), pp. 3–22.

Hoffman, M. 2004. Peace and conflict impact assessment methodology. In: Bloomfield, D., Fischer, M., and Schmelzle, B. (eds), *Berghof Handbook for Conflict Transformation.* Berlin: Berghof Research Center for Constructive Conflict Management. Online at http://edoc.vifapol.de/opus/volltexte/2011/2573/pdf/hoffman_handbook.pdf (accessed 20 May 2021).

Holmes, R. M. 1998. *Fieldwork with Children.* London: Sage.

Hom, A. R. 2018. Timing is everything: Toward a better understanding of time and international politics. *International Studies Quarterly 62*(1), pp. 69–79.

Honwana, A. 2014. 'Waithood': Youth transitions and social change. In: Foeken, D., Dietz, T., de Haan, L., and Johnson, L. (eds), *Development and Equity.* E-book. Rotterdam: Brill, pp. 28–40.

Hovland, C. I., Janis, I. L., and Kelley, H. H. 1953. *Communication and Persuasion.* New Haven: CT. Yale University Press.

Howker, E. and Malik, S. 2013. *Jilted Generation: How Britain Has Bankrupted Its Youth.* London: Icon Books.

Hughes, J. and Donnelly, C. 2003. Community relations in Northern Ireland: a shift in attitudes? *Journal of Ethnic and Migration Studies 29*(4), pp. 643–61.

Hughes, S. and Noblit, G. 2017. Meta-ethnography of autoethnographies: A worked example of the method using educational studies. *Ethnography and Education 12*(2), pp. 211–27.

Hulme, D. and Goodhand, J. 1999. From wars to complex political emergencies: understanding conflict and peace-building in the new world disorder. *Third World Quarterly 20*(1), pp. 13–26.

Hume, E. 2004. *The Media Missionaries: American Support for Journalism Excellence and Press Freedom Around the Globe.* Miami, Florida: John S. and James L. Knight Foundation.

Humphreys, D. 2015. The reconstruction of the Beirut Central District: An urban geography of war and peace. *Spaces and Flows: An International Journal of Urban and Extra Urban Studies 6*(4), pp. 1–14.

Humphreys, M. and Weinstein, J. M. 2007. Demobilization and reintegration. *Journal of Conflict Resolution* 51(4), pp. 531–67.

Hutchings, K. 2007. Happy anniversary! Time and critique in international relations theory. *Review of International Studies 33* (S1), April, pp. 71–89.

Hutchings, K. 2008. *Time and World Politics: Thinking the Present*. Manchester: Manchester University Press.

Hutchings, K. 2018. Time and the study of world politics. *Millennium 46*(3), pp. 253–8.

Hutchinson, F. 1999. Valuing young people's voices on the future as if they really mattered. *Journal of Futures Studies* 3(2), pp. 43–51.

Hutchinson, F. 2005a. Mapping and imagined futures: Beyond colonizing cartography. *Journal of Futures Studies* 9(4), pp. 1–14.

Hutchinson, F. 2005b. *Educating Beyond Violent Futures*. London: Routledge.

Hutchinson, F. P. and Milojević, I. 2012. Worlds without War: Reflections on Elise Boulding's Life, Work and Legacy as a Peace Educator, Feminist and Futurist. *Journal of Peace Education* 9(2), pp. 151–68.

Hutchinson, F., 1997. Our children's futures: Are there lessons for environmental educators?. *Environmental Education Research* 3(2), pp. 189–201.

Igreja, V. 2012. Multiple temporalities in indigenous justice and healing practices in Mozambique. *International Journal of Transitional Justice* 6(3), pp. 404–22.

Iles, K. 2015. *Sri Lanka Post-Closure Evaluation Report*. London: VSO.

Ilievski, Z. and Taleski, D. 2009. Was the EU's role in conflict management in Macedonia a success? *Ethnopolitics* 8(3–4), pp. 355–67.

Inayatullah, S. 1998. Macrohistory and futures studies. *Futures* 30(5), pp. 381–94.

Inayatullah, S., 1997. Future generations thinking. *Futures* 29(8), pp. 701–706.

INTRAC. 2016. Post-closure evaluation: an indulgence or a valuable exercise? Oxford: INTRAC. Online at https://www.intrac.org/resources/ontrac-post-closure-evaluation-an-indulgence-or-a-valuable-exercise/ontrac-61-post-closure-evaluation-an-indulgence-or-a-valuable-exercise/ (accessed 19 January 2021).

Izzi, V., 2013. Just keeping them busy? Youth employment projects as a peacebuilding tool. *International Development Planning Review* 35(2), p.103.

Jachova, Z. 2004. Inclusive education of children with special needs in Republic of Macedonia. *Journal of Special Education and Rehabilitation* 5(1–2), pp. 35–46.

Jackson, P. 2005. Chiefs, money and politicians: Rebuilding local government in post-war Sierra Leone. *Public Administration and Development: The International Journal of Management Research and Practice* 25(1), pp. 49–58.

Jackson, P. 2007. Reshuffling an old deck of cards? The politics of local government reform in Sierra Leone. *African Affairs* 106(422), pp. 95–111.

James, A. 2010. Sustaining a civil society campaign around the chieftaincy reform process in Sierra Leone Final Report. Freetown: SfCG.

James, R. 2015. Is there such a thing as responsible exit? Online at https://www.intrac.org/wpcms/wp-content/uploads/2016/11/Exit-strategies-and-sustainability.-Lessons-for-practitioners.-November-2016.pdf (accessed 28 January 2021).

Jarrett, R. L. 1997. Bringing families back in: Neighborhoods' effects on child development. In: J. Brooks-Gunn, G. J. Duncan, and J. L. Aber (eds), *Neighborhood Poverty: Vol. 2. Policy Implications in Studying Neighbourhoods*. New York: Russell Sage Foundation, pp. 48–64.

Jarstad, A. K. and Belloni, R. 2012. Introducing hybrid peace governance: Impact and prospects of liberal peacebuilding. *Global Governance: A Review of Multilateralism and International Organisations* 18(1), pp. 1–6.

Jeffrey, C. and Dyson, J. 2014. 'I serve therefore I am': Youth and generative politics in India. *Comparative Studies in Society and History 56*(4), pp. 967–94.

Jencks, C. and Mayer, S. 1990. The social consequences of growing up in a poor neighborhood. In: Lynn, L. E. and McGeary, M. F. H. (eds), *Inner-City Poverty in the United States.* Washington, DC: National Academy Press, pp. 111–86.

Jenkins, R. 2008. *The UN Peace-building Commission and the Dissemination of International Norms.* Crisis States Research Centre. Online at https://assets.publishing.service.gov.uk/media/57a08bc3ed915d622c000ea1/wp38.2.pdf (accessed 10 September 2020).

Jennings, K. M. 2008. Unclear ends, unclear means: Reintegration in postwar societies— the case of Liberia. *Global Governance: A Review of Multilateralism and International Organizations 14*(3), pp. 327–45.

Jennings, L. B., Parra-Medina, D. M., Hilfinger-Messias, D. K., and McLoughlin, K. 2006. Toward a critical social theory of youth empowerment. *Journal of Community Practice 14*(1–2), pp. 31–55.

Johnny, T. 2017. *Baseline Survey Report. United for Greater Governance: Empowering Rural Communities to Strengthen Local Governance and Accountability Processes.* Washington, DC: SfCG.

Joireman, S. F., 2018. Intergenerational land conflict in northern Uganda: Children, customary law and return migration. *Africa 88*(1), pp. 81–98.

Jones, H. 2011. Taking responsibility for complexity. How implementation can achieve results in the face of complex problems. ODI Working Paper 330. http://www.odi.org.uk/resources/details.asp?id=5275&title=complex-problems-complexity-implementation-policy (accessed 19 January 2021).

Jordan, A. B. 2005. Learning to use books and television: An exploratory study in the ecological perspective. *American Behavioral Scientist 48*(5), pp. 523–38.

Judah, T. 2020. 'Wildly wrong: North Macedonia's population mystery'. *Balkan Insight.* 14 May. Online at https://balkaninsight.com/2020/05/14/wildly-wrong-north-macedonias-population-mystery/ (accessed 3 September 2021).

Juncos, A. E. and Joseph, J. 2020. Resilient peace: Exploring the theory and practice of resilience in peacebuilding interventions. *Journal of Intervention and Statebuilding 14*(3), pp. 289–302.

Justino, P. 2014. Barriers to education in conflict-affected countries and policy opportunities. Paper commissioned for Fixing the Broken Promise of Education for All: Findings from the Global Initiative on Out-of-School Children. Montreal: UNESCO Institute for Statistics (UIS).

Justino, P., Leone, M., and Salardi, P. 2014. Short-and long-term impact of violence on education: The case of Timor Leste. *The World Bank Economic Review 28*(2), pp. 320–53.

Kabbah, A. 2010. *Coming Back from the Brink in Sierra Leone: A Memoir.* Accra: EPP Book Services.

Kakos, M. and Fritzsche, B. 2017. Meta-ethnography E&E. Editorial of Special Issue on Meta-ethnographic synthesis in education: Challenges, aims and possibilities. *Ethnography and Education 12*(2), pp. 129–33.

Kaldor, M. 1999. *New and Old Wars: Organised Violence in a Global Era.* New York: John Wiley & Sons.

Kalyvas, S. N. 2001. New and old civil wars: A valid distinction? *World Politics 54*(1), pp. 99–118.

Kamatsiko, V. V. 2014. PCIA theory in field practice: World Vision's pursuit of peace impact and programming quality across sectors. *Journal of Peacebuilding & Development 9*(1), pp. 26–43.

Kandeh, J. D. 2008. Rogue incumbents, donor assistance and Sierra Leone's second post-conflict elections of 2007. *The Journal of Modern African Studies* 46(4), pp. 603–35.

Kaplan, M., Sanchez, M., and Hoffman, J. 2017. *Intergenerational Pathways to a Sustainable Society*. Springer International Publishing.

Kaplan, R. D. 1994. The coming anarchy. *Atlantic Monthly* 273(2), pp. 44–76.

Kappler, S. and Lemay-Hébert, N. 2016. What attachment to peace? Exploring the normative and material dimensions of local ownership in peacebuilding. *Review of international studies* 42(5), pp. 895–914.

Karajkov, R. 2008. Macedonia's 2001 ethnic war: Offsetting conflict. What could have been done but was not? *Conflict, Security & Development* 8(4), pp. 451–90.

Kargobai, G. 2017. Community Radio and Women's Empowerment in Sierra Leone. University of Guelph. Unpublished masters' thesis. Online at https://atrium. lib.uoguelph.ca/xmlui/bitstream/handle/10214/16177/KargobaiG_201708_MRP. pdf?sequence=1&isAllowed=y (accessed 19 May 2021).

Katsumata, H. 2011. Mimetic adoption and norm diffusion: 'Western' security cooperation in Southeast Asia? *Review of International Studies* 37(2), pp. 557–76.

Katz, E. and Lazarsfeld, P. F. 1955. *Personal Influence: The Part Played by People in the Flow of Mass Communication*. New York: The Free Press.

Katzenstein, M. F. 1996. *The Culture of National Security: Norms and Identity in World Politics*. New York: Columbia University Press.

Kaufman, S. J. 1996. Preventive peacekeeping, ethnic violence, and Macedonia. *Studies in Conflict & Terrorism* 19(3), pp. 229–46.

Kavaja, K. 2017. Ethnicity, politics, and education in Macedonia. *European Journal of Education Studies* 3(9), pp. 480–94.

Kawano-Chiu, M. 2012. *Starting on the Same Page: A Lessons Report from the Peacebuilding Evaluation Project*. Washington: Alliance for Peacebuilding.

Keck, M. E. and Sikkink, K. 1997. Transnational advocacy networks in the movement society. In: Meyer, D.S. and Tarrow, S. (eds), *The Social Movement Society: Contentious Politics for a New Century*, Oxford: Rowman and Littlefield, pp. 217–38.

Keddie, A. 2012. Refugee education and justice issues of representation, redistribution and recognition. *Cambridge Journal of Education* 42(2), pp. 197–212.

Keen, D. 2000. Incentives and disincentives for violence. In: M. Berdal and D. M. Malone (eds). *Greed and Grievance: Economic Agendas in Civil Wars*. Boulder, CO: Lynne Reinner, pp. 19–42.

Keen, D. 2005. *Conflict and Collusion in Sierra Leone*. London: James Currey (imprint of Boydell & Brewer Ltd).

Keet, A. 2015. It is time: Critical human rights education in an age of counter-hegemonic distrust. *Education as Change* 19(3), pp. 46–64.

Keita, M. 2018. Sierra Leone's path of resilience: Helping democracy deliver. Online at https://sl.usembassy.gov/sierra-leones-path-of-resilience-helping-democracy-deliver/ (accessed 16 September 2021).

Kelman, H. C. 1995. Contributions of an unofficial conflict resolution effort to the Israeli–Palestinian breakthrough. *Negotiation Journal* 11(1), pp. 19–27.

Kelsi, S. 2013. *Final Narrative Report: Sharing a Common Culture: Balkan Theatre Network for EU Integration*. Skopje: Centre for Common Ground. Online at https://www.sfcg.org/wp-content/uploads/2014/08/MKD_EV_Mar13_Sharing-Common-Culture-Balkan-Theatre-Networks-for-EU-Integration.pdf (accessed 22 June 2020).

Ker-Lindsay, J. 2009. From autonomy to independence: The evolution of international thinking on Kosovo, 1998–2005. *Journal of Balkan and Near Eastern Studies 11*(2), pp. 141–56.

Kester, K. 2010. Education for peace: Content, form, and structure: mobilizing youth for civic engagement. *Peace and Conflict Review 4*(2), pp. 1–10.

King, E. 2018. What Kenyan youth want and why it matters for peace. *African Studies Review 61*(1), pp. 134–57.

Kinsbergen, S. and Plaisier, C. 2016. Trust, courage and genuine curiosity: Conducting a post-closure sustainability study. Oxford: *INTRAC Viewpoint, 61*(January), pp. 2–3.

Kirchberger, A., and J. Niessen. 2011. *Integration beyond Migration*. Brussels: European Network Against Racism.

Kirpitchenko, L. and Mansouri, F. 2014. Social engagement among migrant youth: Attitudes and meanings. *Social Inclusion 2*(2), pp. 17–27.

Klapper, J. T. 1960. *The Effects of Mass Communication*. New York: Free Press.

Koinova, M. 2008. Kinstate intervention in ethnic conflicts: Albania and Turkey compared. *Ethnopolitics 7*(4), pp. 373–90.

Koinova, M. 2013. *Ethnonationalist Conflict in Postcommunist States: Varieties of Governance in Bulgaria, Macedonia, and Kosovo*. University of Pennsylvania Press.

Koktsidis, P. I. 2019. The decision to use violence: Opportunity structures and the Albanian insurgency in the Former Yugoslav Republic of Macedonia. *Ethnopolitics 18*(4), pp. 383–405.

Kolb, D. A. 1984. Experiential learning: Experience as the source of learning and development. New Jersey: Prentice-Hall.

Koneska, C. 2012. Vetoes, ethnic bidding, decentralisation: Post-conflict education in Macedonia. *JEMIE 11*, pp. 28–50.

Koneska, C. 2016. *After Ethnic Conflict: Policy-Making in Post-Conflict Bosnia and Herzegovina and Macedonia*. London: Routledge.

Konings, M. and James, A. 2009. Building peace in thin air: The case of search for common ground's talking drum studio in Sierra Leone. In: Zelizer, C. and Rubinstein, R.A. (eds), Zelizer, C. and Rubinstein, R. A. (eds), *Building Peace: Practical. Reflections from the Field*. Sterling, VA: Kumarian Press, pp. 249–65.

Kreci, V. and Ymeri, B. 2010. The impact of territorial re-organisational policy interventions in the Republic of Macedonia. *Local Government Studies 36*(2), pp. 271–90.

Krosnick, J. A. and Petty, R. E. 1995. Attitude strength: An overview. In: Petty, R. E. and Krosnick, J. A. (eds), *Attitude Strength: Antecedents and Consequences*. Mahwah, NJ: Erlbaum, pp. 1–24.

Krstevska-Papic, B., and Zekolli, V. 2013. Integrated education in the Republic of Macedonia. In: C. McGlynn, M. Zembylas and Z. Bekerman (eds), *Integrated Education in Conflicted Societies*. New York: Palgrave Macmillan, pp. 135–45.

Kruglanski, A. W. 2004a. *The Psychology of Closed Mindedness*. New York: Psychology.

Kruglanski, A. W. 2004b. The quest for the gist: On challenges of going abstract in social and personality psychology. *Personality and Social Psychology Review 8*(2), pp. 156–63.

Krupka, E. L. and Weber, R. A. 2013. Identifying social norms using coordination games: Why does dictator game sharing vary? *Journal of the European Economic Association 11*(3), pp. 495–524.

Kumar, K. 2006. International assistance to promote independent media in transition and post-conflict societies. *Democratization 13*(4), pp. 652–67.

Kunda, Z. 1990. The case for motivated reasoning. *Psychological Bulletin 108*(3), pp. 480–98.

Kupermintz, H. and Salomon, G. 2005. Lessons to be learned from research on peace education in the context of intractable conflict. *Theory into Practice 44*(4), pp. 293–302.

Kurian, N. and Kester, K. 2019. Southern voices in peace education: Interrogating race, marginalisation and cultural violence in the field. *Journal of Peace Education 16*(1), pp. 21–48.

Kurtenbach, S. and Pawelz, J. 2015. Voting is not enough: Youth and political citizenship in post-war societies. *Peacebuilding 3*(2), pp. 141–56.

Kvinna till Kvinna. 2011. Making achievements last: Learning from exit experiences. Johanneshov: The Kvinna till Kvinna Foundation.

Labonte, M. T., 2011. From patronage to peacebuilding? Elite capture and governance from below in Sierra Leone. *African Affairs 111*(442), pp. 90–115.

Laffey, M. and Weldes, J. 1997. Beyond belief: Ideas and symbolic technologies in the study of international relations. *European Journal of International Relations 3*(2), pp. 193–237.

Lahai, J. A. 2016. *Equitable Land Rights Promotion. Final Evaluation Report for OSIWA*. Washington, DC: SfCG(April).

Lambourne, M. 2008. Towards sustainable peace and development in Sierra Leone: Civil society and the peacebuilding commission. *Journal of Peacebuilding & Development 4*(2), pp. 47–59.

Lange, M. and Dawson, A. 2010. Education and ethnic violence: A cross-national time-series analysis. *Nationalism and Ethnic Politics 16*(2), pp. 216–39.

Lawrence, M. 2014. United Nations peace building in Sierra Leone: Toward vertical integration? *CIGI Papers 49*, pp. 1–27.

Lazarus, N. 2011. Evaluating Peace Education in the Oslo-Intifada Generation: A Long-term Impact Study of Seeds of Peace 1993–2010. Ph.D. dissertation. American University, International Relations, Washington, DC.

Lederach, J. P. 1995. *Preparing for Peace: Conflict Transformation Across Cultures*. New York: Syracuse University Press.

Lederach, J. P. 1997. *Sustainable Reconciliation in Divided Societies*. Washington, DC: USIP.

Lederach, J. P. and Appleby, R. S. 2010. Strategic peacebuilding: An overview. In: Philpott, D. and Powers, G. (eds), *Strategies of Peace*. Oxford: Oxford University Press, pp. 19–44.

Lederach, J. P., Culbertson, H., and Neufeldt, R. 2007. *Reflective Peacebuilding: A Planning, Monitoring and Learning Toolkit*. Joan B.Kroc Institute for International Peace Studies.

Lee, R. P., Hart, R. I., Watson, R. M., and Rapley, T. 2015. Qualitative synthesis in practice: Some pragmatics of meta-ethnography. *Qualitative Research 15*(3), pp. 334–50.

Leitner, M., Scher, G., and Shuval, K. 1999. Peace-making through recreation: The positive effects of intergenerational activities on the attitudes of Israeli Arabs and Jews toward each other. *World Leisure & Recreation 41*(2), pp. 25–9.

Lemay-Hébert, N. 2011. The 'empty-shell' approach: The setup process of international administrations in Timor-Leste and Kosovo, its consequences and lessons. *International Studies Perspectives 12*(2), pp. 190–211.

Lemish, D. 2005. Guest Editor's introduction: The media gendering of war and conflict. *Feminist Media Studies 5*(3), pp. 275–80.

Lemish, D. and Götz, M. (eds). 2007. *Children and Media in Times of Conflict and War*. New Jersey: Hampton Press.

Lemish, P. 2008. Peacebuilding contributions of Northern Ireland producers of children and youth-oriented media. *Journal of Children and Media 2*(3), pp. 282–99.

Lemon, A. 2017. Presentation on 'Building the Programs That Can Better Build the Peace: Experts Offer Ways to Ensure the Impact of Programs to Halt Violent Conflicts,' online at https://www.usip.org/events/building-programs-can-better-build-peace, 7 March (accessed 17 January 2021).

Lemon, A. and Pinet, M. 2018. Measuring unintended effects in peacebuilding: What the field of international cooperation can learn from innovative approaches shaped by complex contexts. *Evaluation and Program Planning 68* (June), pp. 253–61.

Leonardsson, H. and Rudd, G. 2015. The 'local turn' in peacebuilding: A literature review of effective and emancipatory local peacebuilding. *Third World Quarterly 36*(5), pp. 825–39.

Leone, G. 2018. Beyond historical guilt: Intergenerational narratives of violence and reconciliation. In: Rosa, A. and Valsiner, J. (eds), *The Cambridge Handbook of Sociocultural Psychology*. Cambridge Handbooks in Psychology. Cambridge: Cambridge University Press, pp. 458–78.

Leonhardt, M. 1999. *Improving Capacities and Procedures for Formulating and Implementing Effective Conflict Prevention Strategies: An Overview of Recent Donor Initiatives. Development and Peacebuilding Programme*. London: International Alert.

Leonhardt, M. 2003. Towards a unified methodology: Reframing PCIA. Online at http://dmeforpeace.org/sites/default/files/Leonhardt_Towards%20a%20Unified%20 Methodology.pdf (accessed 17 May 2021).

Levinger, B. and McLeod, J. 2002. *Hello, I Must Be Going: Ensuring Quality Services and Sustainable Benefits through Well-Designed Exit Strategies*. Newton: Education Development Centre and Center for Organisational Learning and Development.

Levitt, B. and March, J. G. 1988. Organisational learning. *Annual Review of Sociology 14*(1), pp. 319–38.

Levy, J. S. 2008. Case studies: Types, designs, and logics of inference. *Conflict Management and Peace Science 25*(1), pp. 1–18.

Lewis, D. 2003. NGOs, organizational culture, and institutional sustainability. *The Annals of the American Academy of Political and Social Science 590*(1), pp. 212–26.

Lewis, S. 2016. Development of a Timeline for Exit Strategies: Experiences from an Action Learning Set with the British Red Cross, EveryChild, Oxfam GB, Sightsavers and WWF-UK. *INTRAC Praxis Paper* 31.

Lijphart, A. 1971. Comparative politics and the comparative method. *The American Political Science Review 65*(3), pp. 682–93.

Lin, N. 2000. Inequality in social capital. *Contemporary Sociology 29*(6), pp. 785–95.

Lin, N. 2008. A network theory of social capital. In: C. Dario, J. W. Van Deth, and G. Wolleb (eds), *The Handbook of Social Capital*. Oxford: Oxford University Press, pp. 50–69.

Linde, R. 2018. Gatekeeper persuasion and issue adoption: Amnesty International and the transnational LGBTQ network. *Journal of Human Rights 17*(2), pp. 245–64.

Lipson, B. and Warren, H. 2006. 'Taking Stock' – A Snapshot of INGO Engagement in Civil Society Capacity Building. INTRAC Civil Society and Capacity Building Conference Paper, Oxford, England.

Loader, R., Hughes, J., Petroska-Beshka, V., and Tomovska-Misoska, A. 2018. Developing social cohesion through schools in Northern Ireland and the former Yugoslav Republic of Macedonia: A study of policy transfer. *Journal on Education in Emergencies 4*(1), pp. 114–40.

Lottholz, P. 2018. Critiquing anthropological imagination in peace and conflict studies: from empiricist positivism to a dialogical approach in ethnographic peace research. *International Peacekeeping 25*(5), pp. 695–720.

Lousley, C., 2016. Humanitarian melodramas, globalist nostalgia: Affective temporalities of globalization and uneven development. *Globalizations 13*(3), pp. 310–328.

Low, W. and Davenport, E. 2002. NGO capacity building and sustainability in the Pacific. *Asia Pacific Viewpoint 43*(3), pp. 367–79.

Lund, M. 2003. What kind of peace is being built? Taking stock of post-conflict peacebuilding and charting future directions. Paper presented on the 10th Anniversary of Agenda for Peace, International Development Research Centre, Ottawa, Canada, pp. 2–55.

Lyon, A. 2011. *Decentralisation and the Delivery of Primary and Secondary Education.* Skopje: Centre for Research and Policy Making.

Lyon, A. 2012. Between the Integration and Accommodation of Ethnic Difference: Decentralisation in the Republic of Macedonia. *Journal on Ethnopolitics and Minority Issues in Europe 11*(3), pp. 80–103.

Lyon, A. 2013. Decentralisation and the provision of primary and secondary education in the former Yugoslav Republic of Macedonia. *International Journal on Minority and Group Rights 20*(4), pp. 491–516.

Lyon, A. 2015. Political decentralisation and the strengthening of consensual, participatory local democracy in the Republic of Macedonia. *Democratization 22*(1), pp. 157–78.

Mac Ginty, R. 2007. Reconstructing post-war Lebanon: A challenge to the liberal peace? Analysis. *Conflict, Security & Development 7*(3), pp. 457–82.

Mac Ginty, R. 2008. Indigenous peace-making versus the liberal peace. *Cooperation and Conflict 43*(2), pp. 139–63.

Mac Ginty, R. 2012a. Routine peace: Technocracy and peacebuilding. *Cooperation and Conflict 47*(3), pp. 287–308.

Mac Ginty, R. 2012b. Between resistance and compliance: Non-participation and the liberal peace. *Journal of Intervention and Statebuilding 6* (2), pp. 167–87.

Mac Ginty, R. 2016. Political versus sociological time: The fraught world of timelines and deadlines. In: Langer, A. and Brown, G. K. (eds), *Building Sustainable Peace: Timing and Sequencing of Post-Conflict Reconstruction and Peacebuilding.* Oxford: Oxford University Press, pp. 15–31.

Mac Ginty, R. and Richmond, O. 2007. Myth or reality: Opposing views on the liberal peace and post-war reconstruction. *Global Society 21*(4), pp. 491–7.

Mac Ginty, R. and Richmond, O. P. 2013. The local turn in peace building: A critical agenda for peace. *Third World Quarterly 34*(5), pp. 763–83.

Mac Ginty, R., 2014. Everyday peace: Bottom-up and local agency in conflict-affected societies. *Security Dialogue 45*(6), pp. 548–64.

Mack, A. 2002. Civil war: Academic research and the policy community. *Journal of Peace Research 39*(5), pp. 515–525.

Maclay, C. and Özerdem, A. 2010. 'Use' them or 'lose' them: Engaging Liberia's disconnected youth through socio-political integration. *International Peacekeeping 17*(3), pp. 343–60.

Maclure, R. and Denov, M. 2006. I didn't want to die so I joined them: Structuration and the process of becoming boy soldiers in Sierra Leone. *Terrorism and Political Violence 18*(1), pp. 119–35.

Magen, A. and L. Morlinoeds. 2009. *International Actors, Democratisation and the Rule of Law: Anchoring Democracy?* Abingdon: Routledge.

Maira, S. and Soep, E. (eds). 2005. *Youthscapes: The Popular, the National, the Global.* Philadelphia: University of Pennsylvania Press.

Malejacq, R. and Mukhopadhyay, D. 2016. The 'tribal politics' of field research: A reflection on power and partiality in 21st-century warzones. *Perspectives on Politics 14*(4), pp. 1011–28.

Mannheim, B. 1988. Social background, schooling, and parental job attitudes as related to adolescents' work values. *Youth & Society 19*(3), pp. 269–93.

Manning, E. R. 2009. Challenging generations: Youths and elders in rural and peri-urban Sierra Leone. Justice and Development Working Paper Series 1(2), Washington DC: World Bank.

Maoz, I. 2000. An experiment in peace: Reconciliation-aimed workshops of Jewish-Israeli and Palestinian youth. *Journal of Peace Research 37*(6), pp. 721–36.

Martens, B., Mummert, U., Murrell, P., and Seabright, P. 2008. *The Institutional Economics of Foreign Aid*. New York: Cambridge University Press.

Maru, V. 2019. Give the people the power to transform institutions. Skoll World Forum, 21 October. Online at https://www.youtube.com/watch?v=WfjUyqV20Jo (accessed 23 May 2021).

Masefield, S. C., Megaw, A., Barlow, M., White, P. C., Altink, H., and Grugel, J. 2020. Re-purposing NGO data for better research outcomes: A scoping review of the use and secondary analysis of NGO data in health policy and systems research. *Health Research Policy and Systems 18*(63), pp. 1–22.

Massey, D. S. 1990. American apartheid: Segregation and the making of the underclass. *American Journal of Sociology 96*(2), pp. 329–58.

Matsumoto, M. 2018. Technical and vocational education and training and marginalised youths in post-conflict Sierra Leone: Trainees' experiences and capacity to aspire. *Research in Comparative and International Education 13*(4), pp. 534–50.

Mayall, B. 2000. The sociology of childhood in relation to children's rights. *The International Journal of Children's Rights 8*(3), pp. 243–59.

Mayer, N. D. and Tormala, Z. L., 2010. 'Think' versus 'feel' framing effects in persuasion. *Personality and Social Psychology Bulletin 36*(4), pp. 443–54.

Mayne, J. 2011. Contribution analysis: Addressing cause and effect. In: Schwartz, R., Forss, K., and Marra, M. (eds), Schwartz, R., Forss, K., and Marra, M. (eds), *Evaluating the Complex*. New Brunswick, NJ: Transaction Publishers, pp. 53–96.

Mayne, J. 2012. Contribution analysis: Coming of age? *Evaluation 18*(3), pp. 270–80.

McCandless, E., Abitbol, E. and Donais, T. 2015. Vertical integration: A dynamic practice promoting transformative peacebuilding. Editorial. *Journal of Peacebuilding and Development 10*(1), pp. 1–9.

McCombs, M. E. and Shaw, D. L. 2017. The agenda-setting function of mass media. *The Agenda Setting Journal. Theory, Practice, Critique 1*(2), pp. 105–16.

McDaniels, T. L. and Gregory, R. 2004. Learning as an objective within a structured risk management decision process. *Environmental Science & Technology 38*(7), pp. 1921–26.

McDowell, L. 1992. Doing gender: Feminism, feminists and research methods in human geography. *Transactions of the Institute of British Geographers 17*(4), 399–416.

McEvoy-Levy, S. (ed.), 2006. *Troublemakers or Peacemakers?: Youth and Post-Accord Peace Building*. Indiana: University of Notre Dame Press.

McEvoy-Levy, S. 2001. Youth, violence and conflict transformation. *Peace Review 13*(1), pp. 89–96.

McEvoy, J. 2014. *Power-Sharing Executives: Governing in Bosnia, Macedonia, and Northern Ireland*. Philadelphia: University of Pennsylvania Press.

McEvoy, S. 2000. Communities and peace: Catholic youth in Northern Ireland. *Journal of Peace Research 37*(1), pp. 85–103.

McGill, M. and Zerla, P. 2017. Final evaluation of the SFCG Project 'Engaging Children and Youth as Partners in Preventing Violence against Children in Liberia, Guinea and Sierra Leone.' Online at https://www.sfcg.org/final-evaluation-jan-2017-engaging-children-youth-partners-preventing-violence-children/ (accessed 9 November 2020).

McGlynn, C. 2009. Negotiating cultural difference in divided societies: An analysis of approaches to integrated education in Northern Ireland. In: McGlynn, C., Zembylas, M., Bekerman, Z., and Gallagher, T. (eds), *Peace Education in Conflict and Post-Conflict Societies: Comparative Perspectives*. New York: Palgrave Macmillan, pp. 9–26.

McGlynn, C. and Zembylas, M. (eds), 2009. *Peace Education in Conflict and Post-Conflict Societies: Comparative Perspectives*. New York: Springer.

McGlynn, C., Zembylas, M., and Bekerman, Z. (eds), 2013. *Integrated Education in Conflicted Societies*. New York: Palgrave Macmillan.

McGuire, W. J. 1968. Personality and attitude change: An information-processing theory. *Psychological Foundations of Attitudes*. In: Greenwald, A., Brock, T., and Ostrom, T. (eds), *Psychological Foundations of Attitudes*. New York: Academic Press, pp. 171–96.

McIntyre, A., Aning, E. K., and Addo, P. N. N. 2002. Politics, war and youth culture in Sierra Leone: An alternative interpretation. *African Security Studies 11*(3), pp. 6–15.

McKechnie, L. 2000. Ethnographic observation of preschool children. *Library and Information Science Research 22*(1), pp. 61–76.

McKeown, S. and Taylor, L. K. 2017. Intergroup contact and peacebuilding: Promoting youth civic engagement in Northern Ireland. *Journal of Social and Political Psychology 5*(2), 415–34.

McLeod, L. 2013. Back to the future: Temporality and gender security narratives in Serbia. *Security Dialogue 44*(2), pp. 165–81.

McMahon, P. C. 2017. *The NGO Game: Post-Conflict Peacebuilding in the Balkans and Beyond*. Ithaca, New York: Cornell University Press.

McMullin, J. R. 2013. Integration or separation? The stigmatisation of ex-combatants after war. *Review of International Studies 39*(2), pp. 385–414.

McQuail, D. 1987. *Mass Communication Theory: An Introduction*. London: Sage Publications.

Meka, E. 2016. Minority protection and democratic consolidation: The role of European integration in the Republic of Macedonia. *Genocide Studies and Prevention: An International Journal 10*(2), pp. 23–37.

Menkhaus, K. 2004. *Impact Assessment in Post-Conflict Peacebuilding Challenges and Future Directions*. Switzerland: Interpeace.

Menzel, A. 2011. Between ex-combatization and opportunities for peace: the double-edged qualities of motorcycle-taxi driving in urban post-war Sierra Leone. *Africa Today 58*(2), pp. 97–127.

Menzel, A. 2015. Foreign Investment, Large-scale Land Deals, and Uncertain Development in Sierra Leone. Impacts, Conflicts, and Security Concerns. *CCS Working Papers*. Marburg: Philipps Universität Marburg.

Messenger Davies, M., 2010. *Children, Media and Culture*. McGraw-Hill Education (UK).

Miall, H. 2004. Conflict transformation: A multidimensional task. Berlin: Berghof Research Centre for Constructive Conflict Management. August. Online at http://edoc.vifapol.de/opus/volltexte/2011/2569/pdf/miall_handbook.pdf (accessed 02 February 2022).

Mignolo, W. D. 2007. Delinking: The rhetoric of modernity, the logic of coloniality and the grammar of de-coloniality. *Cultural Studies 21*(2–3), pp. 449–514.

Mika, H. 2002. Evaluation as peacebuilding?: Transformative values, processes, and outcomes. *Contemporary Justice Review 5*(4), pp. 339–49.

Milcev, V. V. 2013. Building bridges at the earliest age through the *Mozaik* model for multicultural pre-school education in Macedonia. In: McGlynn, C., Zembylas, M., and Bekerman, Z. *Integrated Education in Conflicted Societies*, New York: Palgrave Macmillan, pp. 121–35.

Millar, G. 2013. Expectations and experiences of peacebuilding in Sierra Leone: Parallel peacebuilding processes and compound friction. *International Peacekeeping 20*(2): 189–203.

Millar, G. 2014a. Disaggregating hybridity: Why hybrid institutions do not produce predictable experiences of peace. *Journal of Peace Research 51*(4), pp. 501–14.

Millar, G. 2014b. *An Ethnographic Approach to Peacebuilding: Understanding Local Experiences in Transitional States*. Abingdon: Routledge.

Millar, G. 2015. We have no voice for that: Land rights, power, and gender in rural Sierra Leone. *Journal of Human Rights 14*(4), pp. 445–62.

Millar, G. 2016. Local experiences of liberal peace: Marketisation and emergent conflict dynamics in Sierra Leone. *Journal of Peace Research 53*(4), pp. 569–81.

Millar, G. 2017. For whom do local peace processes function? Maintaining control through conflict management. *Cooperation and Conflict 52*(3), pp. 293–308.

Millar, G. 2018a. Co-opting authority and privatizing force in rural Africa: Ensuring corporate power over land and people. *Rural Sociology 83*(4), pp. 749–71.

Millar, G. 2018b. Engaging ethnographic peace research: Exploring an approach, *International Peacekeeping 25*(5), pp. 597–609.

Millar, G. 2018c. Decentring the intervention experts: Ethnographic peace research and policy engagement. *Cooperation and Conflict 53*(2), pp. 259–76.

Millar, G. 2021. Coordinated ethnographic peace research: Assessing complex peace interventions writ large and over time. *Peacebuilding 9*(2), pp. 145–59.

Millar, G. and Podder, S. 2021. Indigenous Monitoring and Evaluation of Peace Interventions. Unpublished manuscript.

Miller, D. T. and Prentice, D. A.1996. The construction of social norms and standards. In: Higgins, E. T. and Kruglanski, A. W. (eds), *Social Psychology: Handbook of Basic Principles*. New York: The Guilford Press, pp. 799–829.

Miller, N. and Campbell, D. T. 1959. Recency and primacy in persuasion as a function of the timing of speeches and measurements. *The Journal of Abnormal and Social Psychology 59*(1), pp. 1–9.

Ministry of Education and Science. 2006. *National Program for the Development of Education in the Republic of Macedonia 2005–2015*. Skopje: Republic of Macedonia.

Ministry of Education and Science. 2010. *Steps towards Integrated Education in the Educational System of the Republic of Macedonia*. Skopje: Republic of Macedonia.

Ministry of Education and Science. 2018. *Government of Macedonia, Education Strategy for 2018–2025 and Action Plan*. Skopje. Republic of Macedonia.

Minow, M. 2002. Education for co-existence. *Ariz. L. Rev. 44*. Online at https://dash.harvard.edu/bitstream/handle/1/3113767/Minow%20-%20Education%20for%20Co-Existence.pdf?sequence=2&isAllowed=y (accessed 13 January 2021).

Minow, M. 2002. Education for co-existence. *Arizona Law Review 44*(1), pp. 1–30.

Mitchell, A. 2010. Peace beyond process?. *Millennium 38*(3), pp. 641–64.

Mitton, K. 2008. Engaging disengagement: The political reintegration of Sierra Leone's Revolutionary United Front: Analysis. *Conflict, Security & Development 8*(2), pp. 193–222.

Mkandawire, T., 2002. The terrible toll of post-colonial 'rebel movements' in Africa: towards an explanation of the violence against the peasantry. *The Journal of Modern African Studies 40*(2), pp. 181–215.

Moran, M. H. 2006. *The Ethnography of Political Violence – Liberia*. Philadelphia: University of Pennsylvania Press.

Morris, L. 2015. Working at the Sharp End of Programme Closure: Every Child's Responsible Exit Principles. Praxis Note No. 70. Oxford: INTRAC. Online at https://www.intrac.org/wpcms/wp-content/uploads/2016/09/Praxis-Note-70-EveryChilds-Responsible-Exit-Principles-Final-Lucy-Morris-Head-of-Programmes.pdf (accessed 1 February 2021).

Mueller-Hirth, N. and Oyola, S. R. (eds). 2018. *Time and Temporality in Transitional and Post-Conflict Societies.* Abingdon: Routledge.

Mullins, L. 2011. Sierra Leone's Independent Radio Network. Online at https://www.pri. org/stories/2011-04-19/sierra-leones-independent-radio-network (accessed 19 January 2021).

Munive, J. 2010. The army of 'unemployed' young people. *Young 18*(3), pp. 321-38.

Munive, J. and Jakobsen, S. F. 2012. Revisiting DDR in Liberia: Exploring the power, agency and interests of local and international actors in the 'making' and 'unmaking' of combatants. *Conflict, Security & Development 12*(4), pp. 359-85.

Murrar, S. and Brauer, M. 2018. Entertainment-education effectively reduces prejudice. *Group Processes & Intergroup Relations 21*(7), pp. 1053-77.

Murrar, S. and Brauer, M. 2019. Overcoming resistance to change: Using narratives to create more positive intergroup attitudes. *Current Directions in Psychological Science 28*(2), pp. 164-9.

Myers, M. 2009. Radio and Development in Africa: A Concept Paper. Prepared for the IDRC, Canada. Online at https://idl-bnc-idrc.dspacedirect.org/bitstream/handle/10625/41180/129100.pdf?sequence=1 (accessed 12 January 2021).

Myhrvold, R. 2005. Former Yugoslav Republic of Macedonia: Education as a Political Phenomenon. NORDEM Report 04. Oslo: Norwegian Centre for Human Rights.

Nanni, G. 2012. *The Colonisation of Time: Ritual, Routine and Resistance in the British Empire.* Manchester, Manchester University Press.

Naskova, Z. 2014a. Baseline Study of the *Mozaik* Programme in Macedonia. Skopje, Centre for Common Ground.

Naskova, Z. 2014b. Evaluation of the *Mozaik-Model for Integrated, Multicultural Education in FYR Macedonia.* Skopje: Centre for Common Ground.

Natsios, A. 1997. An NGO perspective. In: Zartman, I. W. and Rasmussen, J. L. (eds), *Peacemaking in International Conflict: Methods and Techniques.* Washington, DC: USIP Press, pp. 337-64.

Ndlovu-Gatsheni, S. J. 2013. *Empire, Global Coloniality and African Subjectivity.* Oxford: Berghahn Books.

Ndlovu-Gatsheni, S. J. 2021. The cognitive empire, politics of knowledge and African intellectual productions: reflections on struggles for epistemic freedom and resurgence of decolonisation in the twenty-first century. *Third World Quarterly 42*(5), pp. 882-901.

Neethling, T. 2007. Pursuing sustainable peace through post-conflict peacebuilding: The case of Sierra Leone. *African Security Studies 16*(3), pp. 81-95.

Neufeldt, R. C. 2007. *'Frameworkers' and 'Circlers': Exploring Assumptions in Impact Assessment. Berghof Handbook for Conflict Transformation I and II.* https://dmeforpeace.org/sites/default/files/neufeldt_handbookII.pdf (accessed 12 January 2021).

Nicholson, M. and Hoye, R. (eds). 2008. *Sport and Social Capital.* London: Routledge.

Noblit, G. W. 2018. Meta-ethnography: adaptation and return. In: Urrieta Jr, L. and Noblit, G. W. (eds), *Cultural Constructions of Identity: Meta-ethnography and Theory.* Oxford: Oxford University Press, pp. 34-50.

Noblit, G. W. and Hare, R. D. 1988. *Meta-ethnography: Synthesizing Qualitative Studies* (Vol. 11). London: Sage.

Nordstrom, C. 2006. The jagged edge of peace: The creation of culture and war orphans in Angola. In: McEvoy-Levy, S. (ed.), *Troublemakers or Peacemakers?: Youth and Post-Accord Peace Building.* Indiana: University of Notre Dame Press, pp. 99-116.

Novelli, M. and Smith, A. 2011. The role of education in peacebuilding: A synthesis report of findings from Lebanon, Nepal and Sierra Leone. Online at https://reliefweb.int/sites/

reliefweb.int/files/resources/EEPCT_PeacebuildingSynthesisReport%20%281%29.pdf (accessed 15 September 2021).

Novelli, M., Cardozo, M. L., and Smith, A. 2015. A theoretical framework for analysing the contribution of education to sustainable peacebuilding: 4Rs in conflict-affected contexts. University of Amsterdam. Online at http://learningforpeace.unicef.org/partners/research-consortium/research-outputs (accessed 12 January 2021).

O'Brien, D. B. C. 1996. A lost generation: Youth identity and state decay in West Africa. In: Werbner, R. and Ranger, T. (eds), *Post-Colonial Identities in Africa*. London: Zed, pp. 55–77.

O'Donnell, V. and Kable, J. 1982. *Persuasion: An Interactive-Dependency Approach*. New York: Random House.

O'Keefe, D. J. 2009. Theories of persuasion. Nabi, R. L. and Oliver, M. B. (eds), *The SAGE Handbook of Media Processes and Effects*. London: Sage, pp. 269–82.

Oatley, N. and Thapa, R. 2012. *Media, Youth and Conflict Prevention in Sierra Leone*. Brussels: Initiative for Peacebuilding – Early Warning Analysis to Action.

Oatley, N. 2019. Through the portal and what the peacebuilding field found there: The DME for Peace website and the path to more rigorous design, monitoring, and evaluation practice. In: d'Estrée, T. P. (ed.), *New Directions in Peacebuilding Evaluation*. Rowman & Littlefield International, pp. 191–207.

Ober, H. 2012. Peacebuilding with Impact: Defining theories of change. Research Report for CARE International UK. Online at http://www.careinternational.org.uk/research-centre/conflict-and-peacebuilding/155-peacebuilding-with-impact-defining-theories-of-change (accessed 10 January 2021).

Oda, H. 2007. Peacebuilding from Below: Theoretical and methodological considerations toward an anthropological study on peace. *Journal of the Graduate School of Letters 2*, pp. 1–16.

OECD, n.d. Directorate for Education and Skills Innovative Learning Environments (ILE) System Note: Republic of Macedonia Teacher Education Programme on Early Numeracy and Literacy in the former Yugoslav Republic of Macedonia. Online at https://www.oecd.org/education/ceri/UNICEF.MCD.SystemNote.pdf (accessed 10 November 2020).

OECD. 2010. Evaluation of NGO Partnerships Aimed at Capacity Development. Brussels: Special Evaluation Office of International Cooperation. Online at https://www.oecd.org/derec/belgium/47206244.pdf (accessed 16 September 2021).

OECD. 2012. *Evaluating Peacebuilding Activities in Settings of Conflict and Fragility: Improving Learning for Results*. Paris: OECD-DAC.

OECD. 2015. System Note: Republic of Macedonia Teaching Education Programme on Early Numeracy and Literacy in the former Yugoslav Republic of Macedonia. Skopje: Directorate for Education and Skills Innovative Learning Environments (ILE).

OECD. 2019. *The Education System in the Republic of Macedonia*. Skopje.

OFA Review on Social Cohesion. 2015. Online at http://www.eip.org/sites/default/files/OFA%20Review%20on%20Social%20Cohesion.pdf (accessed 20 April 2019).

OFA. 2001. Online at https://www.osce.org/skopje/100622 (accessed 18 October 2019).

Okumu, P. 2019. How NGOs in Rich Countries Control their Counterparts in Poor Countries...and why they refuse to resolve it. Online at http://www.ipsnews.net/2019/07/ngos-rich-countries-control-counterparts-poor-countries-refuse-resolve/ (accessed 23 May 2021).

Olonisakin, F. 2008. *Peacekeeping in Sierra Leone: The Story of UNAMSIL*. Boulder, CO: Lynne Rienner Publishers.

Oosterom, M. 2018. *Youth Engagement in the Realm of Local Governance: Opportunities for Peace?*. Brighton: IDS. Online at https://opendocs.ids.ac.uk/opendocs/bitstream/handle/20.500.12413/13550/Wp508%20Online.pdf?sequence=1 (accessed 12 September 2021).

Oosterom, M. A. and Shahrokh, T. 2016. *Youth Governance Programming in Fragile Settings*. London: Plan International UK.

OSCE. 2010. *Bridges and Divisions in Education. A Quantitative Overview of Inter-ethnic Realities in Education*. Skopje: OSCE.

Oswald, C., Sauter, M., Weber, S., and Williams, R. 2020. Under the roof of rebels: civilian targeting after territorial takeover in Sierra Leone. *International Studies Quarterly* 64(2), pp. 295–305.

Otterbein, K. F. 2009. *The Anthropology of War*. Long Grove, Illinois: Waveland Press.

Özerdem, A. and Podder, S. 2015. *Youth in Conflict and Peacebuilding: Mobilization, Reintegration and Reconciliation*. London: Springer.

Paffenholz, T. 2005. Third-generation PCIA: Introducing the Aid for Peace Approach. Berlin: Berghof Handbook Dialogue Series No. 4.

Paffenholz, T. 2014. International peacebuilding goes local: Analysing Lederach's conflict transformation theory and its ambivalent encounter with 20 years of practice. *Peacebuilding* 2(1), pp. 11–27.

Paffenholz, T. 2015. Unpacking the local turn in peacebuilding: a critical assessment towards an agenda for future research. *Third World Quarterly* 36(5), pp. 857–74.

Paffenholz, T. 2016. Peacebuilding goes local and the local goes peacebuilding: Conceptual discourses and empirical realities of the local turn in peacebuilding. In: Debiel, T., Held, T., and Schneckener, U. (eds), 2016. *Peacebuilding in Crisis: Rethinking Paradigms and Practices of Transnational Cooperation*. Routledge, pp. 210–26.

Pahlke, E., Bigler, R. S., and Suizzo, M. A. 2012. Relations between colour-blind socialization and children's racial bias: Evidence from European American mothers and their preschool children. *Child Development* 83(4), pp. 1164–79.

Paluck, E. L. 2009a. Reducing intergroup prejudice and conflict using the media: A field experiment in Rwanda. *Journal of Personality and Social Psychology* 96(3), pp. 574–87.

Paluck, E. L. 2009b. What's in a norm? Sources and processes of norm change. *Journal of Personality and Social Psychology* 96(3), pp. 594–600.

Paluck, E. L. 2010b. Is it better not to talk? Group polarization, extended contact, and perspective taking in eastern Democratic Republic of Congo. *Personality and Social Psychology Bulletin* 36(9), pp. 1170–85.

Paluck, E. L. and Green, D. P. 2009a. Deference, dissent, and dispute resolution: An experimental intervention using mass media to change norms and behavior in Rwanda. *American Political Science Review* 103(4), pp. 622–44.

Paluck, E. L. and Green, D. P. 2009b. Prejudice reduction: What works? A review and assessment of research and practice. *Annual Review of Psychology* 60, pp. 339–67.

Paluck, E. L. and Shepherd, H. 2012. The salience of social referents: A field experiment on collective norms and harassment behavior in a school social network. *Journal of Personality and Social Psychology* 103(6), pp. 899–915.

Paluck, E. L., Green, S. A., and Green, D. P. 2019. The contact hypothesis re-evaluated. *Behavioural Public Policy* 3(2), pp. 129–58.

Paris, R. 2004. *At War's End: Building Peace After Civil Conflict*. Cambridge: Cambridge University Press.

Paris, R. 2010. Saving liberal peacebuilding. *Review of International Studies* 36(2), pp. 337–65.

PeaceDirect. 2016. Reflections on PeaceDirect's Approach to Evaluating Local Peace-building Initiatives. Online at https://www.peacedirect.org/wp-content/uploads/2016/11/Evaluation-paper.pdf (accessed 15 November 2020).

Pearson, B. 2002. *Putting Peace into Practice: Can Macedonia's New Government Meet the Challenge?* Washington DC: United States Institute of Peace.

Pelling, M. 2003. *The Vulnerability of Cities: Natural Disasters and Social Resilience.* London: Earthscan.

Pemunta, N. V. 2012. Neoliberal peace and the development deficit in post-conflict Sierra Leone. *International Journal of Development Issues 11*(3), pp. 192–207.

Percy-Smith, B. 2010. Councils, consultations and community: Rethinking the spaces for children and young people's participation. *Children's Geographies 8*(2), pp. 107–22.

Peritore, N. P. and Peritore, A. K. G. 1990. Brazilian attitudes toward agrarian reform: A Q-methodology opinion study of a conflictual issue. *The Journal of Developing Areas* pp. 377–406.

Peters, K. 2006. Footpaths to Reintegration: Armed Conflict, Youth and the Rural Crisis in Sierra Leone. PhD Thesis. Wagenigan University, Netherlands.

Peters, K. 2007a. From weapons to wheels: young Sierra Leonean ex-combatants become motorbike taxi-riders. *Peace, Conflict & Development 10*, pp. 1–23.

Peters, K. 2007b. Reintegration support for young ex-combatants: A right or a privilege? *International Migration 45*(5), pp. 35–59.

Peters, K. 2011a. *War and the Crisis of Youth in Sierra Leone* (Vol. 41). Cambridge University Press.

Peters, K. 2011b. The crisis of youth in post-war Sierra Leone: Problem solved? *Africa Today 58*(2), pp. 128–53.

Peters, K. 2012. Youth, wars and violence in West Africa. *History Compass 10*(12), pp. 879–88.

Peters, K. and Richards, P. 2011. Rebellion and agrarian tensions in Sierra Leone. *Journal of Agrarian Change 11*(3), pp. 377–95.

Petroska-Beska, V. and Najcevska, M. 2004. *Macedonia: Understanding History, Preventing Future Conflict.* Washington DC: United States Institute of Peace.

Petroska-Beska, V. and Osmani, S. 2015. *Report from the Electronic Survey on the Implementation of IIEP.* Online at http://pmio.mk/wp-content/up-loads/2016/03/electronic-survey-report-2015-en.pdf (accessed 12 January 2021).

Petroska-Beska, V., Najcevska, M., Kenig, N., Ballazhi, S., and Tomovska, A. 2009. *Multiculturalism and Inter-ethnic Relations in Education.* Skopje: UNICEF Country Office.

Pettifer, J. 2001. The Albanians in western Macedonia after FYROM independence. In: Pettifer, J. (ed.), *The New Macedonian Question.* Palgrave Macmillan, London, pp. 137–147.

Petty, R. E. and Briñol, P. 2015. Emotion and persuasion: Cognitive and meta-cognitive processes impact attitudes. *Cognition and Emotion 29*(1), pp. 1–26.

Petty, R. E., Wheeler, S. C., and Tormala, Z. L. 2003. Persuasion and attitude change. Millon, T. and Lerner, M. J. (eds), *Handbook of Psychology: Personality and Social Psychology,* Vol. 5, New York: John Wiley & Sons Inc., pp. 353–82.

Pham, J. P. 2007. Making sense of a senseless war. *Human Rights and Human Welfare 7*, pp. 35–51.

Piacentini, A. M. 2019. State ownership and state-sharing: The role of collective identities and the socio-political cleavage between ethnic Macedonians and ethnic Albanians in the Republic of North Macedonia. *Nationalities Papers 47*(3), pp. 461–76.

Podder, S. 2012a. From recruitment to reintegration: communities and ex-combatants in post-conflict Liberia. *International Peacekeeping 19*(2), pp. 186–202.

Podder, S., 2012b. Legitimacy, loyalty and civilian support for the Moro Islamic Liberation Front: changing dynamics in Mindanao, Philippines. *Politics, Religion & Ideology 13*(4), pp. 495–512.

Podder, S. 2013. Bridging the 'conceptual–contextual' divide: Security sector reform in Liberia and UNMIL transition. *Journal of Intervention and Statebuilding 7*(3), pp. 353–80.

Podder, S. 2015. The power in-between: youth's subaltern agency and the post-conflict everyday. *Peacebuilding 3*(1), pp. 36–57.

Podder, S. 2019. Liberia. In: Özerdem, A. and Mac Ginty, R. (eds), *Comparing Peace Processes*. London: Routledge, pp. 144–60.

Podder, S. 2021. Thinking about the legacy of peacebuilding programmes. *Peace Review 33*(1), pp. 106–114.

Podder, S., Prelis, S., and Sankaituah, J. S. 2021. Youth, peace, and programming for change. Global Policy. 31 August. Online at https://www.globalpolicyjournal.com/articles/conflict-and-security/youth-peace-and-programming-change-critical-reflection-between (accessed 30 September 2021).

Pogodda, S., Richmond, O., Tocci, N., Mac Ginty, R., and Vogel, B. 2014. Assessing the impact of EU governmentality in post-conflict countries: pacification or reconciliation? *European Security 23*(3), pp. 227–49.

Popovska, B. and Zhanet, R. 2015. *Process of reconciliation in a post-conflict Macedonia. Academicus* 11, pp. 63–76.

Popplewell, R., James, R., and Lewis, S. 2016. *What Remains: Programming for Sustainability*. Praxis Series Paper No. 1. Oxford: INTRAC.

Pouligny, B. 2005. Civil society and post-conflict peacebuilding: Ambiguities of international programmes aimed at building 'new' societies. *Security Dialogue 36*(4), pp. 495–510.

Pratten, D. 2006. The politics of vigilance in southeastern Nigeria. *Development and Change 37*(4), pp. 707–34.

Prelis, S., Shelper, S., and Sankaituah, J. 2012. *Youth to Youth: Measuring Youth Engagement*. Monrovia: Liberia: SfCG.

Pruitt, L. 2020. Rethinking youth bulge theory in policy and scholarship: Incorporating critical gender analysis. *International Affairs 96*(3), pp. 711–28.

Pugel, J. 2007. *What the Fighters Say: A Survey of Ex-combatants in Liberia*. Monrovia: UNDP Liberia.

Pugh, M., 2005. The political economy of peacebuilding: A critical theory perspective. *International Journal of Peace Studies 10*(2), pp. 23–42.

Purdey, A. F., Adhikari, G. B., Robinson, S. A., and Cox, P. W. 1994. Participatory health development in rural Nepal: Clarifying the process of community empowerment. *Health Education Quarterly 21*(3), 329–43.

Putnam, R. D. 1995. Tuning in, tuning out: The strange disappearance of social capital in America. *PS: Political Science & Politics 28*(4), pp. 664–84.

Putnam, R. D. 2000. Bowling alone: America's declining social capital. In: Carothers, L. and Lockhardt, C. (eds), *Culture and Politics*. New York: Palgrave Macmillan, pp. 223–34.

Ragaru, N. 2008. Macedonia: Between Ohrid and Brussels. *Cahiers de Chaillot*, pp. 41–60. Online at https://hal-sciencespo.archives-ouvertes.fr/file/index/docid/972853/filename/macedonia-between-ohrid-and-brussels-long-version.pdf (accessed 16 January 2021).

Rahall, J. and Schäfter, E. 2011. *The Socfin Land Deal Missing Out on Best Practices: Fact-finding Mission to Malen Chiefdom, Pujehun District, Sierra Leone*. Freetown: Green Scenery.

Ramet, S. P. (ed.). 2013. *Civic and Uncivic Values in Macedonia: Value Transformation, Education and Media*. London: Springer.

Rapley, T. 2007. Exploring documents. In T. Rapley (Ed.), *Doing conversation, discourse and document analysis*. London, England: Sage, pp. 112–124.

Rapley, T. J. 2001. The art (fulness) of open-ended interviewing: Some considerations on analysing interviews. *Qualitative Research 1*(3), pp. 303–23.

Rapoport, A. 1970. Can peace research be applied? *Journal of Conflict Resolution 14*(2), pp. 277–286.

Rashid, I. 1997. Subaltern reactions: Student radicals and lumpen youth in Sierra Leone, 1977–1992. *Africa Development 22* (3/4), pp. 19–43.

Rashid, I. 2004. Smallest victims; youngest killers: Juvenile combatants in Sierra Leone's civil war. In: Ibrahim Abdullah (ed.), *Between Democracy and Terror: The Sierra Leone Civil War*. South Africa: UNISA, pp. 66–89.

Rashid, I. 2006. Silent guns and talking drums: War, radio, and youth social healing in Sierra Leone. In: Sikainga, A.A. and Alidou, O. (eds), *Postconflict Reconstruction in Africa*. Trenton, NJ: Africa World Press Inc., pp. 115–47.

Rawluk, A. J. 2012. Intergenerational Resilience in Aklavik, Northern Territories – Exploring Conceptualisations, Variables, and Change across Generations. Unpublished Masters' Thesis, University of Alberta. Online athttps://era.library.ualberta.ca/items/ea1df372–1cd3–4f37–8b11–077e76fb6057/view/d18d07d9–5d65–4fb6-aa9b-61b183af34bc/Rawluk_Andrea_Fall-202012.pdf (accessed 2 October 2020).

REA Prishtina. 2011. Kosovo Youth for Democracy and Peacebuilding Project. Final Evaluation. September. Online at https://www.sfcg.org/wp-content/uploads/2014/08/KOS_EV_Nov11_Kosovo-Youth-for-Democracy.pdf (accessed 15 September 2021).

Read, R. and Mac Ginty, R. 2017. The temporal dimension in accounts of violent conflict: A case study from Darfur. *Journal of Intervention and Statebuilding 11*(2), pp. 147–65.

Reardon, B. A. 1988. *Comprehensive Peace Education: Educating for Global Responsibility*. Teachers College Press, New York.

Reeler, D. 2007. A three-fold theory of social change. The Community Development Resource Association. Online at https://content.changeroo.com/wp-content/uploads/Academy/2017/09/threefold_theory_of_change_-_and_implications_for_pme_-_doug_reeler_of_the_cdra.pdf (accessed 24 May 2021).

Reimann, C. 2012. Evaluability assessments in peacebuilding programming. Reflecting for Peace Practice Programme. Cambridge, MA.

Reimann, K. D. 2005. Up to no good? Recent critics and critiques of NGOs. In: O. P. Richmond and H. F. Careyeds., O. P. Richmond, and H. F. Carey (eds), *Subcontracting Peace: The Challenges of NGO Peacebuilding*, Burlington, VT: Ashgate, pp. 37–54.

Reka, A. 2008. The Ohrid Agreement: The travails of inter-ethnic relations in Macedonia. *Human Rights Review 9*(1), pp. 55–69.

Reychler, L. 2015a. *Time for Peace: The Essential Role of Time in Conflict and Peace Processes*. University of Queensland Press.

Reychler, L. 2015b. Time, 'temporament' and sustainable peace: The essential role of time in conflict and peace. *Asian Journal of Peacebuilding 3*(1), pp. 19–41.

Richards, P. 2001. War and peace in Sierra Leone. *Fletcher F. World Affairs 25*(2), pp. 41–50.

Richmond, O. P. 2005. *The transformation of peace* (Vol. 110). Basingstoke: Palgrave Macmillan.

Richmond, O.P., 2006. The problem of peace: understanding the 'liberal peace'. *Conflict, security & development* 6(3), pp. 291–314.

Richmond, O.P., 2009a. Becoming liberal, unbecoming liberalism: Liberal-local hybridity via the everyday as a response to the paradoxes of liberal peacebuilding. *Journal of intervention and statebuilding* 3(3), pp. 324–344.

Richmond, O.P., 2009b. A post-liberal peace: Eirenism and the everyday. *Review of international studies* 35(3), pp. 557–580.

Richmond, O.P., 2010. Resistance and the Post-liberal Peace. *Millennium* 38(3), pp. 665–692.

Ricigliano, R. 2003. Networks of effective action: Implementing an integrated approach to peacebuilding. *Security Dialogue* 34(4), pp. 445–62.

Richmond, O. P. 2011. Critical agency, resistance and a post-colonial civil society. *Cooperation and Conflict* 46(4), pp. 419–40.

Richmond, O. P. 2012a. A pedagogy of peacebuilding: Infrapolitics, resistance, and liberation. *International Political Sociology* 6(2), pp. 115–31.

Richmond, O. P. 2012b. Beyond local ownership in the architecture of international peacebuilding. *Ethnopolitics* 11(4), pp. 354–75.

Ricigliano, R. 2015. *Making Peace Last: A Toolbox for Sustainable Peacebuilding.* Routledge.

Riehl, V. 2001. *Who Is Ruling in South Sudan?: The Role of NGOs in Rebuilding Socio-political Order* (Vol. 9). Nordic Africa Institute.

Risse, T. and Sikkink, K. 1999. The socialisation of international human rights norms into domestic practices: Introduction. *Cambridge Studies in International Relations 66* (January), pp. 1–38.

Roche, C. 1999. *Impact Assessment for Development Agencies: Learning to Value Change.* Oxford, UK: Oxfam and Novib.

Rodd, J. 1985. Pre-school children's understanding of war. *Early Child Development and Care 22*(2–3), pp. 109–21.

Rogers, J. D. 2001. *Anarchy in Sierra Leone.* Freetown: Mount Everest Publishing House.

Rogers, M. M. 2012. Evaluating Relevance in Peacebuilding Programs. *Working Papers on Program Review and Evaluation*1. Cambridge, Massachusetts: Reflecting on Peace Practice Program, CDA Collaborative.

Rogers, M., Chassy, A., and Bamat, T. 2010. *Integrating Peacebuilding into Humanitarian and Development Programming.* Catholic Relief Services, Baltimore, MD.

Rogers, P. 2018. How to choose, develop and support innovations in Evaluation. Online at https://www.betterevaluation.org/en/blog/How_to_choose_develop_ and_support_innovation_in_evaluation (accessed 28 January 2021).

Rogers, P. J. 2008. Using programme theory to evaluate complicated and complex aspects of interventions. *Evaluation 14*(1), pp. 29–48.

Romer, D., Jamieson, K. H., and Pasek, J. 2009. Building social capital in young people: The role of mass media and life outlook. *Political Communication 26*(1), pp. 65–83.

Rosandić, R. 2000. *Grappling with Peace Education in Serbia* (Vol. 31, No. 33). Washington, DC: United States Institute for Peace.

Rosenblum-Kumar, G. and Denominator, K. 2018. *Conflict Prevention and Mitigation during the Electoral Cycle in Sierra Leone 2 Mid-term Evaluation – Final Draft.* Online at https://www.un.org/peacebuilding/sites/www.un.org.peacebuilding/files/documents/ sierra_leone_september_2018_project_evaluation_mid-term.pdf (accessed 12 November 2020).

Ross, K. 2017. *Youth Encounter Programs in Israel: Pedagogy, Identity, and Social Change.* New York: Syracuse University Press.

Ross, K. and Lazarus, N. 2015. Tracing the long-term impacts of a generation of Israeli–Palestinian youth encounters. *International Journal of Conflict Engagement and Resolution* 3(2), 116–35.

Rothstein, B. 2005. *Social Traps and the Problem of Trust.* Cambridge: Cambridge University Press.

Roy, E. 2018. Mid-term evaluation, United for Greater Governance and Participation: Empowering Rural Communities to Strengthen Local Governance and Accountability Processes. Online at https://www.sfcg.org/wp-content/uploads/2019/03/SLE504_Mid-Term-Evaluation-Emilie-Roy.pdf (accessed 10 November 2020).

Rushton, S. 2005. Health and peacebuilding: Resuscitating the failed state in Sierra Leone. *International Relations* 19(4), pp. 441–56.

Rusi, I. and Spasovska, K. 2013. Uncertain future: The Albanian-language media in Macedonia. In: Ramet, S. P. (ed.), *Civic and Uncivic Values in Macedonia: Value Transformation, Education and Media.* London: Springer, pp. 235–57.

Russett, B. M. 1974. *Power and Community in World Politics.* San Francisco: WH Freeman.

Ryan, C. 2018. Large-scale land deals in Sierra Leone at the intersection of gender and lineage. *Third World Quarterly* 39(1), pp. 189–206.

Ryffel, F. A., Wirz, D. S., Kühne, R. and Wirth, W. 2014. How emotional media reports influence attitude formation and change: The interplay of attitude base, attitude certainty, and persuasion. *Media Psychology* 17(4), pp. 397–419.

Sabaratnam, M. 2013. Avatars of Eurocentrism in the critique of the liberal peace. *Security Dialogue* 44(3), pp. 259–78.

Saferworld. 2017. Peace Research Partnership. Online at https://www.saferworld.org.uk/projects/peace-research-partnership (accessed 1 Feb 2021).

Sakue-Collins, Y. 2021. (Un) doing development: A postcolonial enquiry of the agenda and agency of NGOs in Africa. *Third World Quarterly* 42(5), pp. 976–95.

Salafsky, N., Margoluis, R., and Redford, K. 2001. Adaptive management. A tool for conservation practitioners. Washington DC: Biodiversity Support Programme.

Salomon, G. 2002. The nature of peace education: not all programs are equal. In: G. Salomon and B. Nevo (eds), *Peace Education: The Concept, Principles, and Practices Around the World.* New York, Lawrence Erlbaum, pp. 3–14.

Salomon, G. 2004. Does peace education make a difference in the context of an intractable conflict? *Peace and Conflict: Journal of Peace Psychology* 10(3), pp. 257–74.

Salomon, G. 2006. Does peace education really make a difference? *Peace and Conflict* 12(1), pp. 37–48.

Salomon, G. 2011. Four major challenges facing peace education in regions of intractable conflict. *Peace and Conflict* 17(1), pp. 46–59.

Salomon, G. and Nevo, B. (eds). 2002. *Peace Education: The Concept, Principles and Practice in the World.* Mahwah, NJ: Lawrence Erlbaum.

Sanyal, P. 2006. Capacity building through partnership: Intermediary nongovernmental organizations as local and global actors. *Nonprofit and Voluntary Sector Quarterly* 35(1), pp. 66–82.

Scharbatke-Church, C. 2011. Evaluating peacebuilding: Not yet all it could be. Online at http://edoc.vifapol.de/opus/volltexte/2013/4688/pdf/scharbatke_church_handbook.pdf (accessed 15 September 2020).

Scheers, G. (ed.). 2008. *Assessing Progress on the Road of Peace: Planning, Monitoring and Evaluating Conflict Prevention and Peacebuilding Activities.* European Centre for Conflict Prevention.

Schiappa, E., Gregg, P. B., and Hewes, D. E. 2006. Can one TV show make a difference? A Will & Grace and the parasocial contact hypothesis. *Journal of Homosexuality 51*(4), pp. 15–37.

Schimmelfennig, F., Engert, S., and Knobel, H. 2006. *International Socialisation in Europe: European Organisations, Political Conditionality and Democratic Change.* London: Springer.

Schirch, L. 2008. *Strategic Peacebuilding: State of the Field.* Women in Security Conflict Management and Peace. Online at http://wiscomp.org/pubn/wiscomp-peace-prints/ 2–1/Lisa%20Schirch.pdf (accessed 15 September 2021).

Schön, D. A. 1987. *Educating the Reflective Practitioner: Toward a New Design for Teaching and Learning in the Professions.* San Francisco: Jossey-Bass.

Schönpflug, U. 2001. Intergenerational transmission of values: The role of transmission belts. *Journal of Cross-cultural Psychology 32*(2), pp. 174–85.

Schütz, A. 1962. On multiple realities. In: *Collected Papers I.* Springer, Dordrecht, pp. 207–59.

Schutz, A. 1966. Some leading concepts of phenomenology. In: *Essays in Phenomenology.* Springer, Dordrecht, pp. 23–39.

Schwartz, B. 1974. Waiting, exchange, and power: The distribution of time in social systems. *American Journal of Sociology 79*(4), pp. 841–70.

Seawright, J. and Gerring, J. 2008. Case selection techniques in case study research: A menu of qualitative and quantitative options. *Political Research Quarterly 61*(2), pp. 294–308.

Segall, G., Birnbaum, D., Deeb, I., and Diesendruck, G. 2015. The intergenerational transmission of ethnic essentialism: How parents talk counts the most. *Developmental Science 18*(4), pp. 543–55.

Sesay, H. and Sesay, D. 2017. Using legal empowerment to fight exploitative land investors in Sierra Leone. Online at https://www.openglobalrights.org/using-legal-empowerment-to-fight-exploitative-land-investors-in-sierra-leone/ (accessed 22 July 2021).

Sesay, M. G. 2006. *Bike Riders in Sierra Leone: A Case Study of Search for Common Ground's Intervention.* Washington, DC: SfCG.

Sesay, M. G. and Hughes, C. 2004. *Go Beyond First Aid: Democracy Assistance and the Challenges of Institution Building in Post-Conflict Sierra Leone.* Hague: Netherlands Institute of International Relations – Clingendael.

Sewell, W. H. 1996. Historical events as transformations of structures: Inventing revolution at the Bastille. *Theory and Society 25*(6), pp. 841–81.

SfCG. 1998. *Baseline for Democracy and Governance Project.* Washington, DC.

SfCG. 2004. *A Final Performance Report on Search for Common Ground in Sierra Leone to the United States Agency for International Development.* Washington, DC.

SfCG. 2005. *Baseline for Democracy and Governance Project.*Washington, DC: SfCG. Online at https://www.sfcg.org/wp-content/uploads/2014/08/SLE_EV_Baseline-for-Democracy-and-Governance-Project.pdf (accessed 15 November, 2020).

SfCG. 2007. *Sisi Aminata: Evaluation Report:* Search for Common Grounds/Talking Drum Studios. December.

SfCG. 2008/2009. Internal evaluation of three projects from Sierra Leone, Burundi, and DRC. Freetown: Sierra Leone.

SfCG. 2018. The Sierra Leone Elections Dialogue Series Project. https://www.sfcg.org/sleds-the-sierra-leone-elections-dialogue-series-project/ (accessed 17 July 2020).

SfCG. 2019. *Mid-term Review of the Advancing Social Cohesion Project*, June. Skopje.

Shapiro, D. L. 2000. Program development for refugee youth. *Peace Review 12*(3), pp. 431–33.

Shapiro, M. 2005. 'Deliberative', 'independent' technocracy v. democratic politics: Will the Globe echo the EU? *Law and Contemporary Problems 68*(3/4), 341–56.

Shaw, R. 2007. Memory frictions: Localizing the truth and reconciliation commission in Sierra Leone. *The International Journal of Transitional Justice 1*(2), pp. 183–207.

Shepler, S. 2005. The rites of the child: Global discourses of youth and reintegrating child soldiers in Sierra Leone. *Journal of Human Rights 4*(2), pp. 197–211.

Shepler, S. 2010. Youth music and politics in post-war Sierra Leone. *The Journal of Modern African Studies 48*(4), pp. 627–42.

Sherif, M. and Sherif, C. W. 1953. *Groups in Harmony and Tension: An Integration of Studies of Intergroup Relations*. New York: Harper& Brothers.

Shinoda, H. 2008. The difficulty and importance of local ownership and capacity development in peacebuilding. *Hiroshima Peace Science 30*, pp. 95–115.

Shipler, M. 2006. *Youth Radio for Peacebuilding: A Guide*. Second Edition. UK: Search for Common Ground.

Shirazi, R. 2011. When projects of 'empowerment' don't liberate: Locating agency in a 'postcolonial'peace education. *Journal of Peace Education 8*(3), pp. 277–94.

Shochat, L. 2003. Our neighborhood: Using entertaining children's television to promote interethnic understanding in Macedonia. *Conflict Resolution Quarterly 21*(1), pp. 79–93.

Sierra Network Salone. 2018. Sierra Leone Police vs Sierra Leone Labour Congress and Bike Riders Union. 14 December. Online at https://snradio.net/sierra-leone-police-vs-sierra-leone-labour-congress-and-bike-riders-union/ (accessed 19 May 2021).

Singhal, A. and Rogers, E. M. 2002. A theoretical agenda for entertainment-education. *Communication Theory 12*(2), pp. 117–35.

Singhal, A., Rao, N., and Pant, S. 2006. Entertainment-education and possibilities for second-order social change. *Journal of Creative Communications 1*(3), pp. 267–83.

Slovak, K., Carlson, K., and Helm, L. 2007. The influence of family violence on youth attitudes. *Child and Adolescent Social Work Journal 24*(1), pp. 77–99.

Smillie, I., Hailey, J., and Hailey, J. M. 2001. *Managing for Change: Leadership, Strategy, and Management in Asian NGOs*. London: Earthscan.

Smith Ellison, C. 2014. The role of education in peacebuilding: An analysis of five change theories in Sierra Leone. *Compare: A Journal of Comparative and International Education 44*(2), pp. 186–207.

Smith, A. 2010. *The Influence of Education on Conflict and Peace Building*. Education for All Global Monitoring Reports. Paris: UNESCO.

Smith, A. 2011. Education and peacebuilding: From 'conflict-analysis' to 'conflict transformation'? Online at https://pure.ulster.ac.uk/ws/files/11269458/FriEnt_Essay_series_Smith%5B1%5D.pdf (accessed 24 May 2021).

Smith, A. and Vaux, T. 2003. *Education, Conflict and International Development*. London: DfiD.

Söderberg Kovacs, M. and Bjarnesen, J. (eds). 2018. *Violence in African Elections: Between Democracy and Big Man Politics*. London: Zed Books.

Soep, E. 2006a. Beyond literacy and voice in youth media production. *McGill Journal of Education 41*(3), pp. 196–214.

Solà-Martín, A., 2009. Is peacebuilding sustainable in Sierra Leone?. *Global Change, Peace & Security 21*(3), pp. 291–307.

Sommers, M. 2012. *Stuck: Rwandan Youth and the Struggle for Adulthood* (Vol. 25). Atlanta: University of Georgia Press.

Sommers, M. 2015. *The Outcast Majority: War, Development, and Youth in Africa.* University of Georgia Press.

Soroos, M. S. 1976. Adding an intergenerational dimension to conceptions of peace. *Journal of Peace Research 13*(3), pp. 173–83.

South, A. and Lall, M. 2016. Schooling and conflict: Ethnic education and mother tongue-based teaching in Myanmar. Online at https://asiafoundation.org/resources/pdfs/SchoolingConflictENG.pdf (accessed 12 January 2021).

Sowa, F. 2013. The Problems of and Prospects for Efficient Media Management in Sierra Leone. Freetown: Unpublished M.Phil thesis, Fourah Bay College.

Spaskovska, L. 2012. The fractured 'we'and the ethno-national 'I': The Macedonian citizenship framework. *Citizenship Studies 16* (3–4), pp. 383–96.

Spasovska, K. and Rusi, I. 2015. From 'chaos' to 'order': The transition of the media in Macedonia from 1989 to 2014. *Southeastern Europe 39*(1), pp. 35–61.

Spreen, M. 1992. Rare populations, hidden populations, and link-tracing designs: What and why? *Bulletin of Sociological Methodology 36*(1), pp. 34–58.

Stasik, M. 2016. Real love versus real life: youth, music and utopia in Freetown, Sierra Leone. *Africa: The Journal of the International African Institute 86*(2), pp. 215–36.

Stave, S. E. 2011. Measuring peacebuilding: challenges, tools, actions. Norwegian Peacebuilding Resource Centre (NOREF) Policy Brief No. 2. Online at http://www.peacebuilding.no/var/ezflow_site/storage/original/application/906762cb32e2eed5dc810bafa139f4ce.pdf (accessed 17 January 2021).

Sukarieh, M. and Tannock, S. 2008. In the best interests of youth or neoliberalism? The World Bank and the New Global Youth Empowerment Project. *Journal of Youth Studies 11*(3), pp. 301–12.

Swartz, S. 2011. 'Going deep'and 'giving back': Strategies for exceeding ethical expectations when researching amongst vulnerable youth. *Qualitative Research 11*(1), pp. 47–68.

Swidler, A. and Watkins, S. C. 2009. 'Teach a man to fish': the sustainability doctrine and its social consequences. *World Development 37*(7), pp. 1182–96.

Sylva, K., Melhuish, E., Sammons, P., Siraj-Blatchford, I. and Taggart, B. (eds). 2010. *Early Childhood Matters: Evidence from the Effective Pre-school and Primary Education Project.* New York: Routledge.

Tankard, M. E. and Paluck, E. L. 2016. Norm perception as a vehicle for social change. *Social Issues and Policy Review 10*(1), pp. 181–211.

Tankersley, D. 2001. Bombs or bilingual programmes?: dual-language immersion, transformative education and community building in Macedonia. *International Journal of Bilingual Education and Bilingualism 4*(2), pp. 107–24.

Taouti-Cherif, R. 2008. Internal Evaluation of TDS Sierra Leone Election Strategy, January. https://www.dmeforpeace.org/resource/internal-evaluation-of-sfcg-sl-election-strategy/ (accessed 15 July 2020).

Taylor, I. 2010. Liberal peace, liberal imperialism: A Gramscian critique. In: Richmond, O. (ed.), *Palgrave Advances in Peacebuilding: Critical Developments and Approaches.* London: Palgrave Macmillan, pp. 154–74.

Taylor, L. K. 2020. The Developmental Peacebuilding Model (DPM) of children's prosocial behaviours in settings of intergroup conflict. *Child Development Perspectives 14*(3), pp. 127–34.

Taylor, L. K., Merrilees, C. E., Baird, R., Goeke-Morey, M. C., Shirlow, P., and Cummings, E. M. 2018. Impact of political conflict on trajectories of adolescent prosocial behaviour: Implications for civic engagement. *Developmental Psychology 54* (9), pp. 1785–94.

Taylor, L., Dautel, J., and Rylander, R. 2019. Contact, conflict and interethnic attitudes among children in North Macedonia. *Primenjena psihologija 12*(4), pp. 409–28.

Teitel, R. G. 2003. Transitional justice genealogy. *Harvard Human Rights Journal 16*, pp. 69–94.

Tholens, S. and Groß, L. 2015. Diffusion, contestation and localisation in post-war states: 20 years of Western Balkans reconstruction. *Journal of International Relations and Development 18*(3), pp. 249–64.

Thompson, L. 2016. *Afrobarometer Despatch 97*(3), June. Online at http://afrobarometer. org/sites/default/files/publications/Dispatches/ab-r6-dispatchno97.pdf (accessed 15 July 2020).

Thorsen, D. 2013. Weaving in and out of employment and self-employment: Young rural migrants in the informal economies of Ouagadougou and Abidjan. *International Development Planning Review 35*(2), pp. 203–18.

Todoroska, K. 2014. Chaulev's considerations on the Albanians and Shqipnia (Albania), *Studia Politologica Ucraino-Polona 4*, pp. 262–9.

Todorov, P. 2016. Teaching history in Macedonia after 2001: Representations of armed conflict between ethnic Macedonians and ethnic Albanians. In: Bentrovato, D., Korostelina, K.V., and Schulze, M. (eds), *History Can Bite: History Education in Divided and Post-war Societies*. Gottingen: V&R Press, pp. 111–24.

Tom, P. 2013. In search for emancipatory hybridity: The case of post-war Sierra Leone. *Peacebuilding 1*(2), pp. 239–55.

Tom, P. 2014. Youth-traditional authorities relations in post-war Sierra Leone. *Children's Geographies 12*(3), pp. 327–38.

Tomovska, A, 2009. Social context and contact hypothesis: Perception and experiences of a contact program for ten to eleven-year old children in the Republic of Macedonia. In: Tomovska, A. 2010. Contact as a tool for peace education? Reconsidering the contact hypothesis from the children's perspectives. *Journal of Peace Education 7*(2), pp. 121–38.

Tomovska, A., Taylor, L. K., Dautel, J., and Rylander, R. 2019. Children's understanding of ethnic group symbols: Piloting an instrument in the Republic of North Macedonia. *Peace and Conflict: Journal of Peace Psychology 26*(1), pp. 82–7.

Tooke, J. 2000. Betweenness at work. *Area 32*, 217–23.

Topuzovska, M., Latkovikj, M., Popovska, B., Serafimovska, E., Cekикj, A., Starova, and N. 2019. *Youth Study North Macedonia 2018/2019*. Bonn: Friedrich Ebert Stiftung. Online at https://www.researchgate.net/profile/Marija_Topuzovska_Latkovikj/ publication/332241977_YOUTH_STUDY_NORTH_MACEDONIA_20182019/links/ 5e20fa01a6fdcc10156f7fa7/YOUTH-STUDY-NORTH-MACEDONIA-2018-2019.pdf (accessed 2 October 2020).

Touliatos, J. and Compton, N. H. 1983. *Approaches to Child Study*. Minneapolis, Minnesota: Burgess Publishing Company.

Tropp, L. R. and Prenovost, M. A. 2008. The role of intergroup contact in predicting children's interethnic attitudes: Evidence from meta-analytic and field studies. In: Levy, S. R. and Killen, M. (eds), *Intergroup Attitudes and Relations in Childhood through Adulthood*. Oxford: Oxford University Press, pp. 236–48.

Truth and Reconciliation Commission. 2004. *Final Report of the Truth and Reconciliation Commission*. 3 Vols. Freetown: TRC.

Tschirgi, N. 2003. *Peacebuilding as the Link between Security and Development: Is the Window of Opportunity Closing?* New York: International Peace Academy.

Tschirgi, N. 2004. *Post-Conflict Peacebuilding Revisited: Achievements, Limitations, Challenges*. New York: International Peace Academy.

Turner, S. 1980. *Sociological Explanation as Translation*. Cambridge: Cambridge University Press.

Tyrer, R. A. and Fazel, M. 2014. School and community-based interventions for refugee and asylum seeking children: a systematic review. *PloS one 9*(5), p. e89359. https://doi.org/10.1371/journal.pone.0097977.

UNDP Sierra Leone. 2018. Consultative Meeting on Community Radio Stations in Sierra Leone. Freetown: 28 August.

United Nations General Assembly. 1991. Convention on the Rights of the Child. Resolution Resolution 44/25 of 20 November 1989. Online at https://www.ohchr.org/en/professionalinterest/pages/crc.aspx (accessed 21 May 2021).

United Nations Security Council. 2015. Resolution 2250. S/RES/2250. 9 December. Online at https://documents-dds-ny.un.org/doc/UNDOC/GEN/N15/413/06/PDF/N1541306.pdf?OpenElement (accessed 12 August 2021).

United Nations Security Council. 2018. Resolution 2419. S/RES/2419. 6 June. Online at https://documents-dds-ny.un.org/doc/UNDOC/GEN/N18/173/81/PDF/N1817381.pdf?OpenElement (accessed 13 August 2021).

United Nations Security Council. 2020. Resolution 2535. S/RES/2535. Online at https://documents-dds-ny.un.org/doc/UNDOC/GEN/N20/182/94/PDF/N2018294.pdf?OpenElement (accessed 12 August 2021).

United Nations. 2015. The challenge of sustaining peace. Report of the Advisory Group of Experts for the 2015 review of the United Nations peacebuilding architecture. A/69/968-S/2015/490. New York.

UNOY Peacebuilders. 2018. *Beyond Dividing Lines: The Reality of Youth-Led Peacebuilding in Afghanistan, Colombia, Libya and Sierra Leone*. The Hague: Netherlands.

Urdal, H. 2006. A clash of generations? Youth bulges and political violence. *International Studies Quarterly 50*(3), pp. 607–29.

USAID. n.d. Macedonia Education. Online at https://www.usaid.gov/macedonia/education (accessed 13 September 2021).

Utas, M. 2005. West-African warscapes: Victimcy, girlfriending, soldiering: Tactic agency in a young woman's social navigation of the Liberian war zone. *Anthropological Quarterly 78*(2), pp. 403–30.

Utas, M. 2012. *African Conflicts and Informal Power: Big Men and Networks*. London: Zed Books.

Valentine, G. 2019. Geographies of youth – a generational perspective. *Children's Geographies 17*(1), pp. 28–31.

Van Balkom, W. D. and Beara, M. 2012. Making or breaking the peace: The role of schools in inter-ethnic peace making. In: Olivera, S. (ed.), *Peace Psychology in the Balkans Dealing with a Violent Past while Building Peace*. London: Springer, pp. 75–87.

Van Hal, A. 2004. Case study: The inter-ethnic project in Gostivar. In: Dimitrijevic, N. and Kovacs, P. (eds), *Managing Hatred and Distrust: The Prognosis for Post-Conflict Settlement in Multiethnic Communities in the Former Yugoslavia*. Budapest: Open Society Institute, pp. 187–204.

Van Hal, A. 2005. Back to the future: The referendum of November 7th in Macedonia. *Helsinki Monitor 16*(1), pp. 36–52.

Van Ham, P. 2010. *Social Power in International Politics*. London: Routledge.

Van Meter, K. 1990. Methodological and design issues: Techniques for assessing the representatives of snowball samples. *NIDA Research Monograph 98*(51.40), pp. 31–43.

Van Rooy, A. (ed.). 1998. *Civil Society and the Aid Industry*. London: Earthscan.

Väyrynen, R. (ed.). 1991. *New Directions in Conflict Theory: Conflict Resolution and Conflict Transformation*. London: Sage.

Väyrynen, R. 2019. From conflict resolution to conflict transformation: a critical review. In: Hon-Won, J. (ed.), *The New Agenda for Peace Research*. New York: Routledge, pp. 135–60.

Verkoren, W. 2010. Learning by southern peace NGOs. *The Journal of Development Studies* 46(4), pp. 790–810.

Visoka, G. 2011. International governance and local resistance in Kosovo: The thin line between ethical, emancipatory and exclusionary politics. *Irish Studies in International Affairs 22*, pp. 99–125.

Vladimirova, K. 2014. The pure intergenerational problem and the UNESCO decade of education for sustainable development. *Ethics in Progress 5*(1), pp. 66–79.

Vogel, I. 2012. *Review of the Use of 'Theory of Change' in International Development*. London: DfiD.

Von Kaltenborn-Stachau, H. 2008. The missing link: Fostering positive citizen-state relations in post-conflict environments. Washington, DC: World Bank. Online at https://elibrary.worldbank.org/doi/abs/10.1596/28229 (accessed 20 October 2020).

Wallerstein, I., 1997. Eurocentrism and its avatars: The dilemmas of social science. *Sociological bulletin 46*(1), pp.21–39.

Walter, B. F. 2004. Does conflict beget conflict? Explaining recurring civil war. *Journal of Peace Research 41*(3), pp. 371–88.

Warshel, Y. 2021. *Experiencing the Israeli-Palestinian Conflict: Children, Peace Communication and Socialisation*. Cambridge: Cambridge University Press.

Watson, A. M. 2006. Children and international relations: A new site of knowledge? *Review of International Studies 32*(2), pp. 237–50.

Watts, W. A. and McGuire, W. J. 1964. Persistence of induced opinion change and retention of the inducing message contents. *The Journal of Abnormal and Social Psychology 68*(3), pp. 233–41.

Weick, K. E. 2001. *Making Sense of the Organisation*. Malden, MA: Blackwell Scientific.

Weinstein, H. M., Freedman, S. W., and Hughson, H. 2007. School voices: Challenges facing education systems after identity-based conflicts. *Education, Citizenship and Social Justice* 2(1), pp. 41–71.

Wellman, B. and Kenneth, F. 2001. Network capital in a multi-level world: Getting support from personal communities. In: Lin, N., Cook, K., and Burt, R. S. (eds), *Social Capital: Theory and Research*. New York: Aldine de Gruyter, pp. 233–73.

Wertsch, J. V. 1991. *Voices of the Mind: A Sociocultural Approach to Mediated Action*, Cambridge, MA: Harvard University Press.

West, A. 2007. Power relationships and adult resistance to children's participation. *Children Youth and Environments 17*(1), pp. 123–35.

Westrick, J. 2011. Transforming early literacy instruction: An effectiveness study of the local literacy provider training program in Macedonia. *European Education 43*(4), pp. 62–87.

Wheeler, W. 2003. Creating structural change to support youth development. *Social Policy Report: Giving Child and Youth Development Knowledge Away 17*(3), p. 7.

Wicker, A. W. 1969. Attitudes versus actions: The relationship of verbal and overt behavioural responses to attitude objects. *Journal of Social Issues 25*(4), pp. 41–78.

Wiener, A. 2004. Contested compliance: Interventions on the normative structure of world politics. *European Journal of International Relations 10*(2), pp. 189–234.

Wiener, A. 2007. Contested meanings of norms: a research framework. *Comparative European Politics 5*(1), pp. 1–17.

Wiener, A. 2014. *A Theory of Contestation*. New York: Springer.

Williams, A. P. and Mengistu, B. 2015. An exploration of the limitations of bureaucratic organisations in implementing contemporary peacebuilding. *Cooperation and Conflict* 50(1), pp. 3–28.

Williams, H. M. A. 2017. Teachers' nascent praxes of care: Potentially decolonizing approaches to school violence in Trinidad. *Journal of Peace Education* 14(1), pp. 69–91.

Winter, J. M. 2006. *Dreams of Peace and Freedom: Utopian Moments in the Twentieth Century*. New Haven: Connecticut: Yale University Press.

Wolff, J. and Zimmermann, L. 2016. Between Banyans and battle scenes: Liberal norms, contestation, and the limits of critique. *Review of International Studies* 42(3), pp. 513–34.

Wood, D. A. 2020. *Epistemic Decolonization: A Critical Investigation into the Anticolonial Politics of Knowledge*. London: Springer Nature.

Woodrow, P. and Chigas, D. 2009. *A Distinction with a Difference: Conflict Sensitivity and Peacebuilding*. Collaborative for Development Action. Online at https://www.dmeforpeace.org/peacexchange/wp-content/uploads/2015/10/A-Distinction-with-a-Difference-Conflict-Sensitivity-and-Peacebuilding.pdf (accessed 11 November 2020).

Yin, R. K. 2003. *Case Study Research*. Sage Publications. Thousand Oaks, CA.

Zack-Williams, A. B. 1990. Sierra Leone: crisis and despair. *Review of African Political Economy* 17(49), pp. 22–33.

Zahar, M. J. 2012. Norm transmission in peace-and statebuilding: Lessons from democracy promotion in Sudan and Lebanon. *Global Governance: A Review of Multilateralism and International Organisations* 18(1), pp. 73–88.

Zakharia, Z. 2017. Getting to 'no': Locating critical peace education within resistance and anti-oppression pedagogy at a Shi'a Islamic school in Lebanon. *Research in Comparative and International Education* 12(1), pp. 46–63.

Zembylas, M. 2010. Children's construction and experience of racism and nationalism in Greek-Cypriot primary schools. *Childhood* 17(3), pp. 312–28.

Zembylas, M. 2017. Re-contextualising human rights education: Some decolonial strategies and pedagogical/curricular possibilities. *Pedagogy, Culture & Society* 25(4), pp. 487–99.

Zembylas, M. 2018. Con-/divergences between postcolonial and critical peace education: Towards pedagogies of decolonization in peace education. *Journal of Peace Education* 15(1), pp. 1–23.

Zembylas, M. and Bekerman, Z. 2013. Integrated education in conflicted societies: Is there a need for new theoretical language?. *European Educational Research Journal* 12(3), pp. 403–15.

Zerubavel, E. 1987. The language of time: Toward a semiotics of temporality. *The Sociological Quarterly* 28(3), pp. 343–56.

Zerubavel, E., 1982. The standardization of time: A sociohistorical perspective. *American journal of sociology* 88(1), pp. 1–23.

Zimmermann, L. 2016. Same same or different? Norm diffusion between resistance, compliance, and localization in post-conflict states. *International Studies Perspectives* 17(1), pp. 98–115.

Evaluation based recommendations and follow-up actions in Macedonia

Year	Recommendation	Adaptation	Results	Action
2004	Families should be the intended focus of inter-cultural communication projects like *Nashe Malo*	Limited	Mixed	Children and youth continued to be the primary focus of future media and theatre projects.
2006	Macedonian was spoken by the Turkish and Albanian children, but the Macedonian children appeared less inclined to use the minority languages.	None	None	Language inequality reflected the contextual reality. No specific remedial action was taken to address this.
2006	Contacts between families and children increased through the *Mozaik* groups. These contacts were mostly superficial in character.	Limited	Limited	Superficial interactions through integrated education projects common for most initiatives. It reflectd the lack of norm resonance and weak norm adoption.
2010	Interorganizational learning was missing across the various donor funded integrated education projects in Macedonia.	None	None	Two evaluations highlighted this shortcoming. Although there were networking opportunities between the different implementing agencies, there was little interorganizational learning in practice.
2013	Media and theatre re-lated outputs like regional networks were often un-sustainable beyond the project funding cycle.	None	None	The return to the use of a television series like *New Heroes* in 2017 suggests that media was used for its donor appeal and for short-term impact, rather than for sustainable effects.

Year	Recommendation	Adaptation	Results	Action
2013	Lack of formal, consistent educational curriculum development in the bilingual immersion groups was a major drawback. Externally aided pedagogical development could create dependency.	Yes	Positive	This area saw the most progress, with a shift towards creating structures and processes for regular M&E. Sustainable and affordable pedagogical development through online training for *Mozaik* methodology (2019) was another positive development.
2013	Media projects had little positive effects on the cultural activities and cultural awareness among both youths, and youth leaders.	None	None	Superficial interactions through structured media exchanges were reflective of interethnic segregation, which was variable depending on the social capital and local history of the different locations.
2013	Dwindling quality following partial institutionalization of the *Mozaik* groups in the state kindergartens	Yes	Mixed	This element could not be remedied. It was part and parcel of institutionalization.
2015	Compliance with national procedures, such as digital record keeping diluted *Mozaik*'s specificities such as bilingual instruction by two teachers.	None	None	Efforts to make an externally designed project to fit the national curricula required inevitable standardization measures that led to a dilution in the quality of provision.
2015	Progressive marginalization of *Mozaik* groups in the context of wider integrated education efforts.	None	None	This reflected a progressive marginalization; and lack of learning from the experience of *Mozaik* in the national context.

Evaluation based recommendations and follow-up actions in Sierra Leone

Year	Recommendation	Action	Results
2002	Producing radio content in local dialects	Yes	Positive
2002	Election related violence	Yes	Positive
2002	Supporting the technical sustainability of the community radio stations.	Mixed	Mixed
2002	Adopting an alliance-building approach	Yes	Mixed
2004	Developing successor local organizations and building alliances with other large INGOs to deliver projects.	No	Weak
2004	Develop IRN	Yes	Positive
2004	Thinking about exit early	No	Weak
2004	Transition from ex-patriot to national staff	No	Delayed
2004	Focus on decentralization	Yes	Positive
2006	Updating training manuals for transport task forces	No	Weak
2006	Preventing the politicization of the transport task forces	No	Weak
2007	Including community leaders in SRH advocacy	Yes	Positive
2008	Strengthening community-based structures for child protection	Yes	Mixed
2008	Monitor and follow up the punitive aspects of formal child protection structures	No	Mixed
2008	Building on existing networks rather than establishing new partnerships	Yes	Mixed
2008	Establishing links with formal agencies to enable sustainable gains	Ad hoc	Weak
2009	Including women and youth in community radio development	Yes	Mixed
2010	Monitoring/sustaining of efforts around CSO advocacy on chieftaincy reform	No	Mixed
2014	Encouraging policy makers to use radio as a feedback mechanism	Yes	Mixed
2016	Women's participation, and inclusion in the deliberations around land deals would be helpful given their exclusion from land ownership in Sierra Leone.	No	Weak
2016	Structures like land management committees created for the purpose of defending land owners' rights. Without external support, these structures would become defunct.	No	Weak

Year	Recommendation	Action	Results
2016	Legal practitioners should be involved in the interpretation of land lease contracts.	No	Weak
2017	Necessary to sustain the relationship with youth re-searchers, create roles like certified Youth Advocate with responsibilities and institutional links to the partner INGO.	No	Weak
2017	Formalizing relationship with the trainees. Follow up with research participants, stakeholders, and youth researchers would be helpful for keeping the momentum on child protection issues going.	No	Weak
2017	Psychosocial support for youth researchers could be pro-vided for children that have conducted research with respondents exposed to WFOV.	No	Weak
2018	Longer implementation timeline for election strategy to complement the national election cycle.	No	Weak
2018	Promote learning and sharing between different CSOs.	Ad hoc	Mixed
2018	Offering financial training to beneficiaries and local CSOs	No	Weak
2018	Establishing links with formal agencies	Ad hoc	Weak

Macedonia meta-ethnographic synthesis and concepts

Evaluation and project details	Project achievements	Programme concepts	Learning concepts	Institutional links	Recommendations for future projects
Evaluation of *Naashe Malo* (NM) by Channel Research 2004 • Edutainment • Fictional narrative • Co-habitation • Linguistic diversity • Cultural tolerance	1,202 children between the ages of 8 and 15 years were surveyed regarding NM. 94.3% had heard about the show, and 91% had watched it at least once. The show was more popular amongst ethnic Macedonians and Serbs. Intended goals as detailed in its curriculum document were only partially met. First show of its kind, intended for children, filled a gap and achieved a high degree of visibility. Children identified with the NM characters. Their preferences permeated into the family environment. Productions like NM have good impact at the individual level.	Theory of change and curriculum development agenda was to include all age groups. Linguistic diversity; cultural tolerance. Mozaik targeted three-seven-year olds, NM targeted eight-12-year olds. Learning about other cultures.	Fictional narrative on TV. Gap between the show and the reality of social interactions. High technical quality appreciated by the viewers. NM logic not applicable to real life, even by the child actors. Cohabitation in same buildings or even as neighbours as shown on the show was not possible in real life. Older children, parents and news media carried contrary messages to NM after the 2001 war. TV better at informing than truly influencing behaviour or attitudes Social change could be slow, gradual, rapid, or all-encompassing depending on the drivers.	N/A	Linguistic diversity; Reducing costs of production in line with Macedonian economic conditions. Public sector funding can be accessed if programmes align with the national priorities. Political dimension of the NM messages not rooted in intra-group dynamic. Families should be the focus of intended outcomes and not just the children.

Thematic Evaluation 2006 (*Mozaik* and complementary Media efforts) • Socialization • Intercultural communication • Intergroup contact	Bridges for the New Balkans (BNB) started in Sep. 2006 as a regional media project. Its outputs included newspaper supplements like *Karavan*: a multi-ethnic forum, and *Balkan Kaleidoscope*. This was complementary to the *Mozaik* bilingual child centred pre-school groups in the public kindergartens. Same topics around intercultural communication were explored through a multiple ethnic perspective.	Child socialization; multicultural exposure, intercultural communication; Multilingual instruction; Increased awareness of languages and commonly used words. Through the children in the Mozaik groups, families were exposed to cultural specificities such as religious festivals etc. Attitudinal, cognitive emotional change sought. Collaboration between journalists and editors of different ethnic groups was an added novelty here.	In an opinion poll survey, of 508 respondents, 67% reported that they had never read the newspaper supplements. Lowest readership was reported in Skopje. Highest readership was reported among men with university degrees. Both direct and indirect project beneficiaries of BNB attested to the fact that their exposure to the project and its outcomes helped the boundaries between different ethnic groups more understandable in general terms. In the Mozaik groups, Macedonian was spoken by the Turkish and Albanian children, although the Macedonian children appeared less inclined to use the other languages.	Newspapers or media production houses in Macedonia, Serbia and Albania could build networks between journalists through BNB. Mozaik worked with the MSLP and was embedded within the state kindergarten system. This networking was helpful in overcoming the biases in reporting the same issues.	Contacts or friendships increased although they remained superficial in character.

Continued

Continued

Evaluation and project details	Project achievements	Programme concepts	Learning concepts	Institutional links	Recommendations for future projects
Balkan Theatre Network (BTN) Evaluation January 2011– November 2012 • Intercultural dialogue • Cultural production	Theatre and cultural arts used for engaging children and youth across borders. Variable uptake across the Balkans. Six new plays, two per country were produced and performed by the youth themselves. The youth teams were involved in writing the plays with a lead professional playwright. Practical approaches to promoting intercultural dialogue. Charter for Balkan Cultural Network signed.	Multi-ethnic democracy posed challenges. Awareness and exposure to the different cultural traditions. Based on formative research conducted among youth from the three countries, about their participation in cultural activities. 525 youth in the age group of 15–19 years took part in the formative research.	Limited effect on attitudes and behaviours were noticed. Social visits during birthdays and religious festivals became more common. Even when attitudes had changed, Mozaik did not translate into increased inter-ethnic contacts or friendships. In adopting an EU centric normative framework, the focus was on promoting co-existence, reconciliation, and intercultural collaboration across the borders. Cultural messages were used to promote regional cooperation. Psychologists used successfully for designing formative research.	BTN Facebook page; Blogs; 10 local CSOs became members of the Network. Curriculum Development for BTN project. Curriculum design groups including representatives of each member CSO. Production of theatre plays, playwright trainings for the participating youth. Partners included Centre for Drama Education (Mostar), CDE, Student Cultural Centre, Nish Produced dramas in Struga and Kumanovo (FYROM)	Thinking through the activities for their long-term significance was necessary. Very little awareness of the 'overall picture.' Broad-brush goals addressed through a documentary film 'Different' to showcase the process of work of the partner organizations. Tendency to quantify activity related output rather than focusing on quality.

Youth Democracy and Peacebuilding Final Evaluation 2011 • Youth leadership • Networking • Community-based projects	Project was funded by the European Commission. It was implemented in the three regions of Prishtina, Prizren, and Mitrovica in Kosovo. Five youth focused CSOs, and 150 young people were trained in mediation, dialogue and reconciliation. 27 youth teams competed for 10 small action grants, to implement community-based projects around music, poetry, and sports.	At baseline, less than 40% respondents felt they had the opportunity to exercise democratic leadership. At the end of the project, 40% of the 150 participants, felt that they were better equipped in developing leadership, conflict resolution, democracy, human rights, organizational capacity and management.	Problems in BiH due to canton-based permission to enter schools. In Serbia, including diverse youth population in the research was challenging. How youth from the three countries, think about culture, how they define it, etc could not be assimilated into a coherent project focus. Small project grants helped community cohesion. Youth were supported by the community members. Unique experiences of developing project proposals and implementing small action grants was valuable for the youth involved.	Partnered with YMCA and four other youth focused CSOs. These projects created links, enabled networking between community groups, government officials and the relevant stakeholders. No concrete link to any government organization, or department, a major weakness of the project. Official links are important to provide a more formalized and meaningful impact. Previous trainings organized by other national NGOs and INGOs did not result in any joint activity with the municipalities. Networks involving other NGOs were created with the potential for future project development.	Nish, Kragujevac (Serbia) Mostar and Bugojno (BiH) More such training activities recommended. Youth from the Prishtina region had more the life opportunities compared with the youth from the more rural areas. This urban–rural divide in terms of life opportunities needed to be addressed. Close cooperation with the local authorities such as newly established municipalities was recommended.

Continued

Continued

Evaluation and project details	Project achievements	Programme concepts	Learning concepts	Institutional links	Recommendations for future projects
Mozaik Baseline study 2013 • Bilingual instruction • Intercultural communication • Enrolment • Demand • Institutionalization	*Mozaik* is the first model of integrated bilingual preschool education in Macedonia. Originally started in 1998, it has been implemented in the state run kindergartens. By 2013, the groups were partially integrated into the state kindergarten system. In 2013, 13 *Mozaik* groups were operating in 10 kindergartens based in 10 municipalities. With funding from the EU's EIDHR instrument, the *Mozaik* programme expanded to three other municipalities. CCG trained new teachers to lead the new *Mozaik* groups. By 2013, the programme had grown to 26 full time *Mozaik* teachers and four volunteers.	Intercultural communication; Bilingual or multilingual instruction; Quality preschool education.	More accessible for youth in urban areas who were more likely to receive donor sponsored and INGO led activities, compared with rural areas, where youth have limited access to such opportunities. Childcare was not central to the original programme design. Once the groups were institutionalized, the model was adapted to imitate standard private nursery hours, and access to younger children was given. The original model required specific training for the teachers. The *Mozaik* groups remained dependent on CCG for this until 2019.	Government has accepted most of the 18 *Mozaik* teachers as state employees, but has yet to take charge of the programme fully. This absorption of the groups is linked to the government's wider integrated education strategy. Since 2003, an agreement with MoLSP was intended to gradually absorb the *Mozaik* groups into the state kindergarten system. In 2010, Swedish funding ceased, and funding for groups shifted to the national government departments and local municipalities.	Lack of formal, consistent, educational curriculum development must be addressed. Government must intensify steps for full institutionalization and quality control.

EIDHR funding February 2014–November 2015 • Pedagogy • Alumni • Quality • Integrated Education					
360 children between three and five years targeted through 13 *Mozaik* groups consisting of 20–24 children in each group.	Capacity building of BDE, SEI and the Counsellors through training in *Mozaik* methodology.	The groups have developed a good reputation, with long waiting lists for child enrolment.	Policy makers at the local and central levels engaged for national institutionalization.	In Kicevo and Radish, teachers' salaries were paid through the local municipal budgets. These Teachers were not fully integrated into the faculty payroll in the respective public kindergartens.
303 kindergarten teachers working in public kindergartens were trained in *Mozaik* methodology.	Monitoring protocol and revision of documents for *Mozaik* daily planning created and approved by the MoLSP.	Development of new groups started to slow down due to a lack of donor funds and limited learning resources for training new staff.	Links with the Ministry of Education and SEI and BDE departments consolidated.	Quality control of integrated model within a segregated education system posed a challenge for sustainability.
73 primary school teachers in first to third grade of participating municipalities were trained.		Supervisors working groups including representatives from the MoLSP were included. Professors from the Institute of Pedagogy, to maintain oversight. A monitoring protocol was developed.	In 2015, MoU signed with BDE and SEI departments.	
For the first time *Mozaik* alumni were targeted.		22 workshops for *Mozaik* parents on communication skills with their children using the *Mozaik* model added another layer to the model dissemination.	Discussions around supervisory visits of the *Mozaik* groups and how the model was to be implemented after being institutionalized were pursued.	
Training for local education counsellors, professional and management staff of the participating kindergartens was offered.			6 BDE, 10 SEI trained in monitoring activities.	
11 training sessions for non-*Mozaik* preschool teachers in 10 multi-ethnic municipalities.				

Continued

Continued

Evaluation and project details	Project achievements	Programme concepts	Learning concepts	Institutional links	Recommendations for future projects
	Taught by current or experienced *Mozaik* teachers.				Universities do not offer professional development programmes to the teachers. This places future support and monitoring in peril.
Final Report *Mozaik* 2014/2015 • Pedagogy • Segregation • Integration • State kinder-gartens • Financing • Budgets	Workshops on the *Mozaik* communication model. Survey with teachers; Protocol for monitoring of *Mozaik* model in the state kindergartens were developed. CPD of *Mozaik* teachers, training for parents and alumni networking were gradually built into the project activities and outreach plans.	Parents targeted through workshops and multi-ethnic communities at large through activities at the schools where the groups were based. A SEI inspector and a BDE Advisor were funded by the EU project to monitor and support the *Mozaik* groups. Compulsory 100 days pre-school attendance since 2012 resulted in a rising demand for the *Mozaik* groups.	With Open Fun Football Schools organized networking activities with the *Mozaik* alumni 1-day workshop for 16 alumni in leadership, 14 community events with students aged 6–10 years were run as well. Improving the status of the *Mozaik* groups. Developing a stronger institutional framework for their support and monitoring.	Shared responsibility over the kindergartens established between the MoLSA, municipalities, and the Ministry of Education and Science, which houses the BDE. State Education Inspectorate for conducting M&E. The municipalities were responsible for maintaining the kindergarten infrastructure.	Compliance with national procedures, digital record keeping, and standardization does not account for *Mozaik*'s specificities such as the intercultural element and the teacher student ratio. Two teachers in each *Mozaik* group versus one teacher in standard kindergarten groups. National Programme for Preschool Education did not

Advancing Social Cohesion (mid-term review) June 2019 • Pedagogy • Media • Training • Monitoring • Social cohesion	A more engaged public outreach strategy enriched the programme and created steps towards its sustainability. USAID funded four-year project between June 2017 and June 2021. Project implemented in 10 municipalities. Training of kindergarten teachers, pedagogical students, parents of the *Mozaik*	*Mozaik* was not specifically listed as a government programme, only mentioned as one of the possible kindergarten projects. Enhancing public awareness of social cohesion; Training in *Mozaik* methodology disseminated across various stakeholder groups.	One of the key successes of the *Mozaik* model was the development of the Monitoring Protocol and assigning a BDE advisor to support the programme. Engagement of SEIs helpful for understanding how to monitor the *Mozaik* groups' administrative procedures.	Municipal, national policies and budgets could affect future development, management and sustainability of the groups. Training of SEI inspectors and BDE cousellors was undertaken.	incorporate the *Mozaik* methodology explicitly. This can pose a possible impediment for the full integration of *Mozaik* groups into the national preschool education system. Shift to online training curriculum for ongoing professional development in *Mozaik* methodology for the kindergarten and *Mozaik* teachers.

Continued

Continued

Evaluation and project details	Project achievements	Programme concepts	Learning concepts	Institutional links	Recommendations for future projects
	students, education inspectors and counsellors from SEI and BDE. 18 community outreach events organized involving 1,141 students in collaboration with the Open Fun Football schools, formerly partners on the EU funded phase of *Mozaik*. A reality TV show *New Heroes* under production/trial in 2019. 97 kindergarten teachers trained during 24 sessions. 18 workshops held with 304 parents across 10 municipalities. Four groups of primary schools involved.	Exchanging of experiences and best practices with teaching colleagues from other locations across North Macedonia. The possibility of establishing further *Mozaik* groups was tabled, by offering funding for training, an element that was flagged as a concern in the final evaluation of the EU funded *Mozaik* phase.	Internal mid-term review to reflect on the project implementation and identify areas for learning and improvement; Trainers were *Mozaik* teachers working with CCG since 1997; Continuity in focus, *Mozaik* remains the central point of efforts, donor focus on enhancing social. Cohesion was being catered to more centrally, rather than simply continuing the previous focus on intercultural communication.	Training of *Mozaik* teachers in public kindergarten groups marked a major extension of the *Mozaik* model and methodology. Negotiations underway with central and local government officials, for the creation of 3–4 new *Mozaik* groups using funds from the ASC project to support the training of new *Mozaik* teachers.	

Sierra Leone meta-ethnographic synthesis and concepts

Evaluation and project details	Project achievements	Programme concepts	Learning concepts	Institutional links	Recommendations for future projects
External review activities in Sierra Leone (2002) • Voice • Democracy promotion	Violence reduction through the promotion of peace, reconciliation, and democratization. Success in capturing dedicated radio listenership. Listenership increased from 40% in December 2000 to 85% in March 2002. Innovation in the use of community theatre, music festivals, radio drama;	Sensitization through radio-based information dissemination. Curbed election related *violence*. Supported reconciliation; empowerment; voice; and capacity-building; Character of programmes were neutral; credible; and were developed in multiple languages.	GKN changed popular perceptions about children's rights. Corporal punishment became less acceptable at home and in schools. Despite very low incidence, and awareness of HIV/AIDs, information on SRH, HIV/AIDS was found to be useful in preventing future infections;	NCDDR partly funded *Tro Away di Gun*. The radio show was hosted by ex-combatants from formerly warring factions. This link helped disseminate information on the DDR of combatants through trusted interlocutors.	The project evaluation underlined the need to work with traditional leaders; Alliance building with different local NGOs was encouraged; A continued focus on elections and election related violence was encouraged. Efforts to link with the truth and reconciliation work of the Special Court was recommended. Issues of governance, corruption and accountable leadership were identified as growing in significance.

	First to train children as reporters in *Golden Kids News* (*GKN*); Ethnic and linguistic diversity of studio staff helped in a broad coverage of social issues.	Focus on community radio; Targets were children youth, and women.	Ex-combatants did not disarm because of sensitization based radio programmes like *Trow Away di Gun*; Information on DDR through radio was helpful nonetheless.		The studio was encouraged to support community radio; Expand staff and to continue its programming focus on human rights and HIV/AIDS education. Finally, efforts to collate data and report on post-conflict violence was also recommended.
Review of activities in Sierra Leone for DfiD by Everett, Williams and Myers (2004) • Accountability • Capacity • Partnerships • Succession	Successful in sensitizing children to refuse sexual advances from teachers in schools. Activities increased enrolment of girls in schools due to the positive impact of *GKN*.	Public accountability and transparency; Decentralization; Critical thinking, self-examination of attitudes and behaviours.	Recognition that long-term social change is complex. It is the product of incentives, legislation, and work by other humanitarian actors.	The consortium established to investigate issues of quality education did not include the Ministry of Education, Science and Technology.	Overstretch particularly in terms of the ability to provide adequate media coverage was noted. For example, the Makeni office had responsibility to cover the entire Northern Province. Six districts including Kono were covered by only five staff.

Continued

Continued

Evaluation and project details	Project achievements	Programme concepts	Learning concepts	Institutional links	Recommendations for future projects
			Building up the capacity of supported organizations like transport stakeholders taskforce;	Forge strategic partnerships with line ministries and government commissions;	Encourage community radio stations. Formal MoUs with 18 out of 20 radio stations.
			Developing successor organizations like the Media Foundation for Peace;	Include smaller local groups of women and youth in the larger consortia on governance and accountability work.	Develop IRN.
			Building up local radio stations rather than expanding regional offices or studios as the more sustainable approach;		Transition from expatriate to national staff and develop middle management.
			Supported community radio stations could not survive on their own;		Focus on decentralization of local governance.
			Capacity building, and investment in continuous staff training was required to ensure sustainability of community radio stations;		Problems with coalition building acknowledged. In the *Na Wi Pot* Alliance, sub-standard reporting by *Radio Moa* criticized.
					Include rural station managers in strategic planning meetings;

| Final Performance Report (2004) in Sierra Leone to USAID (April 2002–2004)

• Governance
• Elections
• Capacity | Supported ex-combatant reintegration under YRTEP through solidarity events.

Focus was on strengthening democracy and governance.

Youth and non-violence campaigns were largely successful in arresting electoral violence.

Inclusion of women on radio, reduced domestic violence and increased community tolerance of rape victims in Kailahun. | • Information
• Trust building
• Role model
• Community mobilization | Neutrality is difficult in a highly politicized space;

Local language programmes more effective in information dissemination in the hinterland;

Regular power cuts meant there was an over-reliance on generators for power supply in Makeni which affected radio programmes.

Peace festivals in Kabala generated revenues that supported the founding of Radio Bintumani, generating multiplier effects. | IRN established. Brought together 10 broadcast media stakeholders to report on elections.

The Diamond Area Community Development Fund coalition was a successful example of community mobilization to focus on accountability and transparency issues.

Transport task force in Bo became a model that was replicated elsewhere to increase traffic safety. | Studio should begin to think of exit;

Scale up media work particularly video

Technical capacity of the local radio stations was weak.

Building on the success of the transport task force in Bo was recommended. |

Continued

Continued

Evaluation and project details	Project achievements	Programme concepts	Learning concepts	Institutional links	Recommendations for future projects
	Programmes like *Parliament Bol Hat* and *Meet the Candidate*, were effective in linking isolated areas like Kailahun to the national dialogue on elections; Education subsidies allocated to head teachers were helpful in eliminating corruption in government agencies like at the level of the Education Secretary. Education Coalition established to support UNICEF and partners in the drive			Local Partnership Board in Bo, enhanced police and community relationships and involved civil society in community security issues.	
Internal Review on Bike Riders in Sierra Leone (2006) • Voice • Sensitization • Information	Conflict reduction between bike riders and the traffic police;	Training in road traffic rules through radio programmes like *Traffic Kotoku* was useful in sensitization and enhancing public information.	Radio programmes cannot resolve traffic related conflicts; Resolving bike rider conflicts required hands-on training and dialogue facilitation.	Limited buy-in from the government authorities in comparison to the high levels of involvement and interest shown by the bike riders.	Political party loyalty determined the outcome of the BRU institutionalization process.

Opened dialogue between bike riders, bike owners, police and traffic wardens; Contributed to a codification of the traffic rules; Traffic discipline and safety improved. Driving licences were introduced.		Short-term training of biker riders in traffic rules did not present a sustainable model. No provision was made for regularly updating the information on traffic regulations.	Limited attention given to the sustainability and organizational development of task forces and the BRU.	Bike riders in Bo were caught up in inter-party conflicts between SLPP and the People's Movement for Democratic Change.
Internal evaluation of *Sisi Aminata* (2007) • Sensitization • Appropriate behaviours	Increased the knowledge around adolescent SRH concerns. High levels of awareness were noted in Koinadugu, although there was little impact in terms of listenership. Some changes in attitudes and behaviour were noted in Bombali district.	Community sensitization, confidence building around sexual and reproductive health of adolescents. Abuse and exploitation of school children was arrested. Teenage pregnancy related stigma was addressed.	Did not increase youth's ability to ask their parents for SRH related advice. Did increase parent's willingness to offer advice on SRH. Radio had to be combined with community engagement activities in schools, live concerts, quizzes etc., to raise awareness.	Ministry of Education, Science and Technology, CARE, UNICEF were partners creating some formal and informal links. CARE was the project financial lead.	Including community leaders to prevent resistance to SRH related sensitization. Providing more advice for out of school youth on the show; and addressing the issues of polygamy would also have been useful.

Continued

Continued

Evaluation and project details	Project achievements	Programme concepts	Learning concepts	Institutional links	Recommendations for future projects
	Reduction in the incidence of early teenage pregnancy was recorded, although this trend was not observed over a longer-time period to check results. The radio programmes aired for three years on Radio Bintumani and Radio Mankneh.		Local language programmes were developed in line with previous project recommendations.		
Internal evaluation of Sierra Leone Election Strategy (2008) • Elections • Accountability	High listenership of election related radio programmes. IRN programmes were well-received. NEW observers were present at the polls, increasing the visibility of the campaign. TV drama called *Insai di Salone*, did not prove as popular and resulted in only a limited audience capture.	Electoral violence, accountability, youth mobilization, trust, anti-corruption, free and fair elections.	Complementarity and coherence between partners was key to success of the strategy. The NEW observers, and IRN radio stations, proved credible and trustworthy. This three-pronged strategy involving advocacy, presence and sensitization through radio was a new model.	Ad hoc engagement with the National Election Commission.	Sustainability of IRN was strengthened by extending the network, and increasing the talent pool of reporters and producers involved in generating community radio content.

	Local radio stations proved their capacity to produce quality programmes, and conduct live reporting.		It introduced partnership between civil society, and the public to encourage their participation in governance.		
	CSO partners like NEW could manage their funds and organize their staff well.				
Internal evaluation of Golden Kids News (2008)	Gave children voice for articulating their concerns publicly;	Child protection;	ID cards and stipends for child reporters;	Ad hoc results. In Bo and Kailahun, the studio was part of the Ministry of Social Welfare (Family Support Unit) child protection meetings.	Strengthening community-based protection structures.
• Voice		Social norms;			Monitor and follow up punitive aspects of formal protection structures.
• Participation	Re-defined social norms around child rights and child protection;	Information on child rights and responsibilities;	New equipment like recorders be provided;		
• Information				Short-term collaboration with other INGOs such as Save the Children and the IRC created links into the broder delivery of child protection activities.	
• Rights and protection	Advocated for the non-use of violence in disciplining children.	Public speaking/voice;	Improve communications with local radio station partners;		
		Formal and informal protection structures.	Timely delivery of tapes and airing of radio programmes.	Involvement of GKN reporters in the Child Welfare Committee structures.	

Continued

Continued

Evaluation and project details	Project achievements	Programme concepts	Learning concepts	Institutional links	Recommendations for future projects
Learning evaluation of Community Radio Development in Sierra Leone and Liberia (2009) • Civil society • Community radio • Capacity • Dependence	Community radio disseminated information relating to development. It helped improve development outcomes. In Kambia, the civil society movement monitored the various development projects to some extent, enhancing local ownership and inclusion.	Radio Wanjei, Pujehun and Radio Kolenten, Kambia were studied as part of this evaluation. Radio Kolenten was established in Dec. 2006 with funding from OSIWA, supported by the community leaders. Action Aid set up the operations in Dec. 2005. Broadcasts were made in all relevant local languages—Krio, Temne, Susu, Limba, and Fullah.	Community radio makes a major contribution to community cohesiveness. Radio is an active agent in diffusing local conflict. The relationship between radio and CSOs enables a grounded and bottom-up reporting approach. Capacity deficits undermine the ability of community radios. CR can promote inclusive development processes. The impact of community radio programmes was reliant on co-operation from the government to avoid the broadcast of politically biased information.	District Council is the key actor in the official development process. Majority of funding comes from central government through line ministries for decentralized development efforts. Traditional leaders are sidelined in this process. Radio used by a range of CSOs, trade unions, women's groups, youth groups etc to communicate messages. International and local NGOs often partner with the government in ad hoc or limited ways.	Inclusion of women and youth could be improved. Broad capacity building required. CR played a strong role in local peace building. Unmet potential for increased quantity and quality of radio led peace building. Community radio allows voices of the ordinary people on issues of governance and politics to filter into radio programmes. Community radio does not allow for strong formal links to be forged with government agencies.

Learning Evaluation of Three Projects from Sierra Leone (Golden Kids and Atunda Ayenda), Burundi and Democratic Republic of Congo (2008/2009). • Voice • Inclusion • Protection	People enjoyed listening to children's voice on the radio, and almost all of them (98%) reported that the programme changed their attitudes towards the role of children in Sierra Leone. The Golden Kids child reporters received respect from elders and community members. Children liked their voices to be heard in the studio. After their training as journalists, they received recognition and respect from their communities.	Voice Respect	Financial struggles and interrupted broadcasts affected the delivery of content. Improved the relationship between youth and community leaders as authorities and the elders in these communities began to feel confidence in young people. They started to involve youth in local decision-making, and in local development initiatives.	Ad hoc links with formal and informal child protection structures set up.	N/A

Continued

Continued

Evaluation and project details	Project achievements	Programme concepts	Learning concepts	Institutional links	Recommendations for future projects
Internal study on Sustaining a Civil Society Campaign around the Chieftaincy Reform Process in Sierra Leone (2010) • Corruption • Governance • Account- ability • Participation • Elections	Support for the PICOT alliance through media-based advocacy around chieftaincy reforms. A national bi-weekly production *Nyu Baray* was launcehd to raise public awareness among policy makers at a national and district level. 14, 30-min radio episodes were produced and aired on 27 radio stations. 75 episodes of *Atunda Ayenda* covered chieftaincy issues. Programmes relating to the the PICOT and NEW alliance members, was aired on radio stations in Bo, Kenema and Bombali	Politicization, tradition, corruption, discrimination against women in governance, leadership, youth participation.	Balance between chiefs' service to the government, and service to the community has shifted too far in favour of the government and national political parties. Limited 'buy in' of PICOT led CSO coalition recommendations by local and national government authorities. Their advocacy challenged traditional concepts that excluded women and youth from running for leadership positions within the traditional authority ranks, and structures. Method of election by a small number of councillors marginalized women's representation. No funding for monitoring and evaluation in the project.	PICOT, a coalition supported by Christian Aid, held meetings with the Ministry of Local Government and community development. Overlapping roles of district councils and chiefdom councils in this area was noted.	Coordination challenges of working with partners in different locations. Shifting focus of the campaign generated confusion in the media campaign.

| Baseline Study for the Democracy and Governance Project (2014)

• Corruption
• Human rights
• Governance
• Sensitization | Youth led survey implemented.

24 youth enumerators were selected through the pre-existing youth group networks.

Six youth selected per district. | Corruption; Human rights; Governance; Education; Sensitization; | Primary source of information was radio for 71% of the population.

The policy makers sources of information and radio listening habits similar to that of the general population.

Policy makers do not use radio as a feedback mechanism from their constituents despite evidenced use of radio for receiving information. | This project built on the pre-existing networks of youth groups in Kailahun, Kono, Kenema, and Koindugu districts. | N/A |
| Equitable Land Rights Promotion: Baseline Report (2014)

• Land rights
• Access to land | Promoting equitable land rights in Bombali, Port Loko, and Pujehun districts.

Problem solving dialogue between community members, local government, and investing companies. | Enhanced local understanding of land rights in the communities affected by corporate land concessions. | Among the 408 respondents interviewed in the three districts, 96.3% said, they had no knowledge about the land policy prepared by the Ministry of Labour.

In Pujehun, chiefs were deciding on land deals on behalf of the community members, creating more tensions. | N/A | Mapping organizations involved in resolving land conflicts.

Increased access to information on land transactions.

Sensitization on inclusive decision-making.

Documentation of land transactions. |

Continued

Continued

Evaluation and project details	Project achievements	Programme concepts	Learning concepts	Institutional links	Recommendations for future projects
			Building on existing CBO/NGO activity to engage the communities instead of establishing new structures		
Equitable Land Rights Promotion: Final Evaluation report for OSIWA (2016) • Information • Account- ability • Rights • Access	36 episodes of *Bush Wahala* produced and broadcasted twice every week on IRN member stations. Land rights issues addressed through 30 screenings of *Atunda Ayenda*. 29 min film in Krio on land rights and land conflicts was produced. 15 community forums held to encourage dialogue between citizens, traditional leaders, local authorities, and foreign companies.	Information on land rights provided to the communities in Bombali, Port Loko, and the Pujehun districts. Through knowledge dissemination on the national land policy, local protection mechanisms were enhanced. The project supported consultative decision-making by the Paramount chief and other traditional authorities. It also aided in peaceful conflict management.	Job creation, employment, livelihoods, and the role of foreign investment companies. Companies have built schools and health facilities as part of CSR commitments. CSR replacing government services provision. Advocacy requires collaborative approach with other organizations.	Limited institutional links a drawback.	Labour law violations were often overlooked. Lawyers needed to be involved to interrogate these labour rights issues. Women's participation, and inclusion in the deliberations around land deals was limited, due to their exclusion from land ownership.

Final Evaluation for the USAID funded project 'Open for business': Promoting equitable land rights protection in Sierra Leone, Liberia and Guinea' (2016) • Land grabs • Civil society	Enabling civil society actors, state actors and investing companies to promote equitable land rights. In Sierra Leone, land lease agreements had a renegotiation clause every seven years. Awareness of these possibilities among the rural communities gave them the hope for change. Green Scenery, the Rural Agency for Community Action Programme in Pujehun benefited from funding through the project.	Knowledge or information on land rights and land demarcation rules.	Participatory theatre, mobile movie projection, radio broadcasting, group discussions were used. Documentation of land holdings without adequate consultation with the government to arrive at a consensus. Legal practitioners should have been involved in the interpretation of the land lease contracts.	Land management committees created for the purpose of defending land owners' rights.	Local land focused CSOs could not continue to operate without external support. Land concession by the government without appropriate local consultation across land owning families had to be probed further.

Continued

Continued

Evaluation and project details	Project achievements	Programme concepts	Learning concepts	Institutional links	Recommendations for future projects
Baseline survey report for the 'United for Greater Governance and Participation: Empowering Rural Communities to Strengthen Local Governance and Accountability Processes' (2017) • Governance • Participation • Accountability	Increase accountability and citizen participation in local decision-making and governance or service delivery.	Local governance; Low levels of knowledge around citizen participation in local decision-making; Fear of political intimidation; Limited involvement of women and youth in community meetings.	Ward committees are the main entry points or legal basis for citizen's participation in development planning or decision-making. Ward committee members are mostly appointed not in line with the statutory requirement of elections. Voluntary nature of members has made them ineffective. Low levels of participation by women and youth.	Ward committees, district budget oversight committees and school management committees exist, but do not meaningfully engage citizens in local governance processes.	N/A

Mid-term evaluation of the project 'United for Greater Governance and Participation: Empowering Rural Communities to Strengthen Local Governance and Accountability Processes' (2018) • Monitoring • Training	Increased understanding of, and demand for greater accountability and participation in democratic governance in the rural communities. 24 youth and women local CSOs in Koinadugu, Port Loko, Kono, Kambia, Pujehan, and Moyamba part of the advocacy process.	Organizing citizens, bringing them and the authorities to deliberate on the issues of governance. Scorecard training (from previous projects) was used. This offered a community based indigenous monitoring of he timely implementation of commitments and activities. Adopted by other school forums	Journalists, CSOs, District and Budget oversight committees (DBOCs), school management (SMCs), and community teachers' associations (CTAs) led monitoring of service delivery. Journalists who took part in the common ground journalism training have applied their skills further. Promoted learning and sharing between CSOs. Monitoring of airing schedules of partner radio stations required. Financial training necessary to build the capacity of CSOs.	DBOCs, SMCs, and CTAs were involved with regard to institutinal links.	WhatsApp groups should be set up for DBOCs, SMCs, CTAs to communicate and share achievements of their respective activities. Link with relevant government ministries was missing. Necessary for advocacy to gain more teeth. Advocacy or engagement required to allow DBOC allowances to be paid on time.

Continued

Continued

Evaluation and project details	Project achievements	Programme concepts	Learning concepts	Institutional links	Recommendations for future projects
Final Evaluation of the Project 'Standing Together for Free, Fair and Peaceful Elections in Sierra Leone' (2018) • Elections • Participation	Effective in facilitating public policy dialogue on electoral integrity. Election related agencies trained to deliver free, fair and peaceful elections. 500,000 direct participants, through the Citizen's Manifesto consultations. Citizen Manifesto created. Three public policy documents developed. People with Disabilities Agenda developed. Election Observers reports drawn up.	Voter civic education on democratic rights and responsibilities. Public policy dialogue. Election observation; Electoral management; Non-violent engagement.	Consortium based project delivery can pool expertise to greater effect, but can present challenges of variable capacity, structure and workflow systems.	Five national CSOs part of the consortium received capacity building training. 700 CSO partners targeted in the citizen manifesto consultation. 35 radio stations received media training and equipment support.	Need for a longer implementation timeline to work alongside with the national election cycle.

Final Evaluation 'Engaging Children and Youth as Partners in Preventing Violence against Children' in Liberia, Guinea, and Sierra Leone (2017) • Children's rights • Violence • Capacity-building	Phase I provided training for youth researchers to conduct research with peers to identify the prevalent and worst forms of violence against children and youth Involvement of youth researchers was a positive; Helped them grow personally and professionally.	Peer support Youth led research Post research actions and follow-up was weak. Worst forms of violence advocacy did not gain traction with elders and the government. Manual or handbook on worst forms of violence against children and youth was the main output.	Beyond youth researchers being involved and the resulting capacity building of children and youth, there was little or no evidence of changes at the country level, or development of a policy on countering worst forms of violence against children and youth. In Sierra Leone, a radio listeners survey suggested that children were motivated by radio messages to prevent violence against peers. 55.4% recalled youth led radio programmes like GKN. 94.3% noted that radio improved their knowledge about these issues.	No specific institutional links with the government. Guide manual produced for stakeholders in the government. Events held in schools, churches and mosques (2016) to disseminate the manual's findings. Limited uptake by these organizations.	Certificate for youth researchers would help them link up with further opportunities of conducting such research. Necessary to sustain the relationship with youth researchers, create roles, such as certified Youth Advocates with responsibilities and institutional links to the studio. Psycho-social support for youth researchers could be provided for children conducting research with respondents who have undergone violent experiences. Follow up with research participants, stakeholders and youth researchers would be helpful for retaining the momentum on these issues.

Index

Tables and figures are indicated by an italic *t* and *f* following the page number.

accountability 10, 16, 21, 199
  public accountability and
    performance 129–37
  see also **financial accountability to donors**
adaptation 35, 36, 44, 49, 94, 148
advocacy 10, 11, 30, 36, 42, 188, 195, 197,
    210–11
  linking informal advocacy with formal
    systems 208–9
alliance building 171–2, 179
Alliance for Peacebuilding 152
animosity 2, 191
appreciative inquiry 15
archival ethnography 13, 54
archival memory 45, 157
atrocities 18
attitudes 183
  attitude change 185, 186, 187, 209, 210, 211
  attitude formation 183, 184, 199
  belief-based models of attitude 185
  persuasion 185

Balkan Theatre Network (BTN) 106–7, 164–5
behaviour change communication 200
beneficiaries 10, 26, 28, 29, 46, 154, 181
'Big Men' 32
Bike Riders Union (BRU) 123, 145, 198
binding social capital 98
bonding social capital 98
bricolage 12
Bridges for the New Balkans (BNB) 105–6, 162
bureaucratic clock-time 28, 205
bureaucratic rationality 15

capacity-building 30, 42, 66, 67, 179, 207, 215
case study research 55–6
Center for Human Rights and Conflict
    Resolution (CHRCR) 86
Centre for the Coordination of Youth Activities
    (CCYA) 123
change agentry 7, 146, 218
chiefdoms in Sierra Leone
  Bagbo 132, 135
  Bum 132

Bureh 131, 135
Kasseh 131, 135
Lugbu 132
Maconteh 64, 131
Malen 64, 132
child labour 128, 195, 200, 211
child marriage 170
child protection 66, 125, 126, 127, 128, 144, 171
children
  child abuse 127, 200
  child development 184
  definition 6
  rights 6, 174
  role in peacebuilding 17–18
  violence against children 127, 128, 174
  see also **youth**
child soldiers 6, 112, 168, 174
'circlers' 150
civic belonging 77
civilians 61, 67, 115, 120, 123, 146
civil war 1, 61, 78, 89, 112, 115, 116, 117, 120,
    186, 199
coercive recruitment 112
community hostility 1
community of practice 152
community radio stations 122, 145, 147
  Radio Gbafth 122, 144
  Radio Moa 122, 144
  Radio Wanjei 145
Conciliation Resources 45, 152
conflict transformation 7, 27, 29, 30, 31, 33, 43,
    47
contact hypothesis 89
continuity in programming 49
contribution analysis 34
corruption 68
  radio programming in Sierra Leone
    governance, accountability and
    anti-corruption 129–37
'critical agency' 38
culture of violence 29
customary courts 130
cyclical time 28, 29

Debar 70
   bilingual use 101
   interethnic relations 101, 102, 103
   Mozaik alumni 73
   Mozaik group 72, 90
decentralization 76, 84, 124, 137, 138, 142, 163, 199
democracy promotion and electoral participation 137–40
democratic politics 199
direct legacies 8, 26
disarmament, demobilization, reintegration (DDR) 1, 2, 34–5
districts in Sierra Leone
   Kambia 136, 175
   Koinadugu 136, 175
   Kono 136, 175
   Moyamba 136, 175
   Port Loko 136, 175
   Pujehun 136, 175
donor rules 180–81
donor time 27
double-loop learning 44–5, 157

early childhood development 6
Ebola 127, 128, 174
ecological model of child development 184, 220
ecological model of peace 220–21
Economic Community of West African States Monitoring Group (ECOMOG) 122
ecosystem 184
elders 11, 62, 66, 69, 115, 116, 122, 125, 128, 130, 141, 142
electoral participation 137–40, 174
electoral violence 139, 172, 199, 200
electronic memory 45, 158
elite-non-elite relations 116
empowerment of children, women, and youth 125–8
endogenous capacity 50
epistemic rigidity 190–91
Equip (Canadian INGO) 2
ethical research 62, 63–4
   feminist ethics 63
ethnographic fieldwork 12–13
   archival ethnography 13, 54
   meta-ethnographic synthesis 12–13, 15, 56–7, 60–61, 74–5, 273–82, 283–301
   reading and translating the studies 58
Eurocentrism 25
European Union 36, 96
evaluation *see* monitoring and evaluation
evaluation research and practice (ERP) 154

EveryChild 46
Everyday Peace Indicators 15
ex-combatants
   reintegration 1, 2, 3, 117, 203
exit strategies 16, 41–2, 50, 151, 171, 204, 213
exo-system 184

family support unit (FSU) 66, 144, 176
feminist ethics 63
fictionalization 61
financial accountability to donors 43, 153
financial sustainability challenges
   INGOs 41
First Balkan War (1912) 102
first-order constructs 189
first-order learning 44
focus group discussions (FGDs) 54, 62, 64, *65t*, 65, 70, 73
follow-up research 10, 46, 151, 168, 181, 207
foreign direct investment (FDI) 132
Fourah Bay College (FBC) 143
Freetown 128
   Kroo Bay 65
   Tombo 128
Freetown Players Group 120
futures thinking 32–3

Galtung, J. 221
gatekeepers 2, 52, 53, 62, 158
Global North 25, 50, 213
Global South 50, 213
Golden Kids News(GKN) 65, 66
governance, accountability and anti-corruption 129–37
'Great Men' 32
Green Scenery 69, 134
group norms 187, 211

handover 208, 209
   see also successor organizations
human memory 45, 157–8
human rights
   Sierra Leone 123–4

illiberal norms 37
images of war 184
'impatient' peace 26
inclusivity 204, 217, 221
Independent Media Commission (IMC) 117, 145
Independent Radio Network (IRN) 122
indigenous monitoring and evaluation (IM&E) 47, 50–51
indirect legacies 8, 26

inner time 28
institutional diagramming analysis 2
institutionalization 8, 9, 10, 42–3, 49, 207, 208
    linking informal advocacy with formal
        systems 208–9
    material and non-material resonance 209
institutionalized ethnicity 20
institutional learning teams (ILTs) 158–9
institutional mapping 159
institutional memory 45–6, 49, 60, 157–8
integrated education 82, 83, 85–6, 110, 168, 193
    see also Mozaik preschool bilingual
        immersion groups
intercultural communication projects 77, 103,
    110, 111
Interethnic Integration in Education Program
    (IIEP) 86
interethnic relations
    Macedonia 79–80, 81, 84–5, 99–100, 108,
        110, 111
intergenerational conflict 10, 11, 32, 112, 115,
    125, 195–6
intergenerational peace 7, 10, 11, 17–18, 31–3,
    206, 211
intergenerational resilience 32
intergenerational responsibility 220
intergenerational transmission of ethnic
    essentialism 78, 109, 111
intergenerational trauma 31–2
intergroup contact 210
internalization of norms 36, 39, 40, 210, 212
Internal Macedonian Revolutionary
    Organization (IMRO) 102
International Alert 45, 152
International NGO Training and Research
    Centre (INTRAC) 46
international non-governmental organizations
    (INGOs)
    country offices 148
        adaptation 148
    criticism of 41, 42
    exit strategies 41–2, 171
    financial sustainability challenges 41
    limited sharing of knowledge between
        INGOs 151–2
    Macedonia country office
        learning from evaluation 167–8
        learning trajectory 159, 160–67, 269–70
        limited inter-organizational learning 168–9
    organizational issues 40–41
    organizational learning 148–9
    Sierra Leone country office
        learning from evaluation 175– 6, 271–2
        learning trajectory 169–75

variation and similarity in country office
        learning behaviour 176–7, 181
    donor rules 180–81
    local partnerships 179–80, 214–15
    national government buy-in 178–9
    staff continuity 177–8, 212
international norms 49–50
International Organization for Migration
    (IOM) 1, 2
inter-organizational learning 45, 49, 168–9
interrupted legacies 8, 26
interviews 2. 54, 58, 60, 61, 64, 65, 70
invested peace constituency 8, 209
iterative incrementalism 45

knowledge production partnerships 3, 52–3
knowledge transfer 213
    barriers to 52
    see also learning and reflection
Kvinna till Kvinna 46–7

land grabs 67, 68, 135, 143, 147
landscape mapping 2
Lean Monitoring, Evaluation, Research and
    Learning (Lean MERL) 152
learning and belief focused programming
    model 9
learning and reflection 10, 14–15, 43–7, 49, 50,
    51, 151, 207–8, 212, 213
    adaptive and agile learning agenda 151
    barriers to learning from evaluation
        disciplinary disconnect 154–5
        fear of failure and the limited consequences
            of not learning 156–7
        managing the institutional memory 157–8
        technocratic dominance 155–6
    documenting field level processes 213–14
    double-loop learning 44–5, 157
    institutional learning teams 158–9
    lack of resources for learning 151
    learning behavior 153
    local partnerships 214–15
    process-driven approach 44, 156–7
    single loop learning 157
    'tick box' learning 153
    triple loop learning 157
    types of organizational learning behavior 159,
        160t
    see also international non-governmental
        organizations
learning diaries 214

legacies
    direct legacies 8, 26, 27, 43
    indirect legacies 8, 26
    interrupted legacies 8, 26
    organizational legacies 10, 212–13
    see also institutionalization; peacebuilding
        legacy
liberal marketization 22, 29–30, 119
liberal norms 3, 66, 119, 124, 136–7, 141
liberal peacebuilding 116, 149, 182
Liberia
    civil conflict 1
    disarmament, demobilization, reintegration
        (DDR) programme 1, 2, 34–5
    Flumpa 2
    Ganta 2
    Kawee 2
    Koon Town 2
    Krahn people 1
    Mamba Point 1
    Mandingo people 1
    Mano people 2
    Margibi county 2
    Monrovia 1
    Sackiebomo 2
    security sector reform (SSR) 1
    Toe's Town 2
Liberian Peace Council 1
Liberians United for Reconciliation and
    Democracy (LURD) 1, 2
lines-of-argument translation 57
linking social capital 98
Local Governance Act (2004) (Sierra
    Leone) 129
localization of norms 38
local legitimacy 37
local ownership 8, 9, 15, 16, 25, 30, 31, 208
local partnerships 179–80, 214–15
'local turn' 30
logical frameworks (logframes) 34, 44, 149, 150
longitudinal studies 46, 48, 50–51, 54, 64, 75
lumpen youth 112, 114

Macedonia
    adoption of new norms 201
    attitude change
contact quality and contact quantity 200–201
    Bitola 84
    bridging ties 99
    citizenship and ethnic identity 79–80, 193–4
        integrated education 193
        minority rights 193
        segregation of the educational system 193,
            194

social cohesion 193
civic belonging 77
Debar 70
    bilingual use 101
    interethnic relations 101, 102, 103
    Mozaik alumni 73
    Mozaik group 72, 90
Director of Children and Youth
    Programmes 3, 4
early years' education policy 87, 88
education in the mother tongue 82
'epistemic rigidity' 77
evaluation based recommendations and
    follow-up actions 269–70
Gostivar 79, 89, 90, 99, 102, 162
integrated education 193
intercultural communication 77, 103, 110,
    111, 164, 165
    attitude change 186, 191
    'building bridges theory' 186
    intergroup contacts 190, 191
    minority language 191
    socialization 190–91
interethnic conflict 78–9, 81, 89–90
    evolution of ethno-national violence 80t
interethnic relations 79–80, 81, 84–5, 99–100,
    108, 110, 111
interethnic separation 76
intergenerational transmission of ethnic
    essentialism 78, 109, 111
Kichevo 92
Kumanovo 106
language rights 76
literature on early years education and
    media 20–21
media and theatre projects 103
    Balkan Theatre Network 106–7, 164–5
    Bridges for the New Balkans 105–6, 162
    institutional legacy 108
    minority language media 104
    Nashe Maalo 104–5, 107, 108, 109, 161,
        162, 163
    New Heroes 166–7
    normative legacy 108–10
    shortcomings of the projects 107–8
meta-ethnographic synthesis and
    concepts 273–82
minority groups 78
minority language 191
minority rights 76, 82, 193
monoethnic schools 83
monolingual instruction 83, 86, 194
Nansen Dialogue Centre 88
networks 99

contact quality and contact quantity (*Continued*)
'otherization' 102
political patronage 192
primary education
quality of instruction in minority
languages 82
quality preschool education 191–3
attitude change, and 192, 193
enrolment 192
institutionalization 192
pedagogy 191, 192
residential segregation 84
school system 83–4
school teachers
requirements 80
segregation of the educational system 83–4,
193, 194
Shtip 105
Skopje 70
interethnic relations 99–100
Mozaik alumni 73–4
Mozaik group 72–3, 92
transition to primary school 100–101
social cohesion 84, 85, 193
Struga 70
interethnic relations 100
Mozaik group 71–2, 90*f*
Strumica 164
Tetovo 106
university education
Albanian language 82
University of Tetovo 80, 81
use of the Albanian language in the judicial
system 194
Veles 106
see also international non-governmental
organizations; *Mozaik* preschool
bilingual immersion groups
Macedonian Civic Education Center 86
macrosystem 184
Malen Affected Land Owners and Users
Association (MALOA) 69, 134
Malen Youth Development Union
(MAYoDU) 134
Margai, Sir Milton 113
media programming 9, 10, 18, 19
mesosystem 184
meta-ethnographic synthesis 12–13, 15, 56–7,
60–61, 74–5, 273–82, 283–301
reading and translating the studies 58
microsystem 184
minority groups 78, 85, 90, 193
minority languages 82, 84, 104, 162, 163, 191

monitoring and evaluation (M&E) 4–5, 24, 43,
44, 151, 152–3, 154
formulaic approach to 153, 153*f*
indigenous monitoring and evaluation 47,
50–51
innovation 12
see also learning and reflection
most significant change (MSC) approach 15
Movement for Democracy in Liberia
(MODEL) 1
Mozaik preschool bilingual immersion
groups 9, 11, 88, 160–66, 216
adaptation process 94
behaviour change 97–8
employment status of teachers 91, 92
enrolment age 94
evolution of 88–9, 91*t*, 91, 92*f*, 92–3
financial problems 91
institutional legacy 110
interethnic conflict (2001), and 89–90
intergenerational values 101
managing conflicts 101
monitoring of the groups' performance 93–4
social capital, and 99, 110
standardization measures 93
teacher to student ratio 93
transition into mainstream education
effect on the children 95
see also Macedonia

Namati 219
Nansen Dialogue Centre (NDC) 88, 168
narod 79
narodnost 79
Nashe Maalo 104–5, 107, 108, 109, 161, 162, 163
National Commission for Disarmament,
Demobilization, Reintegration, and
Rehabilitation (NCDDRR) 1
National Election Commission (NEC) (Sierra
Leone) 139, 199
national government buy-in 178–9
National Liberation Army (NLA) 78–9
National Patriotic Front of Liberia (NPFL) 2
National Telecommunications Commission
(NATCOM) 145
National Youth Commission (Sierra
Leone) 143, 216
'negative peace' 34
neopatrimonialism 32
network capital 98
New Barbarism 112
New Heroes 166–7
Noblit and Hare's model of meta-ethnographic
synthesis 54, 56, 74

non-compliance 21, 39, 39*f*
non-participation 21, 37, 38, 39, 39*f*, 50
norms 36
  adoption of new norms 200
  contestation 37–8
  group norms 187, 211
  international norms 49–50
  liberal norms 3, 66, 119, 124, 136–7, 141
  localization of norms 38
  media interventions triggering norm
    change 188
  models of norm change
    group influence model 187
    learning and beliefs model 187
    social norms model 9, 187
  norm diffusion 36, 37
  norm internalization 36, 39, 40, 210, 212
  norm perception 187
  norm persuasion 184, 186, 187
  norm resonance 37, 39, 40, 50, 206, 210, 212
  norm transmission 9, 36–40, 95–6, 206–7,
    209–11
  peace education interventions and norm
    change 188
  research study
    norm concepts and second-order inter-
      pretations for norm transmission 59,
      59*t*
  retention of norms 37, 39, 40, 50, 206, 210
North Atlantic Treaty Organisation
  (NATO) 76, 81, 85, 179, 193

Ohrid-Debar uprising 102
Ohrid Framework Agreement (OFA) 76, 81, 82
oil palm plantation 132
okada riders 123
  see also Bike Riders Union (BRU)
Open Fun Football schools 166
Open Society Initiative for West Africa
  (OSIWA) 67, 117, 131
organizational learning *see* learning and
  reflection
organizational learning behavior 58, 59*t*
organizational learning routines 15
organizational legacies 10, 212–13
Organization for Economic Cooperation and
  Development (OECD) 153
Organization for Peace, Reconciliation, and
  Development (OPARD) 119
Organization for Security Cooperation in
  Europe (OSCE) 81, 85
outcome mapping technique 15

Paramount Chiefs 67, 68, 69, 115, 132, 133, 135,
  136, 137, 145
participant observation 70–71
participation 197, 217, 218
  non-participation 21, 37, 38, 39, 39*f*, 50
participatory capital 98
participatory rural appraisal (PRA)
  techniques 2
patrimonial politics 112, 113, 114, 116, 136–7
patronage 20, 22, 113, 116, 141, 144, 221
Peacebuilding and Evaluation Consortium
  (PEC) 152
peacebuilding effectiveness
  measurement of 13–14
Peacebuilding Evaluation Project 152
peacebuilding legacy
  conceptualizing 26–7, 36*f*, 205
    intergenerational peace 31–3, 206
    time 27–9, 205
    transformation 29–31, 206
  methodologies for capturing peacebuilding
    legacy 33–5, 206–7
peacebuilding programmes 4, 204
peace education 18–19, 77, 87–8, 96, 111
  norm change, and 188
  see also Mozaik preschool bilingual
    immersion groups
peace festivals 120, 122
'peace from below' 30
Peace Research partnership 45, 152
'peace writ large' 4, 5, 48
performance 34, 44, 48, 74, 155, 156, 205
  public accountability and
    performance 129–37
Plan International 47
policy time 28, 29
political parties in Macedonia
  Democratic Party of Macedonian National
    Unity 194
  Internal Macedonian Revolutionary
    Organization 102, 194
  Left party 194
  United Macedonia Party 194
political parties in Sierra Leone
  Alliance Democratic Party 137
  All People's Congress (APC) 113, 116, 140,
    198
  National Democratic Alliance (NDA) 137
  People's Democratic Party 137
  People's Movement for Democratic Change
    (PMDC) 137
  Sierra Leone People's Party (SLPP) 113, 116,
    129, 132, 140
political time 28

polygamy 170
positionality 12–13, 64
post-closure evaluations (PCEs) 46–7
post-exit studies 10, 181
post-war reconciliation initiatives in Sierra
    Leone 119–20, 122
Poverty Reduction Strategy Paper 132
power
    and time 29
power asymmetries 217
preschool education 88, 95
    see also Mozaik preschool bilingual
        immersion groups
prescriptive messaging 146, 195
'programme disconnect' 42
programming for change 185, 201, 206
project life-cycle 42, 44, 154
prosocial behaviours 188
protest music in Sierra Leone 198
public accountability and performance 129–37
public security 14

radio listening surveys 140, 170, 189
Radio Netherlands 117
radio programmes in Sierra Leone see Sierra
    Leone
randomized control trials (RCTs) 15
rape of minors 170
reciprocal translation 57
reclaimed peace 38
reconciliation
    post-war reconciliation initiatives in Sierra
        Leone 119–20, 122
reflection see learning and reflection
reflexivity 64
refutational translation 57
research ethics see ethical research
research fatigue 62–3
research study 57, 75
    challenges of fieldwork in post-war
        countries 61–3
    data collection and analysis 57–8
    ethical considerations 63–4
    Macedonia 70–71
        Mozaik alumni in Debar and Skopje 73–4
        Mozaik groups in Struga, Debar, and
            Skopje 71–3
    meta-ethnographic synthesis 56–7, 60–61,
        74–5, 273–82, 283–301
    reading and translating the studies 58
    norm concepts and second-order inter-
        pretations for norm transmission 59,
        59t
    potential limitations and biases 74–5

research design 54–5
    archival research 54
    primary data collection 54
    selection of cases 55
Sierra Leone 64–5
    child reporters and young people 65–7
    focus group discussions 64, 65t, 65
    land conflicts and the rural hinterland 67–9
    theory guided diverse case method 55–6
    triangulation of the data and findings 75
'residual caseload' 1, 203
resistance to norm transmission 37–8
resonance
    material and non-material resonance 209
    norm resonance 37, 39, 40, 50, 206, 210, 212
retention of norms 37, 39, 40, 50, 206, 210
Roundtable on Sustainable Palm Oil (RSPO)
    standards 134
rule of law 14, 116, 149

Saferworld 45, 152
Sankoh, F. 114
Save the Children 2
Schütz, A. 189
second-order constructs 189
second-order interpretations on norm
    persuasion and attitude change 188–90
second-order learning 44, 45
secure access 53
segregation in Macedonia
    educational system 83–4, 193, 194
    interethnic separation 76
    residential segregation 84
self-demobilization 2
sensitization 9, 20, 65, 67, 124, 125, 195, 209
sexual and reproductive health 143, 170, 171,
    175, 200
short-termism 11–12, 25, 26
Sierra Leone
    access and acceptance 194–6
        attitude change 195
        dependence 196
        information 195
        sensitization 195
    adoption of new norms 200
    advocacy 195, 197
    agency and behavior 196–8
        attitude change 196, 197
        capacity 197
        participation 197
        voice 198
    attitude change 186, 200
    Bamba 64, 133, 134
    Bike Riders Union 123, 145, 198

Bo 122, 128
chieftaincy reforms 172–3
child rights 174
child soldiers 112
citizenship and democracy 199
  accountability 199
  attitude change 199
  governance 199
  youth participation in elections 199
Civil Defence Forces (CDF) 112
civil war 112, 114–15
  conditions leading to 113–14
coercive recruitment 112
community meetings 68f, 68
Community Peacebuilding Unit (CPU) 118,
  120, 122
democracy promotion 137, 138f
Director of Children and Youth
  Programmes 3, 4
evaluation based recommendations and
  follow-up actions 271–2
ex-combatant reintegration 117
foreign direct investment 132
Freetown 128
human rights 123–4
intergenerational conflict 112, 115, 125,
  195–6
Kabala 120
Kailahun 138, 142–3
Kemen 64, 135, 136, 143
Kono 114, 120
land grabs 67, 68, 135, 143, 147
land rights and conflicts 173
land tenure systems 68–9
liberal peacebuilding 116
literature on post-war peacebuilding 19–20
Local Governance Act (2004) 129
Maconteh 64, 131
Makeni 120, 144
Malen chiefdom 64
meta-ethnographic synthesis and
  concepts 283–301
Mile 91
  internally displaced population (IDP) 119
patrimonial politics 112, 113, 114, 116, 136–7
peace festivals 120, 122
PICOT alliance 172–3
Port Loko 120, 131, 134, 135, 136, 137, 147
post-independence statebuilding process 113
Poverty Reduction Strategy Paper 132
protest music 198
public accountability and
  performance 129–37
Radio Democracy 117

radio programming 146–7, 169–75
  Accountability Now 129
  Atunda Ayenda 125, 126, 127, 128, 131,
    134, 136, 138, 175
  'authentic' to a 'manufactured' peace, shift
    from 124
  Borderline 138, 172
  Bush Wahala 67, 131, 134, 135
  children and youth focused radio 118
  civic educational tool, as 125
  community radio stations 122, 145, 147
  democracy promotion and electoral
    participation 137–40, 174
  empowerment of children, women, and
    youth 125–8
  GKN 125, 126
  governance, accountability and
    anti-corruption 129–37
  Independent Radio Network (IRN) 122
  influence of 116–18
  institutional legacy 119, 143–4, 146, 176
  intervention in the conflicts between *okada*
    riders and the traffic police 123, 197–8
  Lion Mountain 138, 172
  Mugondi Hidesia 129, 170
  normative legacy of 141–3, 146
  Nyu Barray 129
  On the Road 123
  Parliament Bol Hat 138, 170
  Police Tok 144
  post-war reconciliation initiatives 119–20,
    122
  priority themes 124
  Salone Mi Land 134, 135
  Salone Uman 127, 138
  Sisi Aminata 127, 171, 175
  timeline and normative focus 121f
  Traffic Kotoku 123
  Trait Tok 125, 127
  Trow Away di Gun 169
  Uman 4 Uman 175
  Wi Yone Salone 138, 170
Radio UN 117
Revolutionary United Front (RUF) 112, 114,
  115, 119
'shift in consciousness theory' 186
Sinjo 64, 69, 132, 133, 143
youth culture 112, 113
youth empowerment 115–16
  see also **international non-governmental
    organizations**
**Sierra Leone Broadcasting Corporation
  (SLBC)** 117
Sierra Leone Election Dialogue Series 172

Sierra Leone Investment and Export Promotion Agency (SLIEPA) 132
single loop learning 157
Siva Group 135
Skopje 70
  interethnic relations 99–100
  Mozaik alumni 73–4
  Mozaik group 72–3, 92
  transition to primary school 100–101
snowball sampling 62
Socfin Agricultural Company (SAC) 69, 132, 133, 134
social capital 50, 98, 99, 110
  network capital 98
  participatory capital 98
socialization 164, 188, 194, 198, 206, 210
social learning 50, 82
social norms model 9, 187
social referents 187, 188
social reintegration 1
social taboos 127
social time 27, 28
societal transformation 4, 5, 48
socio-cultural anthropology 15
Sri Lanka
  Voluntary Services Overseas 46
staff continuity 177–8, 212
state-citizen relations 17, 23, 205, 206
Steady Bongo 120
Stevens, S. 113
Struga 70
  interethnic relations 100
  Mozaik group 71–2, 90f
successful peacebuilding 24–5
successor organizations 42, 49, 213
sunsetting 55
  near-sunsetting 55
surveys 140, 170, 189
sustainable development goals (SDGs) 150–51
sustainable peace 15–16, 25, 26, 42, 51
Swedish International Development Agency (SIDA) 162–3, 166

targeting 1, 2, 7, 9, 184, 187, 201, 215, 216
Taylor, C. 1, 2, 134
technocratic peacebuilding 17, 34, 149–50, 206
  transformative potential of 8, 24, 47–51, 151, 204, 213
television audience surveys 189
temporality 7, 27
temporament 28
Tetovo 106
  University of Tetovo 80, 81
thematic programming 47, 48

theories of change 43–4, 45, 47, 89, 149, 150, 206
  'revisionist theory of change' 44
theory guided diverse case method 55–6
Third World 25, 38
'tick box' learning 153
timeline exercises 2, 64
traditional leaders 131, 134, 173
transformative peacebuilding 29, 30, 48, 50, 217
  transformative potential of technocratic peacebuilding 8, 24, 47–51, 151, 204, 213
translation 57, 58
  lines-of-argument translation 57
  reciprocal translation 57
  refutational translation 57
transport stakeholders committees 123
triple loop learning 157
trust 61, 62

United Liberation Movement of Liberia for Democracy-Krahn faction (ULIMO-K) 1
United Nations Children's Fund (UNICEF) 2, 86, 169
United Nations Development Programme (UNDP) 2
United Nations Educational, Scientific and Cultural Organization (UNESCO) 88
United Nations High Commissioner for Refugees (UNHCR) 2
United Nations Mission in Liberia (UNMIL) 1
United Nations Mission in Sierra Leone (UNAMSIL) 65
United Nations Peacebuilding Comission (UNPBC) 116
United Nations Security Council (UNSC) resolutions 7
United States Agency for International Development (USAID) 86
  Democracy and Governance project 137, 171
  Interethnic Integration in Education Program (IIEP) 164
  Youth Education and Life Skills (YES) 2
  Youth Training and Education for Peace (YTREP) 126
United States Institute for Peace (USIP) 152

vertical integration 30, 217–18
victimhood 102
victims 6, 26, 28, 77, 127
violence against children 127, 128, 174
  see also rape of minors

Voluntary Services Overseas (VSO) 46
voting 115, 138, 139, 140, 155, 172

West Africa 3, 9, 112, 142, 143, 178
Westminster Foundation for Democracy 138,
    139, 140
women's participation 119
written questionnaires 70

young people's attitudes towards war and
    peace 183–4
  role of media and peace education in norm
    persuasion and attitude change 189–90,
    201, 202
youth
  'at-risk' youth 6, 203
  definition 5–6
  discourse on 6–7
  integrating youth activism into the formal
    sphere 219–20

role in peacebuilding 17–18
  youth as agents of change 217–18
  youth as partners rather than targets 215–16
  youth culture 112, 113
  youth empowerment 115–16, 125–8
  youth insecurity 6
'youth bulge' 6
Youth Democracy and Peacebuilding
    project 165
youth focused media and peace education
    projects 3, 8, 23, 53, 77, 182, 183, 188–9,
    205, 208
youth, peace, and security (YPS) policy
    framework 7
Yugoslavia 79
  interethnic tensions 79
  schools as an instrument of socialist
    propaganda 83